Contents

Introduction

Aims

Soluzioni! is a practical reference grammar which assumes little or no previous knowledge of grammar. It has been designed for learners with differing needs. You can consult *Soluzioni!* to learn the grammar from scratch, to improve your existing knowledge or simply to refresh your memory.

The aim of *Soluzioni!* is to explain and practise the grammar which underpins what people really say and write in everyday situations. Since learning grammar goes hand in hand with vocabulary acquisition, the examples and exercises include a wide range of essential and useful vocabulary with English translations.

Using Soluzioni!

Soluzioni! is a reference book, which means that the list of Contents does not dictate the order you read it in. The book is divided into **26 chapters**, each of which deals with a single topic. For ease of access, the grammar is presented in tabular form, usually with a short eye-catching heading in the left-hand column, plus examples in the middle and explanations on the right. Care has been taken to provide examples that people really want to use and might hear in everyday conversation. Each table is followed by one or more short **exercises**, marked **E** in the margin. The exercises are important because they pinpoint, test and practise the essentials, so that you can use this book on your own as a **teaching grammar**. Answers to the exercises are given in the **answer key**. You will find that some tables and exercises are marked **Level 2** where the language is more complicated. A short **Glossary** defines the additional grammatical terms used in the book, but the key ones are explained at the beginning of each chapter.

Appendix 1 provides the essentials of spelling and pronunciation, while **Appendix 2** lists essential verbs and their irregularities. The **Index** is a vital reference tool and consulting it will help you find what you need and make the most of the material presented.

Language and grammar

Some people find grammar off-putting and insist that the only way to learn a language is by immersion in the foreign country. There is no doubt that direct contact with a foreign language is really crucial, but this does not mean that grammar has no part to play. Unlike children, most adults cannot simply 'pick up' a second language with no reference to rules. Grammar provides rules and patterns: it explains how the different components of a language can be put together 'correctly' to make sense. As such it is a kind of organising agent which helps learners to make sense of a language and to use it independently.

It is important to realise, however, that although most languages have a more or less standard body of grammar which is taught, in reality there are acceptable 'deviations' from this. In any language what is 'acceptable' grammar may vary considerably. This is most obvious in the difference between the grammar of the spoken and written language and is particularly true of Italian, where regional dialects have had a strong influence. (As late as the early 1950s it is estimated that at least two-thirds of the Italian population habitually spoke regional dialects to family and friends rather than standard Italian.) Learners of Italian need to be aware that there are regional differences and variations, both of grammar and vocabulary, many of which are equally acceptable or 'correct'.

Soluzioni! focuses on standard Italian grammar and explains it from the point of view of the English learner, contrasting the different structures of the two languages. It presents the most useful and common language patterns and does not try to account for all possible contexts and all varieties of Italian. However, you will find that the numerous examples and exercises in the book expose you to the way Italian language is used today. It is a rich and fascinating language: enjoy it!

Acknowledgements

The author and publisher would like to thank The Estate of Italo Calvino and Arnoldo Mondadori Editore spa for permission to use copyright material from Italo Calvino, *Marcovaldo*, 1963.

Nouns

Nouns (**i sostantivi**) are used for naming people, animals, places, things, or abstractions such as emotions and ideas. In Italian all nouns have a gender: they are either masculine or feminine and most of them have a different form for the singular and the plural. In addition nouns are often accompanied by articles – words for *the* and for *a/an*. These are dealt with in Chapter 2. In this chapter the examples are given with definite articles (words for *the*), but these are not translated.

1.1 REGULAR NOUNS: GENDER AND THE FORMATION OF PLURALS

The important thing to know about a noun is how to identify its gender and how to form its plural. Regular nouns always follow a common and predictable pattern depending on their ending and on whether they are masculine or feminine.

(a) Nouns ending in -o

Most regular masculine nouns end in **-o**.

Endings	Examples	Explanations
-o/-io → -i	il treno → i treni *train/s* lo sconto → gli sconti *discount/s* l'aereo → gli aerei *plane/s* **But**: l'uomo gli uomini *man/men*	The **-o** is substituted with **-i**. Note the irregular noun: la mano le mani *hand/s*
	il cucchiaio → i cucchiai *spoon/s* il figlio → i figli *sons/children* lo zio [stressed **i**] → gli z**ii** *uncle/s*	The **-o** is dropped, leaving **-i**, but if the final **-i** is stressed the word ends in **-ii**.
-go → -ghi	l'albergo → gli alberghi *hotel/s* il chirurgo → i chirurghi *surgeon/s* il catalogo → i cataloghi *catalogue/s* **But**: l'asparago gli asparagi	An **h** is needed before **-i** to keep the hard sound of the singular. This is the most common **-go** plural.
-ologo (people only) **→ -ologi**	il biologo → i biologi *biologist/s* lo psicologo → gli psicologi *pyschologist/s*	In spoken Italian some people use **-ghi** plurals.

Endings	Examples	Explanations
Consonant + **-co → -chi**	il bosco → i boschi *wood/s* il turco → i turchi *Turk/s* **But**: il porco i porci *pig/s*	The **h** keeps the hard sound of the singular.
Vowel + **-co → -ci**	il sindaco → i sindaci *mayor/s* l'amico → gli amici *friend/s* il greco → i greci *Greek/s* **But**: il buco i buchi *hole/s* il cuoco i cuochi *cook/s* il fico i fichi *fig/s* il fuoco i fuochi *fire/s* **and**: l'eco (m. or f.) gli echi *echo/es*	Most nouns ending in **-aco**, **-eco**, **-ico**, **-oco** and **-uco** have plurals in **-ci** but there are significant exceptions.

(b) Nouns ending in -a

Most regular feminine nouns end in -a.

Endings	Examples	Explanations
-a → -e	la casa → le case *house/s* l'idea → le idee *idea/s* **But**: l'ala le ali *wing/s* l'arma le armi *weapon/s*	The **-a** is substituted with **-e**.
-ca → -che **-ga → -ghe**	l'amica → le amiche *friend/s* la giacca → le giacche *jacket/s* la collega → le colleghe *colleague/s* la paga → le paghe *pay (packet/s)*	An **h** is inserted before **e** to keep the hard sound.
Consonant + **-cia → -ce** **-gia → -ge**	l'arancia → le arance *orange/s* la pelliccia → le pellicce *furcoat/s* l'orgia → le orge *orgy/ies* la spiaggia → le spiagge *beach/es*	The **i** is usually dropped from the plural.
Vowel + **-cia → -cie** **-gia → -gie**	la farmacia → le farmacie *chemist/s* la bugia → le bugie *lie/s* (stressed final **-i**) la ciliegia → le ciliegie *cherry/ies* la valigia → le valigie *suitcase/s*	The **i** is normally kept. The plural is sometimes made without the **i** but never if it is stressed, e.g. **ciliege** but <u>not</u> **buge**.

(c) Nouns ending in -e

Many regular nouns end in -e. Some are masculine and others feminine.

-e → -i	il padre → i padri *father/s* il leone → i leoni *lion/s* la madre → le madri *mother/s* la tigre → le tigri *tiger/s* **But**: il bue i buoi *ox/oxen*	The masculine and feminine forms differ only in the use of the articles.

E **I** You're setting up a house. Say what you need. Begin, 'Ho bisogno di …' and make each noun plural.

lampada   letto   armadio   tavolo   sedia   poltrona   tendina   specchio   tappeto

2   Now say what you need to bring for the picnic. Begin, 'Abbiamo bisogno di ...'

piatto   coltello   forchetta   cucchiaio   bicchiere   tazza   scodella   tovagliolo

3   You're buying fruit and vegetables. Draw up your shopping list by making the nouns plural.

lattuga   asparago   fungo   peperone   fico   albicocca   limone   pesca
arancia   ciliegia

4   The following nouns refer to people. Half of them form their plural in **-ci** and half in **-chi**. Which is which?

greco   polacco   idraulico   medico   cuoco   tedesco   parroco   turco

5   All except two of the following nouns form their plural in **-gi**. Which two end in **-ghi**?

biologo   chirurgo   dermatologo   drammaturgo   psicologo   archeologo   sociologo

The gender of nouns ending in -e

Many -e nouns refer to people, in which case the gender is obvious, e.g. **il/la cantante** *singer/s*, **l'ospite** (m. & f.)/**gli/le ospiti** *guests*. Some common -e endings are mostly masculine or mostly feminine and are worth learning.

(a) Masculine gender patterns

Endings	Examples		Explanations
-ame **-iere** **-ile** **-one** **-ore** **-tore**	il pollame *poultry* il cortile *courtyard* il cuore *heart* **But**: la fame *hunger*	il quartiere *district* il balcone *balcony* il motore *motor* la bile *bile* la canzone *song*	There are very few exceptions.
-ale	l'animale *animal* il giornale *newspaper* il segnale *sign* **But**: la cattedrale *cathedral* la capitale *capital city*	il capitale *capital (sum)* l'ospedale *hospital* il canale *canal, TV channel* la vocale *vowel*	Mostly masculine, but some common nouns are feminine.
-ante **-ente**	l'atlante *atlas* il pulsante *push button* il dente *tooth* il torrente *river/torrent* **But**: la consonante *consonant* la corrente *current* la mente *mind*	l'elefante *elephant* l'ambiente *environment* l'incidente *accident* la stampante *printer* la gente *people*	Mostly masculine, but some common nouns are feminine.

(b) Feminine gender patterns

Endings	Examples		Explanations
-gione **-sione** **-zione** **-trice** **-udine**	la ragione *reason* la stazione *station* l'abitudine *habit*	la tensione *tension* la pittrice *painter* la gratitudine *gratitude*	

Endings	Examples		Explanations
-ine	la grandine *hail* l'indagine *enquiry* la ruggine *rust* **But**: l'argine *river bank* il fulmine *lightening* il margine *margin*	l'immagine *picture/image* l'origine *origin* il cardine *hinge* l'ordine (m.) *order* il pettine *comb*	Mostly feminine but some common nouns are masculine.
-ione	l'alluvione *flood* l'opinione *opinion* **But**: il campione *champion, sample* il lampione *lamp post/street light* il milione *million*	la comunione *communion* la riunione *meeting* l'unione *union* il rione *district*	More likely to be feminine but some important words are masculine.

(c) Masculine and feminine gender patterns

-ice	*masculine*: il codice *code* il giudice *judge* l'indice *index/index finger* il pollice *thumb*	**-ice** nouns are m. if the stress falls before the ending and f. if the stress is on the final **-i**.
	feminine: l'appendice *appendix* la cornice *frame* la narice *nostril* la radice *root*	

E **6** It is important to learn the gender of **-e** nouns beginning with a vowel, since it cannot be deduced from the singular article, **l'**. Group the following nouns into masculine or feminine, using the endings as a guide.

> abitudine   amore   animale   appendice   azione   elefante   esame   immagine
> incidente   indagine   indice   infermiere   ordine   origine   opinione   unione

1.2 IRREGULAR NOUNS: GENDER AND THE FORMATION OF PLURALS

Although irregular nouns do not follow the predictable patterns shown above, their forms are governed by clear rules.

Irregular nouns ending in -a

| Referring to people:
 ↗ **-i** (m.)
 -a (m. or f.)
 ↘ **-e** (f.) | il/la giornalista → i giornalisti/le giornaliste *journalist/s*
 lo/la specialista → gli specialisti/le specialiste *specialist/s*
 l'atleta → gli atleti/le atlete *athlete/s*
 il/la collega → i colleghi/le colleghe *colleague/s*
 il/la belga → i belgi/le belghe *Belgian/s*
 lo/la psichiatra → gli psichiatri/le psichiatre *psychiatrist/s* | The most common ending is **-ista**. The singular forms are identical but not the plurals, which are regularly formed. |

Masculine nouns: -a → -i	il clima → i climi *climate/s* il diploma → i diplomi *diploma/s* il panorama → i panorami *view/s* il problema → i problemi *problem/s* il sistema → i sistemi *system/s* il trauma → i traumi *trauma/s* il programma → i programmi *programme/s* il pianeta → i pianeti *planet/s* il poeta → i poeti *poet/s* il duca → i duchi *duke/s* il pesticida → i pesticidi *pesticide/s* il parassita → i parassiti *parasite/s*	Many masculine nouns in -**ma**, -**ta**, -**ca**, -**ida** and -**ita** have a regular plural in -**i**. A few are invariable (see next section).

- Many nouns ending in -**ma** and -**ta** are regular feminine nouns, e.g. la firma/le firme *signature/s,* la cometa/le comete *comet/s.*

Invariable nouns

Invariable nouns have the same singular and plural forms except for the article, and have a variety of different endings. Here are some common examples.

(a) Masculine

Endings	Examples	Explanations
-a	il/i cinema *cinema/s* il/i cobra *cobra* il/i delta *delta/s* il/i gorilla *gorilla/s* il/i koala *Koala bear/s* il/i vaglia *money order/s* il/i pigiama *pyjamas*	Some common invariable nouns in -**a** are of foreign origin.
-è -é -ì -ò	il/i caffè *coffee/s* il karatè *karate* il/i soufflé *soufflé/s* il/i lunedì *Monday/s* il/i tassì *taxi/s* **But**: la pipì *wee* il/i comò *chest of drawers* il/i falò *bonfire/s*	This is a small group.
One syllable	lo/gli gnu *gnu/s* il/i re *king/s* il/i tè *tea/s* lo/gli sci *ski/s* **But**: la/le gru *crane/s*	Nouns of one syllable are mostly masculine.

(b) Feminine

Endings	Examples	Explanations
-à	l'attività/le attività *activity/ies* l'età/le età *age/s* la/le città *town/s* la/le società *society/ies* **But**: il/i papà *Daddy/ies* lo/gli scià *Shah/s* il/i sofà *sofa/s*	This is a very large group.
-o	l'auto/le auto *car/s* la/le biro *biro/s* la/le foto *photo/s* la/le moto *motorbike/s* la/le radio *radio/s*	Many are shortened nouns (e.g. l'**automobile** → l'**auto**).
	il/i frigo *fridge/s* il/i lavabo *wash basin/s* il/i video lo/gli stereo **Note**: il/i bancomat *cash dispenser/s* (*from* banco automatico)	A few invariable nouns in -**o** are masculine.

-i	l'analisi/le analisi *analysis/es* la/le crisi *crisis/es* la/le diagnosi *diagnosis/es* l'eclissi/le eclissi *eclipse/s* la/le tesi *thesis/es* l'ipotesi/le ipotesi *hypothesis/es* la/le metropoli *metropolis/es* l'oasi/le oasi *oasis/es*	Feminine nouns in **-i** are generally of Greek origin – the masculine ones are not.
	il/i brindisi *toast/s (drink)* il/i bisturi *scalpel/s* l'alibi/gli alibi *alibi/s* il/i safari *safari/s*	A few invariable nouns in **-i** are masculine.
-ie	la/le serie *series* la/le specie *type/s, species* **But**: la moglie le mogli *wife/wives* la superficie le superfici *surface/s*	A small group. Note the important exceptions.

(c) Masculine and feminine

-ù	il/i bambù *bamboo* l'emù/gli emù *emus/s* il/i menù *menu/s* il/i ragù *meat sauce/s* il/i tabù *taboo/s* **and**: la gioventù *youth* la/le tivù *TV/s* la/le tribù *tribe/s* la/le virtù *virtue/s*	The genders of nouns in **-ù** must be learned.

(d) Foreign nouns

Masculine foreign nouns are more numerous than feminine ones.

Masculine foreign words	l'AIDS *(no plural)* l'/gli autobus il/i compact disc/CD il/i computer il/i film il/i flashback il/i modem il/i pacemaker il/i record lo/gli sport il/i takeover	Most end in a consonant, but some end in a vowel.
	il/i data base l'/gli Ecu l'/gli Euro il/i file il/i kiwi il software il reggae *(no plurals)*	Ending in a vowel.
Feminine foreign words	la/le brioche *(a kind of croissant)* l'/le élite la/le hit-parade la/le moquette *(fitted carpet/s)* l'/le overdose la/le routine la/le toilette la/le roulotte *(caravan)*	Most end in a vowel, but a few end in a consonant.
	l'/le email la/le jeep la/le holding la/le hostess la/le reception	Ending in a consonant.

E **1** The following are people. Make them plural, giving two plurals where necessary.

l'atleta   l'automobilista   il collega   il ginnasta   il pilota   il poeta

2 Make these plural nouns singular.

le analisi   le crisi   i dilemmi   i diplomi   le mogli   i problemi   i programmi   i sistemi

3 The following nouns relate to the natural world. Identify their gender and make each one plural.

clima   cometa   delta   eclissi   oasi   pianeta

4 Sort the nouns below into masculine and feminine.

auto   foto   frigo   moto   stereo   video

5 Words for the workplace. Give their gender. Which is the odd one out?

computer   database   email   fax   file   software   mouse   modem

1.3 COMPOUND NOUNS

Compound nouns are common in Italian. They are made up of two or more separate
words combined as one and are nearly always masculine. There are complicated rules
for forming their plurals, so it is easier to learn them individually, always referring to
a dictionary. Italians themselves may vary in their use of compound plurals and so
occasionally do dictionaries! Below are some general guidelines.

Regular plural	il/i passaporto/i *passport/s*		Nouns with normal plurals are often composed of a verb + singular masculine noun or two nouns of the same gender.
	il/i portafoglio/i *wallet/s*		
	il/i reggiseno/i *bra/s*		
	il/i capoluogo/ghi *capital town/s*		
	la/le calzamaglia/e *tights*		
Invariable	l'/gli apriscatole *tin opener/s*	il/i portamonete *purse/s*	The most common noun of this type consists of a verb + plural or feminine singular noun. Also common is the combination of a verb or preposition + uncountable noun (e.g. **neve**) or a noun which is not normally plural in the context (e.g. **legge**).
	lo/gli stuzzicadenti *toothpick/s*		
	la/le lavastoviglie *dishwasher/s*		
	il/i battiscopa *skirting board/s*		
	il/i cavalcavia *flyover/s*		
	l'/gli aspirapolvere *vacuum cleaner/s*		
	il/la/i/le portavoce *spokesperson/s*		
	lo/gli spazzaneve *snowplough/s*		
	il/la/i/le senzatetto *homeless person/s*		
	il/i dopobarba *aftershave/s*	il/i fuorilegge *outlaw/s*	

E

1 Make the following gadgets plural.

l'accendisigaro   l'apribottiglie   l'aspirapolvere   il cavatappi   il giradischi
il portacenere   il portasapone   lo stuzzicadenti   il tagliaerba   il tritacarne (*mincer*)
il tritarifiuti (*waste disposal unit*)

2 Group these nouns into those with a regular plural ending and those that are invariable.

il portachiavi   il portafoglio   il portamonete   il/la portavoce
il doposcuola   il dopobarba   il senzatetto   il sottotitolo

1.4 DEFECTIVE NOUNS

Very few nouns are truly defective, i.e. with only a singular or only a plural form.
However, many are used defectively, i.e. mainly in the singular or mainly in the plural.
In both Italian and English their use sometimes coincides in the plural form,
e.g. **le forbici** *scissors*, **gli occhiali** *glasses*, **i vestiti** *clothes*, but this is not always the case.

Italian plural, English singular	gli affari *business*; i bagagli *luggage*; i capelli *hair*; i compiti *homework*; i consigli *advice*; le dimissioni *resignation*; le informazioni *information*; i lavori di casa *housework*; i mass media *mass media*; i mobili *furniture*; le notizie *news*; le nozze *wedding*; le posate *cutlery*; i progressi *progress*; i soldi *money*; gli spaghetti *spaghetti*; gli spiccioli *change*; gli spinaci *spinach*; le stoviglie *crockery* e.g. Come vanno gli affari? *How is business?* Ho bisogno di consigli *I need advice*

Italian singular, English plural	la gente *people*; l'uva *grapes*; la roba *things/stuff* e.g. C'è molta gente qui *There are a lot of people here* L'uva è buonissima *The grapes are delicious*

E I Express the following in Italian.

(a) *The luggage is here.* (d) *I have no change.*
(b) *I need information.* (e) *Are they seedless grapes?* (senza semi)
(c) *He has too much money.* (f) *There are too many people here.*

1.5 COLLECTIVE NOUNS

Collective nouns are used to refer to people, animals or things as a group.

Collective nouns	la famiglia *family* il governo *government* il partito *party* la polizia *police* il popolo *people* e.g. Il governo è stato sconfitto *The government was/were defeated* Il popolo norvegese ha votato a favore dell'UE *The Norwegian people have voted for the EU*	Italian collective nouns are generally used with a singular verb.
Numerical collectives	la maggioranza *the majority* un centinaio *about a hundred* un migliaio *about a thousand* e.g. La maggioranza della Camera ha votato a favore *The majority of the Chamber have/has voted in favour* **But**: La maggioranza degli inquilini ha/hanno protestato *The majority of the tenants have protested*	In English the preference is for a plural verb. When there is a clear reference to plural subjects, plural agreements are also possible in Italian.

- For the use of singular or plural verbs with percentages, fractions and other collective numbers, see Numerals, pp. 186–7.
  For **la maggior parte** *most*, see Indefinites, p. 134.

E I Choose the appropriate verb(s) to complete the sentences in Italian.

(a) Il popolo danese era/erano contro la UE. (*The Danish people were against the EU.*)
(b) La polizia non c'era/c'erano. (*The police wasn't/weren't there.*)
(c) È arrivato/Sono arrivati un centinaio di ospiti. (*A hundred or so guests have arrived.*)
(d) La maggioranza dei prigionieri è stata torturata/sono stati torturati. (*The majority of the prisoners were tortured.*)

Level 2 1.6 THE GENDER OF NOUNS

The gender of nouns in Italian is important because it affects both the form and meaning. It affects the form of articles, pronouns, adjectives and participles.
In addition, different genders can give the same word a different meaning.

Meaning and gender

(a) Different gender, same or similar meaning

Occasionally a difference in gender has little significant impact on the meaning, although in practice the different nouns are rarely interchangeable in all contexts.

il mattino/la mattina *morning*	These are basically interchangeable. Their use depends on individual preference and on the speaker's origin.
l'orecchio/l'orecchia *ear*	It is more common to use the masculine singular, but in the plural the feminine **orecchie** is normally used.
il tavolo/la tavola *table*	**Tavolo** usually refers to the item of furniture, or to a table in a restaurant. **Tavola** has a wider range of meanings, e.g. **sedersi a tavola** *to sit down to eat*; **apparecchiare la tavola** *to lay the table*.

(b) Little or slight change in meaning

il centinaio → le centinaia *about a hundred/hundreds* il migliaio → le migliaia *about a thousand/thousands* il miglio → le miglia *mile/s* il paio → le paia *pair/s* il riso → le risa *laugh/s* l'uovo → le uova *egg/s*	A few masculine nouns have an irregular feminine plural ending in **-a**. There is a slight shift in meaning with the numbers.

(c) Different gender, related meaning

il ciliegio *cherry tree* il melo *apple tree* il pero *pear tree* il fico *fig tree* il mandarino *mandarin tree* il cioccolato *chocolate*	Some nouns differ in gender but have closely related meanings.
la ciliegia *cherry* la mela *apple* la pera *pear* la cioccolata *eating/drinking chocolate* **But**: il fico *fig* il mandarino *mandarin*	
il frutto *a (piece of) fruit/fruit (of labour)* la frutta *fruit (in general)* i frutti *fruits* il legno *wood* la legna *firewood* i legni *types of wood, woodwind (orchestra)*	A few nouns with related meanings have two singular forms and one plural.

(d) Different gender, related meaning: masculine nouns with two plurals

Some masculine nouns with related meanings have a masculine plural and a feminine plural. The masculine plural usually – but not always – expresses the figurative (non-literal) meaning. Here are the most common.

il braccio	le braccia *arms*	i bracci *arms (of chair, lake, cross, etc.)*
il ciglio	le ciglia *eyelashes*	i cigli *edges (of road/ditch)*
il gesto	le gesta *exploits*	i gesti *gestures*
il grido	le grida *cry, cries*	i gridi *cries (of animals)*
il labbro	le labbra *lips*	i labbri *rim, edge (e.g. of cup, jug, wound)*
il membro	le membra *member, limbs (of body)*	i membri *members (of family, club, etc.)*
il muro	le mura *city/castle walls*	i muri *walls*

l'osso	le ossa *bones (of person)*	gli ossi *bones (of animals, e.g. chicken)*
l'urlo	le urla *yell/s, roar (of crowd)*	gli urli *yells (of an individual)*
il ginocchio	le ginocchia *knee/s (both knees)*	i ginocchi *individual knees*
il lenzuolo	le lenzuola *sheet/s (a pair of sheets)*	i lenzuoli *separate sheets*

(e) Different gender, different meaning

Many nouns with quite different meanings are identical or very similar in form except for their gender. Here are some examples.

il banco *counter, desk*	il fronte *front (war)*	il partito *party (political)*
la banca *bank*	la fronte *forehead*	la partita *match (game)*
il boa *boa constrictor*	il lama *llama, lama*	il pasto *meal*
la boa *buoy*	la lama *blade*	la pasta *pasta, cake*
il capitale *capital (funds)*	il morale *morale*	il soffitto *ceiling*
la capitale *capital (city)*	la morale *morality*	la soffitta *attic*
il fine *aim*	il mostro *monster*	il testo *text*
la fine *end, aim*	la mostra *exhibition*	la testa *head*

E 1 Complete the following sentences in Italian by putting the nouns given into the plural, including an appropriate article if necessary.

(a) Mi fanno male (orecchio).
(b) Ho comprato una dozzina di (uovo).
(c) Il calzolaio fabbricava tante (paio) di scarpe.
(d) Il giornalaio vendeva (migliaio) di giornali.
(e) Il fioraio vende (centinaio) di fiori al giorno.

2 The following are trees. Give the names of their fruits.

l'arancio   il fico   il pesco   il mandorlo   l'olivo

3 Make these parts of the body plural. Which is the odd one out?

il braccio   il ciglio   il dito   il ginocchio   il labbro   la mano

4 Complete the sentences by putting the words in brackets into Italian, choosing the word with the correct gender.

(a) È (*the end*) dell'anno scolastico.
(b) Gli manca (*the capital*) per comprare la ditta.
(c) (*The capital*) dell'Australia non è Sydney.

The gender of nouns referring to people

Most nouns referring to people are either masculine or feminine according to the sex of the person and many have separate, though similar forms:

l'attore, l'attrice;   il cugino, la cugina;   il padrone, la padrona;   il nipote, la nipote;
lo studente, la studentessa

Some nouns, however, have a single gender for both men and women.

Single gender nouns

Feminine only	la guida *guide* la guardia *guard* l'icona *icon* la persona *person* la spia *spy* la star *star* la vittima *victim* e.g. Guy Burgess è stato/Mata Hari è stata una spia famosa	These are some of the most common. Note that the adjectives are always feminine.
Masculine only	il braccio destro *right-hand man* il fantasma *ghost* il monarca *monarch* il sosia *double* il mezzosoprano *mezzosoprano* il contralto *contralto* **But: il/la** soprano *soprano* (**la** is more common) e.g. Pino/Pina è diventato/a il mio braccio destro È diventata un mezzosoprano famoso È una soprano giovanissima	These can refer to either sex apart from the singers. The adjectives are always masculine.
Masculine for most professions	l'architetto *architect* l'avvocato *lawyer* il capo *boss* il designer *designer* il ministro *minister* il redattore *editor* e.g. Mia zia è un noto avvocato (*not* avvocatessa) Giulia è diventata capo redattore (*not* redattrice)	Nowadays the masculine form is usually preferred for women as well as men, even where feminine forms exist.

E   **5**   The following nouns are all masculine, although most of them can refer to both men and women. Which two refer only to women?

     architetto   capo   contralto   direttore   ministro   presidente   medico
     mezzosoprano

   6   The nouns below are all feminine but most of them can refer to men as well. Spot the two that refer only to women.

     comparsa   guardia   guida   icona   levatrice   persona   regina   spia   star   vittima

   7   Complete the following sentences making the correct agreement of adjectives and participles.

     (a)   Maria è diventato/a un architetto molto bravo/a.
     (b)   Mio figlio è diventato/a una guida molto conosciuto/a.
     (c)   James Bond, l'agente 007, è una spia famoso/a inventato/a da Ian Fleming.
     (d)   Le vittime più tragici/tragiche sono stati/e i bambini.

The gender of geographical names

The gender of geographical names is important, as this affects the use of other parts of speech such as the agreement of adjectives and the article used with the prepositions **di, da, a, su** and **in**. (See Section 2.3, p. 22.)

Masculine geographical names	seas	l'Atlantico, lo Jonio, il Mediterraneo **But**: la Manica *the Channel*
	rivers	il Po, il Tevere, il Tamigi *the Thames* **But**: la Senna *the Seine*, la Loira
	mountains	gli Appennini, l'Everest, i Pirenei, il Monte Bianco, il Gran Sasso, l'Himalaia **But**: le Alpi, le Ande, le Dolomiti
	lakes	il Garda, il Trasimeno

Feminine geographical names	continents	l'Africa, l'Europa
	towns	Londra, Milano, Parigi **But**: il Cairo, il Pireo *Piraeus*
	islands	la Sicilia, le Canarie **But**: il Madagascar
Feminine and masculine	regions	la Toscana, le Marche, la Cornovaglia *Cornwall,* il Friuli, il Lazio, il Piemonte, gli Abruzzi, lo Yorkshire, il Texas
	countries	l'Arabia Saudita, l'Australia, la Francia, la Germania, l'Inghilterra, l'Irlanda, l'Italia, la Nuova Zelanda, la Scozia, la Spagna, la Svizzera
		il Belgio, il Brasile, il Canada, il Galles, il Pakistan, lo Sri Lanka, il Sudafrica, lo Zambia

2

Articles

Articles (**gli articoli**) can be definite, indefinite, prepositional or partitive. In English there is one definite article, *the*, and there are two indefinite articles, *a/an*. Prepositional articles are combinations of prepositions with the definite article, e.g. *on the, to the*, etc. and have special forms in Italian. Partitive articles correspond to *some/any* and also have special forms in Italian.

2.1 THE INDEFINITE ARTICLE

FORMS

There are four indefinite articles in Italian: two masculine and two feminine.
They can be used before singular nouns, e.g. *a dog, an animal*, and sometimes before an accompanying adjective, e.g. *a big dog, a tiny animal*. In Italian their form depends on the gender and spelling of the noun or adjective which follows.

(a) Before nouns: masculine forms

un	un treno *a train* un negozio *a shop* un signore *a man* un amico *a friend* un operaio *a worker* un impermeabile *a raincoat*	Used before most consonants and all vowels.
uno	uno sbaglio *a mistake* uno sconto *a discount* uno straniero *a foreigner* uno psicologo *a pyschologist* uno zio *an uncle* uno yogurt *a yoghurt* uno gnomo *a gnome* uno xilofono *a xylophone* uno chalet *a chalet*	Used before **s** + consonant, **ps, z, y, gn,** **x** and a few French words beginning with **ch**.

(b) Before nouns: feminine forms

una	una casa *a house* una straniera a *foreigner* una zia *an aunt* una psichiatra *a pyschiatrist*	Used before all consonants.
un'	un'amica *a friend* un'elezione *an election* un'idea *an idea* un'operaia *a worker* un'uniforme *a uniform*	Used before all vowels.

E

1   You're a busy cook. Say what you've made. Begin, 'Ho fatto un/uno/una/un' ...'

   frullato di frutta   arrosto   insalata   zabaglione   zuppa inglese   spezzatino
   sugo di pomodoro

2   **Un or uno?** The nouns below are all masculine and refer to people. Which require **un** and which require **uno**?

   studente   scienziato   signore   spettatore   soldato   sacerdote
   psichiatra   pediatra   profugo   produttore   psicologo   poliziotto

3   **Un or un'?** These nouns all begin with a vowel. Which require **un** and which require **un'**?

amico	amica	appartamento	automobile
elicottero	enciclopedia	etto	estate
inchiesta	ingresso	isola	ispettore
offerta	ombrello	operaio	opinione
uccello	ufficio	uscita	uniforme

(c) Before adjectives

un → uno	un castello → uno splendido castello *a splendid castle*	When an indefinite article is directly followed by an adjective rather than by a noun, its form depends on the gender and initial letter(s) of the <u>adjective</u>. The same noun may therefore require a different article if it is preceded by an adjective.
uno → un	uno studente → un ottimo studente *an excellent student*	
una → un'	una casa → un'immensa casa *an immense house*	
un' → una	un'idea → una buona idea *a good idea*	

E   4   Describe these people and places by using an appropriate indefinite article.

   (a) È ... signora elegante.   È ... elegante signora spagnola.
   (b) È ... chef famoso.   È ... famoso chef francese.
   (c) È ... palazzo strano.   È ... strano palazzo barocco.
   (d) È ... isola meravigliosa.   È ... meravigliosa isola mediterranea.

Omission of the indefinite article

The indefinite article is used much as the English *a/an*, but there are some important cases in which it is omitted.

Occupation, status or religion	Sono ingegnere *I am an engineer* Mia zia è vedova *My aunt is a widow* Sandro è diventato buddista *Sandro has become a Buddist* **But**: È **un** ingegnere **molto bravo** *He is an excellent engineer*	No article is required unless an adjective or adjectival phrase is used.
Exclamations	Che peccato! *What **a** shame/pity!* Che bella ragazza! *What **a** beautiful girl!*	No article with exclamations.

- For other uses, see pp. 20 and 21, and Numbers, pp. 183 and 186.

5 Complete the following sentences, inserting an indefinite article where necessary. Then translate into English.

(a) Sono (...) medico.
(b) È (...) bravo medico.
(c) È (...) studente che studia tanto.
(d) Sono (...) studente.
(e) È (...) cattolica tua zia?
(f) Mia zia è (...) cattolica molto tradizionale.

2.2 THE DEFINITE ARTICLE

FORMS

The definite article in Italian has four singular forms and three plural forms, all of which correspond to *the* in English. Like indefinite articles they come before a noun and sometimes before an adjective. Their form depends on the gender, number and initial letter(s) of the following word.

(a) Before nouns: masculine singular and plural forms

sing. → pl.

il → i	il bambino → i bambini *the child, children* il sugo → i sughi *the sauce/s*	Used before most consonants.
l' → gli	l'amico → gli amici *the friend/s* l'esercizio → gli esercizi *the exercise/s*	Used before vowels.
lo → gli	lo sciopero → gli scioperi *the strike/s* lo psichiatra → gli psichiatri *the pyschiatrist/s* lo zoo → gli zoo *the zoo/s* lo yacht → gli yacht *the yacht/s* lo gnocco → gli gnocchi *the gnocco/i* lo xilofono → gli xilofoni *the xylophone/s* lo chef → gli chef *the chef/s*	Used before **s** + consonant, **ps, z, y, gn, x** and a few words beginning with **ch** (usually of French origin).

(b) Before nouns: feminine singular and plural forms

sing. → pl.

la → le	la bicicletta → le biciclette *the bicycle/s* la scuola → le scuole *the school/s* la zanzara → le zanzare *the mosquito/es*	Used before all consonants.
l' → le	l'amica → le amiche *the friend/s* l'opinione → le opinioni *the opinion/s* l'università → le università *the university/ies*	Used before all vowels.

E I Name some of the contents of the bathroom, using the singular definite article.

asciugamano   carta igienica   dentifricio   sapone   shampoo   spugna   rasoio

2 The following nouns refer to animals. Give their singular definite articles.

gnu   scimmia   scoiattolo   serpente   struzzo   yak   zanzara

3 Give the definite article for the signs of the zodiac, beginning with *zodiac* itself.

zodiaco Capricorno Acquario Pesci Ariete Toro Gemelli Cancro Leone Vergine Bilancia Scorpione Sagittario

4 Say you would like to see these different types of shoe, using the plural definite articles. Begin, **Mi fa vedere i/gli/le ...**

l'espadrille (f.) il mocassino la pantofola il sandalo la scarpa da tennis lo scarpone lo stivale lo zoccolo

(c) Before adjectives

il → l'/lo	il giorno → l'ultimo giorno → lo stesso giorno	When a definite article
	the day → the last/the same day	is directly followed by
l' → il/lo	l'esercizio → il seguente esercizio → lo stesso esercizio	an adjective rather than
	the exercise → the next/the same exercise	by a noun, its form
lo → il/l'	lo stipendio → il mio stipendio → l'ultimo stipendio	depends on the gender
	the salary → my/the last salary	and initial letter(s) of
	i bambini → gli altri bambini	the adjective. This means
i → gli	*the children → the other children*	the same noun may
gli → i	gli zii → i vecchi zii	require a different article
	the uncles (and aunts) → the old uncles (and aunts)	if it is preceded by an
la → l'	la scuola → l'enorme scuola	adjective.
	the school → the enormous school	
l' → la	l'opinione → la mia opinione *the opinion → my opinion*	

E **5** Use the appropriate definite article with the following phrases.

(a) ... edificio grande   ... grande edificio moderno
(b) ... palazzo stupendo   ... stupendo palazzo rinascimentale
(c) ... messaggio urgente   ... urgente messaggio telefonico
(d) ... invito strano   ... strano invito illeggibile

SOME USES

In Italian, as in English, the definite article is used to refer to something known or specific.

A specific or known thing	Mi piace **la** camicia verde *I like the green shirt* **I** bambini sono stanchi *The children are tired* È **il** gatto di Nina *It's Nina's cat (the cat of Nina)*	Definite articles indicate a specific or known thing, person, or creature.

In Italian the definite article is also used in many cases which do not correspond to the English. They include the following.

Proper names with titles	C'è **la** dottoressa Poli? *Is Dr Poli in?* **I** signori Velli sono partiti *Mr and Mrs Velli have left*	Used with titles when talking <u>about</u> a person.
	Buongiorno, dottoressa Poli *Good morning Dr Poli* Come sta, signor Velli? *How are you, Mr Velli?*	No article when talking directly <u>to</u> a person.
Languages	Studiano **il** tedesco *They are studying German* Non capisco **il** cinese *I don't understand Chinese* Parla tedesco *He speaks German* Ha studiato inglese alle medie *He has studied English in middle school* ***But***: Parla bene **il** tedesco *She speaks German well*	Used to name a language. Not normally used with **parlare** or when referring to a school subject. With **bene** the article is more commonly used.
With possessive adjectives and pronouns	Mi piace **il tuo** CD *I like **your** CD* Qual è **il mio** biglietto? *Which is **my** ticket?* Questo non è **il tuo** *This isn't **yours*** Qual è **il nostro**? *Which is **ours**?*	The article is nearly always used. For exceptions see pp. 19 and 105–7.
The time of day	Sono **le** undici *It's eleven o'clock* È partito **all'** una *He left at one*	The time of day requires a definite article.
Years and dates	**Il** 1321 è la data della sua nascita *1321 is the year of his birth* È nato **il** 25 aprile 1945 *He was born on 25 April 1945* Si sposeranno sabato 16 giugno *They will get married on Saturday 16 June*	The article is used with years unless the date precedes it. It is used with dates unless the day of the week is included.
Days of the week	**La** domenica mi riposo *On Sundays I rest* **Il** martedì mattina vado in palestra *On Tuesday mornings I go to the gym* ***But***: Domenica vado al cinema *On Sunday I'm going to the cinema* È partito martedì mattina *He left on Tuesday morning*	The article is used only to express habitual action (i.e. where 'every' is implied). See also p. 157.
Some expressions with ***fare***	Fa **il** medico *He is **a** doctor* Vorrebbe fare **l'**infermiera *She would like to be **a** nurse* Sta facendo **il** bagno *He is having **a** bath* Bisogna fare **il** biglietto *You have to buy **a** ticket*	**Fare** takes the definite article before the name of many professions and in some set expressions. Others include **fare la doccia** to *shower*, **farsi la barba** to *(have a) shave*.
Continents, countries, regions and groups of islands	**L'**Europa non è unita *Europe is not united* **L'**America confina con **il** Messico *America borders on Mexico* **La** Sardegna e **il** Piemonte sono regioni italiane *Sardinia and Piedmont are Italian regions* **La** Corsica fa parte della Francia *Corsica is part of France* **Le** Canarie appartengono alla Spagna *The Canaries belong to Spain*	Exceptions are **Israele** *Israel* and most countries which are islands: e.g. **Cuba, Haiti, Malta**. Islands which are regions mostly require the article.
Mountains, volcanoes, lakes, rivers and seas	**il** Monte Bianco *Mont Blanc* **il** Vesuvio *Vesuvius* **il** Lago Maggiore *Lake Maggiore* **il** Po *the Po* **il** Tamigi *the Thames* **il** Mediterrraneo *the Mediterranean*	For rivers and seas only, the use of the article coincides with English.

E

6 Insert a definite article where necessary.

(a) Dottor Binni, le presento signor Giusti.
(b) Mi piace italiano.
(c) Parli greco? – No, ma parlo bene spagnolo.
(d) Al liceo studio tedesco e inglese.

7 Now do the same with these places.

(a) Gran Bretagna è un'isola.
(b) Messico confina con Stati Uniti.
(c) Cuba e Haiti non sono paesi ricchi.
(d) Sardegna e Sicilia sono isole e regioni italiane.

8 In which sentences is there an article missing? Supply the correct one.

(a) Dammi tuo libro.
(b) Mi presti la tua penna?
(c) Avete visto mio cappotto?
(d) Questa è la tua giacca e questa è la mia.

9 When? Complete the following sentences by translating the English phrases into Italian.

(a) Vado a teatro (*on Friday*).
(b) Vado in palestra (*on Tuesdays*).
(c) Ci vediamo (*on 27 May*).
(d) Siamo arrivati (*on 5 February 1993*).
(e) Partono (*on Monday 10 June*).

10 Express the following in Italian. The first part has been done.

(a) *I am a doctor.*   Faccio ...
(b) *Maria is having a bath.*   Maria sta facendo ...
(c) *I need to have a shower.*   Ho bisogno di ...
(d) *I haven't bought a/my ticket.*   Non ho fatto ...

Omission of the definite article

| Towns and most single islands | Roma, Torino, Firenze e Napoli sono città italiane
Capri, Lampedusa e Lipari sono isole italiane
***But*:**
Mi affascina **la vecchia** Torino
Old Turin fascinates me
Note the names of the following towns and islands:
l'Aia (*the Hague*)   l'Aquila   il Cairo   l'Havana
la Mecca   il Pireo (*Pireus*)   il Giglio   la Capraia
l'isola d'Elba | No articles are used with towns and most single islands (as opposed to groups of islands) unless they are modified by an adjective or adjectival phrase or are part of the name itself. |

Expressions with *a* and *in*	Vado **a** casa (mia) *I'm going home* Ci vediamo **a** scuola *See you at school* **But:** Si trova vicino **alla** casa **di Mario** *It is near Mario's house*	The article is usually omitted with certain expressions of place and time requiring **a** and **in** unless they are modified by an adjective or adjectival phrase. See also p. 24 and Prepositions, p. 155.
	Ci vediamo **in** centro *I'll see you in town* È nato/arriva **in** autunno *He was born/he is coming in autumn* **But**: Si trova **nel** centro **storico** *It is in the historic centre* È nato **nell'**autunno **del** 1948 *He was born in the autumn of 1948* Arriva **l'**autunno **prossimo** *He's coming next autumn*	
Possessives + singular family members	Questo è mio fratello *This is my brother* Questa è mia moglie *This is my wife* Questo è **il** mio fratellino/**il** mio fratello più piccolo *This is my little/youngest/er brother*	No article unless the singular family members are modified. For more details see Possessives, p. 106.

11 Articles have been used with nearly all the nouns below. Remove any unnecessary definite articles.

(a) La Roma è una bella città.
(b) L'Aia si trova in Olanda.
(c) Il Lipari è un'isola affascinante.
(d) Mi ha fatto vedere la Parigi di Sartre e Camus.
(e) Oggi non è andato alla scuola.
(f) Studia alla scuola del suo fratello.
(g) Siamo arrivati la primavera dell'anno scorso.
(h) Siamo arrivati nella primavera.

FURTHER USES

In most of the following cases the Italian article is used whereas in English there is none.

Plural nouns used in a general sense	Mi piacciono **i** bambini *I like children* **Gli** animali selvaggi sono pericolosi *Wild animals are dangerous* **But**: I leoni sono animali selvaggi *Lions are wild animals*	When plural nouns indicate a category, the article is used unless the noun comes after **essere**.
Singular nouns	**Il** gatto è un animale domestico *The cat is a domestic animal* **La** tigre è una specie minacciata *The tiger is a threatened species*	Singular nouns can indicate a category, as in English.
Specific categories	**L'**ossigeno è un gas *Oxygen is a gas* **Lo** zucchero fa ingrassare *Sugar makes you fat* **L'**Aids e **la** tubercolosi sono molto diffusi *Aids and tuberculosis are very widespread* **Il** tennis fa bene *Tennis is good for you* È arrivata **la** primavera *Spring has arrived*	Substances and materials, food, diseases, sports and seasons are all used with the definite article.

Abstract nouns	**L'**arte è la mia materia preferita *Art is my favourite subject* **La** gelosia è un brutto vizio *Jealousy is an ugly vice* Mi piace **l'**insegnamento *I like teaching*	Abstract nouns refer to things which are not physical entities.
Proper names: institutions, clubs, and famous people	**La** Fiat è stata fondata a Torino *Fiat was founded in Turin* **La** Juventus e **il** Milan sono in serie A *Juventus and Milan are in the Premier league*	**La** is used with companies, but both **il** and **la** are used with clubs. They are best learned individually.
	La Loren e **la** Callas sono famose *Sophia Loren and Maria Callas are famous* **Il** Petrarca e **il** Boccaccio sono scrittori del Trecento *Petrarch and Boccaccio are 14th-century writers* **But**: Dante fu un grande poeta *Dante was a great poet*	The article must be used with surnames of famous women. With masculine surnames it is optional. The article cannot be used with Dante, Leonardo, Michelangelo or Raffaello, as these are not surnames.
Approximation	Avrà tra **gli** 11 e i 13 anni *He must be between 11 and 13* La temperatura si aggira **sui** 30 gradi *The temperature is around 30°* Partiamo fra **un** 35 minuti *We're leaving in about 35 minutes* Si trova a **un** 200 chilometri da qui *It's about 200 km from here*	The definite article + a preposition is used for age and temperature. The indefinite article is used colloquially to express approximate time, distance and quantity.

E 12 Use the definite article where appropriate and translate each sentence into English.

(a) Cani sono animali fedeli.
(b) Cani che abbiamo visto erano adorabili.
(c) In Italia bambini vanno a scuola a sei anni.
(d) Ieri bambini erano stanchi.
(e) Guerra risolve poco.
(f) Guerra nei Balcani è stata una tragedia.

13 Give the Italian equivalent of the following.

(a) *I don't like tea but I love coffee.*
(b) *I love tennis but I don't like football.*
(c) *I hate winter but I love spring.*

14 Insert definite articles as appropriate.

(a) Olivetti, Pirelli e Fiat sono famose società italiane.
(b) Juventus è in testa alla serie A.
(c) Leonardo e Michelangelo erano grandi artisti.
(d) Petrarca e Leopardi erano grandi poeti.
(e) Morante e Ginzburg sono note scrittrici italiane.
(f) Giuseppe Verdi è morto fra 86 e 87 anni, credo.

Use of articles with the body, clothing and personal belongings

Italian definite article, English possessive	Ha **gli** occhi azzurri *His eyes are blue, He's got blue eyes* Hanno **i** capelli biondi *Their hair is blond, They've got blond hair*	Description of parts of the body require the definite article.
	Mi sto lavando **le** mani *I'm washing my hands* Mettiti **le** scarpe *Put on your shoes*	When reflexive verbs are used with parts of the body and clothing the definite article is used. See also p. 109.
	Ho perso **l'**ombrello *I've lost my umbrella*	The Italian definite article expresses an English possessive when the ownership of the object is obvious.

- The definite article is often used with the names of familiar things:
  Non ho **la** macchina/**la** TV satellite *I haven't got a car/satellite TV.*

Special use of definite and indefinite articles: illnesses and ailments

These are used with definite and indefinite articles and sometimes with none at all.

Illnesses and ailments	Ho **la** febbre/**la** tosse/**il** raffreddore/**l'**emicrania *I've got a temperature/a cough/a cold/a migraine* Ho **la** pressione alta/**la** diarrea/**l'**influenza *I've got high blood pressure/diarrhoea/'flu.*	Illnesses require a definite article in Italian.
	Ho mal di gola/di denti/di testa/d'orecchio/di pancia/di schiena *I've got a sore throat/tooth/head/ear/stomach/I've got backache*	Aches and pains require no article in Italian.
	Ho **un** brutto raffreddore *I've got a bad cold* Ho **un** terribile mal di testa *I've got an awful headache*	If the above ailments are modified the indefinite article is used.

- For the use of the articles with numbers, see pp. 184–7. For the use of the article in expressions involving the Italian equivalents of *most* and *all*, see Indefinites, pp. 130 and 134.

E **15** Describe this man and his condition by using the definite article where appropriate. Give English equivalents.

(a) Ha capelli biondi, occhi azzurri, pelle chiara e orecchie a sventola.
(b) Ha raffreddore e mal di gola ma non ha tosse.
(c) Purtroppo si è rotto gamba!

2.3 THE PREPOSITIONAL ARTICLE

When the prepositions **a, da, di, in, su** precede a definite article they combine with it to form one word and are known as prepositional articles. With the preposition **con** the combination is optional and less common.

FORMS

	Masculine definite articles					Feminine definite articles		
	il	**lo**	**l'**	**i**	**gli**	**la**	**l'**	**le**
a	al	allo	all'	ai	agli	alla	all'	alle
da	dal	dallo	dall'	dai	dagli	dalla	dall'	dalle
di	del	dello	dell'	dei	degli	della	dell'	delle
in	nel	nello	nell'	nei	negli	nella	nell'	nelle
su	sul	sullo	sull'	sui	sugli	sulla	sull'	sulle
con	col	collo	coll'	coi	cogli	colla	coll'	colle

USES

Lavoro **dalle** nove fino **alle** cinque *I work from nine until five* La chiave non è **nel** cassetto, è **sulla** vecchia scrivania *The key isn't in the drawer, it's on the old desk*	Prepositional articles are required when a preposition is used before a definite article + noun/adjective.
La casa **dei** miei amici è bellissima *My friends' house is beautiful* La casa **degli** svedesi è bellissima *The Swedish people's house is beautiful*	Note that, as with indefinite and definite articles, its form depends on the gender and initial letter(s) of the word it precedes.

- For the omission of prepositional articles see pp. 23–4.

E 1 Provide the correct form of the appropriate prepositional article.

    (a) **To the** ... Say where you are going, using **a** and a definite article. Begin, 'Vado ...'

        il mercato   l'aeroporto   lo stadio   la stazione

    (b) **In the** ... Say where these items are, using **in** and the definite article. Begin, 'La carta è ... '

        la carta (il cassetto)   i biscotti (l'armadio)   la lampada (lo studio)
        le matite (la scatola)

    (c) **On the** ... Say what these items are on.

        il pane (il tavolo)   la chiave (l'armadietto)   il dizionario (lo scaffale)
        la penna (la scrivania)

    (d) **From the** ... What can be seen from these places? Begin, 'Dai/dalle, etc. ... si vede ...'

        i giardini (la casa)   gli scalini (la fontana)   le montagne (la pianura)

2 Provide the correct form of the prepositional article **di** in the second sentence each time.

(a) Ad Arezzo ho visto **degli** affreschi meravigliosi. Ho visto ... meravigliosi affreschi del Cinquecento.

(b) A Firenze ho visto **dei** dipinti eccezionali. Ho visto ... incredibili dipinti del Seicento.

(c) A Dresden ho visto **della** porcellana antica. Ho visto ... antica porcellana settecentesca.

3 Complete these extracts from a guide to the Highlands by supplying the correct form of the prepositional article where required.

(a) **Centro visitatori (di) distilleria (di) Talisker**

L'unica distilleria (di) isola di Skye, situata in una zona di grande bellezza naturale (su) riva di Loch Harport. Aperta tutto l'anno (da) lunedì (a) venerdì, (da) 9.30 (a) 16.30.

(b) **Centro visitatori (di) distilleria (di) Oban**

Costruita (in) 1794, la nostra favolosa ubicazione (in) centro (di) città ci rende una (di) distillerie più interessanti (di) Scozia. Aperta tutto l'anno (da) lunedì (a) venerdì. (Da) dicembre (a) febbraio ore limitate (di) apertura. Ingresso (a) pagamento.

2. 4 ARTICLES WITH GEOGRAPHICAL NAMES

The use of definite articles and prepositional articles with geographical names differs in English and Italian. (For the definite article see pp. 17–18.) In Italian it depends largely on the category of the geographical place.

(a) Continents, countries, regions and groups of islands

Viaggia **dall'**Africa **all'**Asia *He travels from Africa to Asia* Arriva **dal** Sudafrica/**dal** Trentino/**dalla** Corsica *He is arriving from South Africa/Trentino/Corsica* La capitale **del** Galles è Cardiff *The capital of Wales is Cardiff* Il capoluogo **della** Sicilia è Palermo *The capital of Sicily is Palermo* Andiamo **alle** Maldive *We are going to the Maldives*	Since the definite article is used with continents, countries, regions and groups of islands (see p. 17), it combines with most prepositions to form a prepositional article.
È partito **da** Israele/Cuba *He left from Israel/Cuba* La capitale **di** Haiti è Port au Prince *The capital of Haiti is Port au Prince*	Israel and most countries which are islands require no article.

Level 2

(b) Omission of the article with *di*

La capitale **d'**Italia, le capitali **d'**Europa, etc. Luigi XIV, re **di** Francia, Elisabetta **d'**Inghilterra, il Granduca **di** Toscana, Cosimo I ***But***: Ferdinando II **delle** Due Sicilie La capitale **dell'**Italia **unita**, le capitali **dell'**Europa **centrale** Paola **del** Belgio, Carlo, Principe **del** Galles	**Di** is mostly used with an article but is often omitted with **Italia** and **Europa** or after a noble title + a singular place name. If the place name is plural, modified by an adjective or masculine, the article is mostly used.

(c) Omission of the article with *in*

È nato **in** Australia/Gran Bretagna/Sicilia *He was born in Australia/Great Britain/Sicily* Andiamo **in** Canada/Piemonte *We are going to Canada/Piedmont* **But**: Andrò **nell'**Australia **del nord** *I'll go to northern Australia* Abito **nei** Paesi Bassi/**nelle** Marche/ **nelle** Seychelles/**nel** Regno Unito *I live in the Netherlands/the Marche/ the Seychelles/the UK*	**In** is used to mean both *to* and *in*. The article is omitted after **in** unless the place name is modified by an adjective, is plural or is a masculine compound name such as **il Regno Unito**.
Sono nato **in/nel** Belgio *I was born in Belgium* Sono nato **nel** Veneto *I was born in the Veneto* Ho una casa **nel** Molise/Texas *I have a house in the Molise/Texas*	The article may be used with some masculine countries and regions even when they are not modified.

(d) Towns, single islands and groups of islands

È nato **a**/Andrà **a** Firenze *He was born in/He'll go to Florence* Le fontane **di** Roma sono belle *Rome's fountains are beautiful* **But**: Lavoro **al** Cairo/**all'**Aia *I work in Cairo/in the Hague* Scrive **sulla** Berlino **degli anni Venti** *He writes on Berlin in the '20s*	**A** is used with towns to mean both *to* and *in*. Prepositions only combine with the article when this is part of the name or when the town is modified.
Siamo andati **a** Malta e **a** Gozo *We went to Malta and Gozo* Gli abitanti **di** Creta sono simpatici *Crete's inhabitants are nice* L'aereo è partito **da** Cuba *The plane left from Cuba* **But**: Ha parlato **della** Creta **antica** *He talked about ancient Crete* Andiamo **al** Giglio/**alla** Capraia *We're going to Giglio/Capraia*	No article is used unless it is part of the name itself (e.g. **l'Elba**) or unless the name of the island is modified. A few important islands, e.g. **la Sicilia**, are used with the article, like regions.
Andrò **alle** Canarie *I'll go to the Canaries* Abita **nelle** Seychelles *He lives in the Seychelles* Andrò **all'**Isola Bella *I'll go to Isola Bella* Abita **nell'**/**sull'**Isola di Man *She lives on the Isle of Man*	**a** + article = *to* with groups of islands and islands where **isola** is part of the name. **in** + the article = *in* or *on*. **Su** + article is also used for *on*.

- For the gender of geographical names, see Nouns, pp. 11–12.

1   Combine **di** with the definite article where necessary.

   (a) La capitale (di) Scozia è Edimburgo.
   (b) La capitale (di) Italia è Roma.
   (c) La capitale (di) Israele è Gerusalemme.
   (d) La capitale (di) Canada è Ottawa.
   (e) La capitale (di) Cuba è l'Avana.
   (f) La capitale (di) Filippine è Manila.

2   Now choose the appropriate form of **di**.

   (a) Il futuro re di/dell'Inghilterra è Carlo, Principe di/del Galles.
   (b) Carlo Alberto di/della Savoia abdicò nel 1849.
   (c) Nel 1861 Vittorio Emanuele II, re di/della Sardegna, fu proclamato Re d'/dell'Italia.

3   Combine **in** and **di** with the definite article where necessary.

   (a) Torino è (in) Piemonte. È il capoluogo (di) Piemonte.
   (b) L'Aquila è (in) Abruzzi. È il capoluogo (di) Abruzzi.
   (c) Cagliari è (in) Sardegna. È il capoluogo (di) Sardegna.

4   Use prepositional articles where appropriate.

   (a) Passo sempre le ferie (in) Francia, (in) Francia del sud.
   (b) Io lavoro (in) Gran Bretagna.
   (c) Carlo è nato (in) Regno Unito.

5   Give the Italian equivalent of the English.

   (a) *Fiona lives in the island of Skye.*
   (b) *Donald lives in the Orkneys.* (Le Orcadi)
   (c) *Alberto lives in Capri.*
   (d) *Barbara is going to the Isle of Man.*
   (e) *Alistair is going to the Hebrides.* (Le Ebridi)
   (f) *Sandra is going to Cuba.*

2.5 THE PARTITIVE ARTICLE

Partitive articles express *some, any* and are formed by combining **di** and the definite article (see p. 22).

FORMS

Masculine partitive articles		Feminine partitive articles	
di + il	**del** pane	**di + la**	**della** carta
di + lo	**dello** zucchero	**di + l'**	**dell'**acqua
di + l'	**dell'**olio		
di + i	**dei** pantaloni	**di + le**	**delle** matite
di + gli	**degli** amici		

SOME USES

Expressing some	Mi serve **dell'**olio d'oliva *I need some olive oil* Ho incontrato **degli** amici inglesi *I met some English friends*	In Italian there is no distinction between *some* for statements and *any* for questions.
Expressing any	Avete **dell'**olio d'oliva? *Have you got any olive oil?* Ha **degli** amici o no? *Has she got any friends or not?*	

Omission of the partitive article

No partitive article	Non hanno bambini *They don't have any children/They have no children*	No article with negatives, lists, and some constructions taking **di** (to avoid repetition of **di**), and none if the noun is emphasised or contrasted.
	Ho comprato pane, burro e marmellata *I bought bread, butter and jam*	
	Ho bisogno di scarpe nuove *I need (some) new shoes* Invece di soldi mi ha mandato un regalo *Instead of money he sent me a present*	
	Hai fratelli? *Have you got any brothers or sisters?* Mi servono viti, non chiodi *I need (some) screws, not nails*	

- For other ways of saying *some/any* and for other partitive expressions, see 2.6 below.

E I Use the correct partitive article to complete the following, leaving blank where necessary. Give the English equivalents.

(a) Mi dà ... caffè macinato?
(b) Avete ... pasta fresca?
(c) Devo comprare ... camicie nuove.
(d) Ho comprato ... pantaloni neri.
(e) Mi ha prestato ... scarponi da sci.
(f) Mi serve ... sciroppo per la tosse.

(g) Ho bisogno ... aspirina.
(h) Non ho ... fratelli.
(i) Devo comprare ... olio, ... aceto, ... sale e ... pepe.
(j) Volevo ... mandarini, non ... arance.

2.6 PARTITIVE EXPRESSIONS AND THEIR ALTERNATIVES

Partitive articles (see above) are often replaced by other expressions. Their use depends on whether the nouns they accompany are countable or uncountable. Uncountable nouns are used mostly in the singular (they often refer to foods and substances). Countable nouns refer to objects or people that can be counted and have singular and plural forms.

Countable and uncountable nouns

un po' di *a bit/a little of/* *some/a few*	Vorrei **del/un po' di** formaggio *I would like some/a bit of cheese* È rimasta **della/un po' di** pasta? *Is there any/a bit of pasta left?* Ho comprato **dei/un po' di** formaggi francesi *I bought some/a few French cheeses* Mi sono portato **delle/un po' di** pesche *I brought along some/a few peaches*	Both countable and uncountable nouns can be used with **un po' di**. With countable nouns (e.g. **formaggi**, **pesche**) **un** **po' di** is fairly colloquial.
Negatives: **essere senza** *to be without*	Siamo senza pane (Non abbiamo pane) *We haven't got any bread* Sono senza soldi (Non ho soldi) *I've got no money*	**Essere senza** is commonly used in speech instead of **non** + the noun without the article. See p. 26.
mancare *to be lacking*	Manca il sapone? (Non c'è sapone?/Il sapone non c'è?) *Is there no soap?* Mancano gli asciugamani (Non ci sono asciugamani/Gli asciugamani non ci sono) *There are no towels*	It tends to be equivalent to **non c'è/non ci sono** used with a noun. It implies that you expect the item to be there.

Countable nouns

Alcuni/e and **qualche** cannot be used with uncountable nouns such as **pane**,
benzina, etc.

alcuni/e *some/a few*	Ho comprato **delle/alcune** riviste *I have bought some/a few magazines* Mi ha dato **dei/alcuni** suggerimenti *He has given me some/a few suggestions*	Note that **alcuni/e** is not generally used in questions.
qualche + sing. noun with a plural, meaning *some/a few*	Hai comprato **qualche** rivista? *Have you bought any magazines?* Mi ha dato **qualche** suggerimento *He has given me some suggestions/the odd* *suggestion*	**Qualche** usually has a plural meaning but is followed by the singular form of a countable noun only (i.e. you cannot say 'Hai comprato qualche pane?').
nessuno/a *not any,* *no (at all)*	Non ho fatto **nessuno** sbaglio *I didn't make a single mistake/any mistakes (at all)* Non c'è **nessun'**alternativa? *Is there absolutely no alternative?* *Are there absolutely no alternatives?*	In negative statements and questions **nessun/a/o**, used with singular nouns only, is an emphatic alternative to omitting the partitive.
alcuno/a *not any,* *no ... whatsoever*	Non c'è **alcun'**alternativa *There is no alternative whatsoever* Non c'è **alcun** dubbio *There is no doubt whatsoever*	**Alcuno/a** is used instead of **nessuno** for emphasis.

- For more on **qualche** and **alcuni/e** see Indefinites, pp. 126, 131. For more on
  nessuno, see Indefinites, p. 133 and Negatives, p. 146.

E

1   Find an alternative way in Italian of expressing each sentence below.

(a) Mi dà dello zucchero?

(b) Mi porti dell'acqua frizzante?

(c) Mi dà dei fagiolini?

(d) Non abbiamo burro.

(e) Non ho soldi.

(f) Non ci sono lenzuola.

2   Find alternatives for these sentences. There is sometimes more than one possibility.

(a) Ho delle lettere da scrivere.

(b) Ho dei dubbi da chiarire.

(c) Hai degli articoli da leggere?

(d) Avete degli impegni per domani?

(e) Non ho dubbi.

(f) Non ci sono altre possibilità?

Descriptive adjectives

Descriptive adjectives (**gli aggettivi qualificativi**) tell you what things are like. They describe nouns and pronouns: *a **tall** boy, an **important** book, the weather is **nice**, a **white** one, those **new** ones*. In Italian adjectives change their form to agree in number and gender with the noun or pronoun they describe.

3.1 REGULAR ADJECTIVES

There are two main groups of regular adjectives. These have masculine singular endings in -**o** and in -**e**. There is also a small group whose masculine singular ends in -**a**. In dictionaries adjectives are listed in their masculine singular form and it is this form which is used to identify the group to which an adjective belongs.

Adjectives ending in -o

There are four different vowel endings: two singular and two plural. Endings in -**io**, -**co**, -**go**, -**cio** or -**gio** require some spelling changes.

Masculine		Feminine		Meaning	Explanations
Singular	**Plural**	**Singular**	**Plural**		
-o → -i		-a → -e			
biondo	biondi	bionda	bionde	*blond*	If the ending is -**eo** the
europeo	europei	europea	europee	*European*	-**e** is always retained.
necessario	necessari	necessaria	necessarie	*necessary*	-**io** ending: **i** is dropped
vecchio	vecchi	vecchia	vecchie	*old*	in the masculine plural
But:					unless it is stressed in
pio	pii	pia	pie	*pious*	speech.
sudicio	sudici	sudicia	sudicie/sudice	*dirty*	-**cio** and -**gio**: **i** is dropped
grigio	grigi	grigia	grigie/grige	*grey*	in the m. plural. In the
But:					f. plural it is also dropped
liscio	lisci	liscia	lisce	*smooth*	if a consonant precedes
saggio	saggi	saggia	sagge	*wise*	-**cio/-gio**. Otherwise it
					may be kept or dropped.

Masculine		Feminine		Meaning	Explanations
Singular	**Plural**	**Singular**	**Plural**		
-o → -i		**-a → -e**			
lungo	lunghi	lunga	lunghe	*long*	**-co** and **-go**: an **h** is
stanco	stanchi	stanca	stanche	*tired*	required to maintain the hard sound.
comico	comici	comica	comiche	*comic*	**Vowel + -co** ending:
simpatico	simpatici	simpatica	simpatiche	*nice*	if **-co** is preceded by a
But:					vowel the masculine
ubriaco	ubriachi	ubriaca	ubriache	*drunk*	plural is usually **-ci**.

Adjectives ending in -e

Many adjectives end in -e and have two forms only: a singular and a plural.

Singular	Plural	Meaning	Explanations
-e → -i			
difficile	difficili	*difficult*	A few adjectives in **-e** can be invariable or have a
felice	felici	*happy*	regular plural, e.g. **marrone** *brown* and **arancione**
giovane	giovani	*young*	*orange*. **Grande** *big* can have spelling changes
importante	importanti	*important*	(see p. 32).

Adjectives ending in -a

Singular	m. plural	f. plural	Meaning	Explanations
-a	**-i**	**-e**		
egoista	egoisti	egoiste	*selfish*	Adjectives in **-a** are usually
razzista	razzisti	razziste	*racist*	also nouns. They end mostly
entusiasta	entusiasti	entusiaste	*enthusiastic*	in **-ista**, with a few in **-asta**,
cosmopolita	cosmopoliti	cosmopolite	*cosmopolitan*	**-ida, -ita** and **-ota**.

E I Using the adjectives given, make the necessary agreements with the nouns and then make them plural.

(a) **un uomo/una donna:** alto vecchio stanco simpatico ubriaco importante pessimista

(b) **un discorso/una vacanza:** assurdo necessario lungo breve

(c) **un cappotto/una giacca:** nero grigio sudicio magnifico marrone

(d) **il pesce/la pera:** squisito fresco straordinario marcio inglese

Some irregularities of -o and -e adjectives

(a) Bello and buono

Bello and **buono** are regular in form except when they precede nouns.

The forms of **bello** change to resemble those of the definite article.

	Masculine and feminine singular			m. and f. plural
il	un **bel** palazzo *a lovely block of flats*	i		dei **bei** palazzi
l'	un **bell'**appartamento *a lovely flat*	gli		dei **begli** appartamenti
lo	un **bello** studio *a beautiful study*			dei **begli** studi
l'	una **bell'**isola **or**: una bella isola *a beautiful island*	le		delle belle isole
la	una bella stanza *a lovely room* (no change)			delle belle stanze

Before a singular noun the forms of **buono** are similar to those of the indefinite article. The plurals **buoni** (m. pl.) and **buone** (f. pl.) are regular in form whatever the position of the noun.

un	un **buon** libro *a good book*	un'	una **buon'**idea *a good idea*
un	un **buon** ospedale *a good hospital*	una	**or** una buona idea
uno	un **buono** sconto *a good discount*		una buona pizza *a good pizza* (no change)

(b) Santo

Santo is regular in form except when it precedes a noun and means *saint*.

	Masculine	Feminine	Explanations
Santo *Saint*: before the noun	San Giorgio San Zeno San Severo Santo Stefano Sant'Antonio	Santa Lucia Sant'Elisabetta	**San** goes before all consonants but **Santo** goes before s + consonant. **Santa** is used for female saints and **Sant'** for those whose name begins with a vowel.
santo *holy*: after the noun	Lo Spirito Santo *The Holy Spirit* **But**: il santo Natale *Holy Christmas* Santo cielo/dio! *Good heavens!*	La Settimana santa *Holy Week* **But**: la santa Messa *Holy Mass*	**Santo** *holy* follows the regular pattern for **-o** adjectives and it nearly always follows the noun.

2 Complete the sentences using the appropriate form of **bello**.

    (a) Ho scoperto un posto molto bello: un ... posto di villeggiatura.
    (b) Ho trovato un appartamento molto bello: un ... appartamento spazioso.
    (c) Ho affittato una stanza veramente bella: una ... stanza luminosa.
    (d) Ho visto dei sandali molto belli: dei ... sandali di cuoio.
    (e) Ho comprato degli armadi molto belli: dei ... armadi di mogano. (*mahogany*)

3 Insert the correct forms of **buono** to complete these sentences.

(a) Il dolce è veramente buono: è un ... dolce di cioccolato.
(b) Lo zabaglione è veramente buono: è un ... zabaglione leggero.
(c) L'insalata è molto buona: è una ... insalata mista.
(d) I biscotti sono molto buoni: sono dei ... biscotti casalinghi.
(e) Le tagliatelle sono proprio buone: sono delle ... tagliatelle fatte in casa.

4 Use **santo** correctly in these sentences.

(a) ... Giorgio è il santo patrono dell'Inghilterra.
(b) ... Andrea è il santo patrono della Scozia.
(c) ... Agata è la santa patrona del nostro paese. (*village*)
(d) A Roma tante chiese sono dedicate a ... Pietro ma nessuna a ... Zeno.
(e) La chiesa di ... Spirito a Firenze è famosa.

(c) *Grande*

Grande is mostly regular in form but it may change its spelling before singular nouns.

Before m. nouns	un **gran** palazzo **or**: un grande palazzo un **grand'**appartamento **or**: un grande appartamento un grande studio (no change) un grande zaino (no change)	The spelling changes of **grande** depend on the initial letter of the following word and are optional. The plural **grandi** never changes.
Before f. nouns	una **gran** confusione **or**: una grande confusione una **grand'**isola **or**: una grande isola	
Special meanings of **gran**	La Gran Bretagna *Great Britain* Il Gran San Bernardo *The Great St Bernard* Ho una gran voglia di uscire *I'm desperate/really keen to go out* C'è un gran freddo *It's freezing cold* Non è gran che *It's not up to much/no great shakes*	**Gran** has come to have meanings of its own. It is most commonly used with masculine or feminine geographical names meaning *great*, or as an intensifier in emphatic phrases.

Adjectival phrases

Adjectival phrases perform the same function as descriptive adjectives.

un albergo di lusso *a luxury hotel*; un compagno di scuola *a school friend*; una cintura di sicurezza *a seat/safety belt*; orecchini di valore *valuable earrings*; una camicia a righe/a quadretti/a fiori *a striped/checked/flowery shirt*; una torta al limone/alla fragola *a lemon/strawberry cake*	Adjectival phrases are invariable and always follow the noun. The most common ones are made up of **di** + noun and a few are composed of **a** + noun.

3.2 MAKING AGREEMENTS

An adjective takes the same number and gender as the noun or pronoun it describes, but the endings of the nouns and adjectives are not necessarily identical. This depends on the group of the adjective and also on the form of the noun.

(a) Masculine agreements

m. singular noun	m. singular adjective	m. plural noun	m. plural adjective
un ragazzo	alto giovane ottimista	ragazzi	alti giovani ottimisti
un cantante un artista	alto giovane ottimista	cantanti artisti	alti giovani ottimisti

(b) Feminine agreements

f. singular noun	f. singular adjective	f. plural noun	f. plural adjective
una ragazza	alta giovane ottimista	ragazze	alte giovani ottimiste
una cantante un'artista	alta giovane ottimista	cantanti artiste	alte giovani ottimiste

(c) Agreements with more than one noun

m. and f. nouns: ↓ m. pl. adjective	La casa e il giardino sono **stupendi** Ho comprato una camicia, delle scarpe e dei pantaloni **nuovi**	If more than one noun is described by a single adjective, the adjective is always plural. If both masculine and feminine nouns are described, the adjective is masculine plural.
m. nouns: ↓ m. pl. adjective	Mio fratello e mio cugino sono **alti** I quadri, gli arazzi e i mobili sono **antichi**	
f. nouns: ↓ f. pl. adjective	Mia sorella e mia cugina sono **alte** La lavapiatti, la lavatrice e la tivù sono **rotte**	

E **I** Here is how three different people see the same person. Complete the descriptions by making the necessary agreements. Which person is there clear disagreement about?

(a) È una collega   depresso   lunatico   squilibrato

(b) Sua sorella è   aggressivo   sensibile   dolce

(c) La professoressa è	timido	pedante	conformista
(d) I miei cugini sono	vanitoso	ignorante	egoista
(e) Le mie zie sono	colto	intelligente	cosmopolita
(f) Gina e Franco sono	bravo	simpatico	gentile

(d) Agreements with pronouns

Questa (gonna) è cara *This is expensive* Alcuni (giornali) sono cari *Some are expensive* Le tue (scarpe) sono belle *Yours are lovely* Lei (Angela) è contenta *She is pleased* **But also**: Lei è contenta, signora? *Are you pleased, Madam?* Lei è contento, signore? *Are you pleased, Sir?*	When adjectives are used with any type of pronoun they agree in number and gender. When **Lei** is the formal *you*, the masculine form of the adjective is used for a man and the feminine form for a woman.

(e) Agreements with pronoun + *di* + adjective

Before an adjective a few common pronouns are followed by **di**.

Ho mangiato qualcosa **di** strano *I ate something strange* Non è niente/nulla **di** grave *It's nothing serious* Che cosa c'è **di** nuovo? *What's new?/Is there anything new?* Che cosa fai **di** bello? *What are you doing (that's nice)?* Quello che c'è **di** buono è la sua onestà *What's good/the good thing is his honesty*	**Qualcosa** *something*, **niente/nulla** *nothing*, **che cosa? che? cosa?** *what?* **quello che** *what* all require a masculine singular agreement and are preceded by **di**.
Non ho fatto niente **di** male *I haven't done anything wrong* Ha fatto qualcosa **di** peggio *He did something worse*	The adverbs **male** and **peggio** can also be similarly used.

E **2** Complete the Italian sentences with an appropriate adjective using the English version as a guide.

(a) Che cosa fai ... oggi?	*Are you doing anything nice today?*
(b) Vorrei bere qualcosa	*I want to drink something hot.*
(c) Non ho fatto niente	*I haven't done anything wrong.*
(d) Non danno nulla ... al cinema stasera.	*There is nothing good on at the cinema tonight.*
(e) Che cosa c'è ... in tutto questo?	*What's extraordinary in all this?*
(f) Quello che c'è ... è la sua indifferenza.	*What's odd is his/her indifference.*

(f) Agreement with the impersonal *si* and with the infinitive

Quando **si** è malat**i**, **si** è spesso depress**i** *When one is ill, one is often depressed* Se **si sta** attent**i**, **si sente** il mare *If you pay attention, you can hear the sea*	The impersonal **si** (*one/you*) refers to an indeterminate number of people, so adjectives are m. plural. Note that the verb is singular (è, **sta**). See also p. 266.

Bisogna sempre essere onest**i** *One/you must always be honest* Non è il caso di essere offes**i** *There's no need to be offended* Basta stare zitt**i** *All you have to do is keep quiet*	When impersonal expressions are used with infinitives, adjectives are also always m. plural.	

E **3** Complete the sentences, making the correct adjectival agreements.

    (a) È importante essere (tollerante).   *It's important to be tolerant.*

    (b) Non è il caso di essere (scortese).   *There's no need to be rude.*

    (c) È meglio essere (onesto).   *It's best to be honest.*

    (d) Per rimanere (giovane) bisogna essere   *To stay young you have to be optimistic.*
         (ottimista).

3.3 SOME IRREGULAR ADJECTIVES

Invariable adjectives

The adjectives in the following categories do not change their form.

Foreign adjectives	la musica folk/pop/rock *folk/pop/rock music* una moda gay/sexy/liberty *a gay/sexy/art nouveau fashion* l'italiano standard *standard Italian* l'ingresso gratis *free entry*	
Colours of foreign origin and derived from plants	la maglia/i pantaloni beige/blu *the beige/blue jumper/trousers* i cappelli lilla/rosa/viola *the lilac/pink/violet hats* la borsa/i calzini nocciola *the light brown bag/socks*	Colours of foreign origin or with names derived from plants are invariable.
Compound colours	una maglia verde scuro *a dark green jumper* degli occhi grigio chiaro *light grey eyes* una maglietta blu marino *a navy blue top* delle sciarpe verde smeraldo *emerald green scarves* **But**: delle giacche grigioverdi *grey-green jackets* la squadra bianconera *the black and white team* (Juventus)	Colours of more than one word are invariable. If the colour is a single word it agrees with the accompanying noun.
Other invariable adjectives	Dieci è un numero **pari** *Ten is an even number* Tre è un numero **dispari** *Three is an odd number* È una ragazza **perbene** *She is a respectable girl* Ho mangiato pollo/carne **arrosto** *I ate roast chicken/meat*	

E **I** What did you come across at the flea market? Give the Italian equivalent of the English adjectives given, making any necessary agreements. Begin, 'Ho visto …'

    (a) una lampada (*art nouveau*)   (e) dei pantaloni (*grey-green*)

    (b) tappeti (*multicoloured*)   (f) un parasole (*purple*)

    (c) delle riviste (*gay*)   (g) dei vestitini (*sexy*)

    (d) dei pappagalli (*emerald green*)   (h) un boa con piume (*pink*)

Compound adjectives

una sostanza biodegradabile *a biodegradable substance* paesi extraeuropei *non-European countries* una donna straricca *a mega-rich woman* una bottiglia mezza/o vuota *a half-full bottle*	Compound adjectives formed with a prefix such as **bio**, **extra**, **super**, **stra**, etc. mostly have regular endings. When **mezzo** is used, its ending may, optionally, change.
idee anticonformistiche *non-conformist ideas* rifugi antiaerei *airaid shelters* pregiudizi antifemministi *antifeminist prejudices* **But**: uno shampoo antiforfora *an antidandruff shampoo* dispositivi antifurto *antitheft devices* una task force antiterrorismo *an antiterrorist task force*	**Anti** + adjective (or noun which can also be an adjective): regular ending. **But**: **Anti** + noun: invariable ending.
la chiesa greco-ortodossa *the Greek Orthodox church* una ragazza italo-americana *an Italian-American girl* tendenze piccolo-borghesi *petty bourgeois tendencies* **But**: partiti marxisti-leninisti *marxist-leninist parties*	In hyphenated adjectives, only the second part changes to agree with the noun. Some may be written as one word: **socioeconomico, anglosassone**.

E **2** Invariable or regular? Complete the sentences using one of the adjectives given below.

> anticarro • antiaereo • antidroga • angloamericano • russo-afgano • antinucleare

(a) I centri ... curano i tossicodipendenti.
(b) A Hiroshima ci sono state delle manifestazioni ....
(c) I rifugi ... non servono molto contro le esplosioni nucleari.
(d) Le mine ... uccidono anche i civili.
(e) Nel luglio del 1943, le truppe ... sono sbarcate in Sicilia.
(f) La guerra ... ha rovinato l'Afganistan.

3.4 THE POSITION OF ADJECTIVES

Unlike English (where adjectives precede the noun), in Italian it is possible for most descriptive adjectives to come before or after a noun, depending on their function.

Adjectives after verbs

In Italian, as in English, adjectives can be used after verbs.

La sua ragazza è bella, giovane e affascinante *His girlfriend is beautiful, young and fascinating* Il risultato dell'esame lo rese euforico *The exam result made him euphoric* Ho lasciato la finestra spalancata e la porta chiusa *I've left the window wide open and the door closed*	Adjectives follow **essere, diventare, sembrare, rendere, sentirsi, lasciare**.

Adjectives after the noun

In Italian the majority of descriptive adjectives follow the noun because they usually have what is termed a specifying function – i.e. they highlight specific characteristics or distinguishing features of the noun.

un vestito rosso *a red dress* una scatola rettangolare *a rectangular box* una strada polverosa/sabbiosa *a dusty/sandy road*	Colour, shape, material.
una donna tedesca *a German woman* una chiesa protestante *a Protestant church* il partito socialista *the socialist party*	Nationality. Religion. Ideology.
lo schermo televisivo *the TV screen* una scuola elementare *a primary school* la guerra mondiale *the world war*	Adjectives specifying any category.
una società tollerante *a tolerant society* acqua bollente *boiling water* uno straccio bagnato *a wet rag* un fazzoletto pulito *a clean handkerchief*	Adjectives ending in **-ante** or **-ente** derived from a present participle. Adjectives derived from a past participle usually ending in **-ato, -ito, -uto.**
un bambino piccolino *a tiny child* un bambino furbetto *a crafty child*	Adjectives with a suffix such as **-ino** or **-etto.**
una ragazza molto bella *a very beautiful girl* un film abbastanza buono *quite a good film* un viaggio piuttosto lungo *a rather long journey*	Adjectives in adverbial phrases, i.e. any adjective used with an adverb such as **molto** *very*, **abbastanza** *quite*, **piuttosto** *rather*, **troppo** *too*.
una porta di vetro *a glass door* un paese di montagna *a mountain village* una storia d'amore *a love story*	Adjectival phrases.

E   **I**   Who or what did you see at the airport? Use the English version as a guide and complete these descriptions, placing the adjectives given below in an appropriate position and making the correct agreements.

> americano • annoiato • buddista • di seta • giallo • indiano • molto grande •
> piccolino • sorridente • strano • triangolare • ubriaco

(a) dei soldati   *some American soldiers*
(b) un gruppo di suore   *a group of smiling nuns*
(c) dei bambini   *some bored children*
(d) dei giovani   *some drunken youths*
(e) un monaco con la veste   *a Buddhist monk in a yellow robe*
(f) una signora con il sari   *an Indian lady in a silk sari*
(g) una donna con un cappello   *a weird woman in a triangular hat*
(h) un gatto in una gabbia   *a tiny cat in a very large cage*

Adjectives before or after the noun

Some adjectives are regularly used either before or after the noun, depending on their meaning. The adjectives tend to precede the noun when quantity is implicit (e.g. **diverso, unico, vario**) or when they can be used in a non-literal sense (e.g. **alto, basso**). They tend to come after the noun when highlighting its distinguishing features. However, the rules of position are not watertight and are best learned through use or by consulting a dictionary.

(a) Changes in meaning

Before the noun	Meaning	After the noun	Meaning
un **caro** amico	*a dear friend*	un albergo **caro**	*an expensive/dear hotel*
gli **antichi** romani	*the ancient Romans*	un orologio **antico**	*an old/antique clock*
l'**antica** lugoslavia	*the old/former Yugoslavia*	l'argenteria **antica**	*antique silver*
un **alto** ufficiale	*a high-ranking officer*	un ragazzo **alto**	*a tall boy*
l'**alta** Italia	*Northern Italy*	un muro **alto**	*a high wall*
l'**alto** Po	*the upper Po*	uno stipendio **alto**	*a high salary*
la **bassa** Italia	*Southern Italy*	un uomo **basso**	*a short man*
il **basso** Po	*the lower Po*	un voto **basso**	*a low mark*
diversi libri	*several books*	libri **diversi**	*different books*
una **leggera** ferita	*a slight wound*	una borsa **leggera**	*a light bag*
il **massimo** rispetto	*the utmost respect*	la velocità **massima**	*the maximum speed*
un **nuovo** problema	*another/a new problem*	un film/libro **nuovo**	*a (brand) new film/book*
un **povero** uomo	*a poor (unfortunate) man*	un uomo **povero**	*a poor (financially) man*
lo **stesso** ragazzo	*the same boy*	il ragazzo **stesso**	*the boy himself*
la **stessa** situazione	*the same situation*	la situazione **stessa**	*the situation itself*
una **semplice** domanda	*just a question*	una domanda **semplice**	*an easy question*
l'**unica** occasione	*the only opportunity*	un'occasione **unica**	*a unique opportunity*
l'**unico** figlio	*the only child*	figlio **unico**	*an only child (i.e. unique)*
varie volte	*several times*	un paesaggio **vario**	*a varied landscape*
un **vecchio** amico	*an old (longstanding) friend*	un amico **vecchio**	*an old (in years) friend*

- Similar adjectives include: **amaro, certo, puro, vero.**

E **2** Give the Italian equivalent of the sentences below, taking care to place the adjectives correctly.

(a) *She is a dear friend.* (caro)   *I bought an expensive jacket.*
(b) *There are several solutions.* (diverso)   *There are different solutions.*
(c) *I talked to the same manager.* (stesso)   *I talked to the manager himself.*
(d) *I admire her, she is a unique woman.* (unico)   *It's the only solution possible.*

(b) Little change in meaning

Very common adjectives whose meaning is often not clearly defined (e.g. **lungo, giovane, bello, buono, grande, piccolo**), have particularly variable positions. They often precede the noun for very general description, but normally follow it for more precise specification when choice, contrast or particular emphasis is implied.

Before noun: general description	After noun: specifying function
È un **grande** amico *He is a great friend*	Mi dà una birra **grande**? *Can I have a large beer?*
C'era una **lunga** fila *There was a long queue*	Ho scelto la gonna **lunga** *I chose the long skirt*
Mi sono comprato delle **belle** scarpe	Mettiti le scarpe **belle** stasera
I bought myself some lovely shoes	*Put on your good/best shoes tonight*
È una **buona** soluzione *It's a good solution*	Hai trovato la soluzione **buona**
L'olio di ricino ha un **cattivo** sapore	*You've found the right/a good solution*
Castor oil has a horrible taste	Quel vino ha un sapore **cattivo**, l'altro no
	This wine tastes horrible, the other one doesn't

E **3** Look at these pairs of sentences. Mark each sentence D or S according to whether the adjective is used for general description or for precise specification.

(a) In centro c'è una grande piazza. Ci vediamo nella piazza grande.
(b) È un film bello, ma deprimente. Mi piace: è un bel film.
(c) Mi fa vedere quel vaso strano? Ha avuto una strana reazione.
(d) È una brutta giornata. È una sedia brutta, ma comoda.

4 Complete the sentences below using the adjectives given and placing them appropriately.

(a) Due ... buste ... e tre ... buste ..., per piacere. (grande, piccolo)
   Two large envelopes and three small envelopes, please.
(b) Un ... caffè ... in una ... tazza ..., per piacere. (lungo, grande)
   A weak coffee in a large cup, please.
(c) Prendo il ... caffè ... per piacere e un ... tè .... (solito, freddo)
   I'll have my/the usual coffee please and a cold tea.

3.5 USING TWO OR MORE ADJECTIVES

Level 2 *Several adjectives after the noun*

When a noun is followed by two adjectives they are usually of equal descriptive importance.

Specifying adjectives	un sostantivo maschile irregolare *an irregular masculine noun* la comunità economica europea *the European economic community* una camicia bianca pulita *a clean white shirt* un vestito di seta rossa/un vestito rosso di seta *a red silk dress/a red dress of silk*	The adjective which most closely specifies the noun immediately follows it. This is in reverse order to the English.
Generic and value judgement adjectives	una signora giovane e simpatica *a young (and) friendly woman* una discussione politica affascinante *a fascinating political discussion* un film poliziesco banale *a banal detective film* un corso d'inglese noioso *a boring English course*	These may also go before the noun; see Adjectives before and after the noun, p. 40.

| Adjectives of the same type | un vestito bianco e nero *a black and white dress*
 i conflitti etnici, religiosi e politici
 ethnic, religious and political conflicts
 una notte gelida, buia e tempestosa
 a dark, freezing, stormy night | These are linked by **e** *and*. 'Black and white' is 'white and black' in Italian. |
| Adjectives + adverb | un esame francese **abbastanza** difficile
 quite a difficult French exam
 un signore anziano e **molto** gentile
 a very nice elderly man
 occhi piccoli e **tanto** tristi *such little, sad eyes* | All adjectives used with an adverb come last. |

E   **I**   Describe some of your wardrobe using the adjectives given.

    (a) guanti   nero, di pelle   *black leather gloves*

    (b) un golf   verde, di cachemire   *a green cashmere sweater*

    (c) una camicetta   bianco, nero, di cotone   *a black and white cotton blouse*

    (d) una giacca   nero, giallo, a quadretti   *a black and yellow checked jacket*

2   Give the Italian for the following.

    (a) *a French airline company*   (c) *a Russian nuclear power station* (impianto)

    (b) *a well-known multinational company*   (d) *quite a complicated technical problem*

3   Explain some of the things you did last week, using the adjectives given.

    (a) *I went out with some extremely nice school friends.* (simpaticissimo, di scuola)

    (b) *I saw a boring historical documentary.* (noioso, storico)

    (c) *I went to a really wonderful rock concert.* (meraviglioso, rock)

    (d) *I met a very interesting Canadian couple.* (canadese, interessante)

Level 2

Adjectives before and after the noun

Sometimes one adjective precedes the noun and another or others follow, giving a different descriptive emphasis.

Porta delle **nuove** scarpe **rosse** e **vecchi** pantaloni **neri** *She is wearing new red shoes and old black trousers* Ho conosciuto una **giovane** coppia **gallese** *I met a young Welsh couple*	Common generic adjectives precede the noun when they have a general descriptive function rather than a specifying or emphatic function (see the table above).
È un **banale** film **poliziesco**, non perdere tempo a vederlo *It's a banal detective film, don't waste time watching it* Con lui ho sempre avuto delle **affascinanti** discussioni **politiche** *I've always had fascinating political discussions with him*	Adjectives involving value judgements precede the noun when they have a descriptive, more emotive function rather than a specifying one (see also the table above).
una **bella** casa **grande** *a lovely big house* un **piccolo** albergo **antico** *a small old hotel* un **grande** albergo **nuovo** *a large new hotel* un **gentile** signore **anziano** *a kind elderly man*	When one or more generic adjectives are used together the most specific one usually follows the noun.

E

4 Complete the sentences by giving the Italian equivalent of the English. Place the adjectives according to whether you believe they have equal or different descriptive importance. You may need to refer to the table on p. 39 as well as the previous table.

(a) Tiziana era bellissima, con ... capelli ... e ... occhi ... (*long, dark hair and big blue eyes*).
(b) Stanno cercando una ... donna ... dai ... capelli ... (*a young woman with long dark hair*).
(c) È stata una ... decisione ... (*an absurd bureaucratic decision*).
(d) Non si può mica accettare quell' ... decisione ...! (*that absurd bureaucratic decision*).
(e) Siamo stati in un ... albergo ... (*a wonderful old Scottish hotel*).

5 Describe where some of your friends and acquaintances live placing one of the adjectives before the noun. In two cases there is a second possibility. Begin, 'Abita in ...'

(a) un bungalow (moderno, piccolo)
(b) un quartiere (di Roma, vecchio)
(c) una casa (bello, grande)
(d) una stanza (affittato, enorme)
(e) un attico (antico, stupendo)

Level 2

Several adjectives before the noun

It is less common in spoken Italian for several adjectives to go before the noun, but they may do so even in speech when there is a subjective or emotive focus. In literature this is common.

È proprio una giovane e simpatica signora *She's a really nice young woman* È veramente un caro e bravo ragazzo *He really is a dear, good boy*	There is a particularly subjective focus.
le placide e austere abbazie benedettine *quiet, austere Benedictine abbeys* il sanguinoso e tragico attentato di Firenze *the bloody, tragic bomb attack in Florence*	In literary language, in journalism and in travel literature, adjectives frequently precede the noun since they often have an emotive force.

3.6 NOTES ON MEANING

Level 2

(a) *Bello, buono* and *bravo*: good

The following are broad guidelines to the use of these common adjectives. For further examples consult an Italian monolingual dictionary.

| bello
and
buono | È una bella casa *It is a beautiful/lovely house*
È un buona casa editrice *It is a good publishing house*
È un bel lavoro *a great/good job*
(i.e. impressive/looks good)
È un buon lavoro *a great/good job*
(i.e. well done or worthwhile)
È un bel romanzo *It's a great/good novel (i.e. enjoyable)*
È un buon romanzo *It's a good novel (i.e. well written)* | **Bello** defines visual or aural beauty, what is aesthetic, pleasant or impressive.
Buono defines what is physically good, e.g. to taste or smell, and what is morally good or worthwhile. It can convey the idea of something well done. |

bravo and buono	È un ragazzo bravo *He is a clever boy* È un bravo ragazzo *He is a good boy* *(i.e. well behaved, moral)* È un bravo insegnante **or**: un insegnante bravo *He's a good teacher (i.e. he is skilled and clever)* È un bravo bambino **or** un bambino bravo *a well-behaved child* È un ragazzo buono *He is a good-natured/kind boy* È un buon insegnante *He is a good teacher*	Often both used for describing people. **Bravo** defines skill, cleverness and (good) behaviour. **Buono** tends to describe inherent qualities, e.g. good nature. It can also be used instead of **bravo** to mean experienced/skilled.
Well done! *Good!*	**Bravo!** Hai fatto un buon lavoro *Good/well done! You've done a good job* Domani arriverò presto. – **Bene** *Tomorrow I'll arrive early. – Good*	**Bravo** is used as a compliment. Note that the adverb **bene** (*well*), not the adjective **buono**, is used to express pleasure and approval.

E 1 **Bello**, **bravo** or **buono**? Select the most appropriate adjective for *good* and complete the sentences by giving the Italian equivalent of the English phrases. You may find that you can use more than one adjective.

(a) *It's a good painting,* è un dipinto magnifico.
(b) *It's a good wine,* è un vino stagionato.
(c) *He's a good cook,* è un cuoco geniale.
(d) *It's a good textbook,* è un libro di testo utile.
(e) *It's a good novel,* è un romanzo originale.
(f) *They are good children,* sono bambini educati.
(g) *He is a good person,* aiuta sempre gli altri.
(h) *He's a good student,* che studia tanto.

Level 2 **(b)** *Brutto and cattivo*

Brutto *ugly/bad* and **cattivo** *bad* are sometimes but not always interchangeable. The following are broad guidelines to their use.

cattivo	Non è un cattivo ragazzo *He's not a naughty/badly behaved boy* È di cattivo umore *He's in a bad mood* È un cattivo insegnante *He's a bad teacher*	Can describe behaviour and skill.
brutto	È una brutta città industriale *It's an ugly industrial town* Ha un brutto naso *He has an ugly nose* Che brutta giornata! *What a horrible day!* Ho un brutto mal di testa *I've got a bad headache* È un brutto voto *It's a bad mark* **But**: Questa carne è cattiva *This meat is bad/off*	Used when the emphasis is on physical unpleasantness or ugliness, but this does not apply to taste or smell (where **cattivo** is more usual).
brutto and cattivo	una brutta/cattiva abitudine *a bad habit* una brutta/cattiva impressione *a bad impression* brutto/cattivo tempo *bad weather*	Both used to convey the idea of something bad or unpleasant in many different contexts.

2   Give the Italian equivalent of the following, choosing either **brutto** or **cattivo**. In some
instances either is possible.

(a) *It's an ugly painting.*   (f) *It's a bad textbook.*
(b) *It's a horrible wine.*   (g) *It's a bad novel.*
(c) *He's a terrible cook.*   (h) *They are naughty children.*
(d) *He's a nasty person.*   (i) *He's a bad student.*
(e) *The weather is bad.*   (j) *It's a bad essay.* (saggio)

3.7 ADJECTIVES AS OTHER PARTS OF SPEECH

Adjectives used as nouns

Il bello è che non ho dovuto pagare *The good thing/best bit/joke is I didn't have to pay* Ha fatto tutto **il possibile** *He did everything possible* **Il peggio** è che ho perso la ricevuta *The worst thing is I've lost the receipt* Non chiedere **l'impossibile** *Don't ask for the impossible* Devi fare **del** tuo **meglio** *You must do your best*	Some adjectives used as nouns express abstract concepts. They are masculine singular and preceded by the masculine definite article.
È un ambizioso/un'ambiziosa *He is an ambitious man/She's an ambitious woman* Odiano **i ricchi** *They hate rich people/the rich* **I pentiti** hanno paura *The (ex-terrorist/mafia) informers are afraid* **I neri** sono stati sconfitti *The fascists were defeated* Hanno vinto **gli azzurri** *The Italian team won*	Some adjectives used as nouns describe people or groups of people.

●   For adjectives used as adverbs see Adverbs, pp. 45, 56.

I   Give the English equivalent of the following.
(a) Abbiamo fatto il possibile per aiutarlo.
(b) Il bello è che alla fine mi hanno fatto uno sconto.
(c) Il peggio è che le banche sono chiuse.
(d) È il meglio che sai fare?

4

Adverbs

Adverbs (**gli avverbi**) are invariable words with a wide variety of uses. For example, they answer such questions as *how? when? where? to what extent?* They provide more information about verbs, e.g. *he eats **slowly*** – but they also modify adjectives, other adverbs or even a whole sentence: *it's **quite** difficult, he speaks **really** well, I **usually** get up at seven.*

4.1 THE FORMS OF ADVERBS

Adverbs are varied in form and many are linked to other parts of speech, such as adjectives.

Adverbs derived from adjectives

Most adverbs derived from adjectives are adverbs of manner and have a characteristic -**mente** ending which usually corresponds to the English *-ly*.

Regular adverbs derived from adjectives	rapido → rapidamente *rapidly* semplice → semplicemente *simply*	-**mente** is added to the feminine singular form of -**o** adjectives and to the m./f. singular form of -**e** adjectives.
	But: leggero legger**mente** benevolo benvol**mente** violento violente**mente** altro altri**menti**	
	facile → facilmente *easily* particolare → particolarmente *particularly*	Adjectives ending in -**le** and -**re** drop the -**e** before -**mente** unless preceded by a consonant.
	But: folle folle**mente** *madly* mediocre mediocr**emente** *in a mediocre way*	
Irregular adverbs derived from adjectives	buono *good* → bene *well* cattivo *bad* → male *badly* migliore *better/best* → meglio *better/best* peggiore *worse/worst* → peggio *worse/worst*	Some common adverbs are very different in form from the adjectives they are derived from.

Other parts of speech used as adverbs

Prepositions: e.g. **dentro, fuori, sotto, sopra**	Vera è andata **dentro** *Vera went inside* Mangiamo **fuori** *Let's eat outside*	Many important adverbs borrow their form from other parts of speech, e.g. adjectives, pronouns
Indefinite adjectives and pronouns: e.g. **molto, poco, tanto, troppo**	Angela mangia **molto** *Angela eats a lot* Susi dorme **troppo** *Susi sleeps too much*	and prepositions. The masculine singular forms are used and the adverb does not change.
Adjectives: e.g. **lontano, sodo, forte, piano**	Maria vive **lontano** *Maria lives a long way away* Lavorano sempre **sodo** *They always work hard* La ragazza lo guardò, **indignata** *The girl looked at him indignantly* Arrivano sempre **puntuali** *They always arrive punctually*	Adverbs are normally invariable, but occasionally, when an Italian adjective is used as an adverb, it is made to agree with the subject. This happens when it refers to both the subject and the verb.

Other adverbial forms

Adverbs of independent formation	abbastanza *quite/enough* almeno *at least* così *so* già *already* piuttosto *fairly* volentieri *gladly/willingly*	Many adverbs have forms of their own and are not derived from other parts of speech.
Adverbial phrases	con cautela *cautiously* in fretta *quickly/in a hurry* all'incirca *about, approximately* del tutto *completely* per sbaglio *by mistake* per lo più *mostly* senza entusiasmo *unenthusiastically* in modo strano *strangely* in maniera vergognosa *shamefully* ogni tanto *occasionally, now and again* poco a poco *gradually*	Most adverbial phrases consist of **con, in, a, di, per, senza** + noun or adjective. Others begin with **in modo** or **in maniera** (more formal) followed by an adjective. A few are differently formed, for example by two adverbs together.

E 1 Describe the actions below by transforming the given adjectives into adverbs.

(a) Ha risposto **onesto**
(b) Ha parlato **breve**
(c) Mi ha salutato **cordiale**
(d) Rideva **volgare**
(e) Gioca **buono**
(f) Parla **cattivo**
(g) Si sente **migliore**
(h) È andato **peggiore**

2 (a) Which of the words in bold (below) are used as adjectives, not adverbs?
(b) Which two adverbs do not modify a verb?

(i) Studia **poco**.
(ii) Non fuma **molto**.
(iii) Abita **lontano**.
(iv) Abita in una città **lontana**.
(v) Mettilo **dentro**.
(vi) C'è **poco** vento.
(vii) Suona **tanto** male.
(viii) È **troppo** caro.
(ix) Hanno vissuto **felici** e **contenti**.

4.2 ADVERBS OF MANNER, QUANTITY AND DEGREE

USES

Lo ha punito **severamente** *He punished him severely* Lo abbiamo fatto **apposta** *We did it on purpose* Andiamo **insieme**? *Shall we go together?*	Adverbs or adverbial phrases of manner answer the question *how?*
Lavoro **poco** *I don't work much* Ti sento **appena** *I can hardly hear you* È piuttosto **difficile** *It's quite difficult*	Adverbs of quantity explain *how much* and *to what extent*.

- Typical adverbs of quantity and degree include:

  molto *very, a lot*, poco *not very, not much/a lot*, parecchio *a lot*, tanto *so, so much*, troppo *too, too much*, altrettanto *just as much*, abbastanza *quite/fairly, enough*, così *so*, piuttosto *rather*, almeno *at least*, circa *about*, appena *not quite/barely/ hardly*, ancora *some more*, quasi *almost/nearly*, più/meno *more/less*.

Distinguishing adverbs from adjectives

Molto, poco, tanto, troppo, parecchio, altrettanto

Many adverbs of quantity can also be adjectives. In order to distinguish between their adverbial and adjectival uses it is important to remember that adverbs normally modify verbs, adjectives or adverbs, while adjectives modify nouns.

Adverbial use: no agreement	Maria è **molto** stanca/triste *Maria is very tired/sad* Lucia lavora **tanto** bene/rapidamente *Lucia works so well/quickly*	**Molto** is an adverb modifying the adjectives **stanca/triste**, <u>not</u> **Maria**. **Tanto** is an adverb modifying the adverbs **bene/ rapidamente**, <u>not</u> **Lucia**.
Adjectival use: agreement	Carla ha **molta** pazienza *Carla has a lot of patience* I bambini hanno **pochi/tanti** compiti *The children have little/so much homework*	Here **molto** and **tanto** are adjectives which modify the nouns **pazienza** and **compiti**.

E I Complete the sentences using the appropriate forms of **molto** and **tanto**.

(a) Maria è ... stanca. (*very*)
(b) Giuliana legge ... la sera. (*a lot*)
(c) Anna ha ... amiche. (*many, lots of*)
(d) Paolo ha ... voglia di uscire. (*very much wants: lit. has much desire*)
(e) I tuoi amici sono ... simpatici. (*so*)
(f) Luciana lavora .... (*so much, such a lot*)
(g) Silvano ha ... amici. (*so many, such a lot of*)
(h) Hanno ... fame la sera. (*so: lit. have so much hunger*)

Position of adverbs

There are few hard and fast rules regarding the position of adverbs. The ones that
follow apply to the most standard, neutral positions and take no account of variations
in style.

After the verb and before adjectives and other adverbs	Sta dormendo	**tranquillamente**		He is sleeping peacefully
	La lezione è stata	**insolitamente**	noiosa	The lesson was unusually boring
	Mi è piaciuto	**parecchio**		I liked it quite a lot
	Vai	**troppo**	forte	You are going too fast
Before a direct noun object: this is not always the case in English	Parla	**perfettamente**	italiano	He speaks Italian perfectly
	Hai chiuso	**bene**	la porta?	Have you closed the door properly?
	Non aiuta	**abbastanza**	i genitori	He doesn't help his parents enough
	Mi è piaciuto	**molto**	il concerto	I liked the concert a lot

- Adverbial phrases or long adverbs may follow the direct object.

  Ha aperto la porta **pian piano** *He opened the door very quietly*
  Ha vinto il premio **inaspettatamente** *He won the prize unexpectedly*

2 Rewrite the Italian sentences using the adverbs given, to make them equivalent to
the English.

(a) Giocano a calcio. (bene)   *They play football well.*
(b) Suona la chitarra. (molto)   *He plays the guitar a lot.*
(c) Amava i gatti. (tanto)   *She loved cats so much.*
(d) Mi è piaciuto quel film. (parecchio)   *I liked that film quite a lot.*
(e) Ha sbattuto la porta. (forte)   *He slammed the door hard.*

Position and change of meaning

Ha aperto appena **la finestra** *He barely/only just opened the window* **Ha** appena **aperto la finestra** *He has just opened the window* (adverb of time)	The position of some adverbs can depend on their meaning.
Gli piace **molto** giocare a tennis *He likes playing tennis a lot* *(He is very fond of playing tennis)* Gli piace giocare **molto** a tennis *He likes to play tennis a lot (i.e. often)* Vorrei **tanto** mangiare a casa *I would so much like to eat at home* Vorrei mangiare **tanto** *I would like to eat a great deal/such a lot*	When a verb such as **piacere** or **volere** is followed by an infinitive, adverbs such as **molto**, **tanto**, **spesso** (adverb of frequency) follow either the main verb or the infinitive verb, depending on which one it refers to.

E

3   Place the adverbs appropriately so that the Italian is equivalent to the English.

     (a)   Siamo arrivati. (appena)   *We have just arrived.*

     (b)   Ti sento. (appena)   *I can hardly hear you.*

     (c)   Gli piace mangiare. (molto)   *He likes to eat a lot.*

     (d)   Mi piacerebbe mangiare adesso. (molto)   *I would very much like to eat now.*

4.3 ADVERBS OF TIME, FREQUENCY AND PLACE

USES

Partiamo **adesso** *We're leaving now* Ci vediamo **spesso** *We often see each other* Il treno è arrivato **in orario** *The train arrived on time*	Adverbs of time and frequency answer the questions *when?* or *how often?*
Il pane è **qui** *The bread is here* Mettilo **là** *Put it there* Siediti **dietro** *Sit behind/in the back* Non lo trovo **da nessuna parte** *I can't find it anywhere*	Adverbs of place answer the question *where?*

- Typical adverbs of time and frequency include:

  adesso/ora *now*, ormai *by now*, fino a *until*, finora *until now/so far*, allora *then, at that time*, poi *then, next*, dopo *after(wards), later*, prima *first*, oggi *today*, domani *tomorrow*, ieri *yesterday*, fa *ago*, fra *in*, ancora *still, again*, appena *just*, già *already, yet*, subito *at once*, tardi *late*, presto *early/soon*, frequentemente *frequently*, raramente *rarely, not often*, spesso *often*, sempre *always*, non ... ancora *not ... yet*, non ... mai *never*, non ... più *not any more, no longer*, non ... mai più *never again*.

- Typical adverbs of place include:

  fino a *as far as*, qui/qua* *here*, lì/là* *there*, quaggiù *down here*, quassù *up here*, lassù *up there*, laggiù *down there*, avanti *on, forward*, indietro *back*, davanti *in front*, dietro *behind*, dappertutto *everywhere*, altrove *elsewhere*.

  ⋆ qui and qua are virtually synonymous, though qui may suggest somewhere closer and more precise.

  ⋆ lì and là are also almost synonymous, though lì indicates somewhere slightly more precise and often closer.

E   I   Identify the adverbs of frequency in the list of adverbs of time and frequency above.

Position of adverbs

In Italian, as in English, the position of adverbs of time is particularly variable and often depends on style, emphasis and context. The same adverb can have several positions.

Beginning a sentence	Che cosa fai domani? **Domani** vado a Firenze *What are you doing tomorrow? Tomorrow I'm going to Florence*

| Ending a sentence | Quando vai a Firenze? Vado a Firenze **domani**
 When are you going to Florence? I'm going to Florence tomorrow |
| Directly after the verb | Vai oggi a Firenze? No, vado **domani** a Firenze
 Are you going to Florence today? No, I'm going to Florence tomorrow/
 It's tomorrow I'm going to Florence |

Given the variety of positions in both languages, the following examples focus on generally accepted standard usage rather than on all possible permutations.

After the verb	Arriverò **tardi/fra poco** *I'll arrive late/soon* È venuto **raramente** qui *He has rarely come here* Stanno giocando **lassù** *They are playing up there* Devo partire **subito** *I have to leave right away* Lavoro **sempre/spesso** per lui *I always/often work for him* **But**: Ho **sempre** lavorato per lui *I have always worked for him* Sta **ancora** giocando con Enrico *He is still playing with Enrico* Devi **già** partire? *Must you leave already/yet?*	The most common position, including compound tenses and verb + infinitive. In English adverbs of frequency tend to <u>precede</u> the verb. Note that: **sempre**, **ancora**, **già** and **mai** come <u>between</u> the auxiliary and participle, or verb and dependent infinitive.
Before a direct noun object: time and frequency	Chiudete **sempre** il cancello *Always shut the gate* Ho letto **di nuovo** l'articolo *I read the article again* Ho letto l'articolo **di nuovo** *I again read the article* Anna ha acceso **subito** la luce *Anna immediately turned on the light* Anna ha acceso la luce **subito** *Anna turned on the light immediately*	Unlike English, adverbs of frequency usually come <u>before</u> a direct noun object but this is not a rigid rule, especially with adverbs of time.
Before or after a direct noun object: place	Hai buttato **via** le bottiglie? *Have you thrown the bottles away?* Devi mandare **indietro** il pacco *You have to return/send the parcel back* **But**: Perché non metti i bagagli lì sopra?/Perché non metti lì sopra i bagagli? *Why don't you put the luggage up there?*	Adverbs of place often go before the direct object when they are an integral part of the meaning of the verb, e.g. **buttare via**. Otherwise their position is flexible.
Beginning and ending a sentence	**Qualche volta** esco con mia sorella/ Esco con mia sorella **qualche volta** *Sometimes I go out with my sister/* *I go out with my sister sometimes* **Qui** fa molto caldo/Fa molto caldo **qui** *Here it's very hot/It's very hot here*	Especially common if the adverb modifies a sentence, e.g. **adesso**, **dopo**, **ogni tanto**, **quà**, **là**.

- For interrogative adverbs come? *how?*, quando? *when?*, dove? *where?*, quanto? *how much?*, perché? *why?*, come mai? *why/how come?*, see Interrogatives, pp. 117–18.

E

2 Complete (a)–(e) by inserting the adverb of time or frequency given into each sentence. You must use the adverb twice each time. Give English equivalents.

(a) Marco è a casa. Sta studiando. (ancora *still*)
(b) Davide frequenta l'università? Ha dato gli esami? (già *yet/already*)
(c) Studi in biblioteca? Devi studiare in bibioteca? (sempre *always*)
(d) Suo marito non aiuta in casa. Non ha aiutato in vita sua. (mai *never*)
(e) Usciamo la sera. Siamo usciti la sera. (spesso *often*)

3 Give the Italian equivalent of the English, taking care to place the adverbs of frequency correctly.

(a) *I always do the shopping.*
(b) *We often eat out.*
(c) *I rarely watch TV.*
(d) *We never eat meat.*
(e) *I like to play tennis often.*
(f) *We often like to play tennis.*

4 Place these adverbs of time and place correctly. In two of the sentences there is a choice.

(a) Bisogna chiudere la porta a chiave. (sempre)
(b) Ha chiuso la finestra. (subito)
(c) Hai portato i piatti? (dentro)
(d) Ho mandato il pacco. (indietro)
(e) Ho messo i documenti. (qui dentro)

SPECIAL USES

(a) Using *in ritardo/tardi, in anticipo/presto*

In Italian there is more than one way of saying *late* and *early*.

late: **in ritardo (di)** **con un ritardo di**	Sei **in ritardo**, abbiamo già mangiato *You're late, we've already eaten* Il treno è **in ritardo di** dieci minuti *The train is ten minutes late* È arrivato **con** un quarto d'ora **di ritardo** *He arrived a quarter of an hour late*	Used when a timetable is directly or indirectly implied. **In ritardo** means 'not on time'.
early: **in anticipo (di)** **con un anticipo di**	Arriva sempre a scuola **in anticipo** *He always arrives at school early* L'aereo è **in anticipo di** dieci minuti *The plane is ten minutes early* Il treno è arrivato **con un anticipo di** cinque minuti *The train arrived five minutes early*	**In anticipo** means 'ahead of the appointed time/in advance'.
late: **tardi**	Ceniamo sempre **tardi** *We always have supper late* È troppo **tardi** per andare al cinema *It's too late to go to the cinema*	When the meaning is more general, **tardi** and **presto** are used. **Note**: *It's late/early*
early: **presto**	Preferisco partire **presto** per non perdere il treno *I prefer to leave early so I don't miss the train* È un po' **presto** per pranzare *It's a bit early to have lunch*	È **tardi/presto** **But**: *I'm late/early* Sono in ritardo/in anticipo

5 Complete the sentences using the Italian equivalent of the English.

(a) Sei (*late*), abbiamo finito di cenare.
(b) Sei (*early*), non sono ancora pronto.
(c) È un po' (*late*), perché non usciamo domani?
(d) È troppo (*early*) per partire.
(e) L'aereo arriva (*an hour late*).
(f) Gli ospiti sono arrivati (*ten minutes early*).

(b) Using *ancora – non più : già? – non ancora*

Care must be taken when making **ancora** and **già?** negative. **Non ancora** is <u>not</u> the negative of **ancora**.

ancora → non ... più *again → not again* *still → not any more*	Ti ha chiamato **ancora**? *Has he rung you again?* No, **non** mi ha **più** chiamato *No, he hasn't rung me again* Giochi **ancora** a tennis? *Do you still play tennis?* No, **non** gioco **più** a tennis *No, I don't play tennis any more*
già? → non ... ancora/ancora ... non → non ... finora/finora ... non *yet? → not yet/still not* → *not (as) yet/so far*	Ti ha **già** chiamato? *Has he rung you yet?* No, **non ancora**. **Non** mi ha **ancora** chiamato *No, not yet. He hasn't called me yet* No, **ancora non** ha chiamato *No, he still hasn't called (yet)* **Finora non** ha chiamato *He hasn't rung as yet/so far*

• The difference between **non ancora/ancora non** and **non finora/finora non** is very slight. For more on **ancora** see pp. 52–3. See also Negatives, p. 146.

6 Answer these questions negatively by giving the Italian equivalent of the English.

(a) Lo hai visto ancora/di nuovo? *No, I haven't seen him again.*
(b) Vuoi provare ancora/di nuovo? *No, I don't want to try again/any more.*
(c) Hai già rifatto il letto? *No, I haven't made the bed yet.*
(d) Ti ha già scritto? *No, he hasn't written yet.*
(e) Sono già arrivati? *No, they still haven't arrived/they haven't arrived yet.*
(f) Non hai ancora avuto notizie? *No, I haven't had any news so far/as yet.*

(c) Using *sempre* and *ancora*

Sempre and **ancora** have several meanings. These depend on the context, the tense they are used in, or their position.

sempre: *always*	Lavoro **sempre** la mattina *I always work in the morning* Ho **sempre** lavorato di sera *I have always worked in the evening* Non lavoravo **sempre** tardi *I didn't always use to work late* Non farò **sempre** lo stesso lavoro *I won't always do the same job*	The main meaning of **sempre** in all tenses is *always*.

| sempre: *still* | Hai cambiato lavoro? No, faccio **sempre** lo stesso lavoro *Have you changed jobs? No, I still do the same job*
 Quest'anno dove andrete in vacanza? Mah, penso che andremo **sempre** nello stesso posto. *Where will you go on holiday this year? Well, I expect we'll still be going to the same place*
 Aveva cambiato idea? No, era **sempre** della stessa idea *Had he changed his mind? No, he was still of the same opinion* | In the affirmative present, future and imperfect only, **sempre** can also mean *still*. The key word is usually **stesso**. If in doubt use **ancora** for *still*. |

E   **7**   Give the meaning of **sempre** in the following sentences.

(a) Il giovedì Fabrizio arriva sempre in ritardo.
(b) La mattina mia zia andava sempre a messa.
(c) Ti amerò sempre.
(d) Abiti sempre nella stessa strada?
(e) Angelo mi ha detto che lavorava sempre per la stessa ditta.
(f) Domani avremo sempre le stesse difficoltà.
(g) Non prendo sempre il caffè la mattina.
(h) Non lavoravano sempre a casa.

ancora: *still*	È **ancora** malato *He is still ill* A mezzanotte saremo **ancora** in piedi *We will still be up at midnight* Era **ancora** a letto *He was still in bed*	**Ancora** is the most common way of expressing *still* and is used in the present, future and imperfect only.
	Stiamo **ancora** facendo colazione *We're still having breakfast* Devo **ancora** fare i compiti *I've still got to do my homework* Hai **ancora** voglia di uscire? *Do you still feel like going out?*	It generally comes between auxiliaries and participles, verbs and dependent infinitives or verb phrases.
ancora: *again*	Dimmi **ancora** com'è andato *Tell me again how it went* Proverò **ancora**, se vuoi *I'll try again if you want* Te lo spiego **ancora**? *Shall I explain it to you again?*	**Ancora** is one way of expressing *again*, although there are more common alternatives (see p. 53). It tends to follow the complete verb in all tenses and constructions, but this is not a hard and fast rule.
	Hai voglia di uscire **ancora**? *Do you feel like going out again?* Sì, mi piacerebbe incontrarlo **ancora** (una volta) *I'd like to meet him (once) again*	
ancora: *(some) more*	Ne vuoi **ancora**? *Do you want some more?* Ci sono **ancora** tre fette *There are three more slices* Puoi rimanere **ancora** una settimana/un po' *You can stay another week/a bit longer* Sono rimasto **ancora** guindici giorni *I stayed two more/another two weeks*	As an adverb of quantity **ancora** usually follows the complete verb in all constructions and comes before the amount referred to.

8 Give the Italian equivalent of the following.

(a) *Is he still asleep?*
(b) *Is Paolo still out?*
(c) *Will you still go to Milan?*
(d) *He still had to go to the bank.* (doveva andare)

9 *Still* or *again*? Say which meaning of **ancora** is used in each sentence below. Its position is the clue.

(a) Mi piace ancora suonare la tromba.
(b) Mi piacerebbe vederlo ancora.
(c) Devo ancora fare i letti.
(d) Devo parlargli ancora domani.
(e) Hai ancora voglia di uscire?
(f) Hai voglia di uscire ancora?

10 *More*. Provide Italian equivalents of the English, using **ancora**.

(a) *Would you like some more?*
(b) *Can you give me four more slices?* (fette)
(c) *I'm staying ten more days.*
(d) *I would like to stay a bit longer.*

(d) Alternatives for *ancora*

again: **di nuovo,** **un'altra volta**	Te lo spiego **di nuovo/un'altra volta**, allora? *Shall I explain it to you again, then?* Sì, mi piacerebbe sentirlo **di nuovo/un'altra volta** *Yes, I would like to hear it again*	**Ancora** is often not the most natural way of expressing *again*.
again: Verbs beginning with **ri-**	Si è risposata *She got married again* Non lo rifare! *Don't do it/that again!* Bisogna riprovare *We'll have to try again* Ricominciamo? *Shall we start again/do it again?*	Verbs expressing the idea of *again* are very common.
more: **altro**	Ne vuoi un **altro** po'? *Do you want a bit more?* Mi ha dato **altri** cinquanta euro *He gave me fifty euros more* Rimango **altri** quindici giorni/**un'altra** settimana *I'm staying two more weeks/another week*	An alternative to **ancora** is the adjective **altro**, which must agree with any accompanying noun.

- For **altro**, see also Indefinites, p. 131.

11 Rewrite the sentences in Italian without using **ancora** for *again*. There is more than one possibility.

(a) Mi si è bloccato il computer!   *My computer's crashed again!*
(b) Ho perso le chiavi dell'ufficio.   *I've lost the office keys again!*
(c) Mi si è rotta la stampante.   *My printer's broken again!*

12 Produce Italian equivalents of the responses, using appropriate verbs to express 'again'.

(a) Il fax non è arrivato. – *Shall I send it again?*
(b) È stato bocciato. – *He'll have to take the exam again.* (dare l'esame)
(c) Il mio compito è andato male. – *You'll have to do it again.*

13 *Again*. Rewrite the sentences in exercise 12 above using **altro**.

14 *More*. Rewrite the sentences in exercise 10 above using **altro** instead of **ancora**.

4.4 OTHER ADVERBS AND THEIR USES

(a) Adverbs of affirmation

Vieni? – **Sì/Certo/Sicuro** *Are you coming? – Yes/Of course/Definitely* Dobbiamo aiutare. – **Appunto**, ma come? *We have to help. Precisely/Quite, but how?* Arriva alle cinque, allora. – **Esatto** *So he's arriving at five – That's right* Ti chiamerò **senz'altro** *I'll definitely call you*	These adverbs and adverbial phrases express agreement in varying ways. The English equivalents depend to a large extent on context.

- Other adverbs of affirmation include:

  certamente *certainly*, sicuramente/sicuro/di sicuro *definitely/certainly*, volentieri *gladly/it's a pleasure*, d'accordo *agreed/all right*, senza dubbio *undoubtedly*, come no? *but of course.*

(b) Adverbs of doubt and possibility

Forse verrà stasera *Perhaps/Maybe he'll come this evening* Tornerò presto, **probabilmente** domani *I'll come back soon, probably tomorrow* Vieni? – **Può darsi** *Are you coming? – Maybe/Perhaps/I might* Ci vediamo presto, **magari** domani *We'll see each other soon, possibly/maybe tomorrow* Se c'è sciopero possiamo **magari** andare in macchina *If there's a strike we could maybe go by car* Se l'aereo è troppo caro possiamo **eventualmente** prendere il treno *If the plane is too expensive we might possibly/could perhaps take the train*	These convey degrees of uncertainty. **Può darsi** + **che** is used with the subjunctive (p. 248).

E **I** Use the adverbs below in place of the English ones and complete the sentences.

> appunto • certo • d'accordo • esatto • magari • può darsi • senz'altro

(a) È molto difficile! – (*Exactly*), te l'avevo detto.
(b) Siete pronti? – (*Of course*), arriviamo subito.
(c) Se sei libera domani possiamo (*maybe*) andare al cinema.
(d) Venite domani? – (*We might/maybe*), se non piove.
(e) L'appuntamento è per giovedì, vero? – (*That's right*), per giovedì alle dieci.
(f) Vieni martedì? – (*Definitely*), ma ti chiamerò prima.
(g) Ci vediamo più tardi. – (*All right*), alle due allora.

(c) Comment and viewpoint adverbs

Sinceramente, non vale la pena di andarci *It **honestly** isn't worth going* **Francamente** non mi dispiace ***Frankly** I don't mind* **Ovviamente** viene anche lui ***Obviously** he's coming too* **Psicologicamente** è rimasto un bambino ***Psychologically** he's still a child* **Economicamente** è stato un disastro ***Economically** it was a disaster* **But**: La amava sinceramente *He sincerely/genuinely loved her* (adverb of manner)	Used for comment on what is being said, to express value judgements, or to specify a viewpoint. They usually modify a whole sentence but if they are used as adverbs of manner, they directly follow the verb.

(d) Focus adverbs

Mi ha **perfino/persino** scritto *He **even** wrote to me* Costa **solo** trenta euro *It **only** costs thirty euros* Vado **anche** a Torino *I'm going to Turin **as well*** Ti piacerebbe **davvero**? *Would you **really** like it?* Lo ha lasciato **proprio** davanti alla porta *He left it **right** in front of the door* Me l'ha detto **proprio** prima di partire *He told me **just** before he left* Non capisco **proprio** *I **simply/just** don't understand* **Sul serio**, mi hanno dato il posto ***Seriously/honestly**, they gave me the job*	These adverbs focus on and emphasise a particular word or phrase.

- Some focus adverbs can also be intensifiers. See next section. For more on **solo** and **anche** see pp. 57–8.

2   Put your own slant on things and complete the sentences below using the English as a guideline.

   (a) Ha perso la chiave. (*unfortunately*)
   (b) Non si è fatto male. (*luckily*)
   (c) Non capiscono niente. (*obviously/clearly*)
   (d) Lo trovo antipatico. (*frankly*)
   (e) Non mi sembra necessario. (*honestly*)

3   Now choose one or more of the adverbs below to complete the sentences.

> proprio • davvero • addirittura • solo • perfino/persino

   (a) Non ho capito niente. (*really*)
   (b) Lo ha insultato! (*actually/even*)
   (c) Mi ha aiutato. (*even*)
   (d) Lo troverai davanti alla porta. (*right/just*)
   (e) È un gioco. (*only*)

Intensifiers

These adverbs intensify the meaning of adjectives and other adverbs and are all close in meaning.

Intensifiers with adjectives and adverbs	Mi sento **proprio** male *I feel really/absolutely awful* È **proprio** impossibile *It's quite/really/just/totally impossible* È **davvero** interessante *It's truly interesting* Canta **davvero** bene *He sings really well* È **assolutamente** impossibile *It's absolutely/utterly impossible* È **addirittura** assurdo *It's absolutely/quite simply absurd*	The adverb used depends on the collocation, i.e. which adverbs and adjectives are normally found together. If in doubt, use **proprio**.
	Sei **incredibilmente** testardo *You're incredibly stubborn* Sono ragazzi **spaventosamente** viziati *They are horribly spoilt children*	Some adverbs of manner can be used as intensifiers.

Other adverbial intensifiers: Italian adjective + noun = English adverb + adjective	È di una bellezza straordinaria *She is **extraordinarily** beautiful* È di una volgarità sorprendente *He's **surprisingly** vulgar* Sono di un'ignoranza paurosa *They're **frighteningly** ignorant* Fa un freddo incredibile *It's **incredibly/unbelievably** cold*	In Italian an adjective is often used with a noun as an intensifier, but the English equivalent of these constructions is an adverb + adjective, e.g. *extraordinarily beautiful*.
tutto: adjective used as intensifier	Maria è tornata **tutta** bagnata *Maria came back all wet/totally soaked* Era **tutta** orgogliosa, aveva vinto la gara *She was really proud, she had won the competition* Sei **tutto** sudato, Mario *You're all/really sweaty, Mario* Sono **tutti** eccitati *They are all/really excited*	With plural subjects the meaning may be ambiguous as in English, e.g. the last sentence can also mean *All of them are excited*.

- For adverbs of negation such as **no** *no*, **neanche** *not even*, see Negatives, pp. 145–7. For connecting adverbs such as **invece** *instead, on the other hand*, **di conseguenza** *consequently*, **altrimenti** *otherwise*, see pp. 171–3, 175.

E   4   Intensify your statements by using **addirittura**, **proprio** or **assolutamente** in the sentences below. There is often more than one possibility. Give the English equivalents.

    (a) È incredibile!   (c) Sono matti!

    (b) Non è possibile!   (d) Sono seccati.

5 Form adverbs of manner from the adjectives below and use them as intensifiers in the sentences given.

> eccessivo • eccezionale • forte • terribile

(a) Suonava (*exceptionally*) bene il flauto.
(b) La lezione è stata (*terribly*) noiosa.
(c) Lo trovo (*excessively*) sensibile (*sensitive*).
(d) È stato (*extremely/greatly/strongly*) influenzato dal padre.

6 Below, Italian adjectives are used adverbially as intensifiers. Give the English equivalents of these sentences.

(a) Fa un caldo incredibile.
(b) È un ragazzo di un'intelligenza eccezionale.
(c) Quel film è di una stupidità deprimente.
(d) Quell'uomo è di un'ignoranza spaventosa.
(e) La bambina era tutta triste: aveva perso il gattino.

Using *anche* and *solo*

Different positions of **anche** and **solo** may affect the meaning.

anche: *also, too, as well*	Ho **anche** parlato con Maria *I also spoke to Maria* (i.e. in addition to the other things I did) Ho parlato **anche** con Maria *I also spoke to Maria/I spoke to Maria as well/too* (in addition to speaking to other people) **Anch'io** ho parlato con Maria *I also spoke to Maria/ I too spoke to Maria* (I spoke, as well as others)	**Anche** must be placed before the word or phrase it refers to. In English, on the other hand, the position is more flexible.
	Ieri mi sono alzato tardi, sono andato in piscina e poi ho studiato un po'. **Inoltre**, la sera, sono andato al cinema. *Yesterday I got up late, went swimming and then studied a bit. Also, in the evening I went to the cinema*	When *also* refers to a whole sentence or phrase, **inoltre** is used instead.

7 Give the Italian equivalent of the English, using **anche** each time.

(a) *I went to Rome, Milan, Bergamo, Trento and Turin and then I also went to Bari.*
(b) *Really? You went to Bari as well?*
(c) *Marta is intelligent. – Yes, but Marina is also intelligent/Marina is intelligent too.*
(d) *Marina is sensitive. – Yes, but she's also cheerful* (allegra).

solo: *only*	Mangio **solo** pesce *I only eat fish* Ho mangiato **solo** pesce *or* Ho **solo** mangiato pesce *I only ate fish* Vieni domani? – No, vengo **solo** stasera *Are you coming tomorrow? No, I'm only coming this evening* Puoi venire domani? – No, posso venire **solo** stasera *or* Posso **solo** venire stasera *Can you come tomorrow? – I can only come this evening*	**Solo** comes before the word or phrase it refers to. When used with compound tenses or a verb + infinitive its position may be flexible, but if a word is especially emphasised, **solo** will precede that word.

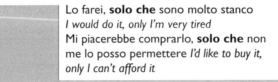

Lo farei, **solo che** sono molto stanco
I would do it, only I'm very tired
Mi piacerebbe comprarlo, **solo che** non
me lo posso permettere *I'd like to buy it,
only I can't afford it*

When *only* refers to a
whole phrase or sentence
it is translated as **solo che**.

E   **8**   Give an Italian equivalent of the English using **solo** each time.

(a) *We've only got one car.*
(b) *Today I'm only studying geography. (and no other subject)*
(c) *We're only free next Monday, because after (that) we're leaving.*
(d) *Yesterday I only read two chapters. (and no more)*
(e) *Did you buy any rolls? – No, I only bought bread.*
(f) *They can only come next week, not before.*

5

Comparatives and superlatives

Comparatives and superlatives (**i comparativi e i superlativi**) are particular forms of some adjectives and adverbs: they are expressed in English by *more/less*, or the suffix *-er* (comparatives), and by *(the) most/least* or the suffix *-est* (relative superlatives). A second superlative, known as an absolute superlative, is expressed by *extremely/very* in English.

5.1 ADJECTIVES: COMPARATIVES AND RELATIVE SUPERLATIVES

Most descriptive adjectives have comparative and superlative forms.

Regular forms

Comparative and relative superlative forms differ only in the use of the definite article with **più** and **meno**.

Comparative adjectives	**più/meno** antico *older/less old* **più/meno** utile *more/less useful*	Comparative adjectives are formed by placing **più** and **meno** before the adjective.
Superlative adjectives	**il più/il meno** antico *the oldest/least old* **il più/il meno** utile *the most/least useful*	Superlative adjectives are formed by placing **più** and **meno** before the adjective, <u>plus</u> the relevant definite article, **il**, **la**, **i** or **le**.

USES

More/less	La chiesa di San Clemente è **più** antica della Cappella Sistina *The church of San Clemente is older than the Sistine Chapel* Questi libri sono **meno** utili degli altri *These books are less useful than/not as useful as the others*	**Più/meno** are invariable, but the adjectives change to agree with the word they refer to. Note that with comparatives **di** often means *than* or occasionally *as*. For **che** as *than*, see p. 67.

The most/ the least	È **la** chiesa **più** antica della città/di Roma *It is the oldest church in the city/in Rome* Questi sono **i** libri **meno** utili di tutti *These are the least useful books of all* **or**: Questi libri sono **i meno** utili di tutti *These books are the least useful of all*	The definite article usually goes before the noun. It may sometimes go before **più/meno**, but not both: you never say 'la chiesa la più antica'. Note that **di** expresses *in* (**della città** *in the city*) as well as *of* (**di tutti** *of all*).
One of the most/least	La regina d'Inghilterra è **una delle** donne **più** ricche del mondo *The queen of England is one of the richest women in the world* La Gioconda è **fra i** dipinti **più** famosi del mondo *The Mona Lisa is one of the most famous paintings in the world*	This is expressed by **uno/a di** + definite article or, very often, by **fra** + **i/gli/le** (lit. *amongst the* ...).
Some of the most/least	**Fra le** squadre di calcio **più** famose d'Italia ci sono la Juventus, il Milan e il Lazio *Some of the/Amongst the most famous football teams in Italy are J., M. and L.*	This is expressed by **fra i/gli/le** or else by **alcuni dei/alcuni degli/ alcune delle**.

E 1 Form regular comparative and relative superlative adjectives by filling in the table below with the Italian equivalent of the English, using the masculine singular form of the adjective.

Adjective	Comparative	Relative superlative
bello *beautiful*	. . . *more beautiful*	. . . *most beautiful*
pesante *heavy*	. . . *heavier*	. . . *(the) heaviest*
ottimista *optimistic*	. . . *more optimistic*	. . . *(the) most optimistic*

2 Complete the sentences using the correct comparative or superlative form of the adjective.

(a) Lorenzo è (*nicer than*) Franco.
(b) La mia macchina è (*not as old as/less old than*) la tua.
(c) È il ragazzo (*nicest in the*) classe.
(d) È la spiaggia (*least busy on the*) costa. (frequentato)
(e) Sono i negozi (*most expensive in the*) quartiere.

3 ***One of the most, some of the most.*** Rewrite the sentences below without changing the meaning.

e.g. Verdi, Puccini e Rossini sono alcuni dei compositori italiani più rinomati.
    Verdi, Puccini e Rossini sono fra i compositori italiani più rinomati.

(a) Gli Stati Uniti sono uno dei paesi più ricchi del mondo.
(b) Marilyn Monroe era una delle attrici più belle di Hollywood.
(c) Stromboli, Lipari e Capri sono fra le isole più affascinanti d'Italia.
(d) Il parmigiano è fra i formaggi italiani più conosciuti.

Irregular forms

Buono, cattivo, grande, piccolo

With **più**, but not **meno**, the following adjectives have both a regular and an irregular comparative and superlative form.

Adjective	Comparative	Relative superlative
buono *good*	più buono/**migliore** *better* meno buono *less good*	il più buono/**il migliore** *the best* il meno buono *the least good*
cattivo *bad*	più cattivo/**peggiore** *worse* meno cattivo *less bad*	il più cattivo/**il peggiore** *the worst* il meno cattivo *the least bad*
grande *big*	più grande/**maggiore** *bigger* meno grande *less big*	il più grande/**il maggiore** *the biggest* il meno grande *the least big*
piccolo *small*	più piccolo/**minore** *smaller* meno piccolo *less small*	il più piccolo/**il minore** *the smallest* il meno piccolo *the least small*

USES

The choice of regular or irregular forms depends on style and what you are talking about. **Migliore/peggiore** are more or less interchangeable with **più buono, più cattivo** only when it comes to food. **Più grande/più piccolo** are more common than **maggiore/minore** (which are often used with numbers or quantity and correspond to *greater/lesser*). However, older or younger brothers and sisters can be described as **maggiore** or **minore**.

Comparative	Relative superlative
Quel libro è **migliore** dell'altro *That book is better than the other one* Oggi la pasta è **migliore/più buona** *Today the pasta is better/nicer*	Lo trovo **il libro migliore** *I find it the best book* È sicuramente **la** pasta **migliore/più buona** *It's definitely the best/nicest pasta*
La casa di Carlo è **più grande** *Carlo's house is bigger* Enrico ha una sorella **maggiore/più grande** *Enrico has an older sister* È stata una spesa **maggiore** del previsto *It was a greater/bigger expense than expected*	La casa di Carlo è **la più grande** *Carlo's house is the biggest* Gemma è **la** sorella **maggiore/più grande** *Gemma is the elder/eldest sister* È stata **la** spesa **maggiore** *It was the biggest/greatest expense*

Molto, poco

The adjectives **molto** and **poco** have an irregular comparative form but no relative superlative form at all.

Adjective	Comparative	Relative superlative
molto *much/many*	più *more*	... *the most*
poco *not much/not many/few*	meno *less/fewer*	... *the least*

The most/the least are expressed in two ways: **più/meno di tutti** or **il maggior/minor numero di** + noun (*the greatest/least number of*).

Comparative	Relative superlative
Ha **più/meno** libri **di** me *He's got more/fewer books than me*	Ha **più/meno** libri **di tutti** *He has the most/fewest books (of all)* Ha **il maggior numero/minor numero di** libri *He has the most/least/fewest books*

- **Molto** and **poco** both have regular absolute superlative forms. See 5.2 below.

E **4** Fill in the table below with the Italian equivalent(s) of the English adjectives given.

Adjective		Comparative		Relative superlative	
good	**buono**	*better*	...	*best*	...
bad	**cattivo**	*worse*	...	*worse*	...
big	**grande**	*bigger*	...	*the biggest*	...
small	**piccolo**	*smaller*	...	*the smallest*	...
much/many	**molto**	*more*	...	*(the) most*	...
not much/many/ little/few	**poco**	*lesser/fewer* ...		*(the) least/fewest* ...	

5 *Comparatives.* Complete the sentences by providing the correct Italian equivalent(s) of the English.

(a) Le lasagne della mamma sono (*good*), ma quelle della nonna sono (*better/nicer*).
(b) È un (*good*) restaurant ma trovo che quell'altro è (*better*).
(c) La minestra era (*bad/horrible*), ma la bistecca era ancora (*worse/more horrible*).
(d) Ho due fratelli: il (*older/bigger*) si chiama Andrea e il (*younger/smaller*) si chiama Bruno.
(e) Non abbiamo (*more*) soldi di loro, perché abbiamo (*fewer*) risparmi.

6 *Superlatives.* Complete the Italian sentences inserting an appropriate superlative.

(a) Chi è il tuo amico ...? — *Who is your best friend?*
(b) Qual è la stagione ... dell'anno? — *Which is the worst season of the year?*
(c) È (il) mio fratello .... — *He is my eldest/biggest brother.*
(d) Chi ha ... carte ...? — *Who has the most cards?*
(e) Ho ... carte .... — *I have the fewest cards (of all).*

5.2 ADJECTIVES: ABSOLUTE SUPERLATIVES

Absolute superlatives are so called because they are used with no other terms of reference. Like all adjectives, absolute superlatives agree in gender and number with the nouns they refer to.

Adjective	Absolute superlative	Explanations
antico *old* utile *useful* molto *much/many*	antichissimo *very/extremely old* utilissimo *very/extremely useful* moltissimo *very much/many*	**-issimo** is added to the adjective, minus the final vowel. To keep the hard sound, *h* precedes **-issimo** if the adjective ends in **-co**.
	molto antico *very ancient/old* molto utile *very useful*	**Molto** + a normal adjective can substitute absolute superlatives except in the case of the adjective **molto**. You cannot say **molto molto**.
egoista *selfish*	molto egoista *very/extremely selfish*	Adjectives in **-a** do not have **-issimo** suffixes. **Molto** is used instead.
buono *good*	buonissimo/**ottimo** *very good/extremely good/excellent*	**Buono, cattivo, grande** and **piccolo** have irregular as well as regular absolute superlatives.
cattivo *bad*	cattivissimo/**pessimo** *very bad/extremely bad/terrible*	
grande *big*	grandissimo/**massimo** *very big/extremely big/maximum*	
piccolo *small*	piccolissimo/**minimo** *very small/extremely small/minimum*	

USES

Examples	Explanations
La pasta è **buonissima/ottima** *The pasta is extremely good/excellent* È una **grandissima** casa *It is an extremely big house* Ha fatto **il massimo** sforzo *He made the utmost/maximum effort* Sono gattini **piccolissimi** *They are tiny kittens* Non ho **la minima** idea *I don't have the slightest idea*	The irregular forms are rarely synonymous with the regular forms, though **buonissimo** and **ottimo** are often interchangeable. **Cattivissimo** is rarely used for people unless it means *very vicious* or *naughty*. **Massimo** and **minimo** are used with the definite article.
È una persona straordinaria *He/She is an extraordinary person* È un artista eccellente *He/She is an excellent artist*	Adjectives which already express a superlative concept do not form the absolute superlative.

1   ***The most …; very/extremely ….*** Complete the descriptions below by giving the Italian equivalent of the English. There are sometimes several possibilities.

(a) Chiara è la ragazza più allegra della classe. *She's an extremely happy girl.*
(b) Gemma è la studentessa meno simpatica della classe. *She's a very selfish person.*
(c) Riccardo è l'artista più dotato della classe. *He's a very good/excellent artist.*
(d) Pietro è il linguista meno bravo della classe. *He's a terrible linguist.*
(e) Il signor De Stefano è l'insegnante più gentile della scuola. *He's a very good person.*
(f) Nerone è il cane più antipatico di tutti. *He is a very bad/vicious dog.*

5.3 ADVERBS: COMPARATIVES, RELATIVE AND ABSOLUTE SUPERLATIVES

Most adverbs of manner and a few adverbs of time, place and quantity have comparative and superlative forms.

Regular forms

Comparative adverbs	**più/meno** lontano *further/less far* **più/meno** tardi *later/less late* **più/meno** rapidamente *more/less quickly*	Comparative adverbs are formed by placing **più** and **meno** before the adverb.
Relative superlative adverbs	**il più/il meno** lontano possibile *the furthest/least far* **il più/il meno** tardi possibile *the latest/least late* **il più/il meno** rapidamente possibile *the most/least quickly*	Relative superlative adverbs are formed by placing **più** and **meno** before the adverb, <u>plus</u> the definite article **il**. They are often accompanied by **possibile**.
Absolute superlative adverbs	lontan**issimo** *very/extremely far* tard**issimo** *very/extremely late* rapid**issima**mente/molto rapidamente *extremely/very quickly*	Absolute superlative adverbs are formed by placing **molto** before the adverb, or by adding **-issimo** to the adverb minus the final vowel. When an adverb ends in **-mente**, **-issima** goes <u>before</u> the **-mente** ending and the final vowel is dropped.

USES

Perché non vieni **più** tardi? *Why don't you come later?* È arrivata tardi, ma **meno** tardi di te *She arrived late, but not as late as (less late than) you* L'hanno fatto **più** rapidamente **di tutti** *They did it the fastest of all* Maria abita **lontanissimo/molto lontano** *Maria lives very far away*	Like most adverbs, comparative and superlative adverbs are invariable. Nearly all absolute superlatives except **moltissimo** can be substituted by **molto** + the normal adverb. (You cannot say **molto molto**.)

E 1 Form regular comparative and relative superlative adverbs by filling in the table below with the Italian equivalent of the English.

Adverb		Comparative	Relative superlative	Absolute superlative
gentilmente	*kindly*	*... more kindly*	*... (the) most kindly*	*... very kindly*
forte	*loudly*	*... more loudly/louder*	*... (the) most loudly/ loudest*	*... very loudly*
tardi	*late*	*... later*	*... (the) latest*	*... very late*
vicino	*near*	*... nearer*	*... (the) nearest*	*... very near*

2 Complete these sentences by using comparative adverbs each time.

  (a) Susanna abita lontano, ma (*not as far/less far*) di te.

  (b) Oggi Piera mi ha salutato cordialmente, (*in a friendlier/more cordial manner*) del solito.

  (c) Ieri Francesca e Giuliana sono partite presto, (*earlier*) del previsto.

3 Use the relative superlative and the **-issimo** form of the absolute superlative to answer these questions.

  (a) Sono tornati molto tardi? – *Yes, they came back extremely late, later than everyone.*

  (b) Ha lavorato veramente veloce? – *Yes, he worked extremely quickly, the most quickly of everyone/all.*

  (c) Ti ha scritto molto regolarmente? – *Yes, she wrote very regularly, the most regularly of all.*

Irregular forms

Bene, male, molto, poco

The article is nearly always omitted in the relative superlative form, making it identical to the comparative.

Adverb	Comparative	Relative superlative	Absolute superlative
bene *well*	meglio *better*	meglio *best*	benissimo *extremely/very well*
male *badly*	peggio *worse*	peggio *worst*	malissimo *extremely/very badly*
molto *much,*	(di) più *more*	(di) più *most*	moltissimo *very much/a great deal*
poco *not much, little*	(di) meno *less*	(di) meno *least*	pochissimo *very little/not very much*

USES

Mi piace molto Roma, ma Bologna mi piace **di più** *I like Rome very much, but I like Bologna more* Mi piacciono Roma, Bologna e Firenze, ma Napoli è la città che mi piace **di più** *I like Rome, Bologna and Florence, but the town I like most is Naples* Napoli mi piace **moltissimo** *I like Naples very much*	The comparative and relative superlative forms are the same, but the context usually makes it clear which form is intended.
Devi mangiare **il più possibile** *You must eat as much as possible.* (lit. *the most possible*) Lui studia **il meno possibile** *He studies as little as possible* Lo farò **il meglio possibile** *I'll do it as best I can/as well as I can*	**Il ... possibile**: *as ... as possible.* The article **il** is necessary with the relative superlative.
Ho finito – **Bene/Benissimo**, andiamo *I've finished – Good/Fine, Excellent/Very good, let's go*	**Bene** and **benissimo** can also mean *good/very good.*

E

4 Complete the sentences by giving the correct Italian comparative forms of the English adverbs.

(a) Si mangia (*well*) in Francia, ma in Italia si mangia (*better*).
(b) Io mi sento (*bad*), ma mio marito si sente (*worse*).
(c) Le mie sorelle studiano (*little, not much*), ma io studio (*less*).
(d) Qui piove (*a lot*), ma da voi piove (*more*).

5 Answer these questions by giving the Italian equivalent of the English, using relative and **-issimo** absolute superlative forms.

(a) Hanno lavorato molto bene? – *Yes, they worked extremely well, better than anyone/ the best of all.*
(b) Ti ha aiutato molto poco? – *Yes, he helped very little, he helped least of all.*
(c) Insegna molto male? – *Yes, he teaches extremely badly, he teaches worst of all the teachers.*
(d) Ti piace veramente molto? – *Yes, I like it very much, I like it most of all.*

6 Give the Italian equivalent of the following.

(a) *You must come as soon as possible.*
(b) *You must eat as little as possible.*
(c) *You must do it as well as/as best you can.*

7 Revision: **better, best, worse, worst**. Distinguish between the Italian adverbial and adjectival forms.

(a) Parla italiano (*better*) di me. I suoi voti sono sempre (*better*) dei miei.
(b) È diventato il violinista (*best*) dell'orchestra. Suona (*best*) of all.
(c) La squadra gioca (*worse*) dell'anno scorso. I risultati sono (*worse*) del previsto.
(d) È diventato il giocatore (*worst*) della squadra. Gioca (*worst*) di tutti.

5.4 MAKING COMPARISONS OF INEQUALITY

Comparisons of inequality are so called because they describe things or actions in terms of *more* or *less ... than* something else. When comparing actions, a comparative adverb is used and when comparing qualities, a comparative adjective is used. In Italian *than* corresponds to **di** or **che. Di** is more frequently used than **che.**

(a) Using *di* (than)

Carlo è **più** simpatico **di** Paolo *Carlo is nicer than Paolo* Carlo si comporta **meglio di** Paolo *Carlo behaves better than Paolo* Le fragole mi piacciono **meno dei** lamponi *I like strawberries less than raspberries* Questo ristorante è **migliore dell'**altro *This restaurant is better than the other one*	**Di** expresses *than* when comparing a <u>single</u> quality or action between two people or things. It tends to be required before nouns and pronouns and is joined to the relevant definite article.
Luigi è **più** giovane **di** te/lei *Luigi is younger than you (are)/she (is)* Franca mangia **più** velocemente **di** me *Franca eats faster than me/I do*	Before emphatic personal pronouns: *than me/you*, etc.

Ho speso **più di** 100 euro *I spent more than 100 euros* Sandra ha **meno di** dieci anni *Sandra is under/less than ten*	Before numbers.
Fa **meno** freddo **di** ieri *It is less cold than yesterday* Sono **più** felici **di** prima/una volta *They are happier than before* **But**: Sono più stanco **che** mai *I am more tired than ever*	Before most adverbs of time except **mai**.
La lezione è stata **meno** interessante **del previsto/ del solito** *The lesson was less interesting than expected/than usual*	With set expressions: **del previsto, del solito, del normale**.
La popolazione italiana è **più alta di quella** svizzera *Italy's population is higher than Switzerland's (population)* I treni inglesi sono **meno puntuali di quelli** italiani *English trains are less punctual than Italian ones/trains*	**Di** + **quello/a/i/e**: to avoid repeating the same noun in a comparison the relevant form of **quello** may be used after **di**.

(b) Using *che*

Che meaning *than* is less common than **di**.

Sono scarpe **più** eleganti **che** comode *The shoes are more elegant than comfortable* Mangiamo **più** pesce **che** carne *We eat more fish than (we eat) meat* Ho **più** fame **che** sete *I'm more hungry than thirsty* Vado **meno** spesso a Milano **che** a Torino *I go to Milan less often than (I go) to Turin* È **più** facile capire **che** parlare una lingua straniera *It's easier to understand a foreign language than to speak it*	Used when directly comparing two qualities, activities, entities in relation to a single activity, person or thing. **Che** can go before nouns, pronouns, adverbs, adjectives. Only **che** (and not **di**) can go before prepositions, and infinitives. For *than* before a finite verb, see p. 72.

1 Give the Italian equivalent of the English, using **di** for *than* in all but one case.

(a) *Ada is less tall than (not as tall as) her sister.*
(b) *Gina studies more than me/than I do.*
(c) *My grandfather is more than eighty years old.*
(d) *It's hotter than yesterday.*
(e) *I get up earlier than my parents.*
(f) *Public transport is more expensive in England than in Italy.*

2 Complete the sentences by giving the Italian equivalent of the English.

(a) Ho più fratelli (*than sisters*).
(b) Bevo più tè (*than coffee*).
(c) È più difficile (*than ever*).
(d) È meno difficile (*than the last time*).
(e) Guidare a Londra è meno stressante (*than driving in Rome*).
(f) È un tipo più simpatico (*than [he is] intelligent*).

5.5 EMPHATIC COMPARATIVES

sempre più sempre meno	È **sempre più** difficile trovare un lavoro *It's increasingly hard/harder and harder to find a job* Ha cominciato a tornare a casa **sempre più** tardi *He has begun to come home increasingly late/later and later* Ho **sempre meno** voglia di studiare *I feel less and less like studying*	**Sempre più** *more and more/increasingly* and **sempre meno** *less and less* are placed before adjectives, adverbs or nouns to form an emphatic comparative.
ancora più ancora meno	Angelo è **ancora più** antipatico di Luigi *Angelo is even more unpleasant than Luigi* Lisa lavora **ancora meno** bene di prima *Lisa is working even less well than before* Fa **ancora più** freddo di ieri *It's even colder than yesterday*	**Ancora più** *even more* and **ancora meno** *even less* are placed before adjectives, adverbs or nouns.
sempre with meglio peggio migliore peggiore	La clientela aumenta e gli affari vanno **sempre meglio** *The clientele is increasing and business is going better and better* In genere Giorgio ottiene voti buoni ma quelli di Luisa sono **ancora migliori** *On the whole Giorgio gets good marks but Luisa's are even better*	**Sempre** and **ancora** may also be used before **meglio/migliore** and **peggio/peggiore**.
	La cucina francese è buona, ma quella italiana è **ancora meglio/migliore** *French cooking is good, but Italian cooking is even better* La situazione politica qua è brutta ma da voi è **ancora peggio/peggiore** *The political situation where you are is bad but it's even worse where we are* Ogni volta che rifaccio il compito mi sembra **ancora peggio/peggiore** *Every time I redo the work it seems even worse*	Note that after the verbs **essere**, **sembrare** and **parere**, the adverbs **meglio** and **peggio** may be used as adjectives instead of **migliore** and **peggiore**.

E I Rewrite these statements twice to make them more emphatic, using the English as a guide.

(a) È difficile trovare un lavoro   *increasingly hard/harder and harder*   *even harder*
(b) L'idea mi piace meno   *less and less*   *even less*
(c) È diventato triste   *sadder and sadder*   *even more sad*
(d) Ottiene dei voti brutti   *worse and worse*   *even worse*

5.6 MAKING COMPARISONS OF EQUALITY

Comparisons of equality involve likening one thing or action to another, and in English this is done by using the phrase *as ... as*. In Italian this is done in a variety of ways which do not always directly correspond to English. Below are some of the most basic phrases used.

(a) Using *tanto ... quanto, altrettanto ... che*

tanto ... quanto No agreements if **tanto** refers to: adjectives	Carlo è (**tanto**) <u>alto</u> **quanto** Luigi *Carlo is as tall as Luigi* Ida è (**tanto**) <u>brava</u> **quanto** me *Ida is as clever as me/as I am* Carla è **tanto** <u>simpatica</u> **quanto** <u>brava</u> *Carla is as nice as she is clever* Lavorare è **tanto** <u>difficile</u> **quanto** <u>studiare</u> *It is as hard to work as to study*	**Tanto** is very often omitted, but not when two adjectives or infinitive verbs are compared. Note that after **quanto**, personal pronouns are disjunctive (**me, te,** etc.).
verbs	Ida <u>guadagna</u> **quanto** te *Ida earns as much as you* Quel disgraziato <u>beve</u> **tanto quanto** <u>mangia</u> *That idiot drinks as much as he eats* Milano <u>dista</u> da Genova **tanto quanto** Torino *Milan is as far from Genoa as Turin*	**Tanto** is usually omitted except when two verbs are compared directly or indirectly.
tanto ... quanto Agreements are made if **tanto** refers to nouns	Ho **tanti** soldi **quanti** Maria/**quanti** ne ha Maria *I have as much money as Maria (has)* Ho comprato **tante** pere **quante** mele *I bought as many pears as apples* Ho mangiato **tanta** pasta **quanta** ne hai mangiata tu *I ate as much pasta as you/you did*	Before nouns, **tanto ... quanto** mean *as much/as many as* and they usually agree with the nouns they refer to. **Tanto** is never omitted.
tanto ... come Agreements are made with nouns	Ho mangiato **tanta** pasta **come** te *I ate as much pasta as you/as you did*	**Tanto ... come** may be colloquially used instead of **tanto ... quanto**, especially if the second part comes before a pronoun. See also **così ... come,** p. 70.
altrettanto che with infinitive verbs: No agreements	Trovare un idraulico è **altrettanto** difficile **che** trovare un buon medico *Finding a plumber is just as hard as finding a good doctor* È **altrettanto** impossibile parlare al manager **che** (parlare) al direttore *It's (just) as impossible to speak to the manager as (it is) to the director*	**Altrettanto** is commonly used with **che** before infinitives, or when an infinitive is implied (as in the second example here).

(b) Using *così ... come*

Così and come never change their form.

così ... come: with adjectives	Maurizio è (**così**) generoso **come** mio fratello *Maurizio is as generous as my brother* Lui non è (**così**) felice **come** te *He is not as happy as you/as you are* Il mare oggi è liscio **come** l'olio *Today the sea is as flat as a millpond* (lit. *as smooth as oil*) Giovanna è magra **come** un chiodo *Giovanna is as thin as a rake* (lit. *nail*)	**Così ... come** is especially common in similes, as it tends to express similarity. Unlike **tanto ... quanto** it is never used to express *as much/many as.*
with adverbs	Mangia lentamente **come** me *He eats as slowly as me/as I do* Guida bene **come** Luigi *She drives as well as Luigi*	**Così** is usually omitted and **come** is followed by disjunctive pronouns.
come before verb	Angela è davvero (**così**) simpatica **come** pensavo *Angela is really as nice as I thought* Non è (**così**) facile **come** credi tu *It's not as easy as you think*	**Così** is usually omitted. **Come** goes before the verb.
così come before verb	Le cose sono andate **così come** avevo previsto *Things turned out just as I had predicted* È proprio **così come** ti ho detto *It's just as I told you*	**Così** and **come** can be used together when the comparison is stressed.

E 1 You are even-handed in your judgements. Contradict these statements using comparisons of equality.

   (a) Lisa è più generosa di Elena. – No, non è vero. (*Elena is as generous as Lisa.*)

   (b) Mirella è più ingenua che stupida. – Non è vero. (*Mirella is as stupid as she is naïve.*)

   (c) Tu guadagni meno di me. – No, non è vero. (*I earn as much as you do.*)

   (d) Quei ragazzi dormono più di quanto studiano. – No, non è vero. (*They study as much as they sleep.*)

   (e) Rina ha meno amiche di Carla. – Non è vero. (*Carla has as many friends as Rina.*)

   (f) Io lavoro meglio di Lucio. – Non è vero. (*Lucio works as well as you.*)

2 Give the Italian equivalent of these common English similes.

   (a) *She came back from the race as fresh as a daisy.* (use una rosa *a rose*)

   (b) *My grandmother is as deaf as a post.* (use una campana *a bell*)

   (c) *My grandfather is as fit as a fiddle.* (use un pesce *a fish*)

   (d) *You smoke like a chimney.* (use un turco *a turk*)

3 Give the English equivalent of the Italian.

   (a) Non è poi così stupido come pensi.

   (b) Li trovo davvero gentili come mi avevi detto.

   (c) Ti preferisco così come sei.

4 Liken these actions by completing the following sentences.

   (a) È ... pericoloso viaggiare in motocicletta ... in bicicletta.

   (b) È ... comodo prendere l'autobus ... la metropolitana.

   (c) È ... stressante occuparsi dei bambini ... andare a lavorare.

5.7 OTHER COMPARATIVE CONSTRUCTIONS

(a) Using *altrettanto*

Altrettanto is very often used in implicit comparisons of equality. It can be an adverb, an adjective or a pronoun.

| altrettanto: adverb | Elisa è pigra. – Sì, ma Francesca è **altrettanto** pigra *Elisa is lazy. – Yes, but Francesca is just as/equally lazy* Mario ha giocato bene ma Dino ha giocato **altrettanto** bene *Mario played well but Dino played just as/equally well* Mi sono iscritto a una palestra e Sabrina ha fatto **altrettanto** *I've joined a gym and Sabrina has done the same/likewise/and so has Sabrina.* | When **altrettanto** *just as, equally, likewise* is an adverb, it modifies adjectives or other adverbs and verbs. It is invariable. |
| altrettanto: adjective and pronoun | Oggi sono arrivati **altrettanti** ospiti *Today just as many guests arrived* Ho raccolto due chili di ciliegie e Carlo ne ha raccolte **altrettante** *I picked two kilos of cherries and Carlo picked as many (as I did)* | When **altrettanto** is an adjective (Example 1) and a pronoun (Example 2), it agrees with the noun or pronoun it refers to. |

(b) Using *lo stesso di/che* and *piuttosto che*

| lo stesso di/che | Ho comprato **la stessa** gonna **di** Mara *I bought the same skirt as Mara* Ho fatto **lo stesso** errore **di** ieri *I made the same mistake as yesterday* In Italia abbiamo **gli stessi** problemi **che** nel resto del mondo *In Italy we have the same problems as in the rest of the world* | **Lo stesso di/che** *the same as* is often used to compare like. **Che** must be used instead of **di** in front of prepositions. |
| piuttosto che | Molti preferiscono alloggiare in una casa privata **piuttosto che** in un albergo *Many people prefer to stay in a private house rather than in a hotel* Perché non dormi da noi **piuttosto che** prendere l'ultimo treno? *Why don't you sleep at our place rather than catch the last train?* | **Piuttosto che** *rather than* is often used when comparing two options. See also Connectives, p. 170–1. |

E **1** Just the same. Complete the replies by giving the Italian equivalent of the English.

    (a) Mio fratello è altissimo. – Certo, (*but you are just as tall*).
    (b) Mio padre guadagna tantissimo. – Certo, (*but mine earns just as much*).
    (c) Ho raccolto un chilo di funghi. – Bene, (*but I've picked just as many*).
    (d) Ho prenotato per domani. – Bene, (*I've done exactly the same/likewise*).

2 These people are not interested in change. Give the Italian equivalent of the English.

    (a) *Michele is wearing the same shirt as yesterday.*
    (b) *Giovanna votes for the same party as her parents.*
    (c) *Paolo has the same hairdresser as his brother.*

3   Say what the options are, choosing the first one each time, and complete the sentences.

  (a) Preferirei ...   andare a comprare una pizza/andare al ristorante.
  (b) Ho intenzione di ... andare in campeggio/dormire in albergo.
  (c) Ho deciso di ...   partire con il treno/prendere la macchina.

Level 2 *Comparatives:* di quanto/di quello che *before finite verbs*

If *than,* used in a comparative of <u>inequality only</u>, precedes a finite verb (i.e. a verb with a specific subject and tense), the following are used.

Sandro è più simpatico **di quello che** pensi/**di quanto** non pensi *Sandro is nicer than you think* È stato più semplice **di quel che** pensavo/**di quanto** non pensassi *It was simpler than I thought* Lui spende più **di quanto** dovrebbe *He spends more than he should* **But**: Mauro è così simpatico come pensavo/è tanto simpatico quanto pensavo *Mauro is as nice as I thought*	**Di quello che** is normally followed by an indicative tense. **Di quanto (non)** is usually followed by a subjunctive – but a conditional is possible. **Non** is optional as it has no negative meaning. **But**: the above are not used in comparisons of equality.

Level 2 *Superlatives: use before finite verbs*

When a superlative is used before a finite verb, **che** + a subjunctive verb is used (see Chapter 24, p. 254).

È l'uomo **più simpatico che ci sia** *He's the nicest man there is/ever*	The present subjunctive is used.
È **la** città **più bella che io abbia** mai visto *It is the most beautiful city I have ever seen*	The perfect subjunctive is used.
Era **la** cosa **peggiore che potesse** capitare *It was the worst thing that could happen.*	The imperfect subjunctive is used.
Era **la** città **più bella che io avessi** mai visto *It was the most beautiful city I had ever seen*	The pluperfect subjunctive is used.

E **4** Complete the following sentences, giving the Italian for the English phrases beginning with *than.*

  (a) È più tardi (*than you think*).
  (b) Sono più anziani (*than they seem*) lit. *than <u>it</u> seems.*
  (c) Tu mangi meno (*than you should*).

5 Match up the phrases in each column to form complete sentences.

  (a) È il film migliore   (i)   che io abbia mai letto
  (b) È la persona più superficiale (ii)   che ci siano
  (c) Sono i vicini più gentili   (iii) che io abbia mai visto
  (d) È il libro peggiore   (iv)   che conosca

Suffixes

A suffix (**un suffisso**) is a letter or group of letters added to the end of a word to modify its meaning, e.g. *green, greenish*. In Italian, suffixes can be used with nouns, adjectives and a few adverbs and verbs. They are more varied than in English and are a creative part of everyday conversation. There are rarely exact equivalents between the two languages.

6.1 NOUN AND ADJECTIVAL SUFFIXES

In Italian four main groups of suffixes are used with nouns or adjectives.

FORMS AND USES

The suffixes are usually added to the source word, minus the final vowel. Note that not all nouns and adjectives can be used with suffixes and not all suffixes are used with a given word (e.g. **poverino**, **poveretto** and **poveraccio** are common, but **poveruccio** or **poverone** are not). The use of suffixes often depends on a native speaker's personal preference or origin, but the following are basic guidelines.

| Diminutivi (*diminutives*) **-ino/a** **-etto/a** | un maschietto (maschio) *a baby (newborn) boy* un omino, un ometto (uomo) *a tiny little/wee man* un piedino (piede) *a tootsie/footsie* un/a poveretto/a (povero) *a poor devil* un vizietto (vizio) *a minor bad habit, peccadillo* bruttino/a (brutto) *not very good-looking* noiosetto/a (noioso) *a bit boring* piccolino/a, piccoletto/a (piccolo) *teeny-weeny, titchy, tiny* poverino/a! (povero) *poor thing!* | The endings convey smallness but also sympathy, and may suggest something attractive. These suffixes are often used for baby talk, as euphemisms (e.g. **fare il bisognino** *to spend a penny*), or as a way of joking or of avoiding offence. Note that **omino** is the diminutive of **uomo**, but the initial **u** is omitted. |

- Other diminutive suffixes include:

  -ello/a (stupidello *a bit stupid*), **-ellino/a** (fiorellino *little flower*), **-ettino/a** (librettino *small book*)

  -icello/a (grandicello *quite big, grown*, ponticello *small bridge, footbridge*)

  -icino/a (posticino *nice little place*); **-olino/a** (gocciolino *a little drop*)

Vezzeggiativi (no exact English equivalent) **-uccio/a**	una femminuccia (femmina) *a baby (newborn) girl* una boccuccia (bocca) *a sweet little mouth* una cosuccia (cosa) *a trifle, an insignificant thing* deboluccio (debole) *a bit on the weak/dim side*	*Vezzeggiativi* can be terms of endearment often used in children's stories. They express goodwill and affection – which is sometimes patronising. Consequently they can also have connotations of mediocrity or insignificance.

- Other *vezzeggiativi* endings include:

  -uzzo/a (principuzzo *little prince*), **-otto/a** (orsacchiotto *bear cub/teddy*, tigrotto *tiger cub*) and **-olo/a** (figliolo/a *dear boy/girl*).

Accrescitivi (*augmentatives*) **-one/a**	un pancione (pancia) *a huge paunch, stomach* un omone (uomo) *a large man* un librone (libro) *a large/important/difficult/overlong book* un riccone (ricco) *an immensely rich person* un donnone (donna) *a big fat strong woman*	The **-one** ending intensifies the meaning of the source word rather than simply expressing largeness. It can express admiration or have a derogatory meaning. Augmentatives are mostly masculine even if the source word is feminine.

- Other augmentative endings include:

  -accione/a (spendaccione/a *spendthrift*), **-acchione/a** (furbacchione/a *a crafty, sneaky devil*).

Peggiorativi (*pejoratives*) **-accio/a**	un poveraccio/a (povero) *an unfortunate wretch* un omaccio (uomo) *a horrible man* un libraccio (libro) *a horrible/awful/immoral book* tempaccio (tempo) *terrible weather*	These are widely used to convey unpleasantness and have a pejorative meaning.

- Other pejorative suffixes include:

  -astro/a (dolciastro *sickly, cloying*). Colour is often described with the suffixes **-astro/a**, **-ognolo/a** or **-iccio/a**, usually in slightly pejorative terms: verdognolo, verdiccio (*greenish*), giallastro, giallognolo, gialliccio (*yellowish*), etc.

1 Complete the sentences below by substituting the words in brackets, including a suffix each time.

   (a) Mio padre è nato in un (piccolo paese) in montagna.
   (b) Mio figlio va male in francese. È (piuttosto debole).
   (c) Carlo è noioso. Usa sempre (delle lunghe parole complicate).
   (d) Mirella è insopportabile. Usa spesso (delle brutte parole).

2 Choose the appropriate word according to the definitions given. If in doubt, use a dictionary.

   (a) **Difetto: difettuccio, difettaccio.** Which word do you use if you're tolerant about someone's faults?
   (b) **Problema: problemino, problemaccio, problemone.** If you want to make light of the problem, which word do you use?
   (c) **Lavoro: lavoretto, lavoraccio, lavoruccio, lavorone.** If you have had a terrible time, how would you describe the work?
   (d) **Stupido: stupidello, stupidino, stupidone.** If you don't want to cause offence which word/s do you use?
   (e) **Figura: Che figuraccia ha fatto! Ha fatto un figurone. Sembra un figurino.** Which phrase would you use to say someone really made a marvellous impression? What do the others mean?

OTHER USES

Many nouns and adjectives with suffixes have acquired an independent but related meaning. Here are a few.

Suffix	Derived word	Source word
-ino/a	bellino *pretty* un finestrino *a car/train window*	bello *beautiful* una finestra *window*
-etto/a	una manetta *a handcuff, lever*	una mano *hand*
-olo/a -olino/a	un tovagliolo/tovagliolino *a napkin*	una tovaglia *tablecloth*
-uccio/a -uzzo/a	una cannuccia *a straw* una viuzza *an alley*	una canna *a reed* una via *road, street*
-one/a	un copione *a script* un pallone *a football* un portone *a main/front door*	una copia *a copy* una palla *a ball* una porta *a door*
-accio/a	un'erbaccia *a weed* una parolaccia *a swear word*	erba *grass* una parola *a word*
-astro/a	un figliastro *a stepchild/son*	un figlio *child, son*

3 The English equivalents of the words in the middle column (see next page) are all mixed up. Match them up, taking the word of origin into consideration and using a bit of guesswork and imagination. If all else fails, use a dictionary.

Word of origin		Related word		English equivalent
barba	(beard)	A	barbone	1 briefcase
bagno	(bath)	B	bagnino	2 test tube
busta	(envelope)	C	bustina	3 bribe
busta	(envelope)	D	bustarella	4 a) tramp b) poodle
carta	(paper)	E	cartella	5 crisp
padre	(father)	F	padrone	6 lifeguard
padre	(father)	G	padrino	7 audition
patata	(potato)	H	patatina	8 saucer
prova	(test, experiment)	I	provino	9 godfather
prova	(test, experiment)	J	provetta	10 felt tip
piatto	(plate)	K	piattino	11 small packet, e.g. of sugar
penna	(pen)	L	pennarello	12 paintbrush
penna	(pen)	M	pennello	13 owner

6.2 FALSE SUFFIXES

Many Italian nouns have endings that are identical to suffix endings such as -**ino** or -**one**, but bear no relation to the apparent source word. Always check meanings in a dictionary. Here are a few.

lampo *flash*	lampone *raspberry*	mulo *mule*	mulino *mill*
matto *mad*	mattone *brick*	matto *mad*	mattino *morning*
vite *vine*	vitello *calf, veal*	tacco *heel*	tacchino *turkey*

E   **1**   True or false? Say if each statement below is true (T) or false (F). If false, give the meaning of the word.

     (a) Un mattone è una persona molto matta.   (d) Il mulino è un piccolo mulo.

     (b) Un postino è un posto piccolo.   (e) Un bagnino è un piccolo bagno.

     (c) Un posticino è un bel posto che ti piace.   (f) Un rubinetto è un piccolo rubino (*ruby*).

6.3 ADVERBIAL SUFFIXES

Adverbial suffixes are invariable. They are mainly used with **poco**, **tardi**, **male** and **bene**. With the exception of **benino** and **benone** the choice of suffix depends largely on the personal preference of the speaker, as they are so close in meaning.

bene	benino *quite well* benone *extremely well*
male	malino, maluccio *not too well*
tardi	tardino, tardetto, tarduccio *latish*
poco	pochetto, pochettino, pochino *a little/tiny bit*

I   Rewrite the Italian inside brackets, using an adverbial suffix.

(a) Non c'è posto qui. – Ti puoi spostare …? (solo un po')

(b) È andato bene ieri? – Sì, è andato … credo. (abbastanza bene)

(c) Aspettiamo mezz'ora, è ancora … per partire. (un po' presto)

(d) Come stai adesso? – … purtroppo. (Non molto bene)

6.4 VERB SUFFIXES

Some verbal suffixes convey the idea of an incomplete, desultory or intermittent action. They may also suggest a repeated but aimless action and have a pejorative meaning. There are no rules for identifying which suffix conveys which meaning. Check in a dictionary if necessary.

Suffix	Examples
-acchiare -icchiare -ucchiare	ridacchiare *to snigger* (ridere); scribacchiare *to scribble, write rubbish* (scrivere); dormicchiare *doze fitfully* (dormire); mordicchiare *to nibble* (mordere); leggiucchiare *to flick through, read aimlessly* (leggere); mangiucchiare *to nibble, snack on* (mangiare)
-erellare	giocherellare *to pass time playing, to fiddle/toy with sth* (giocare) salterellare *to jump/skip up and down* (saltare); trotterellare *to toddle, trot along* (trottare)
-ettare	fischiettare *to whistle quietly* (fischiare); picchiettare *to tap, drum* (e.g. fingers on table), *to patter* (e.g. rain, hail), *to spatter/splatter* (picchiare)
-igginare	piovigginare *to drizzle, to 'spit'* (piovere)
-onzolare	gironzolare *to wander/dawdle about, to lurk* (girare)
-ottare	parlottare *to talk softly, murmur* (often conspiratorial) (parlare)

7

Personal pronouns

A pronoun is a word which stands in place of nouns or noun phrases. Personal pronouns (**i pronomi personali**) are used to refer to specific people or things. The most important categories of personal pronouns are: subject, reflexive, object (direct and indirect) and disjunctive.

7.1 SUBJECT PRONOUNS

Subject pronouns refer to the subject of a sentence.

FORMS

Main subject pronouns			
Singular		**Plural**	
io	*I*	noi	*we*
tu	*you*	voi	*you*
lui, lei	*he, she*	loro	*they*
lei	*you (formal)*	loro	*you (formal)*

Different forms for 'you'

- **tu** is the singular familiar *you*, used to address a child, a family member or a friend.
- **lei** is the singular formal *you*. It is sometimes spelt with a capital **L** to distinguish it from **lei** meaning *she*.
- **voi** is the familiar plural *you* (i.e. the plural of **tu**). It is now also commonly used for speaking to people you would address individually as **Lei**.
- **loro** is the formal plural *you* (i.e. the plural of **lei**). It is sometimes spelt with a capital **L** to distinguish it from **loro** meaning *they*. It is now uncommon to use **loro** as *you* in spoken Italian.

█ USES

In Italian subject pronouns are less frequently used than in English. In most cases there is no need for the pronoun, as the form of the verb makes the subject clear:

Quando pago, guardo bene il conto *When I pay, I look at the bill carefully.*

Subject pronouns are used, however, in the following cases.

To stress the subject	Pago **io** questa volta *I'll pay this time* È un bel vestito, l'hai fatto **tu?** *It's a lovely dress. Did you make it?*	To stress the subject the pronoun usually follows the verb.
To contrast subjects	**Lui** lavora tanto ma **lei** non fa mai niente *He works so much but she never does anything* L'hai fatto **tu?** – **Io** no, l'ha fatto **lui** *Did you do it? – I didn't, he did*	The pronoun often follows the verb.
To clarify the subject	Credi che **io/lui/lei** abbia dimenticato? *Do you think I have forgotten?/he/she has forgotten?* Vuoi fare **tu** la spesa o preferisci che la faccia **io/lui/lei?** *Do you want to shop or would you rather I/he/she did?*	If the form of the verb does not make the subject obvious (as in the identical singular forms of some subjunctives), the subject pronoun is needed.
No verb	Come sta? – Bene, e **Lei?** *How are you? – Fine, and [what about] you?* Chi l'ha fatto? – **Io.** *Who did it? – Me (I did)*	A subject pronoun has to be used if there is no verb to indicate the subject.
anche **neanche** **nemmeno** **neppure**	Vieni anche **tu?** – Certo che vengo anch'**io** *Are you coming too? – Of course I'm coming too* Non viene neanche **lui** *He's not coming either*	With these emphatic words the subject pronoun must be expressed.
It's me, you, him/her/them, etc.	Chi è? – Sono **io** *Who is it? – It is me (lit. I)* Siete stati **voi** due? *Was it you two? (plural)* Sono stati **loro** a chiamare la polizia? – No, siamo stati **noi.** *Was it them who called the police? – No, it was us*	Note that <u>subject</u> pronouns are used in Italian, after the relevant verb form, whereas in English <u>disjunctive</u> pronouns are used, always with *is* or *was*.
Emphatic use: *I myself,* *you yourself,* *etc.*	È vero, l'hai detto **tu stesso/a** *It's true, you said so yourself* Non so se i Bianchi hanno prenotato, **loro stessi** non si ricordano *I don't know if the Bianchis have booked, they can't remember themselves*	Extra emphasis can be given to the subject with **stesso/a**. This agrees with the subject and can go before or after the verb.

E | **I** **Tu, Lei** or **voi**? Which *you* is appropriate? Choose the correct pronoun to complete each sentence.

(a) Come sta, signore? – Bene, e ...? (c) Noi stiamo bene, e ... due, come state?
(b) Come stai, Aldo? – Non c'è male, e ...?

2 Stress, contrast and contradict. Give the Italian equivalent of the English using appropriate pronouns.

(a) Javier e Fiona di dove sono? – (*He*) è spagnolo e (*she*) è scozzese.

(b) Venite anche (*you*)? – No, (*we*) non veniamo, viene solo Marco.

(c) Che bella lampada! L'hai comprata (*you*), Mariella? – Sì, l'ho comprata (*I*).

(d) È un bel giardino. Lo cura (*you*), signora, o suo marito? – Lo curiamo (*us*) due.

3 Clarify matters. Give the Italian equivalent of the English.

(a) *Mina and Elena, is that you? – No, it's us, Marta and Ida.*

(b) *Is that you, Dario? – No, it's me, Giuseppe.*

(c) *Who paid? Was it her? – No, it was him.*

(d) *We're going to the cinema, what about you two?*

Additional subject pronouns

Egli, esso, essi, ella, essa, esse

These pronouns are almost exclusively used in written Italian. It is important to be able to recognise them.

Masculine **egli** *he* **esso** *it, he* **essi** *they*	Lo scrittore Alberto Moravia morì a ottantadue anni, a Roma. **Egli** fu, per oltre sessant'anni, testimone e interprete del nostro secolo *The writer Alberto Moravia died at 82, in Rome. For over sixty years he witnessed and interpreted (the events of) our century*	**Egli** is very formal and only refers to people. **Esso** refers to animals or things and rarely to people. **Essi** refers to people, animals or things.
Feminine **ella** *she* **essa** *it, she* **esse** *they*	La Costituzione Americana fu approvata nel 1787. **Essa** fu il risultato di un lungo processo politico *The American Constitution was approved in 1787. It was the result of a long political process*	**Ella** is very formal and rare. **Essa** and **esse** refer to people, animals or things.

A note on the impersonal *si*

Si is used as a subject with the third person singular forms of the verb. It is a generic/indefinite subject which has various English equivalents: *one, you, we, they, people*:

In Italia non si beve il cappuccino dopo mangiato *In Italy you don't drink cappuccino after a meal*

For more on *si*, see pp. 99, 266–7.

7.2 REFLEXIVE AND RECIPROCAL PRONOUNS

Reflexive pronouns are used with certain verbs mainly to indicate an action that a person does to himself/herself, e.g. **lavarsi** *to wash oneself*. However, they are also used with some verbs which do not express a reflexive action, e.g. **pentirsi** *to be sorry, to regret*.

Reciprocal pronouns are used when two or more people do the action to each other, not to themselves, e.g. **salutarsi** *to greet each other, to say hello.*

FORMS

mi	myself	ci	ourselves; each other (reciprocal)
ti	yourself	vi	yourselves; each other (reciprocal)
si	himself, herself, oneself, yourself (formal)	si	themselves; yourselves (formal): each other

USES

Reflexive pronouns cannot be omitted in Italian. They mostly precede the verb, but see pp. 91–3.

To indicate a reflexive action	**Mi** sono fatto/a male *I hurt myself* **Vi** siete divertiti? *Did you enjoy yourselves?*	A reflexive action 'reflects' back on the subject and is something you do to yourself.
To express non-reflexive meaning	Non **ti** vergogni? *Aren't you ashamed?* **Si** comporta male *He behaves badly*	Reflexive pronouns are essential even if the verb has no reflexive meaning.
To express possession	**Ti** lavi i capelli? *Are you washing your hair?* **Mi** sono rotto **la** gamba *I broke my leg* **Si** è messo **il** cappotto *He put on his coat*	Reflexive pronouns may be used in place of possessives, usually with reference to the body and clothes.
Reciprocal use	**Vi** vedete spesso? *Do you see each other often?* **Si** scrivono spesso *They often write to each other* **Ci** sentiamo *We'll be in touch (with each other)*	**Ci**, **vi** and **si** can be used reciprocally to mean *each other.*
Si	Bisogna fermar**si** al semaforo *One has to/You have to stop at the lights*	Note that with an infinitive this means *oneself/one/you* (in general).
	S'incontrano spesso *They often meet (each other)*	**Si** can elide to **s'** in front of *i.*
Emphatic use: *I myself, you yourself,* etc.	So che le cose vanno male per loro, ma **mi** trovo **io stesso/a** in difficoltà *I know that things are going badly for them, but I am in trouble myself* Ada ci dice di alzarci presto, ma **lei stessa** **si** alza tardi *Ada tells us to get up early, but she gets up late herself!*	Emphasis is made by using **io/tu/lui/lei stesso/a,** **noi/voi/loro stessi/e** <u>in addition to</u> the reflexive pronouns.

- For the agreement of reflexive pronouns and past participles see p. 102.

E | Complete the sentences using the appropriate pronoun and verb forms.

(a) Di solito (io – truccarsi) poco.
(b) Perché non (tu – togliersi) la giacca?
(c) Non (noi – laccarsi) mai le unghie.
(d) (Voi – lamentarsi) troppo, ragazzi!

2 Use the reflexive verbs below to complete the sentences with the appropriate pronoun and verb forms.

(a) Mio nonno (*falls asleep*) sempre dopo pranzo. (addormentarsi)
(b) I miei figli (*wash themselves and comb their hair*) sempre in fretta. (lavarsi, pettinarsi)
(c) Normalmente io e mia moglie (*wake up*) alle sette e (*we get up*) subito. (svegliarsi, alzarsi)

3 Talk about what people do to each other, using the verbs given.

(a) In Italia quando le persone (incontrarsi), (salutarsi) e (darsi) la mano.
(b) Noi (vedersi) raramente ma (sentirsi) spesso.
(c) Oggi la gente (scriversi) poco. Preferisce (scambiarsi) delle e-mail.

7.3 DIRECT AND INDIRECT OBJECT PRONOUNS

These pronouns refer to the object of a sentence. Direct object pronouns replace direct noun or noun phrase objects. Indirect object pronouns replace indirect noun or noun phrase objects. To understand when to use direct object (DO) and indirect object (IDO) pronouns, it is necessary to be able to identify the nouns they replace.

Identifying direct and indirect objects

This can seem problematic because in English direct and indirect objects often look identical.

Direct object	*I saw* **Mario** *I saw* **him** *I helped* **Maria** *I helped* **her** *I hate* **ice cream** *I hate* **it**	A DO is a person, animal or thing directly affected by, or involved in, the action of the verb. It can sometimes be identified by asking, *Who?* or *What?*
Indirect object	*I sent* **Mario** *a message* *I sent* **him** *a message* *I bought* **Maria** *a book* *I bought* **her** *a book*	An IDO is a person, animal, institution and occasionally a thing less directly involved in the action of the verb than a DO. It may sometimes be identified by asking, *To whom/what? For whom/what?*
	I told **Mario** *(to come)* *I told* **him** *I asked* **Maria** *(a question)* *I asked* **her**	IDOs are mostly used with verbs which also take a DO, whether this is explicitly expressed or not. Of the two objects the IDO is the one which is more distant from the action of the verb. Typical double object verbs are *to give/say sth to sb, to buy/make sth for sb.*

- In Italian it is simple to distinguish between direct and indirect <u>noun</u> objects because the indirect object is nearly always preceded by the prepositions **a** or **per**:

Ho dato un libro **a Mario** *I gave Mario a book* **or** *I gave a book to Mario*
Ho comprato dei fiori **per Maria** *I bought Maria some flowers* **or** *I bought some flowers for Maria*

However, Italian direct and indirect <u>pronoun</u> objects have forms of their own which must be learned. See below.

I   Look at the following sentences. First identify the direct objects (DO) and then the indirect objects (IDO).

(a) *He bought some roses and gave them to his wife.*   (b) *He bought her some roses.*
(c) *Did you ask Francesca to leave?*   (d) *Did you ask her?*

FORMS

In Italian, direct and indirect object pronouns are identical apart from the forms for the formal *you* and for *him/her/them*.

Direct object		Indirect object	
mi	*me*	**mi**	*(to) me*
ti	*you*	**ti**	*(to) you*
lo	*him/it*	**gli**	*(to) him/it/them*
la/La	*her/it/you (formal)*	**le/Le**	*(to) her/you (formal)*
ci	*us*	**ci**	*(to) us*
vi	*you*	**vi**	*(to) you*
li, le	*them*	**loro**	*(to) them/you (formal)*

- **la** *you* (DO) and **le** *(to) you* (IDO) are the formal singular forms of address for a man as well as a woman. They are sometimes spelt with a capital letter.
  Signor Rossi, La accompagno io e Le offro un caffè. *Signor Rossi, I'll take you there and offer you a coffee.*
- **vi** is preferred for both the formal and the informal plural *you*. **Loro** is rarely used as the formal plural *you*.
- **gli** means *to him*. It is also used to mean *to them*, in which case it refers to both men and women. **Loro** *to them* is formal or literary, and follows the verb.
  Tom è qui. Gli parlo io. *Tom is here, I'll talk to him.* Eva e Tom sono qui. Gli parlo io. *Eva and Tom are here. I'll talk to them.* Chi darà loro la notizia? *Who will give them the news?*

Spelling

L'ammiri molto? *Do you admire him/her a lot?* **L'ho/L'abbiamo fatto subito** *I/We did it at once* **But**: Era triste, vero? Sì, **lo** era *He was sad, wasn't he? Yes, he was*	The DO pronouns **lo** and **la** can change to **l'** in front of a word beginning with a vowel or the letter **h**, but this is optional. They are not shortened in front of **è/ero/eri/era**, etc.
Li/Le hai visti/e? *Did you see them?* **Le** ho spiegato la situazione *I explained the situation to her*	The plural DO pronouns **li** and **le** are never shortened, nor are the IDO pronouns.

Identifying direct and indirect object verbs

The key to understanding the use of direct and indirect object pronouns lies in understanding the structure of the verbs they are used with.

(a) Direct object verbs

Verbs with no preposition	Chiamerai **il tassi/Mario**? – Sì, **lo** chiamerò stasera *Will you call the taxi/Mario? – Yes, I'll call it/him tonight* Vedrai **la mostra/l'amica di Paolo**? – Sì, **la** vedrò *Will you see the exhibition/Paolo's friend? – Yes, I'll see it/her*	Verbs typically used with direct objects are those without prepositions, e.g. **chiamare qlco/qlcu** to call sb/sth or **vedere qlco/qlcu** to see sb/sth.
Italian and English differ **pagare**	Ascolti spesso **la radio**? **La** ascolti spesso? *Do you often listen to the radio? Do you often listen to it?* Ho chiesto **il conto. L'**ho chiesto *I have asked for the bill. I have asked for it* Hai pagato **i biglietti**? **Li** hai pagati? *Did you pay for the tickets? Did you pay for them?* Hai visto **Dino**? – **Lo** hai pagato? *Did you see Dino? Did you pay him?* ***But**: **Le** ho pagato il caffè I paid for her coffee*	Some common verbs taking a preposition in English require no preposition in Italian and therefore have direct objects. Note that **pagare** takes a DO whether it means *to pay for sth* or *to pay sb*. However, when it has two objects – a person and a thing – an IDO is used for the person and a DO for the sum or thing paid for.

(b) Indirect object verbs

With few exceptions (e.g. **telefonare a, parlare a**) indirect objects are mostly used with double object verbs, e.g. **dire qlco a qlcu, comprare qlco per qlcu**. These verbs divide into three main groups, with the following functions.

Expressing to	Darai il libro **a Gina**? – Sì, **le** darò il libro *Will you give Gina the book? – Yes, I'll give her the book* Scriverai una lettera **a Pino**? – Sì, **gli** scriverò una lettera *Will you write Pino a letter? – Yes, I'll write him a letter*	Many verbs take **a** before a person, and this is the indirect object, e.g. **dare qlco a qlcu** to give sth to sb, **scrivere qlco a qlcu** to write sth to sb.
Expressing for	**Mi** lavi questa maglia? *Will you wash this jumper for me?* **Gli** scaldi il caffè? *Will you heat up the coffee for him?*	The people for whom the actions are done are the indirect objects: **lavare/scaldare qlco per qlcu** to wash/heat sth for sb.

Indirectly expressing the idea of *to*	**Le** piacciono i film di Fellini *She likes Fellini's films* (lit. *Fellini's films please her*) **Gli** servono altri libri? *Does he need any more books?* (lit. *are other books of use to him?*)	Verbs used impersonally. These require IDO pronouns to express what in English are subject pronouns (*I, you, he, she,* etc.). For full explanations see Chapter 25, p. 261.
Italian and English differ	Chiederai **a Dino** di venire? **Gli** chiederai di venire? *Will you ask Dino to come?* *Will you ask him to come?*	The Italian verb structure does not always match the English. For example, *to ask sb sth* is **chiedere qlco a qlcu**, *to promise sb sth* is **promettere qlco a qlcu**. In Italian the person is the indirect object.

2 Can you identify from their infinitives which of the verbs below are direct object verbs and which are double object or indirect object verbs?

ascoltare qlcu	aspettare qlcu	chiamare qlcu	comprare qlco a/per qlcu
dire qlco a qlcu	guardare qlcu	portare qlco a qlcu	pregare qlcu
scusare qlcu	sentire qlcu	spiegare qlco a qlcu	telefonare a qlcu

Direct object pronouns

▌ USES

Note that the pronouns often precede the verb, unlike English. See the section on position, pp. 91–3.

Replacing DO nouns or noun phrases	La macchina è sporca, **la** devo lavare *The car is dirty, I must wash it* Gli amici di Gianni sono simpatici, **li** inviterò *Gianni's friends are nice, I'll invite them*	The pronouns must agree with the nouns or noun phrases they replace.
Replacing adjectives or a whole sentence	Hai detto che il film era divertente, in realtà non **lo** è *You said the film was amusing, but it isn't really* È innamorata di Mario, **l'**ho sempre detto *She's in love with Mario, I've always said so (it)* Quando partono? – Chi **lo** sa? *When are they leaving? Who knows? (it)*	With verbs such as **sapere** or **dire** the DO pronoun **lo** is used to replace a whole phrase, sentence or adjective. It is rarely expressed in English. See also p. 97.
lo, la, li and **le** with **avere**	Hai la piantina? – Sì, **ce l'**ho *Have you got the map? – Yes, I've got it* Avete i passaporti? – Sì, **ce li** abbiamo *Have you got the passports? Yes, we've got them*	In front of the verb *avere*, **lo**, **la**, **li** and **le** are preceded by **ce**. This is for pronunciation, as it is hard to say **lo ho, la hai**, etc.

| Colloquial use: in addition to a DO noun | **Franco l'**ho già visto, ma Enrico no
 I've already seen Franco, but not Enrico
 (lit. *Franco I've already seen him*)
 I pantaloni, quanto **li** hai pagati?
 How much did you pay for the trousers?
 (lit. *The trousers, how much did you pay (for) them?*) | The use of both the pronoun and the noun it refers to is common and colloquial. There is no exact English equivalent. |

- Note that the past participles of verbs with the auxiliary **avere** agree with the preceding DO pronouns **lo, la, li, le**. For further details, see p. 101.

E 3 Replace the underlined nouns and phrases with the correct pronoun.

(a) I pantaloni bianchi sono bellissimi, perché non ... compri?
(b) Quella macchina costa poco, ho intenzione di comprar ....
(c) Conosce mio figlio? – No, non ... conosco.
(d) Conoscete le mie cugine? – Certo, ... conosciamo da molto tempo.

4 Insert the pronoun corresponding to the English one given.

(a) Angelo, ... posso aiutare? (*you*)
(b) Arriveder ..., signore, ... richiamerò più tardi. (*you – formal*)
(c) Ragazzi, ... ringrazio per la bella serata. (*you – plural*)

5 Replace the underlined phrases with one or two pronouns.

(a) Sai dov'è andato? – No, non ... so.
(b) Il suo matrimonio andrà male, ... ho detto tante volte.
(c) Tu dici che sono tutti disonesti? – Certo, è ovvio che ... sono!
(d) Hai la chiave? – Sì, ... ho.
(e) I clienti hanno i documenti? – Sì, ... hanno.

6 Give the Italian equivalent of the English.

(a) Ascolti spesso la radio? – *Yes, I often listen to it.*
(b) Hai chiesto il conto? – *Yes, I've asked for it.*
(c) Quelle scarpe, quanto le hai pagate? – *I paid 150 euros for them.*

Indirect object pronouns

USES

These mostly follow the same rules of position as DO pronouns. See pp. 91–3.

| Replacing IDO nouns or noun phrases | Ha prestato una penna a Stefano. **Gli** ha prestato una penna
 He lent Stefano a pen. He lent him a pen
 A mia cugina Mirella piace la Francia. **Le** piace la Francia
 My cousin M. likes France. She likes France | IDO pronouns replace nouns or noun phrases which function as the indirect object. |

Colloquial use: in addition to an IDO noun	**A Giovanni** non **gli** ho detto niente *I haven't told Giovanni a thing* **A Susi** non **le** piace la carne *Susie doesn't like meat*	IDO pronouns may be used as well as the IDO noun. This is a colloquial emphatic use with no exact English equivalent.
Instead of the English possessive	**Ti** ho stirato **la** camicia *I've ironed your shirt (for you)* **Le** hanno aggiustato **i** freni *They fixed her brakes* **Mi** ha rotto **il** vaso *He broke my vase* **Le** hanno distrutto **il** giardino *They destroyed her garden*	The IDO is often used in conjunction with the definite article. See also Possessives, p. 109.

- Other verbs of the type **rompere** and **distruggere** above include:

  bruciare *to burn someone's ...*, macchiare *to stain someone's ...*, rovinare *to ruin someone's ...*, rubare *to steal someone's ...*, strappare *to tear/snatch someone's ...*, sporcare *to dirty someone's ...*, togliere *to remove someone's ....*

E

7 Replace the underlined nouns and phrases with the correct pronoun.

(a) Ho prestato 50 euro <u>a Riccardo</u>. Ieri ... ho prestato 50 euro.

(b) Devi restituire i soldi <u>a Rina</u>. ... devi restituire i soldi domani.

(c) Anna deve 100 euro <u>a suo fratello</u>. Purtroppo ... deve 100 euro.

(d) Lucio dovrà pagare 2000 euro <u>alla moglie</u>. È vero, ... dovrà pagare 2000 euro.

8 Insert the correct word for *you*.

(a) Signore, ... consiglio di aspettare.

(b) Signora, ... posso dare una mano?

(c) Ragazzi, ... devo chiedere aiuto.

(d) Carlo, ... presento mio marito.

(e) Signori, ... posso offrire da bere?

9 Helping hand. Complete the sentences using the correct pronoun. Use the English as a guide.

(a) ... puoi aggiustare i freni?   *Can you fix my brakes (for me)?*

(b) ... potresti riparare la bicicletta?   *Could you mend her bicycle (for her)?*

(c) ... può cambiare 1000 euro?   *Can you change 1000 euros (for us)?*

10 Disaster. Complete the sentences using the Italian equivalent of the English pronoun given.

(a) Mio nipote ... ha rotto l'orologio. (*my*)

(b) Giulio è rimasto male, la cameriera ... ha macchiato la camicia. (*his*)

(c) Maria ... ha bruciato la caffettiera. (*their*)

11 Give the Italian equivalent of the English.

(a) *I asked him to buy the bread.*

(b) *Pino, did you tell them (the boys) to come at ten o'clock?*

(c) *Dario, you must answer them (the girls) immediately.*

Direct or indirect pronouns?

12 Insert the correct word for *you*, choosing between direct and indirect object pronouns.

(a) ... ringrazio tanto, signore.
(b) Signore, ... mando la conferma domani.
(c) Signora Rodolfi, ... disturbo?
(d) Signora, ... dispiace se torno più tardi?
(e) ... dispiace aspettare signori?
(f) Signore, ... prego di tornare domani.

13 Rewrite the sentences, substituting the underlined words with the correct pronoun.

(a) Porterò <u>mia nonna</u> al mare. (la/le)
(b) Porterò dei fiori <u>a mia nonna</u>. (la/le)
(c) Manderò <u>il pacco</u> a Carlo. (lo/gli)
(d) Manderò un fax <u>a Carlo</u>. (lo/gli)
(e) Leggerò <u>l'articolo</u> a Dina e a Lucia. (lo/gli/loro)
(f) Leggerò il riassunto <u>a Dina e a Lucia</u>. (li/gli/loro)

14 A challenge. Give the Italian equivalent of the English, using the verbs listed to help decide whether to use a direct or an indirect object pronoun.

(a) *I advised her to leave early.*   consigliare a qlcu di *to advise s.o. to*
(b) *We must persuade her to help.*   convincere qlcu a *to persuade s.o. to*
(c) *You can't force him to come.*   costringere qlcu a *to make/force s.o. to do sth*
(d) *I have allowed him to go to the party.*   permettere a qlcu di *to allow s.o. to*

7.4 *NE*

Ne is an invariable pronoun with no exact English equivalent, whose principal meanings are *of it/of them.*

█ USES

Ne replaces nouns or noun phrases relating to quantity. It follows the same rules of position as object pronouns (p. 91–3).

Specific quantity: *of it, of them*	Vorrei due etti **di prosciutto**. **Ne** vorrei due etti *I would like 200 gr. of ham. I would like 200 gr. (of it)* Vorrei un chilo **di pere**. **Ne** vorrei un chilo *I would like a kilo of pears. I would like a kilo (of them)* Quanto/a **ne** vuole? *How much (of it) do you want?* Quanti/e **ne** vuole? *How many (of them) do you want?*	**Ne** replaces singular or plural nouns which refer to specific quantities. In English this is rarely expressed, but in Italian it is essential. **Ne** must be used with **quanto/a/i/e?**

Unspecific quantity: some, a few, a lot (of), etc.	**I fagiolini** sono buoni, **ne** vuoi? *The beans are good, do you want some/any (of them)?* Hai preso un po' di **salame**? – **Ne** ho preso un po' *Did you have some salami? – I've had a little/some (of it)* **Il pesce** era buono, **ne** ho mangiato troppo *The fish was good, I ate too much (of it)* Quanto **ne** hai preso? – **Ne** ho preso la metà *How much did you have? – I had half (of it)* **But**: **Lo/Li** prendo tutto/i *I'll take all of it/them*	**Ne** also replaces nouns relating to unspecific quantities and cannot be omitted. It must be used with **un po' di**, **poco**, **molto**, **tanto**, **troppo**, **alcuni**, **abbastanza**, **la metà**, **parecchio**, etc Note that **ne** is not used with **tutto**.
Agreements	Mangi molta carne? – No, non **ne** mangio **molta** *No, I don't eat much (of it)* Hai molti amici? – Sì, **ne** ho **moltissimi** *Yes, I have a great many (of them)*	An adjective used with **ne** must agree with the noun it refers to. For the agreement of **ne** with past participles, see p. 102.

1 Shorten the questions and answers below, by substituting **ne** where appropriate.

(a) Quante cipolle prende? – Prendo mezzo chilo di cipolle.

(b) Quanto tonno vuole? – Prendo quattro scatole di tonno.

(c) Quanti meloni vuole? – Prendo due meloni.

2 You too. Give the Italian equivalent of the English replies. Begin each sentence with, 'Anch'io …'.

(a) Consumo pochissimi grassi. – *I eat very little too.*

(b) Consumo tanta frutta e verdura. – *I eat a great deal too.*

(c) Compro molto cibo biologico. – *We buy a lot too.*

3 Insert **ne** where necessary in the sentences below.

(a) La minestra è buona, vuoi un po'?   (c) Il vino è buono, vuole?

(b) La pasta è fresca, quanta vuole?   (d) Le salsicce sono eccezionali, volete?

Other uses

With verbs taking **di**	Hai voglia di **andare al cinema**? **Ne** hai voglia? *Do you feel like going to the cinema? Do you feel like it?* Abbiamo parlato di **Mario/Gina**. **Ne** abbiamo parlato *We talked about Mario/Gina. We talked about him/her* Tu, cosa **ne** sai? *What do you know about it/them?*	Other verbs include: **aver bisogno di** to need, **pensare di** to think about, **fare a meno di** to do without, **sapere di** to know about sb/sth. Note that there is no past participle agreement with verbs taking **di**.
Verbs taking **da**	Sono tornato da Roma. **Ne** sono tornato ieri *I came back from Rome. I came back yesterday*	

4   Provide the Italian equivalent of the English.

(a) Hai bisogno di aiuto? – *No thanks, I don't need any.*

(b) Credi che si dimetterà? – *I am sure of it.* (essere sicuro di)

(c) Abbiamo parlato dei loro problemi – *We talked about them too.*

(d) Dimmi quello che è successo. – *But I don't know anything about it.* (sapere di)

(e) Cosa pensi di quello che ha detto? – *I don't know, what do <u>you</u> think of it?*

7.5 *CI*

Ci is extremely common in Italian. It is used as the object pronoun *us* and *to us*. (See p. 83.) It is also widely used to mean *there* and sometimes *it* or *them*. In this context vi sometimes replaces ci in fairly formal writing.

USES

Replacing phrases of place	Vai a Milano/da Mario/al mare/alla festa? – Sì, ci vado *Are you going to Milan/to Mario's/to the seaside/ to the party? – Yes, I'm going (there)*	The closest equivalent is *there*, but this is not always expressed in English. In Italian ci is essential.
Referring to actions	Sei andato a ballare/a vedere Giulia? – Sì, **ci** sono andato/a *Did you go dancing/to see Giulia? – Yes, I went (there)*	Note that this is usually not expressed in English.
Part of the verb **esserci**	**Ci** sono molti bambini *There are many children* **C'**è tanto rumore *There is so much noise* **C'**è Tina? – No, non **c'**è *Is Tina in? – No, she's not in*	Before è, ci shortens to c'. **C'è/ci sono** are also used to talk about people being in.
With verbs taking the preposition **a**	Sei riuscito **a finire**? – Sì, **ci** sono riuscito *Yes, I managed to (do it)* Penso **alle vacanze**. **Ci** penso *I'm thinking about them.* **But**: Hai risposto **a Eva**? – Sì, **le** ho risposto *Did you answer Eva? – Yes, I answered her* Penso **a Maria** ogni giorno. **La** penso/Penso **a lei** ogni giorno *I think of Maria every day. I think of her every day*	**Ci** means *it* or *them* when it replaces phrases with **a** referring to an action or thing. **But**: If the verb + **a** refers to a person, an IDO pronoun is usual. Note however that **pensare a** + person usually requires a DO pronoun or **a** + disjunctive pronoun.
With **metterci** and **volerci**	Quanto **ci** metti per arrivare? *How long do you take to arrive?* **Ci** metto/mettiamo un'ora *I/we take an hour* **Ci** vuole un'ora *It takes an hour* **Ci** vogliono due ore *It takes two hours* **Ci** vuole un'altra forchetta *Another fork is needed* Che cosa **ci** posso fare? *What can I do about it?*	**Ci** is an integral part of these verbs but is not expressed in English. Note that it can be used colloquially with **fare**. See Chapter 25, p. 265 for **volerci**.

I Insert the appropriate pronouns in the answers to replace the words underlined in the questions.

(a) Sei stato <u>a Roma</u>? – Sì, sono stato tante volte.
(b) Andate <u>in centro</u>? – Sì, andiamo fra poco.
(c) Sei andato <u>a trovare Maria</u>? – Sì, sono andato ieri.
(d) Quand'è che vai <u>a far la spesa</u>? – Vado adesso.

2 Give the Italian equivalent of the English. There are two cases in which you do not use **ci**.

(a) Sei abituato al freddo? – *Yes, I'm used to it.*
(b) Siete riusciti a farlo? – *Yes, we managed to.*
(c) Hai risposto a tuo zio? – *Yes, I've answered him.*
(d) Avete pensato a quello che volete fare? – *No, we haven't thought about it.*
(e) Pensi spesso ai tuoi fratelli? – *Yes, I often think of them.*

3 Using **c'è** or **ci sono** in these sentences, give Italian equivalents of the following.

(a) *In my flat there are six rooms but there is only one bathroom.* (un bagno solo)
(b) *What is there to eat? – There is spaghetti alle vongole and there is salad.*
(c) *Is Piero there/in? – No, he's not here/in.*
(d) *Are Andrea and Massimo in? – No, they're not here/in.*

4 Complete the sentences in Italian using **metterci** and **volerci**.

(a) (*I take an hour*) per arrivare all'università.
(b) (*It takes an hour*) per arrivare in centro.
(c) Quanto (*do they take*) per andare a Genova?

7.6 OBJECT PRONOUN POSITION

The following rules apply to reflexive, DO and IDO pronouns, **ne**, **ci** and combined pronouns (see pp. 80–91).

Invariable positions

Broadly speaking pronouns precede the verb, but there are important exceptions.

Before the verb	**Mi** diverto molto *I enjoy myself a lot* **Ne** prendo due *I'll take two* **Ci** vado spesso *I often go* **Lo** comprerò domani *I'll buy it tomorrow* **Gli** ho dato un libro *I gave him a book*	Apart from **loro** the object pronouns normally precede finite verbs, i.e. verbal forms which indicate subject and tense.
After infinitives	Ho voglia di divertir**mi** *I feel like enjoying myself* Sono venuto per veder**ti** *I came to see you* Sarebbe meglio dir**gli** tutto *It would be best to tell him/them everything* Sto cercando di asciugar**lo** *I am trying to dry it/him*	Apart from **loro** the pronouns are attached to the end of infinitives, whose final **e** is dropped.

After gerunds	È uscito dal bagno, asciugando**si** in fretta *He came out of the bathroom drying himself in a hurry* **But**: Cosa fai? – **Mi** sto asciugando *What are you doing? – I'm drying myself*	When gerunds are used alone (not as part of the continuous tenses with **stare**), the pronouns are attached to the end, apart from **loro**.
After participles	Tornata**ci** dopo tanti anni, Lidia è rimasta delusa *Having gone back there after so many years,* *Lidia was disappointed* **But**: Lidia **ci** è tornata dopo tanti anni *Lidia went back there after so many years*	When past participles are used alone (not as part of compound tenses), the pronouns are attached to the participle.
Imperatives: before and after the verb	**Si** accomodi **But**: Accomoda**ti**/Accomoda**tevi** *Make yourself/selves comfortable* **Li** compri domani **But**: Compra**li**/compra**teli** domani *Buy them tomorrow* Compriamo**li** domani *Let's buy them tomorrow*	The pronouns come before formal **lei** imperatives but are attached to the end of **tu**, **voi** and **noi** imperatives.
Ecco	Ecco**mi** qui *Here I am* Ecco**li** qua *Here they are* Ecco**ne** un altro *Here's another one*	Pronouns are always attached to **ecco** to form one word.
Loro: after the verb	Ha comunicato **loro** le sue intenzioni *He has communicated his intentions to them* Vuole dare (a) **loro** il tempo di pensarci *He wants to give them time to think about it*	**Loro** must follow the verb in all cases and is never attached to it. It is sometimes preceded by **a**.

Variable positions

In the following two cases the different pronoun position is optional and does not normally affect the meaning.

With negative **tu** imperatives	Non **ti** preoccupare/Non preoccupar**ti** *Don't worry* Non **lo** toccare/Non toccar**lo** *Don't touch it*	The pronoun precedes the verb or is joined to the end. The position depends on individual preference.
With modal verbs	**Le** devo dire di venire?/Devo dir**le** di venire? *Must I tell her to come?* **Lo** sai spiegare o no?/Sai spiegar**lo** o no? *Can you explain it or not?*	The pronoun goes before **potere**, **volere**, **dovere** and **sapere**, or is attached to the dependent infinitive.

E 1 Rewrite the sentences below, beginning with the verb or phrase given.

(a) Ti vedo più tardi. (*Preferisco*)
(b) Mi diverto al mare. (*Ho intenzione di*)
(c) Ne compriamo altri. (*Abbiamo bisogno di*)
(d) Ci vado domani. (*È meglio*)

2 Substitute the nouns underlined with pronouns and place them correctly in each sentence.

(a) Angelica è uscita, lasciando aperta <u>la finestra</u>.
(b) Luigi ha scritto pregando <u>mia sorella</u> di rispondere.
(c) È caduto, lasciando cadere <u>i bicchieri</u>.
(d) Sto leggendo un racconto <u>a mio figlio</u>.

3 In the commands below substitute the nouns underlined with pronouns and place them correctly in each sentence.

(a) Gianna, manda <u>la lettera.</u>
(b) Signora, spedisca <u>questo pacco</u>.
(c) Ragazzi, parlate <u>di questo</u> oggi.
(d) Signore, parli <u>a nostro figlio</u> domani.

4 It makes little difference. Rewrite the sentences to mean the same thing, but changing the pronoun order.

(a) Mi sai dire se la cena è pronta?
(b) Mi voglio lavare le mani.
(c) Lo devo finire stasera.
(d) Non li posso aiutare.
(e) Non lo toccare!
(f) Non ti preoccupare.

5 It makes a difference! The position of pronouns can alter what you say. Match up the English and Italian meanings below.

(a) Andiamoci domani.
(b) Ci andiamo domani.
(c) Lo facciamo adesso.
(d) Facciamolo adesso.

(i) *Let's do it now.*
(ii) *Let's go tomorrow.*
(iii) *We're going tomorrow.*
(iv) *We're doing it now.*

7.7 DISJUNCTIVE PRONOUNS

These are sometimes known as stressed pronouns, and their position in a sentence usually corresponds to the English.

FORMS

Disjunctive		Additional disjunctives	
me	*me*		
te	*you*		
lui, lei	*him, her*	sé	*him/her, himself/herself*
Lei	*you* (formal)	sé	*yourself* (formal)
noi	*us*		
voi	*you*		
loro	*them*	sé	*them, themselves*
Loro	*you* (formal pl.)		

USES

After prepositions	Lavora **per te/Lei/voi**? *Does he work for you?* **Secondo me** è troppo difficile *In my view (according to me) it's too hard* Mi diverto molto **con te** *I enjoy myself a lot with you*	Disjunctive pronouns follow prepositions. This is their main use.
For emphasis	Vogliono vedere **lui** stasera *It's him they want to see tonight* (Lo vogliono vedere stasera: *not emphatic*) Devo scrivere a **te**? *Is it you I have to write to?* (Ti devo scrivere?: *not emphatic*).	When the object is emphasised, disjunctive pronouns are used instead of DO or IDO pronouns. They always follow the verb.
For contrast	Vuole **me** o **te**? *Does he want me or you?* (<u>not</u>: Mi vuole o ti vuole?) Parlerò **a te**, non **a lui** *I'll speak to you, not to him* (<u>not</u>: ti parlerò, non gli parlerò) A **lui** piace il teatro ma a **lei** no *He likes the theatre but she doesn't* (<u>not</u>: Gli piace il teatro ma non le piace)	When two direct or indirect objects are contrasted, they have to be replaced by disjunctive pronouns (preceded by **a** if the object is indirect).
With two or more objects	Ha visto **me** e Franco *He saw me and Franco* Ho dato un gelato a **lui** e a Gino *I gave an ice cream to him and to Gino*	Disjunctive pronouns replace DO or IDO pronouns and follow the verb.
Exclamations	Beato **te**! *Lucky you!* Povero **me**! *Poor me!*	After adjectives in exclamations.
Comparisons	È più ricco di **me** *He is richer than me* Sono ricco come/quanto **loro** *I am as rich as them*	After the prepositions **di**, **come** and **quanto**.
Emphatic forms	Fallo per **te stesso** *Do it for yourself* Quando la vedo, vedo **me stesso** *When I see her, I see myself* Angela parla sempre di **se stessa** *Angela always talks about herself*	For added emphasis **stesso/a/i/e** is often used with disjunctive pronouns. When used with **sé** (see below) the accent is usually dropped.

Using sé

Sé is a disjunctive pronoun which sometimes replaces **lui, lei, loro**.

Angelo parla sempre **di sé** *Angelo always talks about himself* Angelo parla sempre di lui *Angelo always talks about him* Lo hanno fatto solo **per sé** *They only did it for themselves* Lo hanno fatto per loro *They did it for them (others)*	**Sé** is used instead of **lui, lei, loro** when the action refers back to the subject. **Lui, lei**, and **loro** are used when the action refers to someone else.
La cosa in **sé** non è grave *In itself it's not a serious matter* Le sue intenzioni di per **sé** sono molto buone. *In themselves his/her intentions are very good*	**Sé** also means *itself/themselves*, referring to things. This can sometimes be expressed in English by *as such*.

1   Complete the sentences using disjunctive pronouns.

(a) C'è una lettera per (*me*) e una fattura per (*you*), dottore.
(b) Esci con (*them*) stasera o solo con (*her*)?
(c) Vuoi venire da (*me/my place*) o devi andare da (*him/his place*)?
(d) Secondo (*us*) è pericoloso farlo, e secondo (*you – plural*)?

2   Link the two sentences using **o** for (a) and (b) and **e anche** for (c) and (d).

(a) Mi porti al cinema? Lo porti al cinema? (*Are you taking me or him to the cinema?*)
(b) Le vuoi telefonare? Gli vuoi telefonare? (*Do you want to ring her or him?*)
(c) Li chiamerò. Chiamerò Gina. (*I'll call them and also Gina.*)
(d) Ti manderò una cartolina. Manderò una cartolina ai miei. (*I'll send a postcard to you and also to my parents.*)

3   Pick the appropriate pronoun to substitute the English: **sé**, **lui** or **lei**.

(a) Edoardo è proprio noioso, parla sempre di (*himself*).
(b) Angela è veramente innamorata, parla sempre di (*him*).
(c) Sono piuttosto antipatici, parlano sempre male di (*her*).
(d) Ida è abbastanza egoista, pensa solo a (*herself*).

7.8 COMBINING DIRECT OBJECT PRONOUNS AND *NE* WITH INDIRECT OBJECT OR REFLEXIVE PRONOUNS

FORMS

Direct object pronouns and **ne** can combine with indirect object or reflexive pronouns. When these pronouns are used together, the indirect object and reflexive pronouns change their spelling, except for **loro**.

IDO and reflexive pronouns	Direct object pronouns				
	lo	**la**	**li**	**le**	**ne**
mi	me lo	me la	me li	me le	me ne
ti	te lo	te la	te li	te le	te ne
gli	glielo	gliela	glieli	gliele	gliene
le	glielo	gliela	glieli	gliele	gliene
si	se lo	se la	se li	se le	se ne
ci	ce lo	ce la	ce li	ce le	ce ne
vi	ve lo	ve la	ve li	ve le	ve ne
loro	lo … loro	la … loro	li … loro	le … loro	ne … loro
si	se lo	se la	se li	se le	se ne

Position

With the exception of **loro** the order of pronouns is as follows.

IDO	+	DO	+	Verb	Reflexive	+	DO	+	Verb
Me		lo		dà	Me		lo		metto
		ne					ne		
To me		it/some		he gives	I		it/some		put on

- **Loro** *to them* never combines with other pronouns and must follow the verb.
  When it is used with another pronoun it is often preceded by **a**:

  Mando la lettera ai miei – La mando (a) loro.

  In speech **gli** usually replaces **loro** (see below).

- *Glie-*: **four meanings**
  When the IDO pronouns **gli** (*to him, to them*) or **le** (*to her, to you*) are used with **lo, la, li, le** or **ne**, they have identical spelling changes and both become **glie-**. Glie- can therefore refer to four different persons: *him, them, her* and the formal *you*. The context usually makes it clear which meaning is expressed.

gli + lo = glielo	Gli do l'indirizzo? *Shall I give him/them the address?*	**Glielo** do? *Shall I give it to him/to them/to her/to you?*
le + lo = glielo	Le do l'indirizzo? *Shall I give her/you the address?*	
gli + ne = gliene	Gli do un bicchiere? *Shall I give him/them a glass?*	**Gliene** do uno? *Shall I give him/them/her/you one?*
le + ne = gliene	Le do un bicchiere? *Shall I give her/you a glass?*	

Level 2

Indirect object pronoun combinations

USES

These are used in the following cases.

To replace two objects, direct and indirect	Preparo le tagliatelle per te. **Te le** preparo ... *I'm preparing them for you* Scriverò la lettera a Carlo. **Gliela** scriverò ... *I'll write it to him* Scriverò una lettera a mia sorella. **Gliene** scriverò una ... *I'll write her one* Mi ha parlato delle vacanze. **Me ne** ha parlato ... *He talked to me about them*	Combinations of two pronouns are typical with double object verbs.

| Italian and English differ | Mi puoi dire chi è? **Me lo** puoi dire?
Can you tell me who he is? Can you tell me? (it)
Puoi chiedere a Lucio di venire? **Glielo** puoi chiedere?
Can you ask Lucio to come? Can you ask him? (it)
Mi prometti di alzarti presto? – Sì, **te lo** prometto
Do you promise (me) you'll get up early? – Yes, I promise (you it)
Hai capito quello che devi fare? – No, **me lo** spieghi?
Have you understood what you must do? – No, can you explain? (it to me) | Two object pronouns are always needed with the double object verbs **dire, chiedere, promettere, ricordare, spiegare, far sapere qlco a qlcu,** but the English equivalents require only the DO pronoun or even no pronoun at all. |

1 Repeat the questions and requests below in shortened form, substituting pronouns for the underlined nouns and phrases.

(a) Mi presti i tuoi appunti? ... presti stasera? (*Will you lend them to me this evening?*)
(b) Ti posso spedire le informazioni? ... spedisco adesso?
(c) Signore, Le posso dare il mio numero di casa? ... posso dare adesso?
(d) Vi mandiamo la chiave, allora? ... mandiamo domani?

2 Allow me! Tell these people you'll do it for them. Use both a direct and an indirect object pronoun.

(a) Devo stirare queste camicie. – ... stiro io, se vuoi. (tu) (*I'll iron them for you if you want.*)
(b) Devo imbucare questa lettera. – ... imbuco io, se vuole. (Lei)
(c) Dobbiamo aprire questo pacco. – ... apro io, se volete. (voi)

3 Complete the sentences below, using **ne** and another pronoun each time. The English is there to help you.

(a) Queste pere sono mature, signora, ... scelgo qualcuna? (*Shall I choose some for you?*)
(b) Sono tre etti di formaggio, signore, ... tolgo un po'? (*Shall I take some off for you?*)
(c) I panini, sono freschi, ragazzi, ... incarto qualcuno? (*Shall I wrap some for you?*)

4 Ask who told you each time, using the appropriate pronouns for *you* and not forgetting **lo**.

(a) Sai che si è sposato Antonio? – Davvero? *Who told you?*
(b) Domani sono chiuso, signore, c'è sciopero. – Davvero? *Who told you?*
(c) Siamo stati bocciati tutti. – Davvero? *Who told you?*

5 I promise! Convince these people of your good intentions. Complete the answers below using appropriate pronouns.

(a) Mi farai sapere quando arrivi? – Sì, ... farò sapere senz'altro, ... prometto!
(b) Scusi, mi sa dire quando sarà pronto il lavoro? – ... dirò domani, signora, ... prometto.
(c) Facci sapere com'è andato, mi raccomando! – Certo, ... racconterò di sicuro, ... prometto!

6 Give the Italian equivalent of the English.

(a) *If you (pl.) can't come, will you tell us?*
(b) *Anna, when you leave, will you let me know?*
(c) *Ivo, if you want to come can you tell him?*
(d) *I'll help you Mina, I promise!*

Level
2 *Reflexive pronoun combinations*

Reflexive pronouns may be combined with another personal pronoun in the following cases.

To replace a direct noun object	**Mi** lavo le mani **Me le** lavo *I wash my hands. I wash them* **Si** compra sempre *La Stampa*. **Se la** compra sempre. *He always buys himself La Stampa. He always buys it for himself* **Si** compra sempre un giornale. **Se ne** compra sempre uno *He always buys himself a newspaper. He always buys himself one*	When a reflexive verb has a direct object this can be replaced by a DO pronoun if it is specific, or by **ne** if the object is unspecific (**un/una**, etc.).
With reflexive verbs taking **di**	**Si** accorge dell'errore? **Se ne** accorge? *Does he see/notice the mistake? Does he notice (it)?* **Vi** rendete conto dell'ora? **Ve ne** rendete conto? *Do you realise the time? Are you aware (of it)?*	**Ne** replaces phrases beginning with **di** and combines with the reflexive pronoun. See p. 89.
Reflexive verbs with **la: cavarsela sentirsela prendersela**	**Ce la** siamo cavata! *We managed it!* **Te la** senti di venire? – No, non **me la** sento *Do you feel like coming? – No, I don't feel like it* Perché **se la** prende? *Why does he/she take offence?*	Some colloquial reflexive verbs have the pronoun **la** as part of the meaning. The reflexive pronouns change to agree with the subject but **la** stays the same.
Reflexive verbs with **ne**	**Te ne** vai? – Sì, **me ne** devo andare *Are you going? – Yes, I've got to go* **Se ne** frega *He/she doesn't care a damn*	Other colloquial reflexive verbs, e.g. **andarsene, fregarsene,** are formed as above with **ne**.

• For past participle agreements see p. 102.

E **7** Using the verbs given below, give the equivalent of the English.

> lavarsi • togliersi • comprarsi • occuparsi di • permettersi

(a) I miei capelli sono proprio sporchi! – *Why don't you wash it (them)?*
(b) Mi tiene troppo caldo questo cappotto! – *Why don't you take it off, signora?*
(c) Sono belle quelle fragole! – *Shall we buy ourselves some, then?*
(d) Che freddo che fa! Chiudiamo la finestra? – *Fine, I'll deal with it.* (occuparsi di)
(e) Perché non fate un viaggio in Messico? – *We can't afford it.* (permettersi di)

8   Give the Italian equivalent of the English, using the following verbs.

> andarsene • fregarsene • sentirsela • prendersela • cavarsela

(a) *It's late, I'm going.*

(b) *But he couldn't care less!*

(c) *Do you feel like coming to the cinema? (tu)*

(d) *Why do you take offence? (tu)*

(e) *I got by in the exam.* (all'esame)

7.9 OTHER PRONOUN COMBINATIONS

Level 2

The impersonal si *with other pronouns*

The impersonal and passive **si** (*one, you, we, they, people*) is combined with other pronouns as follows.

With direct and indirect object pronouns	In Italia **si** mangia **il panettone** a Natale. **Lo si** mangia a Natale *You eat it/It is eaten at Christmas* **Si** dice **a me** che è malato. **Mi si** dice che è malato *They tell me/I am told he is ill*	**Si** follows direct and indirect pronouns and does not change its spelling.
With **ne**	**Si** parla tanto **del nuovo film**. **Se ne** parla tanto *People talk a lot about it*	**Si** precedes **ne** and becomes **se**.
With **ci**	**Si** mangia male **da Gino**. **Ci si** mangia male *You eat badly (there)* **Si** riesce **a soddisfare i clienti**? **Ci si** riesce? *Do you/they manage (it)?*	**Si** follows **ci** and becomes **ci si**.
With the reflexive **si**	**Ci si** diverte/annoia tanto *You enjoy yourself/get bored such a lot* **But note:** **Uno si** diverte tanto **al mare**. **Ci si** diverte tanto *You enjoy yourself such a lot (there)* **Uno si** abitua **al freddo**. **Ci si** abitua *You get used to it*	When the impersonal and reflexive **si** are used together, this becomes **ci si** to avoid an ugly **si si** combination. If phrases such as **al mare** or **al freddo** are included, these cannot be replaced by yet another **ci** and are simply omitted.

E **1**   Wrong end of the stick. Correct these misconceptions about Italy by completing the sentences using **si** and another appropriate pronoun.

(a) In Italia, di solito, il Campari si beve come digestivo. – Ma no, ... beve come aperitivo!

(b) In Italia, di solito, la grappa si beve come aperitivo. – Ma no, ... beve come digestivo!

(c) In Italia, di solito, il sale si vende solo in tabaccheria. – Ma no, adesso ... vende dappertutto!

2   How do I look? Rewrite the following sentences replacing the underlined possessives with an IDO pronoun and combining it with **si**. Refer to p. 109 if necessary.

(a) <u>La tua</u> calza si è bucata.   (c) <u>La sua</u> giacca si è strappata. *(her)*

(b) <u>La sua</u> cravatta si è sporcata. *(his)*   (d) <u>Il mio</u> bottone si è staccato.

3   Complete the sentences, replacing the underlined phrase with a pronoun and combining it with **si**.

(a) <u>Su questo materasso</u> si dorme bene. ... dorme benissimo!

(b) <u>In Italia</u> si sta bene. ... sta benissimo!

(c) <u>In questo compito</u> non si capisce niente. Non ... capisce assolutamente niente!

(d) Si riuscirà <u>a fare un bel lavoro</u>. ... riuscirà.

4   Rewrite the sentences, replacing **uno** with **si**.

(a) Durante le vacanze uno si alza tardi.   (c) D'estate uno si diverte al mare.

(b) Uno si veste bene per andare a messa.   (d) Uno si abitua al cibo inglese.

Level 2

Ci *combined with other pronouns*

Ci precedes some pronouns and follows others. In front of another pronoun it becomes ce.

Before **ne**: **ce ne**	Quanta pasta **c'è?** – **Ce n'è** mezzo chilo *How much pasta is there? – There is half a kilo* **Ci** sono molti negozi qui? – Sì, **ce ne** sono tanti *Are there lots of shops here? – Yes, there are lots of them*	The expressions **c'è**, **ci sono** there is, there are (from the verb **esserci**) are most commonly combined with **ne**. Note that before another -e, **ce** becomes **c'**.
	Quanto latte **ci** vuole? – **Ce ne** vuole un litro *How much milk does one/do you need? – You need a litre* Quante ore ci metteremo? – **Ce ne** metteremo due *How many hours will we take? – We'll take two*	**Ci** also combines with **ne** when used as part of **volerci** to be needed/ to take and of **metterci** to put in, to take.
Before **lo**, **la**, **li**, **le**	Dov'è la piantina, **ce l'**hai tu? ... *have you got it?* Li hai i biglietti? – Sì, **ce li** ho ... *Yes, I've got them*	When **lo**, **la**, **li**, **le** are used with **avere**, **ci** is placed in front for ease of pronunciation. See also p. 85.
	Domani Anna va dal dentista, **(ce)** la porti tu? *Tomorrow Anna is going to the dentist, will you take her (there)?*	When used to replace an expression of place, **ci** is often omitted.
With **la** as part of **farcela** **avercela**	**Ce la** fai a portare la valigia? – Sì, **ce la** faccio *Can you manage to carry the case? – Yes, I can manage* Perché **ce l'**hai con me? *Why have you got it in for me/are you cross with me?*	These common verbs are always used with the invariable pronoun combination **ce la** (**ci** + **la**).

After **mi**, **ti**, **vi** and before the reflexive **si**	Quando mi porti al cinema? – **Ti ci** porto domani *When will you take me to the cinema? – I'm taking you (there) tomorrow* Ti siedi spesso sotto l'albero? – Sì, **mi ci** siedo spesso *Do you often sit under the tree? – Yes, I often sit there* Aldo si trova bene a Roma? – Sì, **ci si** trova bene *Does Aldo like it in Rome? – Yes, he likes it (there)*	**Ci** comes after the direct object and reflexive **mi**, **ti**, **vi** but before the reflexive **si**. In speech it is sometimes omitted.
After the indirect objects **gli** and **le**	Quanto **ti ci** vuole per arrivare? *How long does it take you to arrive?* **Gli ci** è voluto molto tempo *It has taken him a long time*	As part of the verb **volerci**, **ci** combines with indirect object pronouns. (See Chapter 25, p. 265.)

- Note that **ci** (*there*) does not combine with the reflexive **ci** or **ci** meaning *us*. It is normally substituted with **là** or omitted:

  Ci troviamo bene a Roma. Ci troviamo bene (là). *We like it in Rome. We like it there.*
  Aldo ci porta al cinema. Ci porta (là). *Aldo takes us to the cinema. He takes us (there).*

E   **5**   You're making preparations for ten guests, but it's not going well. Give the Italian equivalent of the English.
   (a) Quanti bicchieri ci sono? – *There are five.*
   (b) C'è della birra in casa? – *No, there isn't any.*
   (c) Abbiamo abbastanza formaggio, vero? – *No, there is very little.*
   (d) Ci sono poche candele. – *It's true, there are very few.*
   The situation brightens up just a little ....
   (e) Ho trovato altre candele. – *Good, how many are there?*

6   Give the Italian equivalent of the following.
   (a) *It's too late, I won't make it tonight.*   (c) *Dino, why are you cross with me?*
   (b) *It's too difficult, he can't manage it.*   (d) *Does it take you long to get to school?* (tu)

7.10 DIRECT OBJECT PRONOUN AGREEMENTS

When **ne** and the direct object pronouns **lo**, **la**, **li**, **le** are used with compound tenses of verbs whose auxiliary is **avere**, the past participles generally agree in number and gender with what the pronoun stands for. The past participles of verbs with **avere** do not normally agree with <u>noun</u> direct objects.

Agreement with direct object pronouns	Ho preparato **la cena**. L'ho preparat**a** ... *I prepared it* **Gli** ho preparato **la cena**. **Gliel'**ho preparat**a** ... *I prepared it for him* Avete restituito **i soldi**? **Li** avete restituit**i**? ... *Did you give it back?* **Ti** hanno restituito **i soldi**? Te **li** hanno restituit**i**? ... *Did they give it back to you?*	Agreement of past participles is always made with **lo**, **la**, **li**, **le**, used alone or combined with other pronouns. There is no participle agreement with DO <u>nouns</u>.

Level 2	Agreement with **ne** referring to quantity	Ho venduto **molti libri**. **Ne** ho vendut**i** molti *I've sold lots of books. I've sold lots* Ci aveva dato **tante caramelle**. **Ce ne** aveva dat**e** tante *She had given us loads of sweets. She had given us loads (of them)* **But**: Ha preparato un **po' di minestra** per te. **Te ne** ha preparat**a/o** un po' *She has prepared you some*	The past participle usually agrees in number and gender with what **ne** stands for. However, if **ne** refers to quantities whose number and gender are not clear, agreement is preferred but optional.
		Ho comprato **due chili di patate**. **Ne** ho comprat**i/o** due chili *I've bought two kilos of potatoes. I've bought two kilos* Vi ho tagliato **quattro fette di torta**. **Ve ne** ho tagliat**e/o** quattro fette *I've cut you four slices of cake. I've cut you four slices*	When **ne** refers to a specific amount of something (a kilo, slice, tin, bottle, etc.) agreement is with that specific quantity. Agreement is preferred, but optional.
	Agreement with **ne** as part of verbs taking **di**	Mi ha parlato **di Maria**. **Me ne** ha parlato *He spoke to me about Maria. He spoke to me about her* Si sarà occupato **dei conti**. **Se ne** sarà occupato *He will have taken care of the accounts. He will have taken care of them*	There are no past participle agreements when **ne** is used with verbs taking **di**, e.g. **parlare di, occuparsi di**.
	Agreement with reflexive past participles	Antonio si è slogato **la caviglia**. **Se l'**è slogat**a** *Antonio has sprained his ankle. He has sprained it* Bambini, vi siete lavati **le mani**? – No, non **ce le** siamo lavat**e** *Children, have you washed your hands? – No, we haven't washed them* Maria si è rotta **il braccio**. **Se l'**è rotto *Maria has broken her arm. She has broken it* Mi sono fatto/a tagliare **i capelli**. **Me li** sono fatt**i** tagliare *I got my hair cut. I got it cut*	The past participles of reflexive verbs usually agree with the subject. However, when there is a pronoun direct object, the participle agreement is usually made with the direct object. It is also possible to find agreements with noun direct objects – e.g. **Antonio si è slogata la caviglia**.

- For the agreement of the past participle and the subject, see p. 208.

E   **1**   Not yet! Answer the questions below by saying that nothing has been done yet. Substitute a pronoun for the noun underlined, making the appropriate participle agreements.

     (a) Hanno scelto <u>i libri</u>? – No, non ... hanno ancora ...
     (b) Avete innaffiato <u>le piante</u>? – No, non ... abbiamo ancora ...
     (c) Ha mandato <u>la lettera</u>? – No, non ... ha ancora ...
     (d) Hanno prenotato <u>i biglietti</u>? – No, non ... hanno ancora ...

  2   How much? Making correct participle agreements, say how much you have bought or ordered. There are two answers each time.

     (a) Quanti fagiolini hai comprato? Ne ho comprat– ...   (tanto, due chili)
     (b) Quante pizze hai ordinato? Ne ho ordinat– ...   (molto, quattro)
     (c) Quanto vino hai ordinato? Ne ho ordinat– ...   (parecchio, tre bottiglie)
     (d) Quanta marmellata hai comprato? Ne ho comprat– ...   (poco, un barattolo)

3 What have you done! Express disbelief at this succession of disasters. Complete the sentences below, replacing the underlined words with two pronouns and making the participle agreements.

(a) Sai che ho rotto <u>i piatti nuovi di Giulia</u>? – Come! … hai rott– tutti?
(b) Sai che ho rovinato <u>la lavatrice di Antonio</u>? – Come! … hai rovinat– completamente?
(c) Sai che ho sfasciato <u>la macchina di Rina e Roberto</u>? – Come! … hai sfasciat– del tutto?
(d) Sai che ho distrutto <u>il computer di Fabio</u>? – Come! … hai distrutt– totalmente?

4 Don't you remember? Say it's been done already and complete the replies, using the correct pronouns and participle agreements.

(a) Mi presti i tuoi appunti? – Ma te … ho prestat– l'altro giorno!
(b) Ci mandi le fatture domani? – Ma ve … abbiamo mandat– la settimana scorsa!
(c) Mi puoi comprare degli stuzzicadenti? – Ma te … ho comprat– stamattina!
(d) Ci puoi portare un po' di carta igienica? – Ma ve … abbiamo portat– ieri!

5 Poor things! Express sympathy at these accidents. Finish the sentences by completing all the participle agreements.

(a) Mio figlio si è slogato la caviglia – Poveretto, se l'è slogat– sciando?
(b) Mia figlia si è storta il piede – Poveretta, se l'è stort– correndo?
(c) La mia fidanzata si è bruciata le mani – Poveretta, se le è bruciat– cucinando?
(d) Il mio fidanzato si è rotto la spalla. – Poveretto, se l'è rott– cadendo?

8

Possessives

Possessives (**i possessivi**) are adjectives or pronouns indicating belonging, e.g. *my, mine, your, yours.*

8.1 POSSESSIVE ADJECTIVES AND PRONOUNS

In Italian possessive adjectives and pronouns have the same forms.

English adjectives and pronouns	Singular		Plural	
	Masculine	Feminine	Masculine	Feminine
my, mine	il mio	la mia	i miei	le mie
your, yours (fam.)	il tuo	la tua	i tuoi	le tue
his, her, hers, its	il suo	la sua	i suoi	le sue
your, yours (formal)	il Suo	la Sua	i Suoi	le Sue
our, ours	il nostro	la nostra	i nostri	le nostre
your, yours (pl.)	il vostro	la vostra	i vostri	le vostre
their, theirs	il loro	la loro	i loro	le loro

8.2 POSSESSIVE ADJECTIVES

MAIN USES

È **la tua** camera, Dino?
Is this your room, Dino?
È **il tuo** appartamento, Dino?
Is this your flat, Dino?
Sono **i tuoi** stivali, Anna?
Are these your boots, Anna?
Sono **le tue** scarpe, Anna?
Are these your shoes, Anna?

General points: possessive adjectives are mostly used with the definite article and precede the noun they modify. They agree in number and gender with this noun, <u>not</u> with the possessor.

Silvia ha trovato **il suo** libro/**la sua** penna *Silvia has found <u>her</u> book/<u>her</u> pen* Sandro ha trovato **il suo** libro/**la sua** penna *Sandro has found <u>his</u> book/<u>his</u> pen* Signor/Signora Fante, ha trovato **il suo** portafoglio/ **la sua** agenda? *Signor/Signora Fante, did you find your wallet/diary?*	**Il suo, la sua** both express *his, her, its* and the formal *your*. They refer to singular objects owned and one owner, male or female.
Monica ha perso **i suoi** quaderni/**le sue** chiavi *Monica has lost <u>her</u> exercise books/<u>her</u> keys* Roberto ha perso **i suoi** quaderni/**le sue** chiavi *Roberto has lost <u>his</u> exercise books/<u>his</u> keys* Signor/Signora Fante, ha perso **i suoi** appunti/ **le sue** chiavi? *Signor/Signora Fante, have you lost <u>your</u> notes/<u>your</u> keys?*	**I suoi, le sue** also mean *his, her, its* and the formal *you*, but they refer to plural objects owned and one owner. They never mean *their*.
Silvia e Sandro hanno trovato **il loro** libro/**i loro** libri *Silvia and Sandro have found <u>their</u> book/<u>their</u> books*	**Il/la/i/le loro** *their* can indicate one or more objects owned, but always more than one owner. They are invariable, apart from the definite article.

E 1 **Your ....** You're handing people their possessions as they leave the party. Use the appropriate possessive adjective and definite article with the nouns given.

(a) Claudio, ecco ... giacca.
(b) Letizia, ecco ... ombrello.
(c) Signor Nardi, ecco ... cappotto.
(d) Signori, ecco ... impermeabili.
(e) Ragazzi, ecco ... giacche a vento.
(f) Paolo e Claudia, ecco ... zaino.

2 **His, her, their ....** Rewrite the sentences below, substituting the appropriate form of **suo** or **loro** for the phrase underlined.

(a) Non ho mai visto la casa <u>del signor Pirelli</u>. (*his*)
(b) La casa <u>di Mariella</u> è molto piccola. (*her*)
(c) Ti piace la nuova casa <u>di Emilia e Patrizio</u>? (*their*)
(d) L'appartamento <u>di Gianni</u> ha un balcone enorme. (*his*)
(e) L'appartamento <u>di Gigliola</u> si trova al secondo piano. (*her*)
(f) L'appartamento <u>dei signori Mancini</u> è in via Manin. (*their*)
(g) Non mi piacciono le amiche <u>di Sandra</u>. (*her*)
(h) Siamo usciti con le amiche <u>di Flavia e Fulvio</u>. (*their*)
(i) I figli <u>del signor Vezzani</u> frequentano l'università. (*his*)
(j) I figli <u>dei vicini</u> vivono tutti all'estero. (*their*)

3 Find the Italian equivalent of the English phrases given.

(a) Conosce (*my children*)?
(b) Questi sono (*our grandchildren*).
(c) Queste sono (*my nieces*).
(d) Ti faccio conoscere (*our daughters*).

Use of the article with possessive adjectives

The definite article is not always used with possessives referring to the family, and it may be omitted in some idiomatic phrases.

mia sorella *my sister* **tuo** nonno *your grandfather* *But*: **la mia** sorella **preferita** *my favourite sister* **la mia** sorel**lina** *my little sister* **il tuo bis**nonno *your great-grandfather*	No article is used with singular family members – including **marito** and **moglie** – unless there is an adjective or a suffix/prefix.
le mie sorelle *my sisters* **i tuoi** cugini *your cousins*	The article is always used with plural family members.
la loro sorella *their sister* **le loro** sorelle *their sisters* **il loro** nonno *their grandfather* **i loro** nonni *their grandparents*	**Loro** always requires an article.
Posso parlare con **il tuo** babbo? *Can I speak to your Daddy?* Sono uscita con **(la) mia** mamma *I went out with my mum*	**Papà** *Daddy* and **mamma** *Mummy* may optionally be used with the article. **Babbo** usually requires the article.
Vieni a **casa mia/nostra** *Come to my/our house* È **colpa mia/sua** *It is my/his/her fault* Non è **compito mio/nostro** *It is not my/our job* Sono **affari miei/tuoi** *It is my/your business* Sono a **tua/vostra disposizione** *I am/They are at your disposal* Fa tutto a **modo suo** *He/she does everything his/her way*	Idiomatic expressions: the article is often omitted and the possessive adjective may come after the noun. Here are a few common ones.

E 4 Introduce family and friends using the appropriate form of the possessive.

(a) Questo è (*my*) marito e questa è (*our*) figlia, Laura.
(b) Questo è (*my*) figlio, Claudio e questa è (*his*) fidanzata, Emilia.
(c) Questa è Alessandra, (*our*) figlia più grande, e questo è (*her*) fidanzato, Alessio.
(d) Ti presento (*my*) mamma e (*my*) fratellino, Roberto.
(e) Questa è (*my*) moglie e queste sono (*our*) figlie, Simonetta e Chiara.

8.3 POSSESSIVE PRONOUNS

MAIN USES

Possessive pronouns agree in number and gender with the nouns they refer to.

Hai trovato i tuoi guanti? – No, ma ho trovato **i tuoi** *Did you find your gloves? – No, but I found <u>yours</u>*	Possessive pronouns are mostly used with the definite article.
Mia madre lavora nelle relazioni pubbliche, e **la tua**? *My mother works in public relations, what about <u>yours</u>?*	The article is also used when the pronoun refers to a single family member.

È **suo** questo portafoglio? – Sì, è **mio**, ti piace? *Is this your wallet/this wallet yours? – Yes, it's mine, do you like it?* **But**: Questo è **il mio** portafoglio e questo invece è **il tuo** *This is my wallet and this one is yours/this is the one that's yours*	No article is used with **essere** + a possessive when it means *to belong to*, except for emphasis or clarification
I miei sono in vacanza *My parents are on holiday* Salutami **i tuoi** *Say hello to your parents/family* **I suoi** abitano all'estero *His/her parents live abroad* **I suoi** di dove sono, signora? *Where are your parents/ is your family from, Signora?*	**I miei, i tuoi, i suoi** are often used to refer to one's parents or close family

1 Complete the sentences using appropriate Italian possessive pronouns.

(a) Tu prendi la tua macchina e io prendo (*mine*).
(b) Io ho invitato le mie amiche e lei ha invitato (*hers*).
(c) A me piace il mio professore, a te piace (*yours*)?
(d) Tu porti tuo padre e io porto (*mine*).
(e) Io chiederò il permesso ai miei genitori e tu chiedi il permesso a (*yours/your parents*).

2 Substitute the English with the appropriate Italian form of the possessive pronoun, paying attention to the use of the article.

(a) Enrico, è (*yours*) questo libro? – No, non è (*mine*). (*Mine*) è qui.
(b) Che bella sciarpa! È (*yours*), signora? – No, non è (*mine*). (*Mine*) è quella nera.
(c) Ho trovato delle chiavi. Sono (*his*)? – No, non sono (*his*), sono (*mine*).

8.4 EXPRESSING POSSESSION WITH 'S/S' ENDINGS

The *'s/s'* endings to English nouns are usually expressed in Italian by **di** or **quello di** before the possessor. They are equivalent to both possessive adjectives and pronouns.

L'amica **di** Flavio *Flavio's friend* Le chiavi **di** mio fratello *My brother's keys* La moglie **del** signor Arlacchi *Signor Arlacchi's wife* Il cane **dei** vicini *The neighbours' dog*	**Di** (*of*) expresses the equivalent of the English *'s/s'* ending. If the noun takes a definite article, **di** combines with it.
Sono **di** mio fratello *They are my brother's* È **dei** vicini *It is the neighbours'*	**Essere di** expresses the equivalent of the English *to be somebody's* ....
Pino ha mangiato il suo panino e **quello di** sua sorella *Pino ate his roll and his sister's* (lit. *that of his sister*) Ho perso la mia chiave e anche **quella dei** vicini *I've lost my key and the neighbours' as well*	**Quello di**: to avoid repeating a noun the appropriate form of **quello** is used before **di**.
Vai **da** Fiorella? *Are you going to Fiorella's?* Sono andato **dal** dentista *I went to the dentist's*	**Da** is used for the *'s/s'* ending when this refers to someone's place.

1 Give the Italian for the following.

(a) *Leonardo's mother is ill.*
(b) *Signor Palladino's wife is on holiday.*
(c) *The neighbour's cat is black.*
(d) *I have found Elisabetta's shoes and Antonio's too.*
(e) *I have lost Marta's letter and her sister's too.*
(f) *I'll see you at Giovanni's.*

8.5 POSSESSIVES WITH OTHER DETERMINERS + *PROPRIO*

Possessives are commonly used with other determiners (articles, possessives, demonstratives, etc.). See p. 290.

È **un mio** amico/**una mia** collega *He is a friend of mine/She is a colleague of mine* **or**: È **un** amico **mio**/**una** collega **mia**	Indefinite article + possessive: with common nouns such as **amico** the possessive position is flexible. If placed after the noun it is more emphatic.

Sono ... (**dei**) **nostri** parenti/parenti **nostri** ... *relatives of ours*
  (**dei**) **vostri** amici/(**degli**) amici **vostri** ... *friends of yours*
  (**delle**) **sue** amiche/amiche **sue** ... *(girl)friends of his/hers*
	Partitive article + possessive: the partitive article is often omitted and the possessive position is flexible.

Quel tuo cugino non mi piace *I don't like that cousin of yours* **Quegli** amici **tuoi**/**Quei tuoi** amici non mi piacciono *I don't like those friends of yours* **Questa tua** ossessione è assurda *This obsession of yours is absurd*	Demonstrative + possessive: the demonstrative precedes the possessive and agrees with it.
È arrivato con **tre miei** amici/**tre** amici **miei** *He arrived with three friends of mine* Verrà probabilmente con **qualche suo** amico/**qualche** amico **suo** *He'll probably arrive with some friend(s) of his* Mi ha invitato a cena con **alcuni suoi** parenti/**alcuni** parenti **suoi** *He invited me to dinner with a few relations of his*	With a number or indefinite + possessive: the position of the possessive is flexible.

E | **I** | Explain who the following friends, colleagues and acquaintances (**conoscenti**) are, using a possessive with the appropriate form of the indefinite or partitive article where required.

  (a) Pietro è (*a friend of mine*).
  (b) Stefania è (*a colleague of his*).
  (c) Alberto è (*an acquaintance of theirs*).
  (d) Sono andato al cinema con (*friends of ours*), Pietro, Tommaso e Elisabetta.
  (e) Sono andato a un convegno con (*colleagues of mine*), Sergio e Nadia.

2 Now use an indefinite, a number or a demonstrative with the possessive adjective.

  (a) È arrivato con (*three friends of his*).
  (b) Siamo usciti con (*a few clients of ours*).
  (c) Ho litigato con (*those friends of yours*).

Proprio

È importante occuparsi dei **propri** figli *It is important to look after one's (own) children* Bisogna stabilire un buon rapporto con il **proprio** capo *One has to establish a good relationship with one's boss.* Ciascuno ha il **proprio** computer *They each have their own computer* (or *Everyone/Each person has his own ...*)	**Proprio** is mostly used with impersonal expressions to mean *one's (own)*. With indefinites such as **ciascuno/ognuno** *each/everyone* it can also mean *his, her* or *their own*.

L'ho visto con i miei (**propri**) occhi
I saw it with my (very) own eyes
Trascuri i tuoi (**propri**) interessi
You are neglecting your own interests

However, to say *my own*, *our own* or
your own, **proprio** cannot be used
without **mio**, **tuo**, **nostro** or
vostro and is frequently dropped.

3 Complete the sentences by substituting the English with an appropriate Italian possessive.

(a) È importante trovare soddisfazione nel (*one's*) lavoro.
(b) È necessario esaminare (*one's*) coscienza.
(c) Ognuno ha diritto alla (*one's own*) opinione.
(d) Ho pagato con (*my own*) soldi.

8.6 OMISSION OF THE POSSESSIVES IN ITALIAN

Possessives are used far less frequently in Italian than in English, especially where
it is clear from the context who or what belongs to whom. They are often expressed by
the following:

The definite article	È uscita con **il** marito *She went out with her husband* Avevano **i** vestiti strappati e **le** scarpe bagnate *Their clothes were torn and their shoes were wet* Ho perso **l'**ombrello/**l'**agenda/**gli** occhiali/ **la** patente *I've lost my umbrella/diary/glasses/driving licence* Ha **gli** occhi azzurri e **i** capelli biondi *Her/his eyes are blue and his/her hair is fair*	The definite article is often enough to signify possession on its own. This is usually the case with family, clothes, personal possessions and parts of the body.
Reflexive pronouns	Metti**ti la** giacca/**le** scarpe, Dina *Put your jacket/shoes on, Dina* **Si** è slogato **il** polso/**la** spalla *He sprained his wrist/dislocated his shoulder* Prepara**ti i** bagagli *Pack your suitcases (luggage)*	Reflexive pronouns make it clear who the possessor is and eliminate the need for a possessive adjective. See also p. 81.
Indirect object pronouns	**Gli/le** fa male **il** ginocchio/**la** schiena *His/her knee back/hurts* **Mi** ha stirato **la** camicia *She ironed my shirt* **Ci** ha rubato **l'**orologio *He stole our clock*	Indirect object pronouns may also indicate who the possessor is. See also Chapter 7, p. 87.
IDO pronouns + reflexive *si*	**Mi** si è rotto **il** televisore *My TV has been broken* **Ti** si è bloccato **il** computer? *Has your computer crashed?* **Le** si è staccato **un** bottone *One of her buttons has come off*	IDO pronouns + reflexive **si**: in these constructions the IDO pronouns also denote the possessor. See also p. 100, Ex. 2.

Plural subject, singular possession

Perché non vi togliete **il** cappotto? *Why don't you take off your coats?* Abbiamo perso **la** patente *We've lost our driving licences* Ci ha stretto **la** mano *He shook our hands* Hanno perso **la** testa *They lost their heads*	If several people are referred to but each of them possesses only one item of clothing, part of the body, etc., then in Italian the singular noun is used.

E **I** Give the Italian equivalent of the English possessives and nouns below.

(a) Piove, devi prendere (*your umbrella*).

(b) Angelo arriverà domani con (*his wife*).

(c) Fa freddo, perché non ti metti (*your jumper*)?

(d) Mi fa male (*my foot*).

(e) Si sono tolti (*their hats*).

Demonstratives

Demonstratives (**i dimostrativi**) are adjectives or pronouns which refer to something in terms of whether it is near to or far from the speaker. English demonstratives are *this, these, that* and *those*.

9.1 DEMONSTRATIVE ADJECTIVES AND PRONOUNS

FORMS

(a) *Questo* (this)

The adjective and pronoun **questo** has four endings. The singular adjectives, but not the pronouns, may be shortened to **quest'** in front of a vowel.

	Adjectives		Pronouns
m. sing.	**questo** muro *this wall*	**quest'**edificio *this building*	**questo** *this one*
m. pl.	**questi** muri *these walls*	**questi** edifici *these buildings*	**questi** *these ones*
f. sing.	**questa** fabbrica *this factory*	**quest'**aula *this classroom*	**questa** *this one*
f. pl.	**queste** fabbriche *these houses*	**queste** aule *these classrooms*	**queste** *these ones*

(b) *Quello* (that)

The adjective **quello** has seven forms, whereas the pronoun has only four. Like the definite article, the form of the adjective depends on the gender and initial letter of the word which immediately follows.

	Adjectives			Pronouns
m. sing.	**quel** muro *that wall*	**quello** specchio *that mirror*	**quell'**edificio *that building*	**quello** *that one*
m. pl.	**quei** muri *those walls*	**quegli** specchi/edifici *those mirrors/buildings*		**quelli** *those ones*
f. sing.	**quella** fabbrica *that factory*	**quell'**aula *that classroom*		**quella** *that one*
f. pl.	**quelle** fabbriche *those factories*	**quelle** aule *those classrooms*		**quelle** *those ones*

(c) Spelling changes of *quello*

Before other adjectives	**quella** giacca **quell'**edificio **quel** parco **quei** giornali	**quell'orribile** giacca **quel grande** edificio **quello strano** edificio **quell'immenso** parco **quegli stupidi** giornali	The form of the adjective **quello** changes if it precedes another adjective whose initial letter requires a different form.
Before numbers and **altro**	Dammi **quei due** piatti. Dammi **quei due** *Give me those two plates. Give me those two* Dammi **quegli altri** libri. Dammi **quegli altri** *Give me those other books. Give me those other ones*		In front of numbers and **altro** it is always necessary to use the adjectival forms of **quello** even when it is used as a pronoun.

E 1 You've borrowed many of the contents of your flat. Point out what they are. Begin, 'Ho preso in prestito questo/questa …' etc.

> lampada • sedie • divano • cuscini • armadio • scaffale • specchi

2 You're at the market. Point out the things you want to see. Begin, 'Mi fa vedere quel/quella …' etc.

> borsetta • cravatte • maglione • pantaloni • specchio • anello • orecchini

3 Complete the sentences below using the appropriate form of **quello** each time.
   (a) Ho scelto … gonna. Ho scelto … altra gonna.
   (b) Ho scelto … impermeabile. Ho scelto … altro impermeabile.
   (c) Hai visto … programma? Hai visto … strano programma?
   (d) Hai visto … documentario? Hai visto … interessante documentario cinese?
   (e) Non mi piacciono … colori. Non mi piacciono … altri colori.
   (f) Non mi piacciono … edifici. Non mi piacciono … grandi edifici moderni.

USES

Questo and **quello** are used for pointing things out or for contrasting them.

Questa è mia figlia e **queste** sono le sue amiche *This is my daughter and these are her friends* **Quei** gigli mi piacciono ma non mi piacciono **quelle** dalie *I like those lilies but I don't like those dahlias*	**Questo** *this* and **quello** *that* always agree with the noun they refer to, whether they are pronouns or adjectives.

Quale penna vuoi? **Quella rossa?** *Which pen do you want? The red one?* Gli stivali di cuoio sono belli, ma preferisco **quelli di camoscio** *The leather boots are nice but I prefer the suede ones* Quale giornale preferisci? – **Quello che leggi tu** *Which newspaper do you prefer? – The one you read*	**Quello** is used before adjectives, adjectival phrases and relative pronouns to mean *the … one(s)*.
Questo è il bagno e **questa qua** è la tua camera *This is the bathroom and this is your room right here* Queste quanto costano? E **queste qua**? E **quelle lì**, invece? *How much are these? And these ones (right) here? And what about those ones (over there)?*	**Questo qui/qua** and **Quello lì/là**: **qui** and **qua** (*here*) and **lì** and **là** (*there*) are often added to **questo** and **quello** for contrast or emphasis.

4 Which animals are being pointed out at the zoo? Complete the sentences using **quello**.

(a) Guarda quella tigre! – Quale? – *(That one)* lì.
(b) Guarda quel leone! – Quale? – *(That one)* lì.
(c) Hai visto quegli ippopotami? – Quali? – *(Those ones. Those three)*.
(d) Hai visto quei pappagalli? – Quali? – *(Those ones. The green ones)*.
(e) Hai visto quell'elefante? – Quale? – *(That one?)* No, *(That other smaller one)*.

5 Give the Italian equivalent of the following.

(a) *This is the kitchen and this is the bathroom right here.*
(b) *This is my room here and that's yours there.*
(c) *How much does this one* (una pasta) *cost? And what about that one?*
(d) *How much do those cost?* (cartoline). *And what about those ones?*

9.2 OTHER WAYS OF EXPRESSING *THIS* AND *THAT*

(a) Using *ciò*

Ciò is an invariable demonstrative pronoun used more in writing than in speech.

ciò *that/this*	**Ciò** non m'interessa *That/This doesn't interest me* Ha detto **ciò**? *Did he say that?*	**Ciò** refers to a whole situation or idea. It means *that*, or occasionally *this*.

(b) *That, this, that's*

When *this* and *that* refer to ideas, actions or situations in English they no longer correspond exactly to **questo** and **quello** respectively. Nor do they correspond exactly to the pronoun **ciò**. The use of **questo** or **quello** or **ciò**, referring to ideas and situations, depends essentially on the context and on stylistic considerations. Below are some general observations and guidelines.

that/this	**Questo** non m'interessa *That doesn't interest me* **Questo** non mi sembra giusto *That doesn't seem fair to me*	**Questo** (rather than **quello**) usually means *that* when denoting an idea, an event or a situation. It can more formally be substituted by **ciò**.
that's, what a ...!	Dobbiamo firmare tre volte. È assurdo **questo**! *We have to sign three times. That's absurd!* Si è dimesso – Non è possibile! *He's resigned – That's impossible/not possible!* Ho perso le mie chiavi. **Che** seccatura! *I've lost my keys. That's/What a nuisance!* Ci sposiamo – **Che** bello! *We're getting married – That's/How wonderful!*	**Questo** may follow the verb **essere** for emphasis or be omitted altogether. Note that the emphatic English *that* may be conveyed by an Italian exclamatory **che**!
that's	Grazie, molto gentile/sei molto gentile/ è molto gentile da parte tua *Thank you, that's very kind (of you)*	In personal comments, the English *that is* may become *you are* or *it is* in Italian.

(c) This is where, that is where

In Italian **questo** and **quello** are not normally used to express *this* or *that* with *where*.

È qui che compro la verdura ed **è lì che** prendo il pesce *This is where I buy vegetables and that's where I get the fish* **È qui che** dobbiamo scendere? *Is this where we have to get off?* **Era qui che** giocavi da bambino? *Was this where you used to play as a child?* **Qui** lavoro io e **lì** lavora mio marito *This is where I work and that's where my husband works*	In Italian you say, **È qui/qua che ...** or **È lì/là che ....** This literally means <u>it</u> is where, <u>it</u> is there that ... **Qui**, **qua**, **lì**, or **là** may also express *this is where/that is where*.

E   1   Using **ciò** and **questo**. Give your reactions to the following, and find an Italian equivalent of the English. There may be more than one possibility.

(a) Riccardo è molto depresso. – *That doesn't interest me.*
(b) Sabrina non è ancora arrivata. – *That doesn't mean she won't come.*
(c) Silvia guadagna meno di Umberto. – *That doesn't seem fair.*
(d) Sono divorziati. – *That isn't true.*

2   Saying *That's*. Comment on these situations, using an appropriate Italian equivalent for the English responses below.

(a) Marco si è rotto la gamba. – *That's a pity, he can't go skiing.* (andare a sciare)
(b) I nuovi clienti non hanno pagato. – *That's embarrassing, what shall we do?*
(c) Costerà mezzo milione. – *That's absurd!*
(d) Ho perso le chiavi di casa. – *That's a nuisance! Have you got a spare key?* (una chiave di riserva)
(e) Ti posso dare un passaggio? – *Thank you, that's very kind.*

3   Answer the questions by giving the Italian equivalent of the English.

(a) Questo è il liceo Leopardi. – *Is this where you go to school?*
(b) Quello lì è il mercato coperto. – *Is that where you buy the fruit and vegetables?*

(c) Questa qua è la piazza principale. – *Is this where you had an accident?* (un incidente)
(d) Quella lì è la pasticceria principale. – *Is that where your daughter works?*

(d) Using ecco

Ecco is sometimes termed a demonstrative adverb because it can be used to present and point things out. When used alone its meanings include *behold!*, *there/here is* and *there/here are.*

Ecco il tuo posto! *There is your seat!* Ecco i risultati. *Here are the results.*

It can also be used with other words to demonstrate, present, explain or deduce facts. For **ecco** and personal pronouns, see p. 92.

Ecco perché	Ecco perché sono in ritardo *That's why I'm late* Ecco perché non funziona *That's why it doesn't work* È per questo che sei in ritardo? *Is that why you're late?* È per questo che non funziona *This/That is why it doesn't work*	Ecco perché is used to say *That's why, This is why.* It is not used in questions. Per questo can be an alternative, especially in questions.
Ecco come	Ecco come si fa … *This is how you do it …* Ecco come l'ho saputo … *That is how I found (it) out …* È così che si fa? *Is this/that how you do it?*	Ecco come is used to say *This is how, That is how.* Così can be used for questions, unlike ecco come.
Ecco quello che	Ecco quello che penso io … *This is what I think …* Per cancellare un file, ecco quello che bisogna fare … *To delete a file, this is what you have to do …* Ah, ecco quello che bisogna fare *Ah, that's what you have to do*	Ecco quello che is used to say *This is what, So that's what.*

E **4** Using **ecco perché** and **ecco come** where possible, give an Italian equivalent to the English. There may be more than one possibility.

(a) Il treno si è fermato a Prato. *That's why I am late.*
(b) Manca la benzina. *That's why the car won't start!*
(c) Non lo sai usare? *Look, this is how it works …*
(d) Come lo sai che Tilda si separa dal marito? – *My brother is a friend of her husband, that's how I know (it).*

5 Find Italian equivalents to the following, choosing between **ecco quello che** and **quello che**.

(a) *To access the Internet, this is what you must do …*
(b) *This is what he told me …*
(c) *Yes, that's/it's what I intend to do.* (aver intenzione di)
(d) *That's not what I mean.*

10

Interrogatives

Interrogatives (**gli interrogativi**) are adjectives, pronouns and adverbs used to ask questions. Question words are *why? where? when? how? who? whose? what? which? how much? how many? how long?*

10.1 ASKING QUESTIONS

In Italian there is no special word order for asking questions. A statement and a question have the same word order, but the speaker's rising tone of voice indicates that it is a question.

Direct and indirect questions

Direct questions	Marco può venire? *Can Marco come?*	A direct question represents what the speaker actually said.
Indirect questions	Ho chiesto se Marco può venire *I've asked if Marco can come* Vorrei sapere se Marco può venire *I'd like to know if Marco can come* Non so se Marco può venire *I don't know whether Marco can come* Mi chiedo se Marco potrà venire *I wonder whether Marco will be able to come*	An indirect question does not represent the actual words spoken. It reports what was said or introduces a question indirectly.

Question tags

Si chiama Anna, **vero/non è vero?** *She is called Anna, isn't she?/Her name is Anna, isn't it?* Non puoi venire, **vero?** *You can't come, can you?*	In English many questions end with tags such as *isn't she? won't they? can't you?* In Italian all that is necessary is to add **vero?/non è vero?** to a positive statement and **vero?** to a negative one.

I Convert the indirect questions below into direct questions.

   (a) Vorrei sapere quando viene l'avvocato.
   (b) Non so di dov'è la signorina.
   (c) Non ho capito cosa vuole la dottoressa.

2 You're just checking on the facts. Give the Italian equivalent(s) of the English.

   (a) *The post has arrived, hasn't it?*   (c) *They're leaving on Monday, aren't they?*
   (b) *Your name is Carla, isn't it?*   (d) *You haven't paid, have you? (tu)*

10.2 QUESTION WORDS

Main interrogative adverbs

These are all invariable.

quando? *when?*	**Quando** arrivate? *When are you arriving?* Non so **quando** arrivano *I don't know when they are arriving* Da **quando** sei qui? *Since when have you been here?* Per **quando** lo vuole? *When do you want it by? (lit. for when)*	Prepositions precede **quando**.
dove? *where?*	**Dove** hai comprato il pane? *Where did you buy the bread?* Lei di **dov'è?** *Where are you from?* Non mi ha detto **dove** abita *She hasn't told me where she lives*	In front of **è**, **dove** becomes **dov'è?** Prepositions precede **dove**.
quand'è che? dov'è che?	**Quand'è** che arriva? *When is he arriving?* **Dov'è** che l'hai visto? *Where did you see him?/Where is it you saw him?*	**Quand'è che?** and **dov'è che?** (lit. *when/where is it that?*) are commonly used for emphasis.
perché? *why?*	**Perché** vuoi uscire? *Why do you want to go out?* **Perché** non vieni con noi? *Why don't you come with us?* Non ho capito **perché** non vieni *I don't understand why you're not coming*	In direct questions **perché non?** is used for suggestions.
	Non vuoi venire? **Perché no?** *Don't you want to come? Why not?*	*Why not?* is expressed by **perché no?**
come? *how?*	**Come** sta? *How are you?* Mi ha chiesto **come** funziona *He asked me how it works*	**Come** is used in various ways.
	Come mai sei qui? *How come/Why are you here?* Vorrei sapere **come mai** non è venuta *I'd like to know why (on earth) she didn't come*	**Come mai?** means *how come? why on earth?*

come? how? (contd)	Come fai per arrivare al lavoro? *How do you get to work?* Come fai per/ad alzarti in tempo? *How do you (manage to) get up on time?*	Come? is also used with fare to enquire how people do things.
	Com'è la sua città? *What's your town like?* Come sono i suoi colleghi? *What are your colleagues like?*	Com'è? and Come sono? are used to ask what things are like.
	Come, scusi? *Pardon?/Sorry, what did you say?* Mi presti l'articolo? Come no! *Will you lend me the article? – But of course!*	Come? on its own or with Scusi/a? is a way of saying you don't understand. Followed by no, it is used for emphatic agreement.

- For **quanto**, see p. 120.

E 1 Complete the sentences using one of the following interrogatives: **quando? dove? perché? come?** For one of the sentences there are two possibilities – and two meanings.

(a) ... mai sei in ritardo?
(b) ... fai per andare in centro?
(c) Vorrei sapere ... è il tuo nuovo lavoro.
(d) Dimmi ... e ... parti.
(e) ... è che compri il pane?
(f) Non voglio uscire. – ... no?
(g) Posso prendere un bicchiere d'acqua? – ... no!

Main interrogative pronouns

chi? who?	Chi viene domani? *Who is coming tomorrow?* Mi ha chiesto chi viene *He has asked me who is coming*	Chi? refers to people only.
	A chi appartiene? *Who does it belong to?* (lit. *to whom ...?*) Di chi stai parlando? *Who are you talking about? (about whom ...?)* A chi piace il manzo? *Who likes beef?* (lit. *to whom is beef pleasing?*) Dimmi per chi lavori *Tell me who you work for*	If chi is used with a verb requiring a preposition, this precedes chi. Typical verbs include appartenere a, parlare di, piacere a.
di chi? whose?	Di chi è questa giacca? *Whose jacket is this?* Di chi è quel cappotto? *Whose coat is that?* Non mi ricordo di chi è questo portafoglio *I don't remember whose wallet this is*	Di is used before chi to mean *whose?* (lit. *of whom?*).
	Di chi è quel film/libro? *Who is that book/film by?*	Di chi? can also mean *who by?*
che cosa? what?	Che vuoi? *What do you want?* Che cosa è successo? *What has happened?* Cosa facciamo? *What shall we do?*	Che? is frequently followed by cosa but can be used on its own. Cosa? is often used informally on its own.
	A che serve? *What is it used for?* Per (che) cosa lo vuole? *What do you want it for?*	Che cosa? Che? and Cosa? can be preceded by prepositions.

2 Complete the replies below, using appropriate interrogative words, plus any prepositions required.

(a) *What does he want?* – Non so . . . .
(b) *What is it for?* – Non so . . . . (servire a)
(c) *What is it made of?* – Non so . . . .
(d) *Who does it belong to?* – Non ho capito . . . .
(e) *Who is it for?* – Non ho capito . . . .
(f) *Who is the book by?* – Non ho capito . . . .
(g) *Whose shoes are these?* – Non so . . . .
(h) *Whose car is that?* – Non so . . . .

Interrogative adjectives and pronouns

che? *what?*	**Che** ora è? *What's the time?* **Che** lavoro fa? *What job do you do?* **Che** scuola fa? *What school do you go to?* **Che** tipo è? *What sort of a person is he/she?*	**Che?** is an invariable adjective. It can also be a pronoun. (See p. 118.)
	Di **che** colore è? *What colour is it?* In **che** anno è nato Dante? *What year was Dante born in?* Di **che** anno sei? *What year were you born in?* (i.e. *How old are you?*) Dimmi da **che** parte andate *Tell me which (what) way you're going*	**Che?** can be preceded by prepositions. Note that it may sometimes be expressed as *which?* in English.
quale/ quali? *which (one/s)?*	Dammi il bicchiere. – **Quale?** *Give me the glass. – Which one?* **Quale** vuoi, la mela o la pera? *Which (one) do you want, the apple or the pear?* Non so **quali** prendere, le rose o i garofani *I don't know which (ones) to have, the roses or the carnations*	The plural form of **quale** is **quali**. When **quale/i** are pronouns the meaning is *which one/s?*
	Qual è l'indirizzo/la capitale d'Italia? *What's the address/the capital of Italy?* (lit. *which is … ?*) **Quali** sono i vostri progetti? *What are your plans?*	Note that when the pronoun **quale** is used with the verb **essere** it corresponds to the English *what?* **Quale** shortens to **qual** before **è**.
	Quale pasta vuoi, la brioche o la ciambella? *Which cake do you want, the brioche or the doughnut?* **Quali** riviste hai scelto? *Which magazines did you choose?*	The adjective **quale/i** (but not the pronoun) may be replaced by the adjective **che?** (See below.)
che? or **quale?**	**Che** pasta vuoi? Una brioche o una ciambella? *What (kind of) cake … a brioche or a doughnut?* Da **che/quale** binario parte il treno per Londra? *What/which platform does the London train leave from?* Scusi, da **quale** binario? *Sorry, from which platform?*	As adjectives, **che** and **quale** are very similar. Broadly speaking, **che** is used in a general sense to mean *what?* and **quale** *which?* is more specific. When clarification and precise information are required, **quale?** is used.

E

3 Give the Italian equivalent of the following, choosing between **che?** or **quale?** Use the **Lei** form for *you*.

(a) *What's the time?*
(b) *What job do you do?*
(c) *What's your phone number?*

(d) *What's your favourite sport?*
(e) *What's your teacher like?*
    (two possibilities, one with **come**)

4 In which of the sentences below could **che?** substitute **quale/i?**

(a) Qual è la strada migliore?
(b) Dammi una matita. – Quale vuoi?
(c) Quali giornali compri?

5 Guess what the mystery object is. To do so, match up the questions and answers below.

(a) A che cosa serve questo oggetto?
(b) Di che cosa è fatto?
(c) Che dimensioni ha?
(d) Di che colore è?
(e) Che forma ha?

(i) È rosso.
(ii) Dipende, ma questo qua è abbastanza grande.
(iii) È rotondo.
(iv) È fatto di gomma o di plastica.
(v) Serve per giocare.

Quanto

Quanto can be a pronoun, an adjective and also an adverb.

quanto/a? *how much?* **quanti/e?** *how many?*	Ho preso un po' di benzina – **Quanta?** *I got some petrol – How much?* Ecco le tazze, **quante** ne vuoi? *Here are the cups, how many do you want?* In **quanti** siete? *How many of you are there?*	As a pronoun, **quanto** agrees with the noun it refers to. It can be preceded by prepositions.
	Quanta pizza prendi? *How much pizza are you having?* Non so **quante** persone verranno *I don't know how many people will come*	As an adjective, **quanto** also agrees with the noun it refers to.
	Quanto costano? (i fagliolini, le carote) *How much do they cost?* **Quanto** dura? (il viaggio, la gita) *How long does it last?* **Quant'**è lontano?/alto?/grande? *How far/high/big is it?* Da **quanto** (tempo) abiti qui? *How long/Since when have you lived here?*	**Quanto** may also refer to a verb or adjective, in which case it is an invariable adverb. Before **essere**, **quanto** becomes **quant'**. Note that **quanto** can mean *how long?*

E

6 Give the Italian equivalent of the following, using the **tu** form for *you*:

(a) *How much spaghetti do you want?*
(b) *I don't know how many people there are.*

(c) *How far is it?*
(d) *How long will you take?* (impiegare)

10.3 DISTINGUISHING INTERROGATIVES FROM RELATIVES

In English, interrogative pronouns have some forms in common with relative pronouns, unlike Italian, e.g. *who?/who, which?/which*. Here is a summary of the differences.

	Interrogative			Relative	
who?	→	**chi?**	*who*	→	**che**
with, to, etc. whom?	→	**con, a**, ecc. **chi?**	*with, to, etc. whom*	→	**con, a**, ecc. **cui**
which?	→	**quale?/che?**	*which*	→	**che**
with, to, etc. which?	→	**con, a**, ecc. **quale?/che?**	*with, to, etc. which*	→	**con, a**, ecc. **cui**
what?	→	**che cosa?**	*what*	→	**ciò che/quello che**
whose?	→	**di chi?**	*whose*	→	**il/la/i/le cui**

Interrogatives are used in direct and indirect questions. Note that relative pronouns can be used in questions, but they are <u>not</u> the question word.

who? *whom?*	**Chi** è venuto? *Who came?* **Con chi** esci? *Who are you going out with? (With whom?)* Voglio sapere **chi** è venuto/**con chi** esci *I want to know who came/who you go out with*	Direct questions Indirect question
who *whom*	Il ragazzo **che** è venuto è mio fratello *The boy who came is my brother* La ragazza **con cui** esco è sarda *The girl I go out with is Sardinian (with whom ...)* Il ragazzo **che** è venuto è tuo fratello? *Is the boy who came your brother?*	Relative pronouns Relative pronouns in question
which?	**Quale** macchina ti piace? *Which car do you like?* **Da quale** stazione parti? *Which station do you leave from?* Non so **quale** macchina mi piace *I don't know which car I like*	Direct questions Indirect question
which	La macchina **che** mi piace è la Ferrari *The car (which) I like is the Ferrari* La stazione **da cui** parto è Waterloo *The station I leave from is Waterloo*	Relative pronouns
what?	**Che cosa** hai comprato? *What have you bought?* Mi ha chiesto **che cosa** avevo comprato *He asked what I had bought*	Direct question Indirect question
what	Ti faccio vedere **ciò che/quello che** ho comprato *I'll show you what I bought*	Relative pronoun
whose?	**Di chi** è la Lancia grigia? *Whose is the grey Lancia?* Devo scoprire **di chi** è la Lancia grigia *I have to find out whose the grey Lancia is*	Direct question Indirect question
whose	Mio cugino, **la cui** Lancia è stata rubata, si comprerà una Seicento *My cousin, whose Lancia was stolen, is going to buy himself a Seicento*	Relative pronoun

E   I   Complete the following sentences by selecting the correct pronoun: interrogative
         or relative.

(a) Dimmi ... vuoi. (che cosa/quello che/ciò che) *Tell me what you want.*
(b) Fa' ... ti dico. (che cosa/quello che/ciò che) *Do what I tell you.*
(c) Voglio sapere ... viene. (chi/che) *I want to know who is coming.*
(d) Gli ospiti ... vengono sono italiani. (chi/che) *The guests who are coming are Italian.*
(e) Non mi hai detto con ... giochi a tennis. (con chi/con cui) *You haven't told me who
    you play tennis with.*
(f) La ragazza ... esco è simpaticissima. (con chi/con cui) *The girl I go out with is
    extremely nice.*
(g) Mi dai una penna ... funziona? (quale/che) *Can you give me a pen which works?*
(h) Non so ... penna funziona. (quale/che) *I don't know which pen works.*

11

Exclamations

Exclamations (**gli esclamativi**) can consist of one or several words and they express strong emotions such as horror, disgust, delight and admiration. They do not need the usual structure of a full sentence to make sense, e.g. *How wonderful! What nonsense!*

In Italian, exclamations are mainly expressed by interrogatives. The most commonly used are **che**, **come**, **quanto** and, more rarely, **quale**.

(a) *Che!*

Before nouns	**Che** meraviglia! *How wonderful!* **Che** caldo! *How hot it is!* **Che** peccato! *What a shame!* **Che** sorpresa! *What a surprise!*	The English equivalent is *How!* or *What!*
Before nouns and adjectives	**Che** faccia tosta! *What a cheek!* **Che** bei bambini! *What lovely children!* **Che** meraviglia quella casa! *What a wonderful house!/How lovely that house is!* **Che** giacca favolosa/meravigliosa! *What a fabulous/marvellous jacket!* **Che** vino squisito! *What a delicious wine!*	Emphatic adjectives such as **favoloso, squisito** and **meraviglioso** are always used with a noun: you cannot say 'che favoloso/meraviglioso/squisito'.
Before adjectives	**Che** bello! *Great! How nice!* **Che** strano! *How odd!* **Che** buffo! *How funny!*	**Che** + masculine singular adjectives expresses a general comment.
	Che bella! *How lovely/beautiful she is!* (Com'è bella!) **Che** bravi/e! *How clever (we/you/they are)!/Well done!* (Come siamo/siete/sono bravi/e!) **Che** carina questa borsa! *How nice/pretty this bag is!* (Com'è carina questa borsa!)	**Che!** + an adjective agreeing with the noun it modifies is used for specific people or things. A more formal alternative to this is **come!** + **essere**. See **come!** p. 124.
Che ... **che ...!**	**Che** faccia tosta **che** ha! *What a cheek (that) he's got!* **Che** stupido **che** sei! *How stupid you are!* **Che** male **che** giocano! *How badly they play!*	Note the use of relative pronoun **che** *that*, followed by a verb.

- **Quale!** is a rarely used literary form of **che!** Quale coraggio! *How brave!*

(b) Come!

Before complete sentences	**Come** mi dispiace! *How sorry I am!/I'm so sorry!* **Come** cantano bene! *How well they sing!* **Come** fa freddo qui dentro! *How cold it is in here!* **Com'è** pesante questa valigia! *How heavy this suitcase is!* **Come** sono distratti quei ragazzi! *How careless those boys are!*	**Come!** is used before a complete clause or sentence and is less colloquial than **Che!**

E 1 Express your admiration of the following, using the adjectives given.

(a) il giardino ... bello.

(b) il panorama ... stupendo.

(c) la scrivania antica ... magnifica.

(d) quell'orologio ... bello.

2 Give the Italian equivalent of the English.

(a) *What a shame!*

(b) *How wonderful!*

(c) *What wonderful shoes! (two possibilities)*

(d) *What clever children!*

(e) *How clever they are! (two possibilities)*

(c) Quanto!

Before nouns	**Quanta** gente! *What a lot of people!* **Quante** bugie raccontano! *What a lot of lies they tell!*	**Quanto!** *what a lot* usually emphasises amount. It agrees with the nouns it refers to.
Before verbs	**Quanto** hai speso! *What a lot you've spent!* **Quanto** mi piace! *(How much) I love it!*	Used as an invariable adverb when it modifies verbs.
Before **essere**	**Quant'**è piccola questa stanza! *How small this room is!* **Quant'**è bella tua figlia! *How beautiful your daughter is!* **Quant'**è stato difficile l'esame! *How hard the exam was!*	**Quanto** + **essere** is sometimes used like **come** + **essere**, especially referring to quantity or degrees.

E 3 Rewrite the statements below to make them into exclamations, using **Che!** or **Quanto!** as appropriate. Use the English as a guide.

(a) C'è molto rumore qui dentro.   *What a lot of noise in here!*

(b) È un rumore tremendo.   *What a terrible noise!*

(c) È gente antipatica.   *What horrible people!*

(d) C'è molta gente in giro.   *What a lot of people around!*

4 Use **quanto** or **come** to complete the following. Sometimes either is possible.

(a) ... dorme quel ragazzo!

(b) ... soldi hai speso!

(c) ... sono lenti!

(d) ... mi dispiace!

5 What do you say? Select one or more of the exclamations below to match the situation given.

(a) *You've been invited to a concert.*
  (i) Che bella!   (ii) Che bello!   (iii) Com'è bello!

(b) *That's odd, your friend hasn't turned up.*
  (i) Com'è strano!   (ii) Quant'è strano!   (iii) Che strano!

(c) *The ice cream is delicious.*
  (i) Che squisito!   (ii) Che buono!   (iii) Che gelato squisito!

(d) *That boy's so clever!*
  (i) Com'è bravo!   (ii) Quant'è bravo!   (iii) Che bravo!

12

Indefinites

Indefinites (**gli indefiniti**) refer to unspecific people, things and amounts. They are words like *someone, something, every, all.* They can be pronouns or adjectives and sometimes both.

12.1 INDEFINITE ADJECTIVES

Ogni and **qualche** are both invariable and are widely used in speech.

ogni *every, all*	Elisa mi chiama **ogni** giorno *Elisa calls me every day* C'è un treno **ogni** due ore *There's a train every two hours* **Ogni** cittadino deve votare *Every citizen must vote/All citizens must vote* Ho perso **ogni** rispetto per te *I've lost all respect for you*	**Ogni** is always used with a singular noun and verb, even though it can sometimes mean *all*. See also **tutti/tutte**, which is a little more specific and familiar, p. 130.
qualche *some, any,* *a few*	Ho **qualche** dubbio *I have some/a few doubts.* Ho bisogno di perdere **qualche** chilo *I need to lose the odd kilo/a kilo or two* C'è **qualche** posto libero? *Are there any seats free?/Is there a seat free?* L'ho incontrato in **qualche** bar *I met him in some bar or other*	**Qualche** has a range of meanings. It is always used with a singular noun and verb, although its meaning is mostly plural except when it signifies *some or other.* See also **alcuni**, p. 131.

E 1 Complete the sentences using **ogni** or **qualche**.

(a) Mi saluta ... volta che mi vede.

(b) ... volta mi saluta, ma non sempre.

(c) Vado in Italia ... anno.

(d) Ci vediamo fra ... anno.

(e) ... studente deve munirsi di una tessera.

(f) C'è ... studente che non ha la tessera?

Qualsiasi and qualunque are virtually synonymous and have two main uses.

qualsiasi qualunque *any* *(whatsoever)*	Per me **qualsiasi** giorno va bene *Any day is fine for me*; Mi dà un cognac? – Di quale marca? – Una **qualsiasi** ... *What make? – Any one will do/Any old one*; È una segretaria **qualsiasi** *She's a very average secretary*	Note that when placed after the noun/pronoun the meaning can be pejorative.
	Per lei farei **qualsiasi/qualunque cosa** *I would do anything for her*	**Qualsiasi/qualunque cosa** are used to say *anything (whatsoever, at all).*
whatever, *whichever*	Avrai successo, **qualsiasi** corso tu scelga *You'll be successful whatever/whichever course you choose*; **Qualsiasi** cosa tu possa dire, non ti crederò *Whatever you say I won't believe you*	**Qualsiasi** and **qualunque** are often followed by a verb in the subjunctive. See p. 253.

2 Answer the questions in Italian, taking care to give the correct equivalent of *any*.

(a) A che ora ti chiamo? – *At any time.*   (c) Che vino beviamo? – *Any one you want.*
(b) Che colore preferisci? – *Any colour is fine.*   (d) Un whiskey? Che marca vuoi? –
                                    Any will do.

3 Give the English equivalent of the following.

(a) Accetterò la tua decisione, qualunque sia.   (b) Per lui Elisabetta farebbe qualsiasi cosa.

12.2 INDEFINITE PRONOUNS

(a) *Qualcuno* and *qualcosa*

qualcuno *someone,* *anyone,* *some people,* *some*	Fa' venire **qualcuno** *Get someone to come* C'è **qualcuno** in casa? *Is anyone at home?* **Qualcuno** dice che troppa vitamina C fa male *Some people say that too much vitamin C is harmful* Ho visto i quadri. **Qualcuno** era veramente eccezionale *I've seen the pictures. Some were really outstanding*	**Qualcuno** is always used with a singular verb, although it often refers to plural persons or things. In these cases **alcuni/e** + a plural verb can be used but it is less colloquial. See p. 131.
qualcuno/a (di) *some,* *a few (of)*	Hai incontrato qualche amico a Milano? – Sì, **qualcuno** *Did you meet any friends in Milan? – Yes, a few/the odd one* Mi è piaciuta solo **qualcuna** delle foto *I only liked some/a few of the photos/the odd photo*	**Qualcuno/a** is the pronoun equivalent of **qualche**. It is always singular even if it refers to plural nouns. Note that it can refer to things as well as people.
qualcuno/a di + noi/voi/ loro *some/any of us/* *you/them*	**Qualcuno di** voi ha una penna? *Have any/some of you got a pen?/Has anyone got a pen?* **Qualcuna di** noi ragazze ti accompagnerà *Some/one (or other) of us girls will go with you*	**Qualcuno** can be followed by **di** + **noi**, **voi** or **loro**. The verb is always singular in Italian.
qualcosa *something,* *anything*	Ho mangiato **qualcosa** *I ate something* Hai mangiato **qualcosa?** *Did you eat anything?*	**Qualcosa** is invariable.

(b) *Nessuno, niente* and *nulla*

nessuno no one, not anyone	Non c'è **nessuno** qui *There's no one here* Non c'è **nessuno** qui? *Isn't there anyone here?*	When it means *no one/not anyone*, **nessuno** is invariable.
nessuno/a none/not one, not any	Hai ricevuto qualche regalo/cartolina? – No, **nessuno/nessuna** *Did you receive any presents/postcards? – No, none*	When **nessuno/a** refers to a specific noun it agrees with it in gender and is always singular.
nessuno/a di none (of), neither (of), not either (of)	Ha tre figli. **Nessuno di** loro vuol fare il medico ... *None of them want to become doctors* **Nessuna delle** mie sorelle è sposata *None of my sisters are married* (or, if there are two: *Neither of my sisters*) Ho due cappotti. Non mi piace **nessuno dei** due ... *I don't like either of them*	**Nessuno/a di + noi, voi, loro**, or + a noun or number is always used with a singular verb to refer to things as well as people. See also **né l'uno né l'altro**, p. 129.
niente/nulla nothing, not anything	Non ho detto **niente** *I said nothing* Non hai visto **niente**? *Didn't you see anything?*	**Niente** and **nulla are** both invariable. See also Negatives, p. 146.

- For **nessuno** as an adjective see p. 133.

(c) *Ognuno*

ognuno everyone	**Ognuno** ha il diritto di essere protetto dalla legge *Everyone has the right to be protected by the law*	**Ognuno** refers to a collective whole. See also **tutti** (p. 130), which is more specific and familiar.
ognuno/a every one, all of them	C'erano 18 stanze e in **ognuna** c'era un orologio *There were 18 rooms and in every one/all of them there was a clock.* Ha cinque figli, **ognuno** più simpatico dell'altro *He has five children, each one nicer than the next*	**Ognuno/a** also refers to individual people and things. It agrees with the noun in gender but is always singular. See also **ciascuno**, p. 133.
ognuno/a di all, every one of	**Ognuno di voi** deve dare una mano *All/every one of you must give a hand*	**Ognuno/a di + noi, voi, loro** means *all, every one of*. It is used with a singular verb. See also **ciascuno**, p. 133.

E 1 Give the Italian equivalent of the English, using appropriate indefinite pronouns.

(a) *Do you want anything/something?* (Lei) (d) *I don't want anything.*
(b) *There's someone at the door.* (e) *There's no one at the door.*
(c) *Some people prefer to work at home.* (f) *Everyone has the right to a pension.*

2 Answer the following questions using indefinite pronouns.

(a) Avete scattato delle belle foto? – *Yes, some/a few/the odd one.*
(b) Hai ricevuto qualche bel regalo? – *Yes, some/a few/the odd one.*
(c) Avete dei progetti interessanti per quest'estate? – *No, none.*

3 Give the Italian equivalent of the English, and complete the following sentences using indefinite pronouns.

(a) *(Some of us)* ti potrà accompagnare. (c) *(None of us)* ti può aiutare.
(b) Può venire *(any of you)*? (d) *(All of you)* deve pagare domani.

4 Express the following in Italian.

(a) *None of my friends wants to be a doctor.*
(b) *I don't like any of my aunts.*
(c) *My parents have interesting jobs but neither of them went to university.* (fare l'università)
(d) *My brother took two photos but I don't like either of them.*

(d) *Uno/a* and *l'uno/a*

uno *one, you, someone*	**Uno** potrebbe pensare che non sia vero *One might think it isn't true* Ha telefonato **uno** che ti voleva parlare *Someone (or other) rang wanting to speak to you*	When **uno** is used as the impersonal *you* it is invariable. It occasionally means *someone (or other)*.
uno/a *one*	Se vuoi una penna, ne ho **una** in tasca *If you want a pen, I've got one in my pocket*	When **uno** means *one* (in number) it agrees with the noun it refers to.
l'uno/a *each*	Le cartoline costano 90 centesimi **l'una** *The postcards cost 90 cents each* I piatti? Li ho pagati 60 euro **l'uno** *The plates? I paid 60 euros each for them*	**L'uno/a** agrees in gender with the noun it refers to. See also **ciascuno/a**, p. 133.
l'uno o l'altro *one or the other, either*	**L'una o l'altra** delle ragazze si faranno vive/si farà viva *One or other of the girls will turn up* Quale giornale compro? – Puoi comprare **l'uno o l'altro**, per me è lo stesso *Which paper shall I buy? – You can buy either one/one or the other, it's all the same to me*	When **l'uno/a o l'altro/a** are the subject of the sentence, the verbs can be singular or plural.
l'uno e l'altro *both, either*	Non so quale maglione prendere, mi piacciono **l'uno e l'altro** *I don't know which jumper to have, I like both of them* Sono belle sedie, vanno bene **l'una e l'altra** *They are lovely chairs, either/both will do*	With **l'uno/a e l'altro/a** the verb is usually plural. This is also commonly expressed by **tutt'e due** (p. 134).
né l'uno né l'altro *not either, neither*	Questi orologi non mi piacciono, non voglio **né l'uno né l'altro** *I don't like these watches, I don't want either (of them)* Non funziona/funzionano **né l'una né l'altra** macchina *Neither car works*	With **né l'uno/a né l'altro/a** the verb can be singular or plural. See also **nessuno/a di**, p. 128.

5 Complete the answers below by giving the Italian equivalent of the English.

(a) I bicchieri quanto li hai pagati? – Li ho pagati 65 euro *(each)*.
(b) Quale espressione si usa di più? – Vanno bene *(either one/both)*.
(c) Possono venire Mario e Luciano? – Mi dispiace, puoi far venire *(one or other)*.
(d) Mi presti una di quelle calcolatrici? – Mi dispiace, non funziona *(neither of them)*.

(e) Chiunque

anyone (at all)	**Chiunque** lo sa fare *Anyone can do it* Lo sa fare **chiunque** <u>*Anyone can do it*</u> Non sono cose che puoi dire a **chiunque**! *They aren't things you can say to (just) anyone*	**Chiunque** is invariable and refers only to people. There is more emphasis when it follows the verb.
whoever, no matter who, whichever	Non voglio vederlo, **chiunque** sia *I don't want to see him, no matter who/whoever he is* **Chiunque** di voi verrà/venga, sarà il benvenuto *Whichever of you comes will be welcome*	**Chiunque** is often followed by a verb in the subjunctive.

- Note that the relative pronoun **chi** can express *whoever, anyone who*, but it is slightly more specific than **chiunque**.

> Chi ha freddo può aprire la finestra *Anyone who is/Whoever is/Those who are cold can open the window.*

E **6** Give the English equivalent of the following.

(a) Non è niente: l'avrebbe fatto chiunque.   (c) Chiunque chiami, digli che sono fuori.
(b) È semplice: lo sa fare chiunque.

12.3 INDEFINITE ADJECTIVES AND PRONOUNS

The following indefinites agree in number and gender with the noun they refer to, and all adjectives precede the noun.

tutto everything **tutti** everyone	Ho sistemato **tutto** *I've arranged everything* Lo sanno **tutti** *Everyone knows it*	These pronouns are used in a general sense to mean *everything* and *everyone*.
tutto/a/i/e all	I ragazzi? Sono venuti **tutti** *The boys? They all came* Le ragazze? Non sono venute **tutte** *The girls? They didn't all come* La mangi **tutta**? (la pizza) *Will you eat it all/all of it?*	When the pronoun **tutto** refers to specific people or things, it agrees with the noun it refers to.
tutto + article all, every, the whole	Ho lavorato **tutta la** giornata *I've worked all/the whole day* Lavoro **tutti i** giorni *I work every day* **Tutti i** bambini vanno a scuola *All children go to school*	As an adjective, **tutto** is followed by a noun with the definite article.
tutto/a **quanto/a** absolutely all/every single one	Andiamo **tutti quanti** a Parigi *All/Every (single) one of us is going to Paris* Vengono **tutte quante le** ragazze? *Are absolutely all the girls coming?* **Tutti quanti i** biglietti erano prenotati *Absolutely all the tickets were booked/every single ticket was booked*	**Tutto/a quanto/a** can be a pronoun or an adjective. As an adjective, it is followed by a noun with a definite article. Both **tutto** and **quanto** agree with the noun they refer to.

In the following table examples with adjectives are given first.

tanto, molto, parecchio, troppo, poco	C'è **tanta/troppa/poca** disoccupazione *There is so much/too much/little unemployment* **Molti/parecchi/pochi** miei amici sono disoccupati *Many/lots/few of my friends are unemployed*	**Tanto**, **molto**, **parecchio**, **troppo**, **poco** are all used as both pronouns and adjectives.
alcuni/e *some, a few*	Oggi ho pranzato con **alcune** amiche *Today I had lunch with a few/some friends* Gli operai hanno protestato. **Alcuni** hanno fatto sciopero ... *Some/a few went on strike* **But**: Hai pranzato con qualche amica? *Did you have lunch with some friends?* Qualcuno (di loro) ha fatto sciopero? *Did some (of them) go on strike?*	**Alcuni/e** is most common in the plural. Note that in questions it is usually replaced by **qualche** (adjective) or **qualcuno** (pronoun). For the singular form, **alcuno**, see p. 133.
certi/e *certain, some, a few* **un certo** *a certain*	Ho avuto **certe** difficoltà *I've had certain/some difficulties* Ha telefonato **un certo** signor Barilla *A (certain) Mr Barilla phoned*	**Certi/e** is close in meaning to **alcuni**. In the singular it is used with an indefinite article. See also p. 38.
vari/e, diversi/e *various, several, quite a few, a number of*	Ci sono **varie** soluzioni *There are various/quite a few solutions* Ce ne sono **varie/diverse** *There are quite a few* Abito qui da **diversi** anni *I've lived here for several years* **But**: È malato da **diverso** tempo *He has been ill for quite a while*	**Diversi/e** and **vari/e** are usually only used with plural nouns and are close in meaning. See also p. 38 for different meaning and position.
altrettanto *just as much, just as many*	Lui ha **altrettanta** paura *He is just as frightened* Questo mese ti mando 850 euro e il mese prossimo te ne mando **altrettanti** *This month I'm sending you 850 euros and I'll send you the same next month*	**Altrettanto** is used for comparing like. See also Comparatives, p. 71 and Adverbs, p. 46.
altro *another, other*	C'è **un'altra** possibilità *There is another possibility* Ce n'è **un'altra** *There is another one* Ce ne sono **altre**? *Are there any others?* **But**: C'è **altro**? *Is there anything else?*	In the singular **altro** is used with an indefinite article except when it means *else*. (See below.)

Level 2

(a) Indefinites used with *altro* or *poco*

Most of the indefinites in the previous table can be used with **altro** and a few with **poco**.

Indefinites + **altro** *many/some etc. other*	Ci sono **troppe** altre/**molte** altre/**alcune** altre/**poche** altre possibilità *There are too many other/many other/a few other/few other possibilities*	Indefinites before **altro** are classed as adjectives. Agreement is therefore necessary.
Indefinites + **poco**	Ho comprato **troppo** poca carne *I've bought too little meat* Ci sono **molto** pochi clienti *There are very few clients*	Indefinites before **poco** are adverbs, so no agreement is necessary.

E

I Complete the sentences using appropriate forms of **tutto**.

(a) Abbiamo organizzato (*everything*).
(b) Vengono (*everyone*)?
(c) Siamo (*all*) qui.
(d) Hanno dimenticato (*all the*) libri.
(e) Sono stato a letto (*the whole/all the*) giornata.
(f) Lavoro (*every*) sere.
(g) Vengono (*absolutely everyone*) da noi.
(h) La minestra ti fa bene. La devi mangiare (*the whole lot*).

2 (a) Which of these phrases makes no sense?

(i) Ha pagato tanto
(ii) Ha pagato parecchio
(iii) Ha pagato diverso
(iv) Ha pagato poco
(v) Ha pagato molto

(b) Cecilia has got a lot of work. Which is the odd phrase?

(i) Ho tanto da fare.
(ii) Ho parecchio da fare.
(iii) Ho vario da fare.
(iv) Ho molto da fare.

(c) Angelo has made quite a few mistakes. Which is the odd phrase?

(i) Ho fatto vari errori.
(ii) Ho fatto diversi errori.
(iii) Ho fatto errori diversi.
(iv) Ho fatto alcuni errori.

3 Give the Italian equivalent of the following.

(a) *I've got another exam tomorrow.*
(b) *Are there (any) other problems?*
(c) *Have you got anything else to do?*

Level 2

4 Which of these phrases is grammatically inaccurate?

(a) Ci sono molte altre possibilità.
(b) Hai comprato troppa poca carne.
(c) Ho troppe altre cose da fare.
(d) Ci sono troppo pochi insegnanti.
(e) Hai mangiato molto poca verdura.

Level 2

(b) *Altro* with *qualcuno, qualcosa, nessuno, niente* and *tutto*

The indefinite **altro** is used with some indefinites to mean *else*.

qualcun altro *someone else* **nessun altro** *no one else* **qualcos'altro** *something else* **nient'altro** *nothing else*	C'è **qualcun altro** *There's someone else* Non c'è **nessun altro** *There's no one else* Ho visto **qualcos'altro** *I saw something else* **Altro?/Qualcos'altro?** *Anything else?* Non c'è **(nient')altro** *There's nothing else*	**Qualcuno** and **nessuno** drop their final vowel. **Qualcosa** and **niente** also drop their final vowel and require an apostrophe. On its own, **altro** is short for **qualcos'altro** or **nient'altro**.
tutti gli altri *everyone else* **tutto il resto** *everything else*	**Tutti gli altri** sono a casa *Everyone else is at home* Mi ha lasciato **tutto il resto** *He left me everything else*	**Altro** becomes **gli altri** after **tutti**, but **il resto**, not **altro**, follows **tutto** to mean *everything else* (lit. *all the rest*).

E

5 Give the Italian equivalent of the following. Use **Lei** for *you*.

(a) *Can you ask someone else?* (chiederlo a)
(b) *Are you having anything else?* (prendere)
(c) *No one else can do it.* (saper fare)
(d) *I have nothing else to say.*
(e) *Everyone else has gone home.*
(f) *You can take everything else.*

12.4 SINGULAR INDEFINITE ADJECTIVES AND PRONOUNS: *CIASCUNO, NESSUNO, ALCUNO*

Ciascuno, **nessuno** and **alcuno** are always singular in form and can be both adjectives and pronouns.

ciascuno/a adjective *each*	**ciascun** ragazzo **ciascun** allievo **ciascuno** studente **ciascuna** ragazza **ciascun'**allieva **Ciascun** brillante vale un patrimonio *Each diamond is worth a fortune*	**Ciascuno** has four singular adjectival forms based on the indefinite article.
ciascuno/a pronoun *each*	Le rose costano 4 euro **ciascuna** *The roses each cost 4 euros/cost 4 euros each* Ai ragazzi ho dato una penna **ciascuno** *I gave the boys a pen each (each of the boys)*	The pronoun **ciascuno** agrees in gender with the items or individuals referred to.
ciascuno/a di *each of*	**Ciascuno/a di** voi avrà 250 euro *Each (one) of you will have 250 euros* Ho fatto un regalo a **ciascuna delle** mie amiche *I gave each of my girlfriends a present*	**Ognuno/a di** (p. 128) is sometimes used instead, but **ciascuno** emphasises each individual rather than a collective whole.
nessuno/a adjective *no, not any*	**nessun** ragazzo **nessun** allievo **nessuno** studente **nessuna** ragazza **nessun'**allieva Non vedo **nessuna** difficoltà *I can see no difficulty*	The adjectives **nessuno/a** and **alcuno/a** are formed like **ciascuno/a**. **Alcuno/a** is a more emphatic form of **nessuno**.
alcuno/a adjective *no whatsoever*	Non c'è **alcuna prova** *There is no proof whatsoever/absolutely no proof* Non c'era **alcun** dubbio *There was no doubt whatsoever/absolutely no doubt*	The singular pronoun **alcuno** is rare. For **nessuno** as a pronoun, see p. 128. See also Articles, p. 27; Negatives, p. 149.

I Complete the sentences by supplying the correct forms of the adjective **ciascuno**.

(a) ... concorrente ha ricevuto un premio.

(b) In ... camera c'è un minibar.

(c) ... studente deve superare una prova.

(d) Hanno fatto le stesse domande a ... allieva.

2 Supply the correct form of the adjective **nessuno** to complete the sentences.

(a) Non c'è ... problema.

(b) Non abbiamo ... alternativa.

(c) Non hai fatto ... sforzo!

(d) Non ho ... voglia di farlo.

3 Make sentences (a) and (b) above more emphatic using **alcuno/a**.

4 Complete the sentences using the correct form of the pronoun **ciascuno**.

(a) Le cartoline costano 90 centesimi ....

(b) I panini costano tre euro ....

(c) Alle mie figlie ho dato 200 euro ....

(d) I miei figli hanno un computer ....

12.5 INDEFINITES AND QUANTITY

Both/either, all three, most

tutti/e e due, entrambi/e, ambedue *both/either*	Sono venuti **tutt'e due/entrambi** *They both came* Sono partite **tutt'e due/entrambe le** ragazze *Both girls have left* Vanno bene **tutt'e due/entrambi i** colori *Both colours are fine/either colour is fine* Ci sono case su **entrambi/ambedue i** lati *There are houses on both sides/either side*	**tutti e due** (m.) and **tutte e due** (f.) are often replaced by **tutt'e due** and are more widely used than **entrambi/e**. **Ambedue** is the least common, and invariable. If a noun accompanies any of these it is always preceded by a definite article.
tutti/e e tre/quattro ... *all three, four, etc.*	Sono venuti **tutti e tre** *All three (of them) came* Le mie zie abitano **tutte e quattro** a Foggia *All four of my aunts live in Foggia*	Note that *of* is not expressed in Italian.
la maggior parte di *most*	**La maggior parte della** mia famiglia **abita** all'estero *Most of my family live abroad* **La maggior parte dei** miei amici **sono** stranieri *Most of my friends are foreign* **La maggior parte di** noi non **siamo** d'accordo *Most of us don't agree*	**La maggior parte di** can be followed by nouns or pronouns. After plural nouns the verb is usually in the plural. After pronouns the verb matches the pronoun (e.g. **noi ... siamo**).

E   **1**   Complete the sentences, giving the Italian equivalent of the English and using **entrambi** or **tutt'e due**.

(a) Quali delle due giacche mi sta meglio? – Puoi mettere l'una o l'altra, *they both suit you.*

(b) A chi chiedo aiuto? A Carlo o a Riccardo? – Puoi chiedere all'uno o all'altro, *they are both experts.*

(c) Quale colore ti sembra più adatto? Il bianco o il nero? – *Either is fine, they are both lovely.*

2   Give the Italian equivalent of the English.

(a) *All four of my sisters are teachers.*   (c) *Most of my relatives live in Germany.*

(b) *All four of them smoke. (sisters)*   (d) *Most of them are doctors.*

12.6 INDEFINITES AND PLACE

Level 2   **(a) Somewhere, nowhere, anywhere, etc.**

da qualche parte *somewhere, anywhere*	Ho lasciato i miei occhiali **da qualche parte** *I've left my glasses somewhere* Li hai visti **da qualche parte?** *Have you seen them anywhere?*	Note that in questions **da qualche parte** means *anywhere*.

da nessuna parte *nowhere, not anywhere*	Non si vede **da nessuna parte** *It is nowhere to be seen/You can't see it anywhere* Non li trovi **da nessuna parte**? *Can't you find them anywhere?*	In questions **da nessuna parte** means *not anywhere*.
dappertutto *everywhere*	Li ho cercati **dappertutto** *I've looked everywhere for them*	
dovunque *anywhere*	Li puoi comprare un po' **dovunque/dappertutto** *You can buy them more or less anywhere* Si trovano **dovunque/in qualsiasi posto** *You can find them anywhere*	**Dovunque** may be replaced by **dappertutto** or by **in qualunque/qualsiasi posto**.
dovunque *wherever, everywhere, anywhere*	**Dovunque** siano, li troverai *Wherever they are, you'll find them* **Dovunque** io vada, lo porto con me *I take it with me wherever/everywhere I go* Possiamo andare **dovunque** tu voglia *We can go wherever you like* Possiamo andare **dove** vuoi tu *We can go wherever you like/anywhere you want*	When **dovunque** means *wherever* it is used with the subjunctive and is fairly elevated in style. In speech **dove** avoids the use of **dovunque** + subjunctive.

(b) *Somewhere else, nowhere else, anywhere else, etc.*

da qualche altra parte/ altrove *somewhere else*	Saranno **da qualche altra parte/altrove** *They will/must be somewhere else* Si vendono **altrove/da qualche altra parte/in qualche altro posto**? *Are they sold anywhere else/elsewhere?*	Other meanings are *elsewhere, anywhere else*. **Altrove** is more formal. An informal alternative is **in qualche altro posto**.
da nessun'altra parte *nowhere else*	Non si vede **da nessun'altra parte** *It is nowhere else to be seen/You can't see it anywhere else* Non si trovano **da nessun'altra parte** *You can't find them elsewhere*	Other meanings are *not ... anywhere else, not ... elsewhere*.
da tutte le altre parti *everywhere else*	Ho cercato **da tutte le altre parti** *I've looked everywhere else* Si usa l'euro **da tutte le altre parti**/in ogni altro paese/in tutti gli altri paesi *They use the euro everywhere else/in all other countries*	Alternatives include **in ogni altro posto/luogo** It is also common to use a specific noun and say: *in all other countries/ shops, etc.*

- A note on indefinites and time:

Whenever in Italian is expressed by **ogni volta che**, **tutte le volte che** or simply by **quando**.

> **Ogni volta che** mi vede mi fa un sacco di complimenti *Whenever he sees me he pays me a load of compliments*
> Posso partire quando vuoi *I can leave whenever you want*

I Give the English equivalent of the following.

(a) Ho lasciato la mia agenda da qualche parte.

(b) Andiamo da qualche altra parte.

(c) Non vado da nessuna parte.

(d) Non si vende da nessun'altra parte?

(e) Queste scarpe si trovano dappertutto.

(f) Hanno cercato da tutte le altre parti.

13

Relative pronouns

Relative pronouns (**i relativi**) function as linking or relating words introducing a relative clause which provides additional information about a preceding noun or pronoun. *The girl **who** has arrived is my sister. Who has arrived* is the relative clause telling us more about *the girl*, and it is introduced by the relative pronoun *who*. In English the main relative pronouns are *who, whom, whose, which* and *that*. *When, where* and *why* can also be relative pronouns.

13.1 MAIN RELATIVE PRONOUNS

In Italian relative pronouns can never be omitted, unlike English.

che *who, whom,* *which, that*	È un giovane **che** studia molto *He's a young man who studies a lot* È la ragazza **che** ho incontrato *She's the girl (whom) I met* Ho visto un film **che** mi piace *I've seen a film (that) I like* Ho incontrato qualcuno **che** conosci *I met someone you know*	**Che** is invariable. It can refer to people and things and can be the subject as well as the object of the relative clause. In Italian it is never omitted.
il quale *who, whom,* *which, that*	Alla festa c'era anche il mio ragazzo, **il quale** si è sentito male *My boyfriend, who was also at the party, was taken ill* L'hanno visto due persone, **le quali** hanno chiamato la polizia *He was seen by two people who called the police*	**Il quale** agrees with the noun it refers to and has four forms: **il/la quale** and **i/le quali**. Its meaning is the same but its use more limited than **che**; it can only be used as the subject.
	La sorella di Marco **che** parte domani ... *(Is the sister or Marco leaving?)* **La sorella** di Marco, **la quale** parte ... *(The sister is leaving)* La sorella di **Marco**, **il quale** parte ... *(Marco is leaving)*	However, unlike **che**, **il quale** avoids ambiguity because it agrees with the noun it refers to.

il che *which*	È stato bocciato, **il che** non mi sorprende *He failed the exam, which doesn't surprise me*	**Il che** means *which* when this refers to an entire sentence, concept or action rather than to a single noun.
ciò che quello che *what*	Fa' **quello che** vuoi *Do what you want* Non ho capito **ciò che** hai detto *I haven't understood what you said*	**Ciò che**, **quello che** both literally mean *that which*.
quanto *what*	Apprezzo molto **quanto/quello che** hai fatto *I appreciate a lot what you have done* Le ha dato **quanto/ciò che** poteva *He has given her what he could*	**Quanto** (lit. *how much*) is more formal, and may be used to express *what* when the idea of quantity is implicit.

- When *what* is interrogative it is (**che**) **cosa**? **Che cosa hai fatto**? *What did you do?* See Interrogatives, p. 121.

E   **1**   Link the information about the people and things below into a single sentence. Give an alternative relative pronoun where possible.

   (a) Marta è un'amica. Marta mi è molto simpatica.
   (b) Edoardo è un lontano cugino. Edoardo lavora a Parigi.
   (c) I signori Colucci sono i vicini. I signori Colucci litigano tanto.
   (d) La Rinascente è un grande magazzino. La Rinascente si trova nelle maggiori città italiane.
   (e) *Roma città aperta* è un film di Rossellini. Non ho mai visto *Roma città aperta*.

2   Give the Italian equivalent of the following, taking care to use relative pronouns.

   (a) *The flat I rented is on the first floor.* (affittare)
   (b) *The man you met is the landlady's husband who is leaving today.* (la padrona)
   (c) *They have raised the rent, which isn't fair.* (l'affitto)

3   Identify the four relative pronouns *what* below (the others are exclamations and interrogatives). Then give the Italian equivalent of the English relative sentences, using the **tu** form of address.

   (a) *What you're doing is absurd.*   (e) *What a horrible colour!*
   (b) *You can do what you want.*   (f) *What can I do?*
   (c) *I will do what I can.*   (g) *I don't know what to do.*
   (d) *What I don't like is the colour.*

4   In which one of the sentences in (3) above could **quanto** be used as well as **ciò che** or **quello che**?

13.2 PREPOSITIONS WITH RELATIVE PRONOUNS

When prepositions such as **a, da, di, in, su, con** and **per** are used before the relative **che** (*who, whom, which*), this becomes **cui**. Prepositions precede **il quale** or are joined to the definite article. Here are some examples.

a cui (a + che) *to whom/to which* **per cui** (per + che) *for whom/* *for which*	È l'uomo **a cui** ho scritto *He is the man I wrote to/the man to whom I wrote* La ditta **per cui** lavoro è in centro *The firm I work for/The firm for which I work is in* *the centre of town*	**Cui** is invariable and preceded by the preposition. In Italian it never comes at the end of the sentence.
al quale (a + il quale) **ai quali** (a + i quali) **alla quale** (a + la quale) **alle quali** (a + le quali) *to whom/to which* **per il/la quale** **per i/le quali** *for whom/which*	È l'uomo **al quale** ho scritto *He's the man I wrote to* Sono gli uomini **ai quali** ho scritto *They are the men I wrote to* È la donna **alla quale** ho scritto *She's the woman I wrote to* Sono le donne **alle quali** ho scritto *They are the women I wrote to* La ditta **per la quale** lavoro *The firm I work for*	**Il quale** must agree with the noun it refers to. The definite article is joined to **a**, **da**, **di**, **in**, **su**, and occasionally to **con**, but not to other prepositions such as **per**. See p. 22.

SOME USES

Italian and English differ	I libri **di cui/dei quali** ho bisogno sono troppo cari *The books I need are too expensive* (i.e. *of which* I have need) Sono domande **a cui/alle quali** non posso rispondere *They are questions I can't answer* (i.e. *to which* I cannot reply)	Note that a preposition may be required where in English there is none, e.g. with **aver** **bisogno di**, *to need*, **rispondere a** *to answer*.
Preposition + **il quale** for clarification	*I saw my brother's girlfriend, to whom I gave the* *books* Ho visto la ragazza di mio fratello **a cui** ho dato i libri (*Who got the books?*) Ho visto **la ragazza** di mio fratello **alla quale** ho dato i libri (*The girl*) Ho visto la ragazza di **mio fratello al quale** ho dato i libri (*The brother*)	Prepositions + **il/la quale**, etc. can avoid ambiguity better than a preposition + **cui** because they agree with the noun they refer to.
fuori and **invece** with **il quale**	Questo è il negozio **fuori del quale** ci siamo trovati (**not** fuori di cui) *That's the shop (that) we met outside*	A few prepositions, e.g. **fuori (di)** and **invece di**, are only used with **il/la** **quale**, etc. not with **cui**.

- Note the very common use of **di** with either **cui** or **il quale** (see over).

di + cui/ di + i/le quali	Abbiamo tre computer, **di cui uno/uno dei quali** non funziona *We have three computers one of which doesn't work* Hanno tre figli, **di cui due/due dei quali** sono architetti *They have three sons two of whom are architects* Mia nonna ha vari anelli, **di cui alcuni/alcuni dei quali** sono di valore *My grandmother has quite a few rings, some of which are valuable*	**Di cui** and **dei/delle quali** are used with numbers and quantities (e.g. **alcuni, molti**). **Dei/delle quali** usually follow the number or quantity, but **di cui** precedes it.

E **1** How do you relate to these people? Link the two sentences into one by replacing the underlined phrases with suitable relative pronouns. Provide an alternative one each time.

(a) Il professor Binni è un insegnante. Ho molto rispetto <u>per il Professor Binni</u>.
(b) Carlotta è la nipote. Ho regalato una bicicletta <u>a Carlotta</u>.
(c) Aldo e Stefano sono colleghi. Lavoro <u>con Aldo e Stefano</u> da due anni.
(d) Fiorella è la mia assistente. <u>Senza Fiorella</u> non potrei lavorare.

2 Complete these sentences with appropriate relatives.

(a) Ho due stampanti, ... una non è mia.
(b) Qui ci sono tre calcolatrici, due ... sono rotte.
(c) Mi ha dato delle cartelle, alcune ... sono sparite.
(d) Abbiamo cenato con degli amici ... uno è deputato.

Level 2

(a) Other uses of *cui*

in cui *when, where*	Il 1986 è **l'anno in cui** è nato mio fratello *1986 is the year (when) my brother was born* È **la casa in cui/dove** sono nato/a *It's the house where/in which I was born*	**In cui** (lit. *in which*) can mean *when, where*, and is used after words like **giorno, data, momento. Dove** is also used to mean *where*.
	Non mi piace **il modo in cui** ti parla *I don't like the way (in which) he talks to you*	**In cui** is also used after **modo** or **maniera** to mean *the way (in which)*.
per cui *why*	Non è **la ragione per cui** è venuto *It's not the reason (why) he came* Hai capito **il motivo per cui** l'ha fatto? *Did you understand the reason why he did it?*	**Per cui** can mean *why* (literally *for which*?) It is used with both **la ragione** and **il motivo**, *reason*.
nel quale, per il quale, etc.	È l'anno **nel quale** ... È la casa **nella quale** ... Non è la ragione **per la quale** ...	Prepositions + **il quale**, etc. can replace **cui** in the examples above.

E **3** Family matters. Give the Italian equivalent of the English.

(a) *1905 is the year my grandfather was born.*
(b) *The reasons he emigrated are not clear.*
(c) *The house where he lived was bombed during the war.* (è stata bombardata)

(b) Relatives with *piacere, servire, mancare*, etc.

| a cui
who | Sono gli amici **a cui piace** tanto Roma
They are the friends who like Rome so much (lit. to whom Rome is pleasing)
Il signore **a cui serve** un'altra forchetta è al tavolo due
The man who needs another fork is at table two
È una ragazza viziata **a cui non manca** niente
She's a spoiled girl who lacks nothing/wants for nothing | **Piacere (a), servire (a)** and **mancare (a)** literally mean *to be pleasing to, to be necessary to* and *to be lacking to.* In these examples what is expressed as the subject *who* in English is actually the object *to whom* in Italian, hence the need for **a cui**. |
| al quale,
etc. | Gli amici **ai quali** piace ... Il signore **al quale** serve ...
Una ragazza **alla quale** non manca ... | **Il quale** can replace **cui** in the examples above. |

- It is important to note that **che** is also used with the verbs above when it refers to the Italian grammatical subject:

 È la ragazza **che** mi piace di più *She's the girl (whom) I like most* (lit. *She's the girl* ***who*** *is most pleasing to me*)

 È un libro **che** non mi serve *It's a book (that) I don't need* (lit. *It is a book* ***which*** *is not necessary to me*)

(c) Relatives with some passive constructions

| a cui
who | Gli operai **a cui** hanno rifiutato un aumento sono in sciopero
The workers who were refused a rise are on strike
La signora **a cui** hanno mandato la fattura non ha pagato
The woman who was sent the invoice has not paid | When verbs which require **a** before a person are used with a passive meaning, the English *who* is literally *to whom.* See also Chapter 25, p. 261. |
| al quale,
etc. | Gli operai **ai quali** hanno rifiutato ...
La signora **alla quale** hanno mandato ... | **Il quale** can replace **cui** in the examples above. |

- Note that **a cui** is not used to express *who* when these verbs have no passive meaning.

 Gli operai **che** hanno rifiutato di lavorare *The workers who refused to work*

 La signora **che** ha mandato la fattura *The woman who sent the invoice*

4 **Che** or **cui**? Decide which of the sentences in each pair requires **che** and which **a cui**.

(a) È l'unico studente ... piace l'insegnante.
He's the only student who likes the teacher.
È l'unico insegnante ... mi piace.
He's the only teacher I like.

    (b) I profughi ... hanno concesso l'asilo sono bosniaci.
        The refugees who were given asylum are Bosnian.
        I profughi ... hanno richiesto l'asilo sono bosniaci.
        The refugees who asked for asylum are Bosnian.
    (c) La signora ... mi ha offerto il posto è molto gentile.
        The woman who offered me the job is very nice.
        La signora ... hanno offerto il lavoro lo ha rifiutato.
        The woman who was offered the job turned it down.

Level 2

13.3 WHOSE

In Italian how to say *whose* depends on whether it refers to the subject or the object of a sentence.

(a) Subject of the relative sentence

There are two main forms used as the subject of a sentence.

il cui la cui i cui le cui	La signora, **il cui ombrello** ... *The lady, whose umbrella* ... Il signore, **la cui agenda** ... *The man, whose diary* ...	**Cui** is used with the definite article of the noun denoting who or what is possessed, and is placed <u>before</u> the noun.
di + il/la quale i/le quali	La signora, l'ombrello **della quale** Il signore, l'agenda **del quale** ...	**Di** + quale/i is used with the definite article of the noun denoting the possessor, and is placed <u>after</u> the noun.

- Either of the forms above are commonly used to express *whose*. Where there is ambiguity, the use of **del quale, della quale**, etc. is usually clearer than **il/la cui**, etc.

    Il mio amico, **la cui** casa è in vendita, è simpaticissimo.
    Il mio amico, la casa **del quale** è in vendita, è simpaticissimo.
    My friend, whose house is for sale, is very nice.

- When a verb requiring a preposition is involved (e.g. **contare su, fidarsi di**), the use of **il/la cui**, etc. is more common than **di** + **il/la quale**, etc.

    È una persona sul cui giudizio posso contare. *He's a person whose judgement you can rely on.*
    È un uomo del cui parere mi fido sempre. *He's a man whose opinion I always trust.*

(b) Object of the relative sentence

di cui + verb + definite article	È la signora **di cui** non ricordo mai **il** nome *She's the lady whose name I never remember* È un libro **di cui** conosco bene **l'**autore *It's a book whose author I know well*	When *whose* + noun is the object of the verb in the relative clause, **di cui** is placed before the verb and the definite article + noun come after it.

- When *whose* is interrogative it is **di chi?** e.g. **Di chi** sono questi guanti? *Whose gloves are these?/Whose are these gloves?* See Interrogatives, p. 121.

I   Form a single sentence from the two below by replacing the underlined phrases using a construction with **cui**.

    (a)   Ho appena incontrato una signora. <u>La sua</u> nipotina conosce Anna.
         (*a woman whose granddaughter* ...)
    (b)   Mia cugina si sente molto sola. <u>Le sue</u> figlie abitano a Parigi.
         (*my cousin whose daughters* ...)
    (c)   La signora è all'ospedale. <u>I suoi</u> gioielli sono stati rubati.
         (*the woman whose jewels* ...)
    (d)   Il camion ha provocato l'incidente. <u>I suoi</u> freni non funzionavano.
         (*the lorry whose brakes* ...)
    (e)   Abita in un paesino. Mi sono dimenticato/a il nome <u>del paesino</u>.
         (*a village whose name* ...)

13.4 OTHER RELATIVE PRONOUNS

tutto quello che, **tutto ciò che,** **tutto quanto** *everything, all that, whatever*	Fa **tutto quello/ciò che** vuole *He does everything (that) he wants/whatever he wants* Milano è la vera capitale di **tutto quanto** è nuovo *Milan is the true capital of all that is new*	**Tutto quello che** and **tutto ciò che** are interchangeable. The literal meaning is *all that which*. **Tutto quanto** is more formal.
tutti quelli che *everyone/all those who*	**Tutti quelli che** si trovano in difficoltà mi possono consultare dopo *All those who/Everyone who is having problems can consult me afterwards*	**Tutti quelli che** is used when referring to a general group of people.
tutti/e quelli/e che *all those which*	Le mele sono cadute e ho raccolto **tutte quelle che** non erano marce *The apples have fallen and I gathered all those which weren't rotten*	This is used to refer to specific people or things and must agree with the noun it refers to.
quello/a che **quelli/e che** *those/the one(s) which, whichever*	Ho comprato la rivista, **quella che** compri tu *I bought the magazine, the one (which) you buy* Quale prendo? – **Quello che** vuoi *Which one can I take? – Whichever/the one you want*	Apart from meaning *what* (p. 138), **quello che** is used to refer to specific things or people and must agree with the noun it modifies.
quelli che *those who*	**Quelli che** si trovano in difficoltà mi possono consultare *Those who are having problems can ask me*	This is close in meaning to **chi** below.
chi *people who/those who/anyone who/ whoever/he who*	**Chi** si trova in difficoltà mi può consultare *Whoever is having/Those who are having problems can consult me* C'è **chi** non sa né leggere né scrivere *There are people who can neither read nor write* **Chi** non lavora non mangia *Anyone who/People who/Those who don't work don't eat*	**Chi** is always used with a singular verb, although it may have a plural meaning. It refers to unspecified people only and is commonly used in spoken as well as written Italian.

chi ... chi some ... others	**Chi** leggeva, **chi** dormiva *Some (people) were reading, others were sleeping*	**Chi** ... **chi** is more common in written than spoken Italian.

- **Coloro che** *those who* is mainly used in written Italian, and is less used than **quelli che** and **chi**:

    È un nuovo registratore digitale su disco per **coloro che** desiderano ascoltare un suono stereo digitale. *It is a new digital CD recorder for those who wish to hear a digital stereo sound.*

    Its singular forms, **colui che** (*he who*) and **colei che** (*she who*), are quite rare.

E 1 Use each of the relative pronouns below twice to complete the sentences.

> tutto quello che • tutti quelli che

(a) Grazie per ... hai fatto.
(b) Puoi fare ... vuoi.
(c) ... hanno studiato quest'anno saranno sicuramente promossi.
(d) Questi libri non mi servono più, puoi prendere ... vuoi.

2 (a) In which of the above sentences could **tutto ciò che** be used?
  (b) In which of the sentences could the relative pronoun be translated as *whatever/whichever*?

3 Identify those sentences below in which **chi** is used as a relative pronoun, and provide an English equivalent.

(a) Mi dispiace, ma chi non ha la tessera non può mangiare alla mensa.
(b) Devo sapere entro domani chi vuole iscriversi al corso.
(c) La scadenza per chi vuole iscriversi al corso è il 3 settembre.
(d) È un posto ideale per chi desidera riposarsi.
(e) L'albergo Miramare pensa a chi desidera il relax totale.
(f) C'è chi preferisce i cani e chi invece preferisce i gatti.

4 In which sentence above can **quelli che** not be used instead of **chi**?

Negatives

Negatives (**le negazioni**) are used to contradict the meaning, or part of the meaning, of a sentence. They include various parts of speech such as adverbs or indefinites. Typical negative words are *no*, *not* and *nothing*. In Italian, negatives are sometimes made with single words but more often with two.

14.1 SINGLE NEGATIVES

In Italian the main single negatives are **no** *no* and **non** *not*. Their use does not always correspond to the English.

no **no**	Vieni domani? – **No** *Are you coming tomorrow? – No*	**No** is used like *no* in English to contradict a whole question.
not **non**	Vieni domani? – No, **non** vengo *Are you coming tomorrow? – No, I'm not coming* Lui fuma *He smokes.* **Non** fuma *He doesn't smoke* **Non** lo trovo *I can't (cannot) find it* **Non** mi piace *I don't like it*	**Non** is used within a sentence and placed immediately before the word it negates – usually a verb. If there are any object pronouns, **non** goes before them.
di no	Viene anche Matteo? – Spero/Credo **di no** *Is Matteo coming too? – I hope/think not (i.e. I don't think so)* **Note also**: Vieni domani? – **Non** credo *Are you coming tomorrow? – I don't think so*	To say *I hope/think/believe not*, **(di) no** is used after **sperare**, **credere** and **pensare**. Note that the construction of **non** before the verb is not used with **sperare**, as you cannot say *I don't hope so*.
or not **o no** **o meno**	Vieni **o no**? *Are you coming or not?* Fammi sapere se puoi aiutare **o no/o meno** *Let me know if you can help or not* Non so se viene **o no/o meno** *I don't know if he's coming or not*	The literal equivalent of *or not* is 'or no' and 'or less'. In direct questions **o meno** is not normally used.

E

I Give Italian equivalents of the English replies.

    (a) Ti chiami Edda? – *No, my name isn't Edda, it's Emma.*

    (b) Pioverà domani? – *I don't think so. I hope not!*

    (c) Perché lo chiami? – *Because I'd like to know if he's paid or not.*

14.2 DOUBLE NEGATIVES

In Italian many negatives involve <u>two</u> words because **non** is used with other negative words. They are as follows.

non ... nessuno	(pronoun) *no one, nobody*	**non ... ancora**	*not yet, still*
non ... nessun/o/a	(adj.) *no, not any, none*	**non ... più**	*no longer, not any more, not again*
non ... niente/nulla	*nothing, not anything*	**non ... mai**	*never, not ever*
non ... né ... né	*not (either) ... nor*	**non ... mai più**	*never/not ever again*

non ... neanche		**non ... affatto**	*not at all,*
non ... nemmeno	*not even/not either*	**non ... per niente**	*not in the least*
non ... neppure			
non ... mica	*just/really/actually not*	**non ... assolutamente**	*in no way*

• Many of these are almost synonymous and their use may depend on style or individual preference.

The position of double negatives

The position may vary depending on the tense, the emphasis or the personal style of the speaker. The following examples provide guidelines.

Non inviterò **nessuno** *I won't invite anyone* **Non** ho comprato **niente** *I haven't bought anything* **Non** voglio invitare **né** Maria **né** Anna *I don't want to invite either Maria or Anna*	In most cases **non** goes before the verb and the negative word immediately follows.
Non legge **mai** il giornale *He never reads the paper* **Non** ha **mai** letto un giornale *He has never read a paper* **Non** deve **più** uscire *He must not go out again*	The negatives **ancora, più, mai, mai più** and **mica** directly follow a simple tense verb but usually come before a past participle or infinitive. See also Adverbs, p. 52.
Non mi è piaciuto **per niente/affatto/Non** mi è **affatto** piaciuto *I didn't like it at all* **Non** mi hai **assolutamente** convinto *You haven't convinced me in any way/at all* **Non** può **assolutamente** capire *He just can't understand*	These negatives go before or after past participles and infinitives depending on emphasis or personal style. **Per niente** tends to follow the verb, while **assolutamente** is more likely to come before a past participle or infinitive. **Affatto** is very flexible.

1   Give the Italian equivalent of the English, paying attention to the position of the negatives.

(a) *I haven't seen anyone.*
(b) *He has never seen Mont Blanc.*
(c) *He hasn't left yet.*
(d) *I don't want to eat anything.*
(e) *She never wants to help.*
(f) *I don't want to come any more.*

2   Use the negative words in the box to produce the Italian equivalent of the English given. There may be more than one possibility, but make sure that you use each phrase at least once.

> non ... affatto • non ... assolutamente • non ... per niente

(a) *I don't like it at all.*
(b) *I don't know him at all.*
(c) *He isn't in the least unpleasant.*
(d) *You simply mustn't leave.*

Position and different meaning

The position of **non neanche, non nemmeno** and **non neppure** affects the meaning.

not even non ... neanche non ... nemmeno non ... neppure	**Non** lo so **neanche** *I don't even know* **Non** mi piace **nemmeno** *I don't even like it* **Non** puoi **neanche** telefonare? *Can't you even phone?* **Non** ha **neppure** chiamato *He didn't even call*	When **neanche, nemmeno, neppure** mean *not even*, they have the same position as **ancora, più, mai, mai più** (see p. 146).
not either non ... neanche non ... nemmeno non ... neppure	**Non** lo so **neanch'io** *I don't know either* **Non** piace **nemmeno a me** *I don't like it either* **Non** hai chiamato me e **neppure Tom** *You didn't call me or Tom either* **Non** sa scrivere e **neanche leggere** *He can't write or read either* Ida non vuole telefonare. **Non** puoi telefonare **nemmeno tu?** *Ida doesn't want to phone. Can't you phone either?*	When **neanche, nemmeno** and **neppure** mean *not either*, they are placed immediately before the item they emphasise. If this is the subject, it is placed at the end.

3   What's the difference? Give the English equivalent of the sentences below.

(a) (i) Giacomo non ha nemmeno chiamato.
    (ii) Non ha chiamato nemmeno Giacomo.
(b) (i) Non ci sono andato neppure io.
    (ii) Non ci sono neppure andato.
(c) (i) Non mi piace neanche.
    (ii) Non piace neanche a me.

SOME USES

(a) Non ... mica

Mica is colloquial, and widely used in speech to reinforce **non**.

non ... mica *just, really,* *actually, not*	**Non** è **mica** vero *It's just not/isn't actually true* **Non** è **mica** colpa mia *It's (certainly) not my fault* **Non** mi piace **mica** *I don't really/just don't like it* **Non** sono **mica** venuti *They didn't actually/just didn't come* **Non** vuole **mica** venire *He just doesn't want to come* **Non** ti sei **mica** offeso? *You're not offended, are you?/by any chance?*	**Mica** has the same position as **ancora, più, mai, mai più** (p. 146). In questions **mica** can have the meaning of *by any* *chance?*

E   **4**   Surely not? You're hoping your worst fears won't be realised. Put the following into Italian.

(a) *You haven't forgotten to post the letter, have you?*
(b) *You didn't invite the neighbours, did you?*
(c) *You haven't left the oven on, have you?* (lasciare acceso il forno)

(b) Non ... nessuno/niente/nulla with other negatives

Non nessuno and non niente/nulla can be used with **ancora, mai, mai più, mica** and **più**.

With simple tenses	**Non** legge **mai niente/nulla** *He never reads anything* **Non** vede **più nessuno** *He doesn't see anyone any more* **Non** aiuterà **mai più nessuno** *He will never help anyone ever again* **Non** darò **niente** a **nessuno** *I won't give anyone anything*	**Nessuno** and **niente/nulla** generally come after the second negative word. Note that if they are both used, **nessuno** comes last.
With compound tenses and with verb + infinitive	**Non** ho **ancora** fatto **niente** *I haven't done anything yet* **Non** ho **mica** visto **nessuno** *I didn't actually see anyone* **Non** vuole **più** aiutare **nessuno** *He doesn't want to help anyone again*	**Ancora, mica, mai** and **più** usually go before participles and dependent infinitives, but **nessuno** and **niente** always follow.

E   **5**   Find the Italian equivalent of the English, using two negative words each time.

(a) *He never explains anything.*
(b) *He won't offend anyone again/any more.*
(c) *There is nothing else/more.*
(d) *I haven't found anything yet.*
(e) *I didn't actually find anything.*
(f) *I won't say anything to anyone.*

Negatives with the subjunctive

Using negatives sometimes involves the use of a subjunctive verb. See also pp. 248, 254.

non dico che, etc. ...	**Non dico che** sia una buona *soluzione* *I'm not saying it's a good solution* **Non è detto che** possa venire *He won't necessarily be able to come* **Non è che** sia difficile, ma non mi va di farlo *It's not that it's difficult, but I don't feel like doing it*	Subjunctives are often needed when the reality of what is said is denied. Other expressions include **non è vero/possibile che** and **non perché** (*not because*).
nessuno che niente che	**Non** c'era **nessuno che** lo potesse aiutare *There was no one who could help him*	These require a subjunctive, especially in written Italian.
non sapere/ non capire ... se/come	**Non so come** abbiano fatto *I don't know how they did it* **Non si capisce se** sia vero o meno *It's not clear whether it's true or not* *(lit. One doesn't understand whether ...)*	These are indirect questions. There is an increasing tendency to use the indicative.

For exercises on the subjunctive, see pp. 249, 250, 255.

14.3 NEGATIVES USED WITHOUT *NON*

It is possible to make a sentence negative without **non**, using one of the following negatives.

senza + **infinitive**	È partito **senza** dire niente *He left without saying anything*	**Non** is omitted with **senza**.
nessuno **niente** **neanche** **nemmeno** **neppure** **mica**	**Nessuno** è venuto (**Non** è venuto nessuno) *No one came* **Neanche** loro lo sanno (**Non** lo sanno neanche loro) *They don't know either* **Mica** è venuto, sai *He didn't actually come, you know*	The negative word goes before the verb and is usually more emphatic than with **non**.
ancora no **assolutamente** **(no)/nient'affatto** **mai/mai più** **mica** **per niente**	Sei pronto? – **Ancora no** ... *Not yet* Gli darai i soldi? – **Assolutamente (no)!/** **Nient'affatto** ... *Certainly not!/No way!* Torneresti in quell'albergo? – **Mai più!** ... *Never again/Never ever!* Ti piace? – **Mica** male! ... *Not bad!* Hai capito? – **Per niente** ... *Not at all*	The negative word(s) may often be used without a verb. **Assolutamente** may be followed by **no**.

- Note that in questions **niente** and **nessuno** may be used colloquially with an affirmative meaning:

    Hai bisogno di niente? *Do you need anything?*

E

I The right word for the right situation. Choose the appropriate response from the ones given. There is one case where either will do.

(a) Ti piace l'appartamento? – Mica male!/Meno male!
(b) Hai studiato il testo? – Niente/Nient'affatto!
(c) Che cosa ti ha detto? – Niente/Per niente!
(d) Quand'è che si sposano? – Mai più/Mai!
(e) Ti piacerebbe tornarci? – Mai/Mai più!
(f) Era interessante? – Assolutamente (no)/Per niente!

15

Prepositions

Prepositions (**le preposizioni**) are words like *at, in, to, by*, which are used to express a wide variety of relationships, the most common of which is location in time and place: *in an hour*, *at two o'clock*; *in the drawer*, *at the station*. Other relationships include possession, purpose, cause and manner. Prepositions can be one word, sometimes two and occasionally a whole phrase: e.g. *on the other side of.*

This chapter deals with prepositions used with nouns, pronouns or adjectives. For verbs with prepositions, see Chapter 26.

15.1 THE MAIN PREPOSITIONS

Prepositions often acquire different meanings in different contexts and have a large number of uses that can vary, especially in everyday Italian. Use depends on a number of things, including the region someone is from and the differing degrees of formality or informality being used. The examples in this unit present the most common norms.

There are eight basic prepositions. All except **per** and **fra/tra** can form one word with the definite article (p. 22). They are otherwise invariable.

a	*to, at, in*	**di**	*of*	**su**	*on, onto*
in	*in, into, at, to*	**per**	*for*	**fra/tra**	*between*
da	*from, by, at, to*	**con**	*with*		

The uses of a

(a) To express place, position, motion and direction

Motion and transmisssion to a place/person: *to*	Vado **a** Roma *I'm going to Rome.* (See also p. 155.) Telefono **a** Parigi/a Giorgio *I'm phoning (to) Paris/G.* Darò il libro **a** Anna *I'll give the book to Anna.*

Where: *at, on*	Mi fermo **al** semaforo *I stop at the traffic lights* La casa si trova **all'**angolo/**a** sinistra *The house is on the corner/on the left* Abito **al** primo piano *I live on the first floor*
Direction and distance: *no English equivalent*	È un paesino **a nord est** di Roma *It's a village (to the) north-east of Rome* Abito **a cento chilometri** da Roma *I live 100 km (away) from Rome*
Position on the body: *in, on, round*	È ferito **al** braccio *He is wounded in the arm* **Al** collo aveva una catenina d'oro *She had a gold chain round her neck* *But*: Ha un cappello strano **in testa** *He's got a strange hat on his head*
Non-literal expressions of place: *on, in*	L'ho sentito **alla radio** *I heard it on the radio* Chi c'è **al telefono**? *Who's on the phone?* Sono **a pagina** 17 *I'm on page 17* Mi siedo **al sole/all'**ombra *I sit in the sun/shade* *But*: sotto la pioggia *in the rain*

(b) To express time

The time, time of day, festivals, months: *at, in*	**a** che ora? *At what time?* **a** mezzogiorno/**alle** due *at midday/at two o'clock* all'alba/**al** tramonto *at dawn/sunset* **al** weekend *at the weekend* **a** Natale/**a** Pasqua *at Christmas/Easter* **a** marzo/maggio *in March/May* (also **in** marzo, **in** maggio, etc., see p. 153)
Future time and duration: *until, to*	**A** domani/**A** presto/**A** lunedì *Until tomorrow/See you tomorrow/soon/* *on Monday* Rimandano la riunione **a** martedì *They are postponing the* *meeting until Tuesday* Aperto da lunedì **a** venerdì *Open from Monday to* *Friday*
How often: *per/a*	Mi lavo i denti due volte **al** giorno *I brush my teeth twice per/a day*
a + noun can replace English phrases beginning with *when*	Lo farà **al** suo ritorno *He'll do it when he returns/on his return* **Alla** partenza piansero tutti *When they left/On their departure* *everyone cried*

(c) For description

Distinguishing features – design, construction and food: *no equivalent*	un vestito **a** fiori *a flowered dress* carta **a** righe *lined paper* una casa **a** tre piani *a three-storey house* pattini **a** rotelle *roller-skates* il gelato **al** limone *lemon ice cream* una bistecca **ai** ferri *brace grilled steak*
Manner and means – how things are done or what with: *on, by, in*	**a** cavallo *on horseback* **a** piedi *on foot* **a** memoria *by heart* fatto **a** mano *made by hand* scritto **a** matita *written in pencil* *But*: in corsivo *in italics* in/a stampatello *in capitals*

- For **a** with other prepositions, see p. 162.

E   1   Give the Italian equivalent of the English.

(a) *I live on the top floor.* (ultimo)

(b) *The restaurant is on the corner, on the right.*

(c) *The bookshop is 200 metres from my house.*

(d) *I live in a town south-west of London.* (sud ovest)

(e) *There is an interesting film on television.*

(f) *Your mother's on the phone.*

(g) *See you in December, at Christmas.*

(h) *What time are you coming, Ida?*

For more on **a**, see also Exercise 2, p. 154, Exercises 1 and 2, p. 156, and Exercise 4, p. 157.

The uses of in

(a) To express place, position and motion

Motion and transmisssion to a place: *to, into* Note the use of **in** with **entrare** and **salire**	Vado/telefono **in** Italia *I'm going to Italy/I'm phoning (to) Italy* (See also p. 155.) Sono salito **in** macchina *I got into the car* È entrata **nel** negozio *She went into/entered the shop*
Where: *in, on*	Abito **in** Italia *I live in Italy* (See p. 155.) L'ho messo **nella** busta *I put it in(to) the envelope* Ci vediamo **nel** parco *See you/we'll see each other in the park* Leggo **in** treno/autobus/metropolitana *I read on the train/bus/tube*

(b) To express time

Time taken: *in* **In** does <u>not</u> express future time	È un libro che si legge **in** un paio d'ore *It's a book you read in a couple of hours* **But**: Il lavoro sarà pronto **fra** un paio d'ore *The work will be ready in a couple of hours* (See p. 161.)
Months, seasons, years and centuries: *in*	Sono nato **in** ottobre/**in** autunno/**nel** 1980/**nel** ventesimo secolo *I was born in October/in autumn/in 1980/in the twentieth century* (See also **di** for seasons (p. 156) and **a** for months (p. 152).)

(c) Other uses

Means: transport, colours, materials: *by*	Vado **in** macchina/metropolitana *I go by car/tube* Parto **in** treno/aereo *I'm going by train/plane, I'm taking the train/a plane* Era dipinto **in** nero *It was painted (in) black* I pavimenti sono **in** marmo *The floors are (made of) marble* (See also **con** for transport (p. 159) and **di** for colour/material (p. 156).)
Quantity: *two/three/ ten/many/few of,* etc.	**In** quanti siete? *How many of you are there?* Siamo **in** cinque/**in** pochi *There are five of us/few, not many of us* Sono venuti **in** quattro/venti *Four/twenty of them came* Si gioca **in** tre *Three of you play/It's a game for three*

1 Give the Italian equivalent of the English using **in** with an appropriate verb.

(a) *I must go to France.*

(b) *I must phone Italy.*

(c) *I'm going by plane.*

(d) *Let's go into/enter the shop.*

(e) *Do you live in England?*

(f) *It's in the drawer.* (il cassetto)

(g) *I sleep on the train.*

2 Answer the questions, giving the Italian equivalent of the English using **in** or **a**.

(a) A chi devi telefonare? – *I have to phone my cousin in Italy, in Rome.*
(b) È difficile imparare a guidare? – *No, you can learn in a few months.*
(c) In quanti siete? – *There are six of us.*
(d) Quand'è che sei nato? – *I was born in April at five in the morning, at dawn.*

The uses of da

(a) To express motion to, from and through a place

Motion to: *to*	Vado **dal** medico/**da** Ugo *I'm going to the doctor's/Hugo's* (See p. 155.)
Motion away: *from, out of.* Note the use of **da** with **partire** and **uscire**	Il treno parte **dal** binario 2 *The train leaves from platform 2* Sono partiti **da** Bergamo/**da** qui alle due *They left Bergamo/here at two* (For **di** before **qui**, see p. 157.) È uscito **dalla** stazione *He came out of the station*
Motion from: *out of, off, from*	Lo ha tolto **dalla** borsa *He took it out of/from the bag* Lo ha tolto **dal** muro *He took it off/from the wall* Guardare **dalla** finestra *To look out of the window*
Motion through: *through, by*	È entrato/passato **dalla** finestra *He came/went in through the window* Devi uscire **dalla** porta di dietro *You have to go out/leave by the back door* (See also **per**, p. 158 and **di**, p. 157.)
Distance: *from*	Quanto dista **da** Milano? *How far is it from Milan?*

(b) For actions

Agent (who or what by): *by*	È amato **da** tutti *He is loved by everyone* La città è stata distrutta **dal** terremoto *The town was destroyed by the earthquake* È un libro scritto **da** Pasolini *It's a book written by Pasolini* **But**: un libro/un film **di** Pasolini *a book/a film by Pasolini* (See also p. 156.)
da + infinitive verb: Things to be done	Ho due capitoli **da** leggere *I've got two chapters to read* Vuoi qualcosa **da** mangiare? *Do you want something to eat?* **Note**: Ho **da** fare *I've got a lot to do* Non c'è niente **da** fare *It's no good/hopeless*
How things are done: *like, as*	Mi tratta **da** imbecille *He treats me like an idiot* Devo fare **da** guida *I've got to act as the guide* **Note**: Sono andato **da** solo *I went alone*
Cause	Tremavo **dal** freddo *I was shivering from/with cold* Saltava **dalla** gioia *He was jumping for joy*

(c) To express time

How long: *for, since.* See also pp. 194–5, 214.	Sono qui **da** un'ora/domenica *I have been here for an hour/since Sunday* Studiavo medicina **da** anni *I had been studying medicine for years*
A period in the past: *when, as*	**Da** bambino/**Da** giovane ho vissuto a Roma *As a child/When I was a child/When I was young I lived in Rome*

(d) For descriptions

Purpose: what an object is for. **Da** often does not translate into English	un ferro **da** stiro *an iron* una sala **da** pranzo *a dining room* una tazzina **da** caffè *a coffee cup* una tazzina **di** caffè *a glass of wine, a cup of coffee*	un campo **da** tennis *a tennis court* un bicchiere **da** vino *a wine glass* **But**: un bicchiere **di** vino,
Physical characteristics: *with*	una ragazza **dagli** occhi azzurri *a girl with blue eyes/a blue-eyed girl* La giraffa è un animale **dal** collo lungo *The giraffe is an animal with a long neck* (See also **con**, p. 159.)	
Physical disabilities: *in*	cieco **da** un occhio *blind in one eye* sordo **da** un orecchio *deaf in one ear* zoppo **da** una gamba *lame in one leg*	
The value of objects/ things. **Da** means *worth*	un francobollo **da** 41 centesimi *a 41 cent stamp (a stamp worth …)* un biglietto **da** 100 euro *a 100 euro note (a note worth …)* **But**: una multa **di** 500 euro *a 500 euro fine (i.e. it amounts to)* (see p. 156.)	

I   Give the English equivalent of the following.

(a) Sono partito da Londra ieri.
(b) Sono uscito dall'ufficio alle sette.
(c) L'aereo parte dall'uscita numero 34.
(d) Siamo entrati dalla finestra.

(e) Non guardare dalla finestra.
(f) Da studente mi piaceva viaggiare.
(g) Sono qui da sabato.
(h) Vuoi qualcosa da bere?

2   **Da** or **di**? Complete these sentences using the correct Italian equivalent of *by*.

(a) Il Kosovo è stato distrutto (*by*) la guerra.
(b) Il film è girato (*by*) Franco Zeffirelli.
(c) È un libro (*by*) Leonardo Sciascia.
(d) È un libro scritto (*by*) Umberto Eco.

●   For more on **da** see also Exercises 1 and 2, p. 156; Exercises 3 and 4, p. 157; Exercise 5, p. 158.

In, a, da: in, at, to

In Italian **in**, **a**, and **da** can all be used to talk about being in a place or going to a place. Their use depends mostly on the category of place, but in many cases these must be learned.

in *in, at, to*	**Sono in … /Vado in …** In Europa/in Italia/in Piemonte/in Sicilia/ in farmacia/in città/in ufficio/in banca/ in montagna	With: continents, countries, regions, some islands, shops ending in **-ia**, familiar places.
a *in, at, to*	**Sono a/Vado a …** A Roma/a Capri/alla Standa/allo stadio/ all'università/a scuola/a casa	With: towns, some islands, shops (unless they end in **-ia**), many public places and the word *home*.
da *in, at, to*	**Sono da … /Vado da …** da Gianni/dalla zia/dagli amici/dai Bianchi/ dal medico/dal farmacista/da 'Carlino'/da loro	With: places connected with people, such as family, friends, professional people, shopkeepers and shops or restaurants named after people.

- For more on the use of prepositions and the article with geographical place names see Articles, pp. 23–4.

E **I** Where are you going to? Choose **a**, **da** or **in** – with the definite article if necessary – to say you're going to the following places. Begin: 'Vado ...'

(a) Italia	(e) Bari	(i) piscina	(m) lo zoo
(b) Sicilia	(f) il supermercato	(j) Franco	(n) il mare
(c) Toscana	(g) la Rinascente	(k) il parrucchiere	(o) casa
(d) Capri	(h) farmacia	(l) il medico	(p) campagna

2 Where are you meeting? Choose between **a**, **da** and **in**. Begin: 'Ci vediamo ...'

(a) casa mia	(d) la fermata dell'autobus	(g) il bar	(j) il ristorante
(b) biblioteca	(e) trattoria	(h) banca	(k) 'Gigino'
(c) Franca	(f) mia sorella	(i) fruttivendolo	(l) centro

The uses of di

Di is one of the most frequently used prepositions. Its main function is specification and description: it provides extra information about a noun to define it more precisely.

(a) For possession, specification and description

Possession and relationships: 's	la casa **di** Anna *Anna's house* la figlia **del** padrone *the boss's daughter*
Specification: *of*	la partita **di** calcio *the football match*; un libro **di** geografia *a geography book*; un'uscita **di** sicurezza *an emergency exit*
Authorship: *by*	È un'opera **di** Verdi *It's an opera by Verdi*; Sono dipinti **di** Botticelli *They are paintings by Botticelli*; Regia/musica **di** ... *Production/music by ...*
Colours, materials and substances: *no English equivalent*	**Di** che colore è? (*of*) *What colour is it?* **Di** che cosa è fatto? *What's it made of?* È vestita **di** nero *She is wearing black* Ho una camicetta **di** seta *I have a silk blouse* (See also **in**, p. 153.) È una torta **di** cioccolato *It's a chocolate cake*
Quantities and measurement: *no English equivalent, but di is essential*	un aumento **di** duemila euro *a 2,000 euro rise* un pacco **di** quattro chili *a four-kilo package* La superficie è **di** 350 metri quadrati *The surface area is 350 sq. metres* Il percorso più lungo è **di** 8 km. *The longest route is 8 km.*
Specifying subject/ topic: *about, of*	Parliamo **della** situazione in Italia *Let's talk about the situation in Italy* **Di** che cosa si tratta? *What's it about?*
With comparatives and superlatives: *than, in, of*	È più alto **di** me *He is taller than me* È la donna più simpatica **del** mondo *She is the nicest woman in the world* La più simpatica **di** tutte *The nicest of all*
Duration, age, time, seasons: *no exact English equivalent*	un ragazzo **di** dodici anni *a twelve-year-old boy* il treno/il volo **delle** 1700 *the five o'clock train/flight* le sette **di** mattina/**di** sera *seven in the morning/in the evening* una notte **d'**estate *a summer night*

(b) Relating to time and place

To express the usual time or season: *in, at, on*	Veniva **di** sera/**di** notte/**di** domenica/**d'**estate *He used to come in the evening/at night/on Sundays/in the summer* **Note also**: Veniva **la** sera/**la** domenica (See Articles, p. 17.) Veniva **in** estate/**in** inverno/**in** autunno/**in** primavera (See **in**, p. 153.)
Origin: with the names of towns or areas, not countries or regions: *from*	**Di** dove sei? *Where are you from?* Sono **di** Roma/Sono **del** Sud *I'm from Rome/from the South* **But**: Siamo toscani/italiani *We are Tuscan, from Tuscany/Italian, from Italy*
Distance and motion: *from, through*	Abito a due passi **di** qui *I live a stone's throw from here* Si entra/passa **di** qui/qua *You enter through here/this way* Esco **di** qui/**di** casa alle sette *I leave here/home at seven* (See also **per**, p. 158 and **da** (note below).)

(c) A note on *di*/*da* with *qui*

Di is more usual than **da** before **qui/lì**, **qua/là** or familiar places such as **casa**.

Da is more usual with **partire**, emphatic statements and **lontano**:

> È partito **da** qui ieri sera *He left here last night*
>
> **Da** qui non esci! *You're not leaving here/getting out of here!*
>
> Non è lontano **da** qui *It's not far from here*

See also **da**, p. 154.

1 Give the English equivalent of the following:

(a) una cintura di sicurezza   (c) un dipinto di Leonardo   (e) una bottiglia da due litri
(b) la casa di Mauro   (d) un aumento di 2000 euro   (f) una giornata d'inverno

2 Give the Italian for the following.

(a) *a language teacher*   (d) *a ten-year-old girl*   (f) *a five-hour journey*
(b) *the prime minister's wife*   (e) *the eight o'clock flight*   (g) *eight in the evening*
(c) *a novel by Manzoni*

3 Insert the correct preposition – **di** or **da**.

(a) Vuoi una tazza ... caffè o preferisci un tè?
(b) Mi ha regalato sei tazzine ... caffè.
(c) Ho bisogno di due francobolli ... un euro.
(d) Ha pagato una multa ... 400 euro.
(e) Gina è ... Pisa, è pisana.
(f) Gina è arrivata ... Pisa.

4 Complete the words for clothing and personal effects below using **di**, **a** or **da**. Bear in mind that **a** usually denotes design or how something is made, **da** generally indicates what something is for, while **di** tells you what something consists of.

(a) un anello ... oro (*a gold ring*)   (d) un cappello ... paglia (*a straw hat*)
(b) un abito ... sera (*an evening dress*)   (e) occhiali ... sole (*sunglasses*)
(c) una gonna ... fiori (*a flowery skirt*)   (f) una camicia ... quadretti (*a checked shirt*)

5 **Di** or **da**? Choose the appropriate preposition. In some cases both are possible.

(a) Dobbiamo entrare <u>dalla/della</u> porta principale?
(b) Si può entrare <u>da/di</u> qui?
(c) A che ora uscirai <u>dalla/della</u> riunione?
(d) A che ora esci <u>di/da</u> casa la mattina?
(e) Non passare <u>da/di</u> quella strada.
(f) Parte <u>dal/del</u> binario 7.

The uses of per

(a) For purpose, intention and cause

Purpose – who and what for: *for*	Lavora **per** me *He works for me* Vorrei delle pasticche **per** la gola *I'd like some pastilles for my throat* **Note also**: È andato **per** affari *He went on business* L'ho fatto **per** scherzo *I did it as a joke (for a laugh)*
Inclination: *for*	Ha una passione **per** la musica *He has a passion for music*
Intention: *to, in order to*	Sono venuti **per** aiutare *They have come to help* È uscita **per** fare la spesa *She has gone out to do the shopping* (See also **a**, Chapter 26, p. 273.)
Cause: *because of/ on account of, out of* **Per** indicates why something happens	È **per** questo che non ti piace? *Is that why/is it because of that you don't like it?* Ha sofferto molto **per** il freddo *He suffered a lot on account of the cold* Il traffico è bloccato **per** la nebbia *The traffic is held up because of the fog* L'ha fatto **per** ripicco/**per** curiosità *He did it out of spite/curiosity*

(b) For destination, distances and motion through or around a place

Destination, distance, motion along: *for, along*	Prendo il treno **per** Bolzano *I'm taking the train for/to Bolzano* Ho guidato **per** 500 chilometri *I drove for 500 kilometres* Camminava **per** la strada *He was walking along the street*
Motion through and around: *through, by, about, on* **Per** + **tutto/a** means *thoughout/ all over*	È entrato **per** la porta principale *He came in through the main entrance* È uscito **per** la porta di servizio *He left by the tradesman's entrance* (See also **da**, p. 154.) Il treno passa **per** Milano *The train goes through Milan* Girava **per** la casa *She was wandering through/about the house* Si rotolavano **per** terra *They were rolling around on the ground* Ho viaggiato **per** tutta l'Europa *I've travelled all over Europe*

(c) For time expressions

Duration (how long): *for*	Ha piovuto **per** un'ora/una settimana *It rained for an hour/a week*
Specific point in time: *for, by*	Ho un appuntamento **per** domani *I have an appointment for tomorrow* **Per** quando lo vuole? *When do you want it for/by?* – **Per** sabato/**per** le cinque *For/by Saturday/five o'clock* (See also **entro**, p. 162.)

(d) Other uses

How or by what means: *by*	L'ho mandato **per** posta/**per** via aerea *I sent it by post/by air* È meglio comunicare **per** e-mail *It's best to communicate by e-mail* Mi ha preso **per** il braccio *He took me by the arm* ***Note also***: **per** iscritto *in writing* **per**/in ordine alfabetico *in alphabetical order*
With numbers: *there are various* *English equivalents*	il venti **per** cento *twenty per cent* Due **per** cinque fa dieci *Two by/times five equals ten* Devi dividere **per** dieci *You must divide by ten* Sono entrati due **per** due *They came in two by two* Li ho mangiati poco/uno **per** volta *I ate a few/one at a time*

1 Give the Italian equivalent of the phrases in English.

(a) Che lavoro fa? – *I work for an airline company.* (una compagnia aerea)
(b) Lei è qui in vacanza? – *No, I'm here on business.*
(c) Lei per che cosa è qui? – *I'm here to learn Italian. It's for my job.*
(d) Quanto si trattiene a Milano? – *I'm staying for a month.* (Mi trattengo)
(e) È libero domani? – *I'm sorry, I have lots of appointments for tomorrow.*

2 Match up the phrases to complete the sentences and give the English equivalent.

(a) La macchina non è partita stamattina   (i) per la lontananza del fidanzato.
(b) Non è venuto alla festa   (ii) per il freddo.
(c) Mia figlia soffre molto   (iii) per timidezza.

3 Complete the sentences by giving the Italian equivalent of the English.

(a) I tifosi giravano (*through/about*) la città.
(b) Erano seduti (*on the ground*).
(c) L'ho incontrato (*in the street*).

Main uses of con

In modern Italian **con** does not usually combine with the definite article, though the forms **col** (**con** + **il**) and **coi** (**con** + **i**) are used in speech. Its main meaning is *with*.

Means – who and what with: *with, together with*	Vengo **con** mio fratello *I'm coming with my brother* Prendo il pollo **con** le patate fritte *I'm having chicken with chips* L'ha colpito **con** un martello *He hit it with a hammer*
Transport: *by*	È partito **con** il treno *He went by train/took the train* Andiamo **con** la macchina? *Shall we go by car?* (See also **in**, p. 153.)
Manner (how): *with, to*	Parla **con** entusiasmo *He speaks with enthusiasm* **con** mia sorpresa/mio stupore *to my surprise/amazement*
Description: *with*	È una ragazza **con** i capelli biondi *She is a girl with fair hair* Ho comprato delle scarpe **con** tacchi alti *I bought some high-heeled shoes* (See also **da**, p. 155.)
Cause and effect: *with, in view/because* *of, despite*	**Con** questo temporale non si può uscire *In view of this storm you can't go out* **Con** tutti i problemi che ha, è sempre allegra! *Despite all her problems she is always cheerful!*

I   Link up the pairs.

     (a) una Coca Cola con   (i) servizi

     (b) un appartamento con   (ii) la panna

     (c) un gelato con   (iii) la cannuccia

2   Consequences. Match up the phrases to say what the consequences are.

     (a) Con questi voti ...   (i) non ho voglia di uscire.

     (b) Con questo maltempo ...   (ii) non ti potrai mai laureare.

     (c) Con questo mal di gola ...   (iii) dovresti smettere di fumare.

3   Substitute the preposition **in** with **con**, making any necessary changes.

     (a) Andiamo in macchina.

     (b) Sono partito in treno.

     (c) È un uomo alto dai baffi lunghi.

     (d) È una signora elegante dai capelli biondi tinti.

The uses of su

(a) To express place

Position: *on*	Era seduta **sulla** sedia rossa *She was sitting on the red chair* **Note also**: L'ho letto **sul** giornale *I read it in the newspaper*
Location: *over, above* **Sopra** can sometimes be used instead of **su**	Hanno costruito un ponte **sul** fiume *They have built a bridge over the river* È a mille metri **sul** mare *It's a thousand metres above the sea* Stiamo volando sopra le/**sulle** Alpi *We're flying over the Alps*
Motion onto and up: *onto, up*	Andiamo **sul** balcone *Let's go onto the balcony* La finestra dà **sul** cortile *The window looks onto/overlooks the courtyard* È salito **sulla** collina *He climbed up the hill* Siamo andati **sull'**Etna *We've been up Etna* Ho fatto un viaggio **sul** Nilo *I travelled up the Nile*

(b) Other uses

Topic/subject: *on,* *about, concerning*	È un libro **sulla** Cina *It's a book on/about/concerning China* Ho letto molto **sul** problema *I've read a lot about the problem* Si raccontano molte cose **su di** lei *People say a lot of things about her* (After **su**, **di** is needed before a personal pronoun. See p. 162.)
Approximation: *about, around*	Costa **sui** 300 euro *It costs about/around 300 euros* È un uomo **sui** trent'anni *He is a man of about thirty* Verrò **sul** tardi/presto *I'll come late/fairly early* (In this sense, **su** must be used with the definite article. See p. 20.)
Quantity: *out of*	Ha preso nove **su** dieci *He got nine out of ten* Venti allievi **su** trenta *Twenty out of thirty pupils* Aperto 24 ore **su** 24 *Open 24 hours*

I   Give the English equivalent of the following.

(a) Ho lasciato i documenti sulla scrivania.

(b) Il gatto è salito sul tetto.

(c) *Il ponte sul fiume Kwai* è un film piuttosto vecchio.

(d) È un film sulla guerra in Giappone.

(e) Siamo stati sul Monte Bianco.

(f) Il viaggio costa sui due mila euro.

(g) Ho letto la notizia sul giornale.

(h) Ho lasciato l'ombrello sull'autobus.

The uses of fra and tra

Tra and **fra** are interchangeable. Their basic meaning is *between* and *among*. They express relationships of time and space and relationships between people.

Main uses

Place: *between, among(st)*	La casa si trova **fra** due strade *The house is between two roads* Gli ulivi crescono **tra** i fiori *The olive trees grow amongst the flowers* La luce filtra **fra** i rami *The light filters through (between) the branches* **Note also**: Me lo trovo sempre **fra** i piedi *He's always under my feet*
Time: *between, in* (for future time)	Arrivo **fra** le due e le tre *I'm arriving between two and three* Parto **fra** un'ora *I'm leaving in an hour* Sarò a casa **fra** un mese *I'll be at home in a month* (**Fra/tra** denote a specific point in the future.)
People: *between, among, amongst, amidst*	la guerra **fra** l'Italia e l'Austria *the war between Italy and Austria* **Tra** loro c'è molta stima *There's a lot of respect between them* Siamo **fra** amici *We're among friends* È tornato **tra** noi *He returned amongst us* **Note also**: **Fra** me (e me) pensavo che … *I was thinking to myself that …*
Partitive: *(out) of, amongst/some of*	**Fra** i suoi amici preferisco Enzo *Out of his friends, I prefer Enzo* Sono **fra** gli uomini più ricchi d'Italia *They are some of/amongst the richest men in Italy* (See also p. 60.) **Fra di** loro si capiscono molto bene *They understand each other well* (See p. 162.)

I   Give the English equivalent of the following.

(a) Arrivo fra le cinque e le sei.

(b) Arrivo fra una settimana.

(c) Mario è seduto fra la cugina e il nonno.

(d) Fra i miei cugini preferisco Luciano.

(e) Siamo fra amici.

(f) La nuova casa si trova fra Genova e Livorno.

(g) Si vede la casa fra gli alberi.

(h) Fra di noi c'è un'intesa speciale.

15.2 OTHER PREPOSITIONS

Simple prepositions

These are one-word prepositions. The main ones are:

attraverso *across, through*	**lungo** *along*
contro (di) *against*	**nonostante/malgrado** *despite*
dentro (a/di) *inside*	**oltre** (a) *beyond, over, besides*
dietro (a/di) *behind*	**secondo** *according to*
dopo (di) *after*	**senza** (di) *without*
durante *during*	**sopra** (a/di) *above, over*
eccetto/meno/salvo/tranne *except, apart from*	**sotto** (di) *under, below, beneath*
entro *by, within*	**verso** (di) *towards, at about*
fuori (di/da) *outside*	

(a) Uses of other prepositions with *a* and *di*

Some of the above prepositions can be followed by **a** or **di** depending on the word that follows.

Before a noun	Before a personal pronoun	Explanations
contro il muro *against the wall*	contro di me *against me*	**A** is occasionally used
dentro la (alla) scatola *inside the box*	dentro di sé *within himself*	before a noun or
dietro il (al) negozio *behind the shop*	dietro a/di te *behind you*	pronoun. **Di** is often
dopo la partita *after the match*	dopo di te *after you*	used before pronouns.
senza soldi *without money*	senza (di) te *without you*	
sopra la (alla) porta *above the door*	sopra a/di noi *above us*	
sotto la neve *under the snow*	sotto di lui *below/beneath him*	
verso il fiume *towards the river*	verso di lei *towards her*	

- Note that **su** and **fra/tra** also require **di** before personal pronouns. See pp. 160, 161.

(b) *Fuori*

Abita **fuori** città *He lives out of town*	**Fuori** may be used alone
In questo momento è **fuori** casa/**fuori** città/**fuori** Roma	before nouns in some
At the moment he's not at home/not in town/out of Rome	common expressions.
Non mangiare **fuori** pasto *Don't eat between ('outside') meals*	
L'ha tirato **fuori** del/dal cassetto *He pulled it out of the drawer*	**Fuori** is used with **di** (and
È sconosciuto **fuori** dall'Italia *He's unknown outside Italy*	sometimes **da**) before most
Fuori di qui! *Get out of here!*	other nouns, before **qui** and
È **fuori** di sé *He is beside himself* (lit. *outside himself*)	before personal pronouns.

I   Read the sentences below and add the preposition **di** where necessary.

    (a) Ci vediamo dopo cena.
    (b) Marina andrà in vacanza dopo me.
    (c) Abita verso il centro.
    (d) Non ho nessun obbligo verso lui.
    (e) Mauro è fuori città oggi.
    (f) Non è mai stato fuori Italia.
    (g) Non riesco a lavorare senza un po' di musica.
    (h) Senza te non riesco a lavorare.

2   Add **di** where necessary and also indicate where **a** is possible.

    (a) Il portafoglio è dentro la borsa.
    (b) Dentro me sono molto arrabbiato.
    (c) Le scarpe sono dietro la porta.
    (d) Le chiavi sono dietro te.
    (e) Oltre te non conosco nessuno.
    (f) Oltre i libri, ci hato dato delle videocassette.

Compound prepositions and prepositional phrases

These consist of two or more words. Some of the most common relate to place.

a destra/sinistra di *on the right/left of*
accanto a *beside, next to*
dall'altra parte di *on the other side of*
davanti a *in front of, outside*
di fronte a *opposite*
fino a *as far as, until*
giù per/su per *down/up (along)*
in cima a *at the top of*

in fondo a *at the end/bottom of*
in mezzo a *in the middle of, amongst*
intorno a *around*
lontano da *far from*
nel centro/mezzo di *in the centre of*
vicino a *near (to)*
a causa di *because of*
prima di *before*

Uses

Their use is fairly straightforward. Note the following.

davanti a	Il burro è **davanti a** te *The butter is in front of you*
	Ci vediamo **davanti al** cinema *We'll see each other outside the cinema*
in fondo a	La toilette è **in fondo al** corridoio *The toilet is at the end of the corridor*
	La nave è **in fondo al** mare *The ship is at the bottom of the sea*
	La citazione è **in fondo alla** pagina *The quote is at the bottom of the page*
in mezzo a	Non mi piace stare **in mezzo a** tanta gente
	I don't like being amongst so many people
nel centro di	La fontana è **nel centro della** piazza
	The fountain is in the middle/centre of the square
prima di	Saremo lì **prima di** mezzogiorno *We'll be there before midday*
	Ci sono altri candidati **prima di** te *There are other candidates before you*

3 Using each of the prepositions below once, you tell your friend you're parked in the following places:

> di fronte al ... • accanto alla ... • davanti a ... • nel ... • in fondo alla ... • dall'altra parte della ...

(a) in the courtyard   (c) opposite the cinema   (e) at the end of the street
(b) next to his car   (d) on the other side of the street   (f) outside his house

15.3 ADJECTIVES USED WITH PREPOSITIONS

Many common adjectives are followed by a preposition. Their use often differs from the English.

(a) Adjectives taking *a*

abituato a *accustomed/used to*	indifferente a *indifferent to*
attento a *careful of, aware of*	interessato a *interested in*
costretto a *forced to*	nocivo a *harmful to*
deciso/risoluto a *determined to*	uguale a *like, the same as*
disposto a *prepared/willing to*	

(b) Adjectives taking *di*

ansioso di *anxious/keen to*	innamorato di *in love with*
capace di *capable of*	macchiato di *stained with*
consapevole/conscio di *aware/conscious of*	pieno di *full of*
contento di *pleased to/satisfied with*	responsabile di *responsible for, in charge of*
convinto di *convinced of/about*	sicuro di *sure of/about*
farcito/imbottito di *stuffed with*	soddisfatto di *satisfied with*
felice/lieto di *happy, pleased to*	stanco/stufo di *tired of/sick of, fed up with*
fornito di *equipped with*	vestito di *dressed in/wearing*

(c) Adjectives taking *con*

antipatico con *unpleasant to*	simpatico con *pleasant to*
buono con *kind to*	sposato con *married to*
gentile con *nice to*	

(d) Adjectives taking *da*

diverso da *different from/to*	lontano da *far from*
indipendente da *independent of*	

I Describe these people by completing the sentences using **a** or **di**.

    (a) Pina è molto interessata … imparare il greco.

    (b) Alberta è proprio decisa … cambiare casa.

    (c) Ida è ansiosa … partire ma Delia non sembra disposta … muoversi.

    (d) Diego è molto soddisfatto … suo lavoro, è responsabile … tutto il reparto.

2 Give the Italian equivalent of the English.

    (a) *I am fed up with my job.*

    (b) *I am pleased with the results.*

    (c) *He is nice to me.*

    (d) *She is married to an engineer.*

(e) Adjectives with different dependent prepositions

bravo **a**, bravo **in** *good at*	È bravo **a** scuola *He's good at school* È bravo **a** tennis/**a** scacchi *He's good at tennis/chess* È brava **in** matematica/**in** geografia *She's good at maths/geography*	**Bravo a** with the word 'school' and games you play; **bravo in** followed by subjects of study.
circondato **di**, circondato **da** *surrounded by*	Sono circondati **dal** nemico *They are surrounded by the enemy* È circondato **di** affetto/**di** mistero *He/It is surrounded by affection/by mystery*	Literal meaning. Figurative meaning.
coperto **di** *covered in/with* coperto **con** *covered with* coperto **da** *covered by*	coperto **di** sangue/polvere/neve/cioccolato *covered in blood/dust/snow/chocolate* coperto **con** (pellicola di) alluminio *covered with/wrapped in foil* un corpo coperto **dalla** neve *a body covered by the snow*	**Coperto di** is most common.
costituito **da/di** *comprising/consisting of*	L'appartamento è costituito **da/di** una sola stanza *The flat consists of a single room*	There is no difference.
dipinto **di**/dipinta **in** *painted (in)*	La stanza è dipinta **di** verde *The room is painted green* Ho dipinto la porta **in** nero *I painted the door in black*	Little difference. **In** stresses the colour more.
generoso **con**, generoso **verso** *generous to/towards*	È molto generoso **con** tutti/**con** te *He is very generous to everyone/to you* Si è dimostrato generoso **verso** gli avversari *He proved to be generous towards his adversaries*	**Con** for material generosity; **verso** for moral generosity.
libero **di** *free (to)*, libero **da** *free of*	Sei libero **di** fare quello che vuoi *You are free to do what you want* È libero **da** ogni preoccupazione *He is free of all worries*	**Di** before a verb; **da** before a noun.
pronto **a/per** *ready/willing to/for*	Siamo pronti **a** decollare *We're ready to take off* Sono pronto **a** tutto *I am ready for anything* Siamo pronti **per** il decollo *We are ready for take-off*	**Pronto a** before a verb and **tutto**; **pronto per** before a noun.

3 Complete the sentences using the correct preposition.

    (a) Angelo è bravo ... scacchi.

    (b) Pietro è bravo ... scuola, soprattutto ... italiano.

    (c) L'appartamento è costituito ... tre piccole stanze.

    (d) Il divano è coperto ... una stoffa indiana.

    (e) Il vecchio pianoforte è coperto ... polvere.

    (f) Simona era pronta ... uscire.

15.4 NOUNS AND PREPOSITIONS

Here are just a few nouns that are commonly used with prepositions.

l'amore **per** *a love of*	un esperto **di** *an expert on*
un'antipatia **per** *a dislike of/aversion to*	(un) esperto **in** *expert in/at*
l'assuefazione **a** *addiction to*	l'odio **contro/verso** *hatred of*
la capacità **di** *the ability to*	il responsabile **di** *person in charge of*
la causa **di** *the cause of*	una simpatia **per** *a liking for*
un desiderio **di** *a desire for*	

- A note on **esperto di/in: esperto in** is more common as an adjective.

    È un esperto di cibi transgenici/di Dante/del Medio Oriente *He is an expert on genetically modified food/Dante/the Middle East*

    È esperto nell'uso dei colori/nelle previsioni del tempo *He is expert in the use of colour/in forecasting the weather*

1 Give the Italian equivalent of the English.

    (a) *The cause of the accident is not clear.*   (c) *His love of animals is well known.*

    (b) *My sister is an expert on medieval Italy.*   (d) *Her aversion to cats was extraordinary.*

16

Connectives

Connectives (**i connettivi**) are those all-important words or phrases such as *and, or, but, since, instead of, even if,* that link sentences or different parts of a sentence and which crucially affect the meaning. They are vital linguistic building-blocks which make it possible to develop more fluent, precise and complex language. Their many uses include: adding or clarifying information; giving alternatives or reasons; expressing contrast, conditions or exceptions and defining temporal relationships. They can have co-ordinating or subordinating functions.

Co-ordination

*You can have butter **and** jam. You can have butter or jam.* (Simple sentences. See p. 290.) *I opened the window **and** shut the door. I opened the window **but** shut the door.* (Compound sentences. See p. 289.)	The simplest connectives have a co-ordinating function. They connect or co-ordinate two similar items of equal importance within simple or compound sentences.

Subordination

Subordinating connectives tend to express a more precise meaning than co-ordinating ones.

She called her brother (main clause) **because** *he was ill* (subordinate clause) *She called her brother* (main clause) **although** *he was ill* (subordinate clause)	Many connectives have a subordinating function when used in complex sentences to introduce a dependent or subordinate clause. (See p. 299.)

A sentence can of course contain both co-ordinating and subordinating connectives:

> *She picked up the phone **and** (co-ordinating) called her brother, **although** (subordinating) it was late.*

Traditionally connectives are classified as conjunctions (e.g. *and, but, although, since*), but they also include other grammatical categories such as adverbs, prepositions and pronouns. These categories are included but not discussed here; attention is focused on the various functions of connectives in speech and writing.

16.1 ADDING INFORMATION

Le copulative

The following connectives are known in English as copulative because they couple together two items.

e	Caterina **e** Michela sanno nuotare *Caterina and Michela can swim* Studi con Anna **e** Giulio? *Do you study with Anna and Giulio?*	Used in affirmative statements and questions.
(non) ... né	**Non** studio inglese, **né** voglio farlo *I'm not studying English, nor do I want to/and I do not want to*	Used in negative statements and questions.
anche pure	Va bene, prendo **anche** quello *Fine, I'll also take that one/I'll take that one too/as well* Spero che verranno **pure** loro *I hope they will come too/as well*	See also Adverbs, pp. 55, 57. Can be used like **anche**.
inoltre/ in più per di più	Vado a Roma. **Inoltre/In più** vado a Bari *I'm going to Rome. Also/In addition I'm going to Bari* Non ha pagato l'affitto e **per di più** mi ha insultato *She didn't pay the rent and what's more/on top of that, she insulted me*	Both used to express *also* at the beginning of a sentence. **Per di più** is emphatic.
oltre a a parte	**Oltre a** Roma ho visto Napoli *Besides/As well as/In addition to Rome I saw Naples* **A parte** Sergio, c'erano Marina e Ugo *Apart from/Besides Sergio, Marina and Ugo were there*	**Oltre** and **a parte** can also mean *except*; see p. 175.
come pure	Gli insegnanti fanno sciopero, **come pure** gli studenti *The teachers are on strike and so are the students/ as well as/just like the students* Lucio si è offeso, **come pure** mio marito Lucio *took offence, and so did/just like my husband*	Literally *like also*. It is a common and useful way of avoiding the clumsy repetition of a verb.

Level 2

Le correlative

These connectives (known as correlative) link more than one item and add emphasis.

sia ... sia sia ... che	Possono venire **sia** Caterina **che** Michela *Both Caterina and Michela can come* Vado in piscina **sia** d'inverno **sia/che** d'estate *I go swimming in both summer and winter/in summer and winter alike* Non importa chi cucina oggi: può farlo **sia** l'una **che** l'altra *It doesn't matter who cooks today, either of them can do it*	This generally means *both ... and*, or occasionally *either ... or*. It never expresses opposing, excluding alternatives as with **o ... o** (p. 171).

Level 2

né ... né	Non sono amico **né** di Anna **né** di Giulio **Neither** Anna **nor** Giulio are my friends Non bevono (beve) **né** mia sorella **né** suo marito **Neither** my sister **nor** her husband drink	The plural verb is preferred to the singular.
non solo ... ma (anche)	**Non solo** ha perso l'orologio, **ma** ha **(anche)** dimenticato la riunione **Not only** did he lose his watch **but** he **(also)** forgot the meeting **Non solo** noi **ma anche** loro hanno il diritto di scegliere **Not only** us, **but** they **too** have the right to choose	When **ma anche** is followed by a different subject from the first one, it determines the person of the verb.
non solo	Si è rotto il braccio. **Non solo**: il poveretto si è anche spaccato un dente He's broken his arm **and that's not all**: the poor thing has also broken a tooth	This refers to a whole clause or sentence.
tanto meno	Non si può condannarli, **tanto meno** punirli You can't condemn them, **let alone** punish them	Links verbs and avoids repetition.

I   Complete the text below by using the connectives given.

> e anche • e • inoltre • in più • oltre a

Durante le vacanze sono andato in giro con mio fratello. Abbiamo visitato tutta la Campania, (**and also**) la Sicilia. (**Also/In addition**) siamo stati nelle isole Eolie al largo della Sicilia. In Campania abbiamo visto Napoli, Salerno, Amalfi (**and**) Ravello. In Sicilia siamo stati un po' dappertutto. (**As well as**) visitare le città principali di Messina, Palermo, Catania, Siracusa e Trapani, siamo stati nel centro, a Enna e (**in addition**) abbiamo visitato Erice e il tempio di Segesta.

2   Give the English equivalent of the following sentences.
   (a) Sia Emilio che Elisabetta sono stati promossi.
   (b) Né Emilio né Elisabetta sono stati promossi.
   (c) Emilio è stato promosso, come pure Elisabetta.
   (d) Emilio ha invitato alcuni amici e per di più ha invitato la madre.

16.2 CLARIFYING INFORMATION

Le esplicative

These connectives, known in English as declaratives, are commonly used to define, correct, explain or confirm.

per esempio, ad esempio	Ti posso vedere presto, **per esempio** alle otto I can see you early, **for example** at eight	**Ad esempio** is slightly more formal.

cioè	Torno più tardi, **cioè** all'una *I'll be back later, **that is** at one* Sono proprio stufo – **Cioè?** – **Cioè** non ci voglio andare! *I'm really fed up – **What does that mean?** – **It means** I don't want to go*	Widely used to express and request more specific information.
ossia	È un esperto di micologia, **ossia** dello studio dei funghi *He is an expert in mycology, **that is to say**, in the study of mushrooms*	Very like **cioè**, but typical of formal written Italian.
in altre parole, in altri termini, vale a dire (che)	Il capo mi ha detto di non metter piede nella ditta, **in altre parole** mi ha licenziato *My boss has told me not to set foot inside the firm, **in other words** he has sacked me* È una lettera anonima, **vale a dire** non firmata *It's an anonymous letter, **that is to say** it is not signed*	Both can be used in the same way. **Vale a dire** is typical of written Italian.
o meglio o piuttosto **piuttosto che**	Gli telefonerò – **o meglio/o piuttosto** gli manderò un'e-mail *I'll phone him – **or rather**, I'll send him an e-mail* **Piuttosto che** un conoscente, è un amico *He's a friend **rather than** an acquaintance (more of a friend than …)*	These can be used as a way to specify or to correct oneself.
si tratta di	**Si tratta di** un incendio doloso, non di un semplice incidente **It is** arson, not just an accident **Si tratta dei** problemi di una coppia separata **It's about** the problems of a separated couple **Di** che cosa **si tratta?** *What is it/this about?*	Used to specify what something is about. It literally means *it is a question of* but often translates as *This/It is*.
ecco	**Ecco!** Avevo ragione io, Mauro non ha pagato! **You see!** I was right, Mauro hasn't paid Non m'interessa, **ecco!** *I'm not interested, **so there!/** I'm **just not** interested*	Commonly used to reinforce a point.
già infatti	Pietro viene stasera. – **Già!** Avevo dimenticato *Pietro's coming tonight. – **Of course/That's right.** I had forgotten* Pietro viene stasera. – **Infatti**. Purtroppo non andiamo d'accordo *Pietro is coming tonight. – **That's right/indeed.** Unfortunately we don't get on*	Both express agreement but **già** is used to acknowledge you have remembered something. **Infatti** is used to confirm what has just been said.
infatti in effetti	Hai perso il treno, allora? – **Infatti**. *So did you miss the train then? – **Indeed/That's right!** Yes I did*. È un ragazzo timido. – **Infatti**, l'ho sempre notato. **Infatti/In effetti** non parla mai in classe *He is a shy boy. – **That's right**, I've always noticed it. **In fact/The truth is** that he never talks in class*	These are virtually synonymous, but **in effetti** introduces detail to support the statement. It has the additional meaning of *The truth is*. Compare **in realtà**, p. 173.
anzi	Ti chiedo, **anzi**, ti prego di aspettare *I'm asking you, **in fact** I'm begging you to wait* Sei veramente gentile, **anzi**, sei proprio un angelo! *You're so kind, **in fact** you're an angel!*	Used emphatically to specify. See also p. 173.

I   Make things clear. Substitute the English connectives with an appropriate Italian one, choosing from the list below.

> cioè • già • in effetti • infatti • meglio

(a) Ho telefonato a Marta, (*that is*) a mia cognata.
(b) Ho invitato la suocera, o (*rather*) l'ha invitata mia moglie!
(c) È meglio partire più tardi. – Sì, (*that's right/indeed*), così evitiamo il traffico.
(d) Domani è festa. – (*Of course!*), avevo dimenticato.
(e) Sandra mi sembra piuttosto depressa. – Sì, (*that's right/in fact*) non esce più.

16.3 EXPRESSING ALTERNATIVES

Le avversative *(1)*

These are known as adversative or disjunctive connectives and express choice or alternatives.

o, oppure	Vuoi una birra **o** un caffé? *Would you like a beer **or** a coffee?* Possiamo andare da Mirella **oppure** rimanere qui *We can go to Mirella's **or else** we can stay here/ We can **either** go to Mirella's **or** we can stay here*	All these express opposing alternatives.
o ... o/ oppure	**O** lo faccio io **o/oppure** lo fai tu *Either I do it **or (else)** you do* Vengo **o** con Carlo, **o** con Paolo **o/oppure** con Lino *I'm **either** coming with Carlo, **or** Paolo **or (else)** with Lino*	
altrimenti	Devo andarmene, **altrimenti** sarò in ritardo *I must leave, **otherwise** I'll be late*	**Altrimenti** is used only before a verb.
invece di / piuttosto	**Invece di** scrivergli perché non lo chiami? ***Instead of** writing to him why don't you call him?* **Invece di** Sandro, perché non sposi **piuttosto** Andrea? ***Rather than** Sandro, why don't you marry Andrea **instead**?*	Can also go before nouns/pronouns. **Piuttosto** often comes after the verb.
piuttosto che/(di) / anziché	**Piuttosto che** fare tardi, prenderò un taxi ***Rather than** be late, I'll take a taxi* Secondo me è timido **piuttosto che** freddo *I think he is shy **rather than** cold* Preferisco parlare con te **anziché** con il professore *I prefer to speak to you **instead of** the teacher*	**Che** is more commonly used than **di** with **piuttosto. Anziché** is similar but expresses a more definite alternative.

E

1   Complete the sentences in Italian, substituting the English.

(a) Dobbiamo rispondere subito (*otherwise we'll lose the contract*).
(b) È meglio parlargli direttamente (*instead of sending an email*).
(c) Aldo, (*rather than*) mangiare caramelle, (*eats fruit instead*).
(d) Voglio lavorare con voi (*instead of with them*).

2   Give the Italian equivalent of the following.

(a) *Are you having beer or wine?*
(b) *We can either go to the cinema or stay here.*
(c) *I prefer to go alone rather than wait.*
(d) *Don't drink coffee, have a lemon tea instead.*

16.4 COMPARING, CONTRASTING AND CONTRADICTING

Le avversative *(2)*

These adversative connectives introduce contrasting or opposing ideas.

ma	Noi usciamo, **ma** Lucio non viene *We're going out **but** Lucio's not coming*	
però	Non posso parlare adesso, ti chiamo domani, **però** *I can't talk now, **but/however** I'll call you tomorrow*	**Però** can be used like **ma** and can also end a sentence.
mentre	Io studio a Bari **mentre** Tommaso studia a Milano *I'm studying in Bari **while/whereas** Tommaso is studying in Milan*	These two connectives are used to compare.
invece	Io studio a Bari, Tommaso **invece** studia a Milano *I'm studying in Bari, Tommaso **however/on the other hand** is studying in Milan*	For **invece** see also p. 173.
eppure	Tu dici che è pigro, **eppure** ha ottimi risultati *You say he is lazy, **and yet** he has excellent results*	**Eppure** is preferred in speech.
tuttavia	Era stanco morto, **tuttavia** ha giocato a tennis *He was dead tired, **nevertheless** he played tennis*	**Tuttavia** is more literary.
comunque	È vero che si sta bene qui, **comunque**, domani parto *It's true that it's nice here, **however/anyhow/but anyway** tomorrow I'm leaving* **But**: Fai come vuoi, io parto **comunque** *Do what you want, I'm leaving **anyway***	Precedes the verb. After the verb it means *come what may/anyway.* See also p. 177.
d'altra parte del resto, da un lato ... dall'altro, da una parte ... dall'altra	Non mi piace viaggiare in aereo. **D'altra parte** è rapidissimo *I don't like going by plane. **On the other hand** it is very quick* Antonio si è comportato male, anche Stefania, **del resto** *Antonio behaved badly, **but then/on the other hand** so did S.* **Da un lato** ha ragione, **dall'altro** no *On the one hand he's right, **on the other** he isn't*	These are all used to evaluate and weigh things up. **Del resto** can be used like **d'altra parte** but also has other meanings. **Da un lato ... dall'altro** and **da una parte ... dall'altra** are identical in meaning.

Le oppositive o sostitutive

These are used to contradict and to say that something else is true.

invece	Katia ha promesso di venire, **invece** è andata al cinema. *Katia promised to come **but** she has gone to the cinema instead*	See also p. 172; **in realtà** is used to contradict or correct a previous statement. Do not confuse with **infatti** (p. 170).
in realtà	Sembra un ragazzo timido. **In realtà** è piuttosto aggressivo *He seems a shy boy. **In actual fact/In reality** he is quite aggressive/He's **actually** quite aggressive*	
anzi	Non lo trovo interessante, **anzi**! *I don't find him/it interesting, **far from it/on the contrary!** Disturbo? – **Anzi**, mi fa piacere *Am I interrupting you? – **Not at all**, you're welcome*	Very common. Mostly used to contradict, but also to reinforce/clarify. See also p. 170.
bensì	La crisi non è dovuta a fattori economici, **bensì** a problemi politici. *The crisis is **in fact not** due to economic factors **but** to political problems (instead)*	An emphatic form of **ma**. It is only used after negatives.

1   Contrasting and comparing. Complete the sentences by substituting the English with Italian connectives.

   (a) Io studio medicina (*but*) mia sorella studia architettura.
   (b) Io studio medicina (*whereas*) mia sorella studia architettura.
   (c) Io sono nato a Torino, Leonardo (*on the other hand/however*) è nato a Palermo.
   (d) Non mi piace viaggiare in aereo, (*on the other hand*) è molto comodo.

2   Rewrite the sentences by including the Italian equivalent of the connectives given after **ma**.

   (a) Avevo intenzione di studiare, ma ho cenato da amici. (*instead*)
   (b) Sembra una persona antipatica ma è gentilissima. (*actually/in actual fact*)
   (c) Leopoldo mi ha portato a cena ma non avevo fame. (*in reality/in actual fact*)

16.5 EXPRESSING REASONS, CAUSE AND EFFECT

Le causative

The following connectives are known as causal in English, as they explain reasons or cause.

perché	Non vengo **perché** piove troppo *I'm not coming **because** it's raining too much* **Siccome** fa freddo, mi metto il cappotto ***Because** it's cold I'll wear my coat*	Does not begin a sentence. Instead use **dato che, siccome, visto che, dal momento che.**
a causa di + noun **per colpa mia/tua**	Sono in ritardo **a causa dell'**incidente/**a causa di** Giulio *I am late **because of** the accident/Giulio* ***But**:* Sono in ritardo **per colpa tua** *I am late **because of** you* È colpa sua se sono in ritardo. *It's **because of** him/her that I am late/It's **his/her fault** that I am late*	**A causa di** cannot be followed by a personal pronoun (e.g. **me, lui, lei**). To express *because of me, him*, etc., **per colpa mia,** etc., or **per causa mia,** etc. usually indicates negative causes, while
grazie a	La festa è andata bene **grazie al** bel tempo/**a** Roberto/**a** loro *The party went well **thanks to/because of** the weather/Roberto/them*	**grazie a/è merito tuo/suo** are used when the cause is positive.
è merito tuo/suo, etc.	È merito tuo se la festa è andata bene *It's **thanks to/because of** you the party went well*	
per questo **per**	È **per questo** che sono in ritardo *It's **because of this/that** I'm late* Non siamo venuti **per** il freddo *We didn't come **because of** the cold*	

These causal connectives also focus on the link between cause and effect: the cause is mentioned before the effect, so they usually begin a sentence.

siccome	**Siccome** è ricco, può viaggiare molto ***Because/Since** he is rich, he can travel a lot*	
dato che, dal momento che, visto che	**Dato che/Dal momento che** siamo senza soldi, è assurdo pensare a cambiare casa ***Since/As** we have no money, it's absurd to think about moving* **Visto che** sei qui, mi puoi aiutare ***Since/Seeing that/As** you are here, you can help me*	
poiché	**Poiché** non aveva capito, ha pagato troppo ***Since** he had not understood, he paid too much*	**Poiché** is typical of formal written Italian.
Gerund	**Avendo perso** il treno, sono rimasto da loro ***As/Since** I had missed the train I stayed at their place*	See also Gerunds, p. 242.

E **1** Complete the following sentences. More than one version may be possible.

    (a) *(Since/seeing that)*, sei qui mi puoi aiutare.

    (b) *(Since I had)* perso la chiave, ero chiuso fuori.

    (c) *(Because/since)* la banca è chiusa, sono rimasto senza soldi.

Level 2 **2** Give the Italian equivalent of the following.

    (a) *Because it's your birthday we can eat out.*

    (b) *We can't leave because of the strike.*

    (c) *It's because of you that I passed the exam.* (sono stato promosso)

    (d) *I'm late because of you.*

Le conclusive

These express conclusions and consequences. They focus on outcome.

allora* così quindi* sicché perciò dunque pertanto	Ero senza macchina, **allora/quindi/così** sono venuto a piedi *I didn't have the car **so/therefore** I walked* Il telefono era rotto, **sicché/perciò** non ho potuto chiamare *The phone was broken **and so/therefore** I couldn't call* Penso **dunque** sono *I think **therefore** I am*	These can all be used in very similar ways. **Perciò** is a little more formal. **Pertanto** is really formal and used in writing. For *dunque*, see also p. 180.
per cui di conseguenza tanto che	È caduto per strada, **per cui** è arrivato tardi *He fell in the street, **so that** he arrived late* Si è addormentato. **Di conseguenza** non ha sentito il telefono *He fell asleep. **As a result** he didn't hear the phone* Cinzia lo trova proprio antipatico, **tanto che** non gli parla mai *Cinzia really dislikes him, **to the extent that/so the result is** she never talks to him*	These put more emphasis on the outcome than the above connectives.
in/di modo che in modo da + infinitive	Farò **in modo che** loro possano andare a casa presto *I'll **see to it that** they can go home early* Bisogna organizzarci **in modo da** evitare lavoro inutile *We have to organise ourselves **so that** we avoid unnecessary work*	**In modo che/da** focus on future outcome, and **in modo che** sometimes requires the subjunctive (p. 253).

3 Match up the sentences and give the English equivalents.

    (a) La macchina è guasta ...   (i) in modo da poter risparmiare di più.

    (b) Si è rotto la gamba ...   (ii) quindi la devo portare dal meccanico.

    (c) Sono diminuiti i profitti ...   (iii) per cui non ha potuto andare a sciare.

    (d) Ho organizzato le cose ...   (iv) di conseguenza hanno chiuso una fabbrica.

16.6 MAKING EXCEPTIONS

Le eccettuative

| a parte,
oltre (a)

meno/salvo/tranne | **Oltre** Paolo, non è venuto nessuno
***Apart from/Except for** Paolo no one came*
Ho letto tutto, **a parte** la conclusione
*I've read everything **apart from/except** the conclusion*
Sono partiti tutti, **meno/salvo/tranne** lui
They have all left except him | *Except for/apart from* can be expressed in Italian by any of these. |
| eccetto,
fuorché | Mi puoi chiedere tutto quello che vuoi, **eccetto/fuorché** andare in aereo
*You can ask me to do whatever you want, **apart from** going by plane* | Mostly used with infinitive verbs. |

Level 2	eccetto che, a meno che, salvo che, tranne che	Sono a tua disposizione, **eccetto che/a meno che** qualcuno mi telefoni *I'll be available **except if/unless** somebody phones me*	*Unless* is expressed by any of these + the subjunctive.
	senza + infinitive	È arrivato **senza** dirlo a nessuno *He arrived **without** telling anyone*	The subject must be the same for both verbs.
	senza che + subjunctive	È tornato Angelo **senza che** lo sapessimo *Angelo returned **without** our knowing*	With **senza** + **che** the subjects are *different*.
	a prescindere da	**A prescindere dal fatto che** non abbiamo soldi, non ho voglia di andare all'estero **Apart from the fact/Leaving aside the fact that** *we have no money, I don't feel like going abroad*	Used more in writing.

E 1 Using appropriate connectives complete the following sentences. There may be more than one possibility.

(a) Io mangio di tutto (*except*) il baccalà. (*salt cod*)
(b) Non ha obiettato nessuno, (*except*) tuo fratello.
(c) (*Apart from*) mia madre, nessuno parla inglese.
(d) Chiedimi tutto, (*apart from*) invitare quella gente!

16.7 CONDITIONS AND CONCESSIONS

Condizionali e concessive

Most of these connectives are used in complex sentences and can take the subjunctive.

Level 2	se	**Se** vuoi, ti posso aiutare *If you want, I can help you* **Se** fossi in te, non lo farei *If I were you I wouldn't do it* **Se** avessi studiato avrei passato l'esame *If I had studied I would have passed the exam*	For the use of **se** with the subjunctive, see p. 254. For **se** with the future, see p. 201.
	nel caso che, qualora	**Nel caso che** dovesse dimenticare la chiave, ce n'è un'altra nel vaso *In case/If he forgets/Should he forget his key, there's another one in the vase*	**Qualora** is literary.
	anche se	**Anche se** è mio cugino, mi è antipatico **Even though/Although** *he is my cousin, I don't like him* **Anche se** fosse vero, non ci crederei **Even if** *it were true I wouldn't believe it* **Anche se** l'avesse saputo, non avrebbe cambiato idea **Even if** *he had known he wouldn't have changed his mind*	Used exactly like **se**. Note the use of the subjunctive when a conditional is in the main clause. See also p. 229.
	benché, sebbene	**Benché/Sebbene** sia difficile, ci riuscirai **Although** *it is hard, you will manage*	Used with the subjunctive.
	pur + gerund	**Pur** sapendo che era troppo tardi, gli ho telefonato **Although** *I knew it was too late, I phoned him* **Pur** non **avendo capito** molto, gli è piaciuto il film **Although** *he had not understood much, he liked the film*	Used if the subject of both verbs is the same See Gerunds, p. 242.

malgrado, nonostante	Uscirono, **malgrado/nonostante** facesse freddo *They went out **although** it was cold* È arrivato in tempo **malgrado/nonostante** la neve *He arrived on time **despite** the snow*	Used with a subjunctive verb or with a noun.
a condizione di/a patto di	Accetto di viaggiare con la tua macchina, **a patto di/a condizione di** poter contribuire alle spese di viaggio *I'll accept travelling in your car **on condition that/ as long as** I can contribute to the expenses*	**Di** + infinitive is used when the subject of both clauses is the same. **Che** + subjunctive is used when each clause has a different subject.
a condizione che/a patto che	Ti darò i soldi **a condizione che/a patto che** tu me li restituisca *I'll give you the money **on condition that** you return it*	
purché	Non m'importa quello che fa, **purché** sia felice *I don't mind what he does **as long as/provided that** he's happy*	Used with subjunctive.
a meno che	Lo pulisco io, **a meno che** tu non abbia voglia di farlo *I'll clean it, **unless** you feel like doing it*	Used with subjunctive.
lo stesso, comunque	Io vengo **lo stesso/comunque** *I'm coming **all the same/anyway***	No subjunctive.
ammettendo che	**Ammettendo che** sia vero, cosa farai? ***Supposing** it is true, what will you do?*	Used with subjunctive.
per quanto, comunque	**Per quanto** difficile sia, ci riuscirai ***However** hard it may be, you will manage* Non ti scoraggiare **comunque** vadano le cose *Don't get discouraged **however** things go*	With subjunctive. When it means *however*, **comunque** is only used before verbs. (See also p. 172.)

I Complete the sentences by substituting the English with Italian connectives.

(a) Io voglio andarci (*even though*) è lontano.
(b) (*Although*) sia lontano, vale la pena di andarci.
(c) (*Although*) non avendo studiato francese parla meglio di tutti.
(d) Mi sono divertito (*despite*) la pioggia.

2 Give the English equivalent of the Italian.

(a) Mi va bene qualsiasi orario purché io lo sappia prima.
(b) Ci troviamo in biblioteca a meno che non sia chiusa.
(c) So che c'è sciopero, ma io parto lo stesso.
(d) Andremo in vacanza comunque vadano gli affari.

16.8 TIME SEQUENCE

Le temporali

These important connectives signal when something happens in relation to something else.

| prima, all'inizio, poi, dopo, in seguito, alla fine | **All'inizio** ho rifiutato. **Poi, dopo un po'** ho cambiato idea, e **alla fine** ho accettato *At first I refused. **Then, after a while** I changed my mind and **in the end** I accepted* **Prima** ero impiegato alle poste, **poi, in seguito**, ho lavorato per il Comune *First I was employed in the post office, **then subsequently** I worked for the council* | These basic connectives are used in simple or compound sentences to indicate a sequence of actions or events. |

The following are used to locate points in time.

allora, a quell'epoca, a quel tempo, in quei giorni	**Allora/a quell'epoca** erano poveri *Then/in those days they were poor* Ero a Roma quando è morto mio padre. **In quei giorni** ho sofferto molto *I was in Rome when my father died. I suffered a lot **at that time***	Distant past. Distant past. Distant past in relation to a specific time span/event.
negli ultimi giorni/tempi, nei giorni scorsi	**Negli ultimi tempi** ha smesso di salutarmi *Recently/of late he has stopped saying hello* **Nei giorni scorsi** il tempo è peggiorato *The weather has got worse **in the last few days***	Recent past. Very recent past.
in questi giorni	**In questi giorni** mi occupo io dei suoi bambini *I'm looking after her children **at the moment/at present/these days** (present)* **In questi giorni** ho passato molte ore al computer *In/Over the last few days I've spent many hours at the computer (recent past)* **In questi giorni** avrò molto da fare *In the next few days I'll have a lot to do (future)*	This can be used with reference to the present, to the recent past and also to the future.
nei prossimi giorni	Ho intenzione di vederli **nei prossimi giorni** *I intend to see them **in the next few days***	Future.

The following time connectives are used in complex sentences to introduce subordinate clauses.

Level 2

prima di + infinitive	Li chiamerò **prima di** partire *I'll call them **before** I leave* Ha rifatto il letto **prima di** uscire *She made the bed **before** she left*	**Prima di** is used when the subject of both clauses is the same.
prima che + subjunctive	Li chiamerò **prima che** partano *I'll call them **before** they leave* Ha rifatto il letto **prima che** arrivassero *She made the bed **before** they arrived*	**Prima che** is used when each clause has a different subject. See also Subjunctive, p. 248.
prima che me ne/te ne/se ne dimentichi	*Note also*: **Prima che** me ne dimentichi/**Prima di** dimenticarmene, ti do le chiavi di casa ***Before** I forget, I'll give you the house keys*	**Prima che** is often used with the subjunctive of **dimenticarsi** even when the subjects are the same.
appena	**Appena** arrivi, chiamami *Call me **as soon as** you arrive* **(Non) appena** avrai una risposta, fammelo sapere ***As soon as** you get a reply, let me know*	See pp. 201, 203 and 223 for use with the future, future perfect and past anterior.

dopo che	Riceverà i risultati **dopo che** tu sarai partito *He will receive the results after you (will) have left/leave* Riceverà i risultati **dopo che** sarà partito *He will receive the results after he (will) have left/he leaves*	**Dopo che** can be used whether the subjects of the clauses are different or the same.
dopo + past infinitive	L'ho saputo solo **dopo esser** arrivato (**dopo che** ero arrivato) *I found out only **after arriving**/I had arrived* Ti chiamerò **dopo averlo** visto (**dopo che** l'avrò visto) *I'll call you after having seen him/after I (will) have seen him*	**Dopo** + past infinitive is used when the subject of both clauses is the same. See also pp. 203, 240.
dopo + noun	Riceverà i risultati **dopo** la tua partenza ... *after your departure* L'ho saputo **dopo** il mio arrivo ... *after my arrival*	**Dopo** + noun substituting the verb is a very common alternative
fino a + time expression	Dobbiamo aspettare **fino a** domani/**fino alla** settimana prossima *We must wait **until** tomorrow/next week*	This indicates time *until*.
finché + verb	Puoi rimanere **finché** vuoi *You can stay **as long as** you like* **Finché** fa caldo, sono felice ***As long as** it's hot, I'm happy* **Finché** c'è vita c'è speranza ***While** there's life there's hope*	This is followed by the indicative.
finché/fino a quando (non)	Abbiamo aspettato/Non abbiamo cenato **finché/fino a quando (non)** sono tornati tutti *We waited/We did not eat supper **until** they all returned* Aspettiamo **finché/fino a quando** saranno tornati/non siano tornati *Let's wait **until** they have returned/return*	If the action is not certain to take place, the subjunctive is preferred. The use of **non** is stylistic and has no negative meaning. (See also p. 248.)
che + subjunctive	Aspettiamo **che** tornino *Let's wait **until** they return* Abbiamo aspettato **che** tornassero *We waited **for** them **to** return*	**Che** is often used after **aspettare** instead of **finché**.

I   Pick out all the connectives which make sense in each sentence, then name the odd one out each time.

   (a) Da studente ho vissuto a Firenze. (A quell'epoca/A quel tempo/In questi giorni) avevo pochissimi soldi.

   (b) Spero di vederti (nei giorni scorsi/nei prossimi giorni/in questi giorni).

   (c) (Negli ultimi tempi/Nei prossimi giorni/In questi giorni) ho avuto tanto da fare.

   (d) (In questi giorni/in quel momento) non faccio niente di bello.

2   Match up the two parts of the sentences by finding the equivalent of the English phrase.

   (a) Chiamami (*before you leave*)

   (b) Fammelo sapere (*before they leave*)

   (c) Chiamalo (*as soon as you arrive*)

   (d) Mi metterò in contatto (*after I have seen him*)

   (e) Fammi sapere qualcosa (*after she leaves/has left*)

   (i) appena arrivi.

   (ii) prima di partire.

   (iii) dopo averlo visto/dopo che l'avrò visto.

   (iv) prima che partano.

   (v) dopo che sarà partita/dopo la sua partenza.

3   Complete the sentences by using the appropriate Italian phrases.

   (a) Rimango qui (*until*) sabato.

   (b) Puoi stare da noi (*as long as*) vuoi.

   (c) Starò qui (*until*) siano tornati.

   (d) Abbiamo aspettato (*until*) non sono tornati.

16.9 INITIATING, CONCLUDING AND GENERALISING

The clarity and fluency of speech and writing is enhanced by the ability to use connectives to initiate, conclude, summarise and generalise.

(a) Initiating

prima di tutto, per cominciare	**Prima di tutto/Per cominciare**, vorrei ringraziare tutti *First of all/to begin with, I'd like to thank everyone*	These open out a topic. **Per cominciare** is quite formal.
allora	**Allora**, cominciamo *Right (then), let's begin*	Informal.
anzitutto, innanzitutto	**Anzitutto/Innanzitutto** è necessario chiamare la banca *First and foremost it is necessary to call the bank* **Anzitutto/Innanzitutto** quello che ha detto non è vero, e in ogni caso non ti riguarda *In the first place/First of all/Firstly what he said is not true, and in any case it doesn't concern you (It's none of your business)*	These can be used like the above, but are often used to respond to questions and prioritise things.

These connectives can be used to round off a topic and initiate another one.

dunque, quindi, allora/ora	**Dunque/Quindi**, come dicevo, ci sono tre problemi *So, as I was saying, there are three problems* **Allora/Ora**, a questo punto è essenziale valutare i rischi *Now/so, at this point, it is essential to evaluate the risks*	These tend to begin a sentence and can all be used colloquially.
a proposito	Ho visto Maria ieri. **A proposito**, hai deciso cosa facciamo domani? ... *By the way/Incidentally, have you decided what we're doing tomorrow?*	Switching topics. Used to initiate a totally new topic.

(b) Concluding/summing up

These are all used for drawing things to a close.

infine, per terminare	**Infine/Per terminare**, vorrei ringraziare il dottor Bianchi *Finally/to end with, I'd like to thank Doctor Bianchi*	Quite formal.
tutto sommato, in fin dei conti, in ultima analisi	**Tutto sommato**, è la soluzione migliore *All things considered/All in all it's the best solution* **In fin dei conti/In ultima analisi**, non c'è altro da fare *Ultimately/In the end/When it comes down to it/In the final analysis nothing else can be done*	Can all be used when making a final assessment.
insomma	**Insomma**, dobbiamo prendere una decisione *Basically/In a nutshell/The fact is, we have to make a decision* Alla festa c'erano tanti amici. – È stata una bella serata **insomma** *There were lots of friends at the party. All in all it was a lovely evening* **Insomma**, che vuoi? *Look here/For heaven's sake, what do you want?*	Informal. Used more for summing up than assessing. Colloquially, **insomma** can convey exasperation.

(c) Generalising

in fondo **in sostanza**	**In fondo** non mi piace guidare ***Basically*** *I don't like driving/I don't **actually** like driving* **In sostanza** ci sono due possibilità *There are **essentially** two possibilities*	Used in a similar way. **In fondo** is more colloquial.
per lo più **in linea di massima**	I nostri clienti sono **per lo più** italiani *Our clients **by and large** are Italian/Our clients are **mostly** Italian* **In linea di massima** sono d'accordo *I agree **on the whole***	Used to avoid specifying numbers, often conciliatory/diplomatic.
in generale	Si può dire **in generale** che la nuova politica ha avuto successo ***Generally speaking*** *it can be said that the new policy has been popular*	Used to express a global view, avoiding details.
in genere/ **in generale**	**In genere/In generale** i negozi aprono alle otto ***As a rule*** *shops open at eight*	Used to express norms and habit.

17

Numerals and units of measurement

There are two types of numerals (**i numerali**): cardinal numbers which are used for counting (*one, two, three*, etc.) and ordinal numbers, used to order items in a series (*first, second, third*, etc.).

17.1 CARDINAL NUMBERS

Numbers 0–100

0 zero	**10** dieci	**20** venti	**30** trenta
1 uno	**11** undici	**21** ventuno	**31** trentuno
2 due	**12** dodici	**22** ventidue	**32** trentadue, etc.
3 tre	**13** tredici	**23** ventitré	**40** quaranta
4 quattro	**14** quattordici	**24** ventiquattro	**50** cinquanta
5 cinque	**15** quindici	**25** venticinque	**60** sessanta
6 sei	**16** sedici	**26** ventisei	**70** settanta
7 sette	**17** diciassette	**27** ventisette	**80** ottanta
8 otto	**18** diciotto	**28** ventotto	**90** novanta
9 nove	**19** diciannove	**29** ventinove	**100** cento

FORMS

Quanti piatti ti servono? – **Uno/Un** piatto va bene *How many plates do you want? – One/One plate is fine* Quante tazze ci sono? – **Una** sola/C'è **una** tazza sola *How many cups are there? Only one/There is only one cup*	All cardinal numbers are invariable except for **uno**. This becomes **un** when used before a masculine noun and **una** with a feminine noun.
Quanti studenti hanno firmato? – **Ventotto/Ventotto** studenti; **Cinquantuno/Cinquantun(o)** studenti *How many students have signed? – Twenty-eight/Twenty-eight students; fifty-one/fifty-one students*	When **uno** and **otto** are part of numbers above 20 the final vowel of **venti**, **trenta**, etc. is omitted. The final **-o** of **uno** (but not **otto**) may be omitted when the number is used with a noun.

Mi ha dato **sessantatré** sterline
He gave me sixty-three pounds

When **tre** is part of a number it is
written with an accent.

Numbers from 100

100 cento	**200** duecento	**1.001** milleuno
101 centouno	**201** duecentouno	**1.008** milleotto
102 centodue	**300** trecento	**1.211** milleduecentoundici
108 centootto/cento otto	**400** quattrocento	**2.000** duemila
111 centoundici	**500** cinquecento	**2.001** duemilauno
120 centoventi	**600** seicento	**100.000** centomila
121 centoventuno	**700** settecento	**1.000.000** un milione
128 centoventotto	**800** ottocento	**2.000.000** due milioni
130 centotrenta	**900** novecento	**1.000.000.000** un miliardo
140 centoquaranta	**1.000** mille	**2.000.000.000** due miliardi

FORMS

Cento/duecento euro
A hundred/two hundred euros
Mille/**duemila** euro
A thousand/two thousand euros
Un **milione**/due **milioni di** euro
A million/two million euros
Un **miliardo**/due **miliardi di** euro
But: Un milione (e)duecento euro
Due miliardi(e) cinquecentomila euro

Cento is invariable but **mille, milione**
and **miliardo** change.
Cento and **mille** are <u>not</u> used with a
definite article, unlike English.
Milione and **miliardo** require
the article **un**, and are followed by **di**
unless additional numbers are used.
Un miliardo is a thousand million –
an American billion.

Sono stati uccisi 2.800 prigionieri
2,800 prisoners were killed

In Italian full stops are used where in
English commas are required. The
reverse is true with regard to decimal
points (see Percentages, p. 184).

1 Give the Italian equivalent of these phrases.

(a) *one kilo*
(b) *one slice*
(c) *seventeen books*
(d) *nineteen pages*
(e) *thirty-one students*
(f) *forty-eight hours*

(g) *three chapters*
(h) *twenty-three girls*
(i) *a hundred pounds*
(j) *two hundred pounds*
(k) *a thousand euros*
(l) *ten thousand euros*

(m) *a million yen*
(n) *five million dollars*
(o) *three million five
hundred thousand euros*

USES

Percentages	Solo **il** 35,5 (trentacinque virgola cinque) per cento **della** popolazione ha votato *Only 35.5 (thirty-five point five) per cent of the population has voted* **Il** 53 per cento **degli** intervistati ha/hanno paura del futuro *53 per cent of those interviewed are afraid of the future*	Cardinal numbers are used with the definite article **il/l'** and the preposition **di**. The decimal point is a comma (**virgola**) in Italian. If there is a clear reference to a plural subject a plural verb may sometimes be used.
Price and speed	Costa 30 euro **al/il** chilo *It cost 30 euros per kilo* Viaggiava a 200 chilometri **l'ora/all'**ora *It was going at 200 km per hour*	Cardinal numbers are used with the definite article, which is sometimes combined with **a**.
Years	**Il** duemilaquattro sarà un anno bisestile *Two thousand and four will be a leap year* Sono nato **nel** millenovecentosessantotto *I was born in nineteen sixty-eight*	The year is written as one word and the definite article is required, sometimes combined with **in**.
Dates	È il 29 (ventinove) ottobre, l'8 (otto) settembre, l'11 (undici) marzo *It's the twenty-ninth of October, the eighth of September, the eleventh of March* Arrivo il primo o il due maggio *I'm arriving on May the first or second*	With the exception of the first of the month, cardinal numbers are used, with the definite article **il** – or **l'** before **otto** and **undici**. The first is **il primo** (see ordinal numbers, p. 185).
Phone numbers	Il mio numero è ventuno trentotto zero due *My number is 21 38 02* Il mio fax è quarantacinque sessantasette ottantuno nove *My fax is 45 67 81 9* Il prefisso è zero due zero sette *The prefix is zero two zero seven* Per un'emergenza chiamate **il** centotredici *Call 113 for an emergency*	The main phone number is given in pairs of digits. The prefix or extension tends to be given digit by digit. If the number is three digits it is normally said as one number. Note that numbers tend to be masculine except when telling the time (see below).
Telling the time	È **l'**una *It's one o'clock* Sono **le** cinque *It's five o'clock* La riunione inizia **alle** venti *The meeting begins at eight p.m.*	Cardinal numbers are used with the feminine definite article (which refers to the feminine noun **ora/e** hour/s). The twenty-four-hour clock is very common.

E   2   Insert the correct figure in words each time.

(a) (*Ten per cent of*) automobilisti non sono assicurati.
(b) (*Fifty-one per cent of*) popolazione ha votato.
(c) L'olio costa (*25 euro per*) litro.
(d) (*2002*) è stato un anno brutto per gli agricoltori.
(e) Per chiamare fuori bisogna fare (*9*).
(f) Il mio numero di telefono è (*02 39 24 81*) interno (*750*).

3   Give these times in Italian also, giving the twenty-four-hour clock version where relevant.

(a) *ten o'clock (a.m.)*

(c) *eight o'clock (p.m.)*

(b) *one o'clock (p.m.)*

(d) *eleven o'clock (p.m.)*

17.2 ORDINAL NUMBERS

primo	1st	sesto	6th	undicesimo	11th	sedicesimo	16th
secondo	2nd	settimo	7th	dodicesimo	12th	diciassettesimo	17th
terzo	3rd	ottavo	8th	tredicesimo	13th	diciottesimo	18th
quarto	4th	nono	9th	quattordicesimo	14th	diciannovesimo	19th
quinto	5th	decimo	10th	quindicesimo	15th	ventesimo	20th

FORMS AND USES

I miei hanno festeggiato il **cinquantesimo** anniversario del loro matrimonio *My parents have celebrated their fiftieth wedding anniversary*	Ordinal numbers above **decimo** are formed by adding -**esimo** to a number, minus its final vowel, except if the number ends in -**tré**: **trentesimo** *30th*, **quarantatreesimo** *forty-third*, etc.
I, II, III, …, XXV 1°, 2°, 3°, …, 25° *1st, 2nd, 3rd, …, 25th*	Ordinal numbers can be abbreviated in two ways: with Roman numerals or the symbol °.
Prendi la **terza** (strada) a sinistra *Take the third (road) on the left* **Sono i primi** *They are the first*	Ordinal numbers can be used as adjectives or pronouns, and agree in number and gender with the noun they refer to.
il **Terzo** Mondo *the Third World* il **diciottesimo** secolo *the eighteenth century* **But**: Umberto Secondo (II) *Umberto the Second* Paolo Sesto (VI) *Paul the Sixth*	The numbers go before the noun unless used with the names of monarchs and popes.
Il **primo** secolo a.C. (avanti Cristo) *The first century BC* Il **quinto** secolo d.C. (dopo Cristo) *The fifth century AD*	As in English, ordinal numbers can be used for centuries, but from the thirteenth century onwards cardinal numbers are also used, especially in art and literature. See the following section.

Centuries

There are two ways of expressing centuries. **Il Duecento, il Trecento,** etc. are shortened forms of *twelve hundreds, thirteen hundreds,* etc. They are always spelt with a capital letter, e.g.

Machiavelli è nato nel 1469: è nato nel Quattrocento/nel quindicesimo secolo.

13th c.	Il Duecento	Il tredicesimo secolo
14th c.	Il Trecento	Il quattordicesimo secolo
15th c.	Il Quattrocento	Il quindicesimo secolo
16th c.	Il Cinquecento	Il sedicesimo secolo
17th c.	Il Seicento	Il diciassettesimo secolo
18th c.	Il Settecento	Il diciottesimo secolo
19th c.	L'Ottocento	Il diciannovesimo secolo
20th c.	Il Novecento	Il ventesimo secolo
21st c.	Il Duemila	Il ventunesimo secolo

E

1 Give the Italian for the following.

(a) *the first of October*
(b) *the Second World War*
(c) *the Third World*
(d) *the tenth time*
(e) *the twentieth anniversary*
(f) *Elizabeth II*
(g) *the eighth century AD*

2 Express these centuries in a different way.

(a) il ventesimo secolo
(b) il quattordicesimo secolo
(c) il Quattrocento
(d) l'Ottocento

17.3 OTHER NUMBERS

(a) Fractions

Fractions	un terzo, un quarto, un quinto *a third, a quarter, a fifth* due terzi, tre quarti, due quinti *two-thirds, three-quarters, two-fifths*	Fractions are mostly expressed by using cardinal and ordinal numbers. The denominator (**terzo**, **quarto**, etc.), is plural if the numerator is plural. See also below.
mezzo as an adjective	**mezzo** secolo/chilo *half a century/a kilo* **mezza** bottiglia/porzione *half a bottle/a portion*	(**Un**) **mezzo** is *(one/a) half*. If used as an adjective it agrees with the noun to which it refers and precedes it. Unlike English no article is used.
mezzo as a noun	Ho mangiato una porzione e **mezzo**/e **mezza** *I ate one and a half portions/a portion and a half* Ho preso tre chili e **mezzo** di patate *I got three and a half kilos of potatoes* Sono le due e **mezzo/mezza** *It is half past two*	It comes after the noun it refers to and is usually invariable, although in speech agreement is often used. When used to tell the time it can also agree with **ora**.
Plural fractions	**Sono** rimasti tre quarti della sua fortuna *Three-quarters of his fortune was left* (I)due terzi del territorio **sono** dedicati all'agricoltura *Two-thirds of the territory is given over to agriculture*	With plural fractions note that plural verbs are required and that sometimes the definite article is used as a stylistic choice.

(b) Half and multiples

(la) metà as a noun	**La metà** di otto è quattro *Half of eight is four* **(La) metà degli** invitati erano malati *Half (of) the guests were ill* Ho speso **(la) metà del** mio stipendio *I've spent half (of) my salary*	The noun for *half* is **(la) metà**.
metà as an adjective	Lo vendono a **metà** prezzo *It's (being sold) half-price* Sono a **metà** strada *I'm halfway* Arrivo a **metà** giugno *I'm arriving in mid-June*	When used as an adjective there is never an article with **metà**; **metà** also means *mid*.
Multiples	Ha pagato **il** doppio/triplo **del** prezzo normale *He paid twice/three times the normal price*	Multiples are preceded by **il** and followed by **di**.

(c) Collective numbers

una decina	*about 10/ten or so*		
una dozzina	*about twelve/12 or so; a dozen*	un centinaio	*about a hundred/100 or so*
una quindicina	*about 15/15 or so*	un migliaio	*about a thousand/1000 or so*
una ventina	*about 20/20 or so*		
una trentina etc.	*about 30, etc.*		

Singular collective numbers	C'era/c'erano solo **una decina di** ospiti *There were only about ten guests* È venuto/sono venute **un centinaio di** persone *About a hundred people came* C'è **una dozzina di** uova *There are a dozen/about twelve eggs*	Numbers ending in **-ina** and **-aio** are preceded by the indefinite article and followed by **di**. If they are the subject of the sentence the verb can usually be singular or plural.
Plural collective numbers	Ha scritto **decine di** lettere *He wrote scores of letters* Sono venuti/venute **centinaia di** ospiti *Hundreds of guests came*	**Centinaio** and **migliaio** have plural feminine forms (p. 9). Past participles can agree with these numbers or, more often, with the following noun.

- For expressions involving the Italian equivalents of *both*, *all* and *most*, see Indefinites, pp. 129, 130, 134.

I   Complete these sentences in Italian by substituting the English.

(a) Io risparmio (*a quarter*) del mio stipendio.

(b) Gianni spende (*a third*) della sua paga per l'affitto.

(c) Mio padre ha investito (*three-quarters*) del suo capitale.

(d) (*Two-thirds*) degli impiegati sono stati licenziati.

2   Complete these sentences in Italian choosing between **mezzo/a** and **metà**.

(a) Hanno bevuto (*half a*) bottiglia.

(b) Hanno bevuto una bottiglia (*and a half*).

(c) Hanno bevuto (*half of the*) vino.

(d) Ho letto solo (*half a*) pagina.

(e) Ho letto (*half of the*) libro.

(f) L'ho comprato a (*half*) prezzo.

3   Give the Italian for the following.

(a) *There were about a hundred guests.*

(b) *There were about twenty students.*

(c) *There are about a thousand demonstrators.* (manifestanti)

(d) *There are thousands of demonstrators.*

18

Verbs: the present tense

THE ITALIAN VERB

A verb is a word most typically used to express a physical or mental action or state, such as eating, thinking or being. Its basic form depends on who or what is the subject of the action or state (the person) and when this takes place (the tense). In a dictionary verbs are listed in the infinitive form, e.g. *to hit* **colpire**, *to think* **pensare**, *to be* **essere**. Chapters 18–26 concern aspects of the Italian verb. For any grammatical terms not explained in this and subsequent chapters, see pp. 289–91.

THE PRESENT INDICATIVE TENSE

The present indicative tense (**l'indicativo presente**) is called 'indicative' because it expresses or indicates facts (unlike the present subjunctive tense, p. 245). It has a variety of functions: amongst other things it expresses what is universally the case, what usually happens and what is happening now.

18.1 PRESENT TENSE REGULAR VERBS

Regular forms

	-are portare *to wear, to bring*	**-ere** vendere *to sell*	**-ire** dormire *to sleep*	**-ire** preferire *to prefer*
io	port**o**	vend**o**	dorm**o**	preferis**co**
tu	port**i**	vend**i**	dorm**i**	preferis**ci**
lui lei/Lei	port**a**	vend**e**	dorm**e**	preferis**ce**
noi	port**iamo**	vend**iamo**	dorm**iamo**	prefer**iamo**
voi	port**ate**	vend**ete**	dorm**ite**	prefer**ite**
loro	port**ano**	vend**ono**	dorm**ono**	preferis**cono**

The -ire verbs have two regular patterns. The majority of these take the -isco pattern, so it is worth learning the ones which do not. Below is a list of the main ones.

- Verbs like **dormire** include:

  aprire *to open*, avvertire *to warn, notify*, bollire *to boil*, coprire *to cover*, cucire *to sew*, divertir(si) *to enjoy*, fuggire *to run away*, investire *to invest*, offrire *to offer*, partire *to leave*, pentir(si) *to regret*, scoprire *to discover*, seguire *to follow*, sentire *to feel, to hear*, servire *to serve*, soffrire *to suffer*, vestir(si) *to dress*.

- Verbs which take either ending include:

  applaudire *to applaud*, assorbire *to absorb*, inghiottire *to swallow*, mentire *to lie*, nutrire *to nourish*, starnutire *to sneeze*, tossire *to cough*.

Spelling changes

Ending	tu	noi	Explanation
-ciare -giare	cominci mangi	cominciamo mangiamo	The **i** of the stem is dropped before the **tu** and **noi** endings (which begin with **i**) to avoid forms like comincii, cominciiamo, etc.
-care -gare	giochi paghi	giochiamo paghiamo	An **h** is added to stems ending in **c** or **g** in order to keep the hard sound before **i** endings. (**ci** and **gi** have a soft sound as in *cheese* and *gene*) See p. 279.

Reflexive verbs

Their present tense is exactly like other present tense verbs, but used always with the reflexive pronouns. (See Personal pronouns, p. 81.)

lavarsi *to wash (oneself)*	mettersi *to put on*	divertirsi *to enjoy oneself*	stupirsi *to be amazed*
mi lavo	mi metto	mi diverto	mi stupisco
ti lavi	ti metti	ti diverti	ti stupisci
si lava	si mette	si diverte	si stupisce
ci laviamo	ci mettiamo	ci divertiamo	ci stupiamo
vi lavate	vi mettete	vi divertite	vi stupite
si lavano	si mettono	si divertono	si stupiscono

E **I** Choose which of the forms of the verbs underlined in each sentence is correct.

abitare • leggere • scrivere • studiare • dormire

(a) Dove <u>abitono/abitano</u> i tuoi?
(b) Che cosa <u>leggono/leggano</u> i vostri figli?
(c) Che cosa <u>scrivete/scrivate</u> in classe?
(d) Dove <u>studiete/studiate</u> a Roma?
(e) Giacomo <u>dorma/dorme</u> fuori stasera?
(f) Elena <u>mangia/mangie</u> fuori domani?

2 The verbs used in the sentences below are all **-ire** verbs, but which pattern do they follow, the **-isco** pattern or the **-o** pattern?

(a) Offrono loro da bere.
(b) Preferite il gelato?
(c) Partiamo domani.
(d) Soffrono molto il freddo.
(e) Seguiamo un corso di francese.
(f) Quand'è che finite il lavoro?
(g) Capite quando parlo?
(h) Ci vestiamo sempre in fretta.

3 Spell it right. Give the correct form of the verbs in brackets.

(a) Tu (mangiare) troppo.
(b) Tu (pagare) troppo di affitto.
(c) Perché non (cominciare – noi) subito?
(d) Perché non (giocare – noi) a bridge?

4 Complete the sentences using the appropriate present tense form of the reflexive verbs given in brackets.

(a) Rita e Anna (annoiarsi) a casa nostra.
(b) Renato e Luca (perdersi) sempre a Londra!
(c) Giovanna e Paola (divertirsi) da me.
(d) Aldo (stupirsi) della loro stupidità!

18.2 IRREGULAR VERBS

Irregular present tense forms are important, as other verb forms are based on them (e.g. the imperative and the present subjunctive). The main present tense irregularities can be grouped under the following categories:

A. Common irregular verbs, e.g. **avere, essere, dare, stare.**
B. Contracted infinitive verbs, e.g. **bere, dire, fare, trarre, porre, condurre.**
C. Modal verbs: **dovere, potere, volere, sapere.**
D. Other patterns, which fall mainly into four categories:
  • Verbs with -**g** in 1st person sing. and 3rd person pl., e.g. **rimanere** (rimango), **scegliere** (scelgo), **togliere** (tolgo), **spegnere** (spengo), **salire** (salgo), **valere** (valgo).
  • Verbs with -**g** in 1st person sing. and 3rd person pl. plus a vowel change in the 2nd and 3rd persons sing., e.g. **tenere** (tengo, tieni/e), **venire** (vengo, vieni/e), plus compounds of these, e.g. **contenere, trattenersi** *to stay*, **intervenire.**
  • Verbs with vowel changes in the stem, e.g. **sedere** (siedo), **parere** (paio), **apparire** (appaio), **morire** (muoio), **udire.**
  • Verbs with minor spelling changes, e.g. **piacere** (piaccio).

Below is the present tense of the first three categories. The full present tenses of the other verbs are in Appendix 2, pp. 284–8.

A. Common irregular present tense verbs

Infinitive	Present tense	Similar verbs
avere *to have*	ho hai ha abbiamo avete hanno	
essere *to be*	sono sei è siamo siete sono	
andare *to go*	vado vai va andiamo andate vanno	
uscire *to go out*	esco esci esce usciamo uscite escono	riuscire *to manage, succeed*
dare *to give*	do dai dà diamo date danno	ridare *to give back*
stare *to be, to stay*	sto stai sta stiamo state stanno	sottostare *to underlie*

B. Contracted infinitive verbs

A few verbs have infinitives known as 'contracted' because they are nearly all shortened versions of longer Latin verbs from which they are derived. To form many of the tenses of these verbs it is necessary to learn their expanded stem. The main ones are: bere → **bev-**; dire → **dic-**; fare → **fac-**. Many other contracted infinitive verbs end in **-arre, -orre, -urre** and their stems are as follows: trarre → **tra-**; porre → **pon-**; condurre → **conduc-**.

Infinitive	Present tense	Similar verbs
bere *to drink*	bevo bevi beve beviamo bevete bevono	
dire *to tell, to say*	dico dici dice diciamo dite dicono	contraddire *to contradict*, disdire *to cancel*
fare *to do, to make*	faccio fai fa facciamo fate fanno	rifare *to redo*, stupefare *to amaze*
condurre *to lead*	conduco conduci conduce conduciamo conducete conducono	tradurre *to translate*, produrre *to produce*
porre *to place*	pongo poni pone poniamo ponete pongono	proporre *to propose*, supporre *to suppose*
trarre *to draw, pull*	traggo trai trae traiamo traete traggono	attrarre *to attract*, distrarre *to distract, entertain*

C. Modal verbs

Modal verbs are nearly always used before another infinitive verb to modify its meaning by indicating the attitude of the writer/speaker to the action.

dovere *to have to*	devo/debbo devi deve dobbiamo dovete devono/debbono
potere *to be able to*	posso puoi può possiamo potete possono
sapere *to know how to*	so sai sa sappiamo sapete sanno
volere *to want to*	voglio vuoi vuole vogliamo volete vogliono

- The English equivalents of these verbs often vary according to the tense in which they are used. See pp. 217, 227.

- **Sapere** can be used both as a normal verb without a dependent infinitive (see p. 260) and as a modal verb:

  Sanno scrivere *They know how to write*

  Mi sa dire quando arrivano? *Can you tell me when they are arriving?*

1 Insert the correct forms of the present tense for both question and answer.

(a) Giulio, ... tempo di prendere un caffè? – Mi dispiace, non ... tempo. (avere)

(b) Sandra, dove ... di casa? – ... in via Carducci, numero 12. (stare)

(c) Lucia, che ... domani? – Domani ... una lunga passeggiata in campagna. (fare)

(d) Lino, mi ... una mano? – No, oggi non ti ... una mano. (dare)

(e) Antonella, dove ... stasera? – Stasera ... da Alessandro. (andare)

2 Rewrite the sentences below changing the form of the verb as shown. Give the infinitive of each verb.

(a) Esco spesso la sera. (io → noi)

(b) Vado raramente all'estero. (io → noi)

(c) Cosa propone? (lui/lei → loro)

(d) Ma cosa mi dici? (tu → voi)

(e) Traduciamo un articolo. (noi → io)

(f) Dov'è? (lui/lei → loro)

(g) Siamo in anticipo. (noi → io)

3 Insert the correct present tense form of these modal verbs.

(a) Scusa, (volere – io) partire adesso, non (potere – io) aspettare.

(b) (Potere – tu) venire subito o (dovere – tu) chiedere il permesso?

(c) Non (sapere – noi) ancora se (dovere – noi) lavorare domani.

(d) Se non (volere – voi) aspettare, (potere – voi) mangiare adesso.

4 Using the appendix on pp. 286–8 if necessary, complete the sentences with the correct present tense form of the verb given.

(a) Se tu ... a casa, ... anch'io. (rimanere)

(b) Se lui ... a Milano ... anche loro. (rimanere).

(c) Tu ... sempre i vini migliori, mentre io ... quelli peggiori! (scegliere)

(d) Io ... con mia sorella, tu con chi ...? (venire)

(e) Io ... qui per dieci giorni, ma loro ... per almeno un mese. (trattenersi)

(f) Io ... qua, voi dove ...? (sedersi)

USES OF THE PRESENT

Habitual actions or states	**Vado** spesso in Italia *I often go to Italy* Che lavoro **fai**? *What job do you do?* Mi **piace** leggere *I like reading*	This refers to things that happen regularly. The use is the same as in English.
General truths	Il latte **fa** bene *Milk is good for you* Londra **è** la capitale della Gran Bretagna *London is the capital of Great Britain*	This use is the same as in English.
What is going on now	Cosa **fai**? *What are you doing?* **Leggo** il giornale *I'm reading the paper*	In Italian the present tense is also used to express the English present continuous. See pp. 195–7.

Do/does and can

Note the following differences from Italian.

Do/does	Il pesce lo **mangio**, ma la carne no *I do eat fish but I don't eat meat* **Suoni** la chitarra? *Do you play the guitar?*	There is no Italian equivalent to *do/does*. The present tense is usually enough.
Can: **potere** **sapere** **riuscire a**	Posso venire? *Can I come?* (permission) Posso/riesco a vedere la torre solo se mi metto sul balcone *I can see the tower only if I go onto the balcony* (ability) So nuotare *I can swim* (ability) **But**: Lo **vedi**? – Sì, lo **vedo** benissimo *Can you see him? – Yes, I can see him really well*	When *can* expresses permission and ability it may correspond to the present of **potere, sapere** and **riuscire**. **But**: With verbs of perception (e.g. *to see, to hear*), there is no Italian equivalent of *can* unless permission or ability are involved.

E 5 Give the Italian equivalent of the following, using each of the verbs once.

> alzarsi ● bere ● dire ● essere ● fare colazione ● pranzare ● riuscire a ● sentire

(a) *I get up early and have breakfast at seven.*
(b) *Great Britain is an island and Italy is a peninsula.* (isola, penisola)
(c) *What is he saying? I can't hear him.*
(d) *Do you (voi) drink coffee in the morning?*
(e) *I can't open the window.*
(f) *Are they still having lunch?* (still ancora)

Present instead of future or past

The Italian present tense is very often used to refer to the immediate future and can also refer to the past.

Immediate or definite future	Cosa fate domani? – Andiamo a Pisa *What are you doing tomorrow? – We're going to Pisa* Ti richiamo fra poco *I'll call you back soon*	The present is used to express definite future plans or intentions.
To be about to: **stare per**	**Sta per** piovere *It's about to rain* Non mi posso trattenere, **sto per** andare dal medico *I can't stop, I'm about to go to the doctor's*	When used in the present tense, **stare per** expresses what is about to happen.
How long for and since: **da**	**Da** quanto tempo **sei** qui? – **Sono** qui da un mese *How long have you been here? – I have been here for a month* Aspettate **da** molto tempo? – **Aspettiamo dalle** due *Have you been waiting long? – We have been waiting since two*	**Da** + present tense is used when the verb refers to an action which has not been completed or interrupted. This corresponds to the English perfect tense + *for/since*.

How long for and since: **da** (contd)	**Da** quand'**è che** sei qui? *Since when have you been here?* **È da** molto **che** sei qui? *Have you been here long?* **È** un'ora **che** aspetto *I have been waiting for an hour* **È dal** 1999 **che** abitano a Torino *They have been living in Turin since 1999*	**Essere** + **che** + present tense is more colloquial.
No present tense: **da** + perfect tense	Dal 1945 ci **sono state** varie guerre in Europa *Since 1945 there have been several wars in Europe* Da quando ci **siamo incontrati** gli ho scritto due volte *I have written to him twice since we met*	**Da** + the perfect (passato prossimo) tense is used to express <u>completed</u> past actions.
	Ho portato gli occhiali **per** due anni *I wore glasses for two years (and no longer do)*	The present is not used with **per** *for*, because it expresses actions that are over and done with.
Historic present	**Squilla** il telefono. **Rispondo** e **sento** una voce strana *The phone rings. I answer and hear this strange voice …* Giuseppe Verdi **nasce** nel 1901, a Busseto … *Verdi was born in 1901, in Busseto*	This is often used in speech to make a story more dramatic. In writing it is much used in historical narrative or biography.

6   Give the Italian equivalent of the following, using each of the verbs once.

> andare • chiamare • partire • sentirsi • stare per

(a) *When are you (voi) leaving for Paris?*   (d) *We'll be in touch soon.*
(b) *Tomorrow I'm going to the cinema.*   (e) *We are about to leave.*
(c) *I'll call you (tu) next week.*

7   How long for? Answer the following questions in Italian.

(a) Da quanto tempo impari l'italiano? – *I have been learning Italian for two years.*
(b) Da quand'è che vi conoscete? – *We have known each other for three months.*
(c) È da molto che sei in Italia? – *I have been in Italy since September.*
(d) Lo aspetti da molto tempo? – *I have been waiting for him since Saturday.*

8   Choose the appropriate tense in the sentences below and provide the English equivalent.

(a) <u>Porto/ho portato</u> gli occhiali da due anni.
(b) <u>Porto/ho portato</u> gli occhiali per due anni.
(c) Dal 2000 <u>cambio/ho cambiato</u> casa quattro volte.
(d) Dal 2000 <u>abito/ho abitato</u> nello stesso posto.
(e) Da quando ci conosciamo <u>scrive/ha scritto</u> ogni settimana a sua madre.
(f) Da quando ci conosciamo <u>scrive/ha scritto</u> cinque libri.

18.3 THE PRESENT CONTINUOUS

The English present continuous focuses on an activity in the process of taking place at the time of speaking. In Italian this can be expressed with the normal present tense or with the present tense of the verb **stare**, followed by the gerund of the verb required. The gerund only has two endings -**ando** and -**endo**.

Regular forms

Infinitive	Stare + gerund	
	sto	
parlare	stai	parl**ando**
leggere	sta	legg**endo**
finire	stiamo	fin**endo**
partire	state	part**endo**
	stanno	

Irregular forms

Verbs with contracted infinitives form the gerund by expanding their stem and adding -**endo**.

Infinitive	Stare + gerund	
bere	sto	**bev**endo
dire	stai	**dic**endo
fare	sta	**fac**endo
trarre	stiamo	**tra**endo
proporre	state	**propon**endo
produrre	stanno	**produc**endo

USES OF THE PRESENT CONTINUOUS

Sto + gerund has a far more restricted use than the English present continuous.

Non può venire al telefono, **sta preparando** un rapporto *He can't come to the telephone, he's preparing a report* In questo momento Nina si **sta lavando** *Right now Nina is washing* (or, **si lava**) Oggi Nina **porta** una minigonna *Today Nina is wearing a mini skirt* (the normal present only is possible)	**Sto** + gerund is used when emphasising an action taking place right now. It is not essential and can nearly always be replaced by the normal present. Note that **sto** + gerund is not used to express a state of affairs, i.e. it must emphasise an action in progress.
Si **stanno divertendo** *They are enjoying themselves*	Personal pronouns normally precede **stare** and are not attached to the gerund.

1 In which of the following sentences is it impossible to use 'stare + gerund'?

(a) *What are you doing today?*

(c) *Who are you talking to?*

(b) *What are you doing in Rome?*

(d) *Where are you going tomorrow?*

2 Answer the questions using an appropriate present tense form of the verbs given.

(a) Volete venire a cena con noi? – No, mi dispiace, in questo momento (studiare).

(b) Posso parlarti un attimo? – No, mi dispiace, (leggere) un rapporto.

(c) Vieni al cinema con me? – Adesso non posso, (fare) i compiti.

(d) I bambini, cosa (fare)? – (divertirsi) in giardino.

19

The future

The future indicative tenses are used to express what will happen after the time of speaking. There are two forms: the simple future (**il futuro semplice**) corresponds to the English *will*, e.g. **Will** *you leave?* The future perfect (**il futuro anteriore**) corresponds to *will have*, e.g. **Will** *you* **have** *left?*

19.1 THE SIMPLE FUTURE

Regular forms

There are only two regular future tense forms: -**are** verbs follow the same form as -**ere** verbs, and both types of -**ire** verbs follow the other form.

-**are** and -**ere**		-**ire**	
port**are**	prend**ere**	fin**ire**	dorm**ire**
port**erò**	prend**erò**	fin**irò**	dorm**irò**
pot**erai**	prend**erai**	fin**irai**	dorm**irai**
port**erà**	prend**erà**	fin**irà**	dorm**irà**
port**eremo**	prend**eremo**	fin**iremo**	dorm**iremo**
port**erete**	prend**erete**	fin**irete**	dorm**irete**
port**eranno**	prend**eranno**	fin**iranno**	dorm**iranno**

Spelling changes

Ending	Future forms	Explanation
-**ciare** -**giare**	las**c**erò, las**c**erai, las**c**erà, etc. man**g**erò, man**g**erai, man**g**erà, etc.	The **i** of the stem is omitted in front of **e**, as it is not needed to keep the soft sound of the infinitive.
-**care** -**gare**	cer**ch**erò, cer**ch**erai, cer**ch**erà, etc. pa**gh**erò, pa**gh**erai, pa**gh**erà, etc.	An **h** is added to verb stems ending in **c** and **g** in order to keep the hard sound of the infinitive.

- See p. 279 for notes on spelling.

1 Choose the correct form of the verbs given.

    (a) Fra poco <u>scriverò/scrivirò</u> quella lettera. (scrivere)

    (b) Domani Enrico <u>dormerà/dormirà</u> da me. (dormire)

    (c) <u>Tornaranno/torneranno/tornerano</u> domani con i loro amici. (tornare)

2 Provide the correct future form of the verbs given.

    (a) Se vuoi (io – giocare) con te stasera.

    (b) Se volete vi (noi – spiegare) il gioco.

    (c) Quand'è che (loro – cominciare) a studiare?

    (d) Quand'è che (tu – festeggiare) il tuo successo?

Irregular forms

essere	sarò sarai sarà saremo sarete saranno	**Essere** has an irregular stem.
andare fare potere	andrò andrai andrà andremo andrete andranno farò farai farà faremo farete faranno potrò potrai potrà potremo potrete potranno	Many verbs omit the **e** or **i** of the regular future ending.

- Similar verbs are:

    avere, cadere, dare, dire, dovere, sapere, stare, udire, vedere, vivere.

bere tenere venire trarre porre condurre	berrò berrai berrà berremo berrete berranno terrò terrai terrà terremo terrete terranno verrò verrai verrà verremo verrete verranno trarrò trarrai trarrà trarremo trarrete trarranno porrò porrai porrà porremo porrete porranno condurrò condurrai condurrà condurremo condurrete condurranno	Other verbs, including all those with **-arre, -orre** and **-urre** infinitives, omit the vowel and double the **r**.

- Similar verbs include:

    ottenere (otterrò), parere (parrò), proporre (proporrò), ridurre (ridurrò),
    rimanere (rimarrò), tradurre (tradurrò), valere (varrò), volere (vorrò).

3 Complete the sentences using the correct future tense form of the verb given.

    (a) Fra poco (io – andare) a casa e (fare) il bucato.

    (b) Domani (tu – dovere) stare a casa o (potere) uscire?

    (c) I nostri figli (rimanere) a Rimini e ci (vedere) dopo le vacanze.

    (d) La settimana prossima (io – avere) moltissimo da fare, ma (io – essere) disponibile
        venerdì.

    (e) Martedì vi (noi – dire) se (noi – venire) o no.

    (f) (Tu – tradurre) l'articolo o lo (dare) a qualcun altro?

USES OF THE FUTURE

In Italian the future tense is not always used when referring to future events. (The present is usually preferred for definite future plans and intentions: see p. 194.) Nevertheless the future is likely to be used for the following.

Definite future events/facts	Oggi c'è la partita, non **sarà** mica facile parcheggiare *The match is on today, it won't be at all easy to park* Mi dispiace, **arriverò/sarò** in ritardo *I'm sorry, I'm going to be late*	The future must be used to say what will happen next.
Firm beliefs and predictions	Sono convinto che lui **avrà** successo *I am convinced he will be successful* **Verrà** senz'altro *He will definitely come*	
On-the-spot decisions	Luisa non c'è – La **chiamerò** più tardi, allora *Luisa's not in – I'll call her later then* Oggi c'è sciopero – **Rimarrò** a casa allora *There's a strike today – I'll stay at home then*	
Speculation and probability	Quanti anni **avrà**? *How old could/(will) he be/I wonder how old he is?* **Avrà** settant'anni *He must be/will be/is probably seventy* Dove **saranno**? *Where can/could they be?* **Saranno** in centro *They must be/I expect they are in town*	This is one of the most common uses of the future. Note that there is a range of English equivalents. See also the Future perfect, p. 202.
Concession	**Avranno** ragione, ma sono proprio antipatici *They may be right, but they are really unpleasant* **Sarà** un collega ma non mi fido di lui *He may be a colleague but I don't trust him*	Like the above, this does not actually refer to the future. It is widely used to express scepticism. See also Future perfect, p. 202.
Orders	**Farai** come ti ho detto *You'll do as I say* **Ti scuserai** con lui *You will apologise to him*	Like English, the future can be used as a command.

E **4** Say what is bound to happen next, using the correct future tense forms of the verbs given.

(a) Guarda che nuvoloni! (Piovere) di sicuro.
(b) Marco non ha studiato. (Essere) sicuramente bocciato.
(c) Abbiamo perso il treno. Purtroppo (arrivare) in ritardo.

5 Getting better all the time? When it comes to politics you know better. Make your predictions.

(a) Le tasse (aumentare) e gli stipendi (restare) fermi.
(b) Gli automobilisti (affollare) le strade e (inquinare) l'ambiente.
(c) Per gli anziani la vita (diventare) più dura. (Lavorare) di più e alla fine (ottenere) una pensione più piccola di prima.

6 Make some on-the-spot decisions. Give the Italian equivalent of the English.

(a) Lo sai che Marina è all'ospedale? – *I'll go and see her then.* (andare a trovare)
(b) Hanno chiuso l'autostrada. – *We'll take the statale (road) then.* (prendere la statale)
(c) È il compleanno di Giacomo. – *I'll send him a card then.* (mandare una cartolina di auguri)

7 Say what you're planning to do. Give the Italian equivalent of the English. Take care to use the appropriate tense.

(a) *Tomorrow I'm going to Turin.*
(b) *We're taking the train at five o'clock.*
(c) *I'm sending my mother some flowers.*

8 You're looking at photos of relatives you haven't seen for ages. Give the Italian equivalent of the English, using a future tense each time.

(a) *He must be at least sixty.* (almeno)   (c) *I expect he's married.*
(b) *I wonder what job she does?*   (d) *She may be rich, but she's really stupid!*

Conditions and time clauses

The future after **se**	Se **avrò/ho** tempo, **passerò** a prenderti *If I have time I'll come by and pick you up* Se **bombardano** la città, **uccideranno** molta gente *If they bomb the city they will kill lots of people* **Note**: Se rimani qui, fai tardi *If you stay here, you'll be late*	When the main clause verb is future (e.g. **passerò**), the future or present is used after **se**. The future makes the action less definite. Note that the present in *both* clauses is colloquial and expresses certainty.
The future after connectives of time	Appena lo **saprò** te lo dirò *As soon as I (will) know, I will tell you* Quando **sarò** grande farò il medico *When I am (will be) grown up I'll be a doctor* Fino a quando **rimarrà** qui, non andremo d'accordo! *As long as he stays (will stay) here, we will not get on!* **Note**: Appena lo **sai**, me lo **dici**? *As soon as you know, will you tell me?*	In standard Italian the future is preferred after **appena, dopo che, fino a quando/finché** and **quando** when there is a future in the main clause. Colloquially the present tense is common.

E

9 Here are some definite promises and predictions you have made. Express them in Italian using **tu**.

(a) *If you give me a hand, I'll buy you an ice cream.*
(b) *If you lend me the car, I'll pay for the petrol.*
(c) *If you don't hurry up, we'll be late.* (sbrigarsi, fare tardi)

10 What will happen if ? Give the Italian equivalent of the English.

(a) Se non aumentano gli stipendi quest'anno ... *teachers will go on strike.* (fare sciopero)
(b) Se i rifornimenti non arrivano presto ... *people will starve.* (morire di fame)
(c) Se non riusciranno a salvare le foreste equatoriali ... *the Earth's climate will change.*

11 Using **finché/fino a quando**, **appena** and **quando**, give the Italian equivalent of the following.

(a) *I'll stay as long as he stays.*
(b) *I'll stay until he arrives.*
(c) *I'll phone you as soon as he writes.*
(d) *When they pay me I'll buy you a dress.*

19.2 THE FUTURE PERFECT

Level 2

The future perfect (**il futuro anteriore**) is made up of the future of the auxiliary **avere** or **essere** plus the past participle of the verb. (See p. 206 for which auxiliary to use.)

pagare		tornare	
avrò	pagato	sarò	tornato/a
avrai	pagato	sarai	tornato/a
avrà	pagato	sarà	tornato/a
avremo	pagato	saremo	tornati/e
avrete	pagato	sarete	tornati/e
avranno	pagato	saranno	tornati/e

Level 2

USES OF THE FUTURE PERFECT

What will have happened	Domani a quest'ora **avrò dato** l'esame *By this time tomorrow I will have sat the exam* Le due non ci conviene, **saremo** già **partiti** *Two o'clock is no good for us, we will already have left*	As in English, the future perfect is used in Italian to say what will have taken place by a certain time.
Speculation and supposition	Dove **saranno andati/e**? *Where can/could they have gone?* **Saranno** già **partiti** *They must have/will have already left* Ti **sarà costato** un occhio dalla testa *It must have/I bet it cost you an arm and a leg*	This is one of the most common uses of the future perfect (and the simple future, see p. 200), although it does not strictly refer to the future.
Concession	**Avrà cambiato** idea, ma mi sembra strano *He may have changed his mind but I think it's odd*	See also the Simple future, p. 200.

E

1 Complete the sentences in Italian to say what will have happened.

(a) Fra una settimana ... *you will have forgotten him.*
(b) Quando leggerà questa lettera ... *I will already have left.*
(c) A quest'ora domani ... *Giovanni will have returned/will be back.*

2 A friend hasn't turned up. What could have happened? Give the Italian equivalent of the following.

(a) *Could he have gone the wrong way?* (sbagliare strada)
(b) *He must have had an accident.*
(c) *He may have lost our address.*

Conditions and time clauses

In standard Italian, unlike English, the future perfect may be used with conditions and time expressions.

The future perfect after **se**	Se **avremo finito**, ti **chiameremo** alle quattro *If we have finished we'll call you at four*	A simple future in the main clause (**ti chiameremo …**) is used with the future perfect in a **se** clause. For alternatives to the future perfect, see below.
The future perfect after connectives of time	Non appena **avrò finito**, ti **verrò** a trovare *As soon as I (will) have finished I will come and see you* Quando **sarò arrivato**, ti **chiamerò** *When I (will) arrive I'll call you* **Passerò** a trovarvi una volta che/dopo che **avrò cenato** *I'll call round and visit you once/after I (will) have had supper*	A simple future in the main clause is used with the future perfect after **(non) appena, dopo che, fino a quando/ finché, quando, una volta che**. For colloquial Italian alternatives, see below.
With imperatives	Appena **avrai pagato**, fammelo sapere *Let me know when you (will) have paid*	The future perfect is often replaced by the **passato prossimo** in everyday speech.

Alternatives to the future perfect

In colloquial Italian the future perfect after **se** and connectives of time is often replaced by other tenses.

Simple future or present	Non appena **finirò/ finisco** ti verrò/vengo a trovare *As soon as I finish I'll come and see you* Se **finiremo/finiamo** ti chiameremo alle quattro *If we finish we'll call you at four*	After **se, (non) appena, fino a quando/finché, quando** the future or present are common in speech.
Passato prossimo	Se **abbiamo finito** ti chiamiamo *If we've finished we'll call you* Non appena **ho finito** ti passo a prendere *As soon as I've finished I'll come by and pick you up*	The passato prossimo may be used after **se, (non) appena, quando, dopo che, una volta che**.
dopo + past infinitive	Potrò/Posso venire a trovarvi dopo **aver visto** mia figlia *I can come and see you after I have seen my daughter*	If the subjects in both clauses are the same, **dopo** can be followed by a past infinitive. See pp. 179, 240.

E

3 Give the standard Italian equivalent of the English, using the future perfect.

(a) Potrò passare a prenderti alle sette ... *if I have finished my homework.*

(b) Ti restituirò il libro ... *when I have read it.*

(c) Ti inviterò da me ... *once I have sorted out the flat.* (sistemare)

(d) Ti verrò a trovare ... *after I have done the shopping.*

4 Now make the statements above more colloquial and definite. Do not use the future perfect.

(a) Passo a prenderti ...

(b) Ti restituisco il libro ...

(c) Ti invito da me ...

(d) Ti vengo a trovare ...

20

The past tenses

Past tenses express states or actions and events related to the past. There are four main Italian indicative past tenses: the perfect (**il passato prossimo**), imperfect (**l' imperfetto**), pluperfect (**il trapassato prossimo**) and simple past (**il passato remoto**).

20.1 THE *PASSATO PROSSIMO*

The perfect tense in Italian is called the **passato prossimo** ('near past') and expresses completed past actions which are sometimes related to the present. It can correspond to two main forms of the English past tense: **ci sono andato** = *I have gone* and *I went*. The **passato prossimo** is composed of the present tense of an auxiliary verb – **avere** or **essere** – plus the past participle of the verb required.

Regular past participles

The regular past participles end in: -**ato** (-are verbs), -**uto** (-ere verbs) and -**ito** (-ire verbs).

Verbs with *avere*				**Verbs with *essere***			
	parl**are** *to talk*	ricev**ere** *to receive*	fin**ire** *to finish*		and**are** *to go*	cad**ere** *to fall*	usc**ire** *to go out*
ho				**sono**	andato/a	caduto/a	uscito/a
hai				**sei**	andato/a	caduto/a	uscito/a
ha	parlato	ricevuto	finito	**è**	andato/a	caduto/a	uscito/a
abbiamo				**siamo**	andati/e	caduti/e	usciti/e
avete				**siete**	andati/e	caduti/e	usciti/e
hanno				**sono**	andati/e	caduti/e	usciti/e

- The past participles of verbs taking **essere** change to agree with the subject. (See also reflexive verbs, pp. 206, 208.)

- The verb **avere** itself has a regular past participle (**avuto**) and takes the auxiliary **avere: ho avuto**, etc. **Essere** is irregular. (See p. 207.)

Auxiliaries (1)

Many verbs use **avere** as the auxiliary but there are some important ones which take **essere**. The choice of auxiliary often depends on whether a verb is transitive or intransitive. A transitive verb is a verb which can be used with a direct object, e.g. **comprare** or **vendere**, while an intransitive verb cannot be used with a direct object, e.g. **andare** or **partire**.

- Transitive verbs usually take **avere**. Intransitive verbs usually take **essere**. But some intransitive verbs such as **camminare, dormire, parlare** or **viaggiare** take **avere**.
- Reflexive verbs always take **essere** whether or not they are used with a direct object. There is a list of verbs taking **essere** in Appendix 2, p. 281.
- Some verbs can take either **avere** or **essere**, depending on the context or function of the verb. See Auxiliaries (2), pp. 209–10 and Appendix 2, p. 281.

Reflexive verbs

Reflexive verbs all take **essere** and the past participles are regularly formed. Note that the participles agree with the subject.

	al**zarsi** *to get up*	se**dersi** *to sit down*	diver**tirsi** *to enjoy onself*
mi sono	alzato/a	seduto/a	divertito/a
ti sei	alzato/a	seduto/a	divertito/a
si è	alzato/a	seduto/a	divertito/a
ci siamo	alzati/e	seduti/e	divertiti/e
vi siete	alzati/e	seduti/e	divertiti/e
si sono	alzati/e	seduti/e	divertiti/e

Irregular past participles

Irregularities in the **passato prossimo** concern the form of the past participle. Many common -**ere** verbs have an irregular past participle, as do all contracted infinitive verbs. Only a few -**are** and -**ire** verbs are irregular. Over the page are some common patterns of irregular past participles, together with an example of each. There is a more comprehensive list in Table 1 of Appendix 2 on pp. 282–3.

-asto -esto -isto -osto	rimanere chiedere vedere rispondere	**rimasto** **chiesto** **visto** **risposto**	-anto -ento -into -unto	piangere spegnere vincere giungere	**pianto** **spento** **vinto** **giunto**
-arso -erso -orso	apparire perdere correre	**apparso** **perso** **corso**	-elto -olto	scegliere togliere	**scelto** **tolto**
-atto -etto -itto -otto -utto	fare dire scrivere rompere distruggere	**fatto** **detto** **scritto** **rotto** **distrutto**	-erto -orto	aprire morire	**aperto** **morto**
-aso -eso -iso -oso -uso	persuadere prendere decidere esplodere chiudere	**persuaso** **preso** **deciso** **esploso** **chiuso**	-ato -ito -uto	essere stare esistere bere venire vivere	**stato** **stato** **esistito** **bevuto** **venuto** **vissuto**
-esso -osso -usso	mettere muovere discutere	**messo** **mosso** **discusso**	-iuto	piacere conoscere	**piaciuto** **conosciuto**

1   Complete the questions below using the correct past participle of the verbs given.

(a) Hai … una pizza? (ordinare)
(b) Avete … la lettera? (ricevere)
(c) Hai … il problema? (capire)
(d) Siete … in centro? (andare)
(e) È … per strada? (cadere)
(f) Sei … ieri? (partire)

2   Complete the sentences choosing the correct auxiliary and form of the past participle.

(a) (*I have made*) un errore madornale. (fare)
(b) (*He answered*) subito. (rispondere)
(c) Luca, (*have you opened*) la finestra? (aprire)
(d) Ieri sera (*I stayed*) da Ornella. (stare)
(e) Oggi (*I stayed*) a casa. (rimanere)
(f) L'anno scorso (*they came*) da noi. (venire)

3   Complete the sentences using the correct auxiliary and past participle of the verbs given.

(a) Mi … alle sette. (alzarsi)
(b) Mi … male in autobus. (sentirsi)
(c) Mi … accanto a Rita. (sedersi)
(d) Mi … il cappotto. (mettersi)
(e) Mi … le scarpe in casa. (togliersi)

USES OF THE *PASSATO PROSSIMO*

As mentioned on p. 205 the **passato prossimo** is equivalent to two English tenses. These depend on the context.

Expressing completed actions in the past	Stamattina **ha preso** il treno per Napoli *This morning he took the train for Naples* Ieri mi **ha telefonato** due volte *Yesterday he phoned me twice* Trent'anni fa **sono andato** a Cagliari *Thirty years ago I went to Cagliari*	Despite its name, the **passato prossimo** is the normal tense used for events in the distant past as well as for recent actions.

Expressing an ongoing situation or action	**Non ho mai preso** sonniferi *I have never taken sleeping tablets* Oggi **mi ha già telefonato** dieci volte *He has already phoned me ten times today* Siamo **sempre andati** in Sicilia per Natale *We have always gone to Sicily for Easter*	The **passato prossimo** is often used with words such as **sempre**, **già** or **mai** to express an action that is still being repeated now. Note that in this case the English equivalent is *have/has* …

E 4 Give the English equivalent of the following.

(a) Conosco bene la Sardegna. Ci sono stato molte volte. Mi è sempre piaciuta.

(b) L'anno scorso sono stato in Sardegna. Mi è piaciuta moltissimo.

(c) Hai preso l'aereo o hai viaggiato in treno? – Ho preso la macchina, è più comodo.

(d) Giulia, ho preso la macchina. Te la riporto stasera.

Past participle agreements

Agreements with the subject: verbs taking **essere**	**Ada** dov'è andat**a**? *Where has Ada gone?/Where did Ada go?* **Le ragazze** si sono divertit**e** *The girls enjoyed themselves* **Modena** mi è molto piaciut**a** *I liked Modena a lot (Modena is pleasing to me)*	When **essere** is used, the past participle agrees with the subject. Note that with **piacere** it agrees with the object/person liked, as it is the grammatical subject. See also pp. 261, 263.
Agreements with object pronouns: verbs taking **avere** and reflexive verbs	Ieri ho vist**o** **Ada** (noun direct object, no agreement) **L**'ho vist**a** (pronoun direct object) *I saw Ada yesterday. I saw her* **Ada** si è lavat**a** le mani (agreement with the subject of a reflexive verb) Se **le** è lavat**e** (agreement with pronoun direct object of reflexive verb) *Ada washed her hands. She washed them* **But**: Ho parlato con Ada. **Le** ho parlato (**le** is an indirect object pronoun) *I spoke to Ada. I spoke to her*	Past participles may agree with the pronoun direct objects of verbs taking **avere** and of reflexive verbs. Note that no agreement is made with indirect object pronouns. See also p. 101.

E 5 Your day. You're Giorgio's wife. Say what you did yesterday, using the verbs given and making any necessary participle agreements.

Ieri io e mio marito Giorgio (1 alzarsi) presto e (2 andare) tutti e due a lavorare. Io (3 arrivare) in ufficio alle otto e mezzo e (4 lavorare) tutta la giornata. Io (5 annoiarsi) da morire! (6 tornare) a casa verso le sei e dopo cena io e Giorgio (7 fare) una lunga passeggiata. (8 camminare) per un'ora, dopodiché (9 tornare) a casa e (10 vedere) un bel film che ci (11 piacere) molto. Devo dire che noi (12 dormire) bene!

6 Complete the sentences making participle agreements where necessary.

    (a) Hanno scritt … la lettera? L'hanno scritt …?
    (b) Avete lett … i giornali? Li avete lett …?
    (c) Hai parlat … con Franca? – Non, non le ho parlat ….
    (d) Angelo, ti sei mess … la giacca? – No, non me la sono mess …, fa troppo caldo.

Auxiliaries (2)

(a) Verbs used impersonally

essere must be used	Gli spaghetti non mi **sono piaciuti** *I didn't like the spaghetti* (lit. *the spaghetti were not pleasing to me*) Ci **sono volute** tre ore per arrivare *It took three hours to get there*	All verbs used impersonally take **essere**. The past participle agrees with the Italian grammatical subject. (In English this is the object, i.e. who or what is liked.) See p. 261.

(b) Modal verbs

dovere **potere** **volere**: *avere* preferred	Fausto non **è potuto partire** ieri (**partire** takes essere) *Fausto was not able to leave yesterday* Fausto **ha potuto studiare** in pace (**studiare** takes **avere**) *Fausto was able to study in peace* ***But most usual***: Fausto non **ha potuto partire** ieri	Strictly speaking, modal verbs take the auxiliary normally required by the following infinitive. Increasingly, however, the tendency is to use **avere** even when the following verb takes **essere**.
With modal + **essere**	Non **ho** potuto **essere** presente *I didn't manage to be there*	When **essere** is used after a modal verb the auxiliary is always **avere**.
With modal + reflexive verbs	Ho dovuto alzarmi **or** Mi sono dovuto/a alzare *I had to get up* Hanno voluto riposarsi **or** Si sono voluti/e riposare *They wanted to rest*	Both constructions are used in speech. Note that with **avere** the reflexive pronoun comes last and there are no past participle agreements.

(c) Different auxiliary: shift in meaning

Some verbs can be used either with **avere** or with **essere**, depending on the meaning and on whether they are being used transitively or intransitively (see the definition on p. 206). Some of the most common are: **cominciare, finire, salire, scendere, cambiare, migliorare, toccare.** There is a more complete list in the Verb Appendix on p. 281.

Transitive use: **avere**	**Ho salito** le scale *I climbed the stairs* Non **ha toccato** niente *He didn't touch anything* **Ha cominciato** a gridare *He began to shout* **Hai finito** di criticarlo? *Have you stopped criticising him?*	The verb takes **avere** when the verb is transitive and there is a direct object. When the verb is followed by **a** or **di** + infinitive it is considered transitive.

Intransitive use: **essere**	**Sono salito** in macchina *I got into the car* Gli è **toccato** pagare per loro *He had to pay for them* Il film è **cominciato** tardi *The film began late* La lezione è **finita** *The lesson has finished*	When the verb has no direct object it is intransitive and takes **essere**.

Correre, **saltare** and **volare** do not follow the clear-cut rules for transitive and intransitive use.

Level 2	With **avere**	**Ho corso** cinque chilometri/tanto/per due ore *I ran five kilometres/so much/for two hours* **Ha saltato** il muretto/la cena/dalla gioia *He jumped over the wall/skipped supper/ jumped for joy* **Abbiamo volato** di notte *We flew at night*	**Avere** is the most common auxiliary with these verbs even when there is no obvious direct object.
	With **essere**	**Sono corso** a casa/verso il bosco *I ran (to) home/towards the wood* **È saltato** giù dall'albero *He jumped down from the tree* La vespa è **volata** via *The wasp flew away*	These verbs take **essere** only when they are accompanied by a phrase of direction indicating to or from a place (**a casa**, **dall'albero**, **via**).

(d) Different auxiliary: same meaning

A few verbs can take either auxiliary, irrespective of whether they are transitive or intransitive.

Level 2	vivere	**È vissuto** fino a ottant'anni *He lived until he was eighty* **Ha vissuto** dei brutti momenti *He lived (through) some bad moments* È un tipo che **ha vissuto** molto *He's someone who's lived a lot (i.e. been through a lot)*	**Essere** is possible when **vivere** is intransitive, but **avere** is increasingly common for both transitive and intransitive uses of **vivere**.
	Verbs referring to weather	**Ha/È piovuto** per un'ora *It (has) rained for an hour* Ieri notte **ha/è nevicato** senza sosta *Last night it snowed without stopping*	Either auxiliary is acceptable. In speech **avere** is more common than **essere**.
	Other verbs	L'aereo **ha/è decollato** con un'ora di ritardo *The plane took off an hour late* La messa è **durata/ha durato** tre ore *The mass lasted three hours* Il telefono **ha/è squillato** a mezzanotte *The phone rang at midnight*	The most common are: **atterrare** *to land*, **decollare** *to take off*, **durare** *to last*, **squillare** *to ring*.

E | **7** | Rewrite the sentences below using the **passato prossimo**. Use the correct auxiliary and agreements each time.

    (a) Quella chiave mi serve per aprire il portone.
    (b) Quei soldi non mi bastano per il cinema.
    (c) In quella casa succedono delle cose strane.
    (d) Mi piace quella coppia.

8 There's more than one way of saying the same thing. Which of the verbs below can have a different form?

(a) Non sono potuto partire.   (c) Hai dovuto cambiare treno?
(b) Non ho voluto vederlo.   (d) Sei dovuto tornare a casa?

9 Rewrite the sentences below, making sure the meaning is the same.

(a) Ci siamo dovuti fermare.   (c) Ho potuto sposarmi presto.
(b) Elena si è dovuta riposare.   (d) Marta non ha voluto fidanzarsi.

10 Choose the correct auxiliary to complete the sentences and make any necessary participle agreements.

(a) Ho/sono cambiato casa il mese scorso.   (e) L'ape ha/è volato via.
(b) La casa ha/è molto cambiato.   (f) Ho/Sono volato in prima classe.
(c) La nuova legge non ha/è migliorato niente.   (g) Ho/Sono corso fino all'angolo.
(d) La situazione non ha/è migliorato da ieri.   (h) Ho/Sono corso per molto tempo.

Tense sequence

The **passato prossimo** can be used with different tenses, depending on whether it is referring to the present, to the immediate past or to a more distant past.

(a) Reference to the present or to the very recent past

With the present	Io **ho** sempre **saputo** che è un delinquente *I've always known that he is a criminal* Mi **ha detto** che Anna **piange** spesso *He has told me that Anna cries a lot* Che cosa ti **ha detto**? – Mi **ha detto** che **parte** *What did he say/has he said to you? He has told me that he is leaving*	When the **passato prossimo** is linked to the present or to the very recent past it can be followed by the present tense or by another **passato prossimo**. The present is used to refer to present states or habitual actions and also to the immediate future.
With the **passato prossimo**	**Mi sono** appena **accorto** che lui non **ha pagato** *I've just realised that he hasn't paid*	The **passato prossimo** is used to express recent past actions.

(b) Reference to more distant past

With the imperfect	Le **ha detto** che **si sentiva** male *He told her he felt/was feeling unwell* Le **ha detto** che **partiva** il giorno seguente *He told her he was leaving the following day*	When the **passato prossimo** refers to a more distant past, an imperfect or pluperfect tense follows. The imperfect expresses ongoing states/situations or the immediate future (in the past). See p. 215.
With the pluperfect	Mi sono accorto (ieri) che lui non **aveva pagato** *I realised (yesterday) that he hadn't paid*	The pluperfect expresses completed actions in the past (p. 219).

11 Choose an appropriate tense to complete the sentences, using the English as a guide.

    (a) Ha appena detto che ... (avere) intenzione di dare le dimissioni. (*he intends to*)

    (b) Ha appena detto che ... (dare) le dimissioni. (*he has handed in his notice*)

    (c) Mi ha detto ieri che ... (avere) intenzione di dimettersi. (*he intended/was intending to*)

    (d) Mi ha detto ieri che ... (dare) le dimissioni. (*he had handed in his notice*)

12 Give the Italian equivalent of the following.

    (a) *He has (just) told me that he booked yesterday.*

    (b) *He told me (yesterday) that he hadn't booked.*

    (c) *He told me that he intended to book next week.*

20.2 THE IMPERFECT

The imperfect tense (l'**imperfetto**) is a past tense which expresses unfinished states or actions. It corresponds to four forms of the English past tenses: e.g. **studiavo** = *I used to study, I would study, I was studying, I studied.*

Regular forms

The imperfect is formed by putting the appropriate -**are**/-**ere**/-**ire** endings onto the stem of the infinitive. The stress is on the last but one syllable, except in the **loro** form.

-**are** andare	-**ere** avere	-**ire** uscire
and**avo**	av**evo**	usc**ivo**
and**avi**	av**evi**	usc**ivi**
and**ava**	av**eva**	usc**iva**
and**avamo**	av**evamo**	usc**ivamo**
and**avate**	av**evate**	usc**ivate**
and**avano**	av**evano**	usc**ivano**

Irregular forms

There are few irregularities. These relate to **essere** and to verbs with contracted infinitives. The verbs with contracted infinitives (-**arre**, -**orre**, -**urre** verbs) expand their stem and use the regular -**ere** endings.

essere	ero eri era eravamo eravate **e**rano
-**arre** verbs (**trarre**)	tra**evo** tra**evi** tra**eva** tra**evamo** tra**evate** tra**e**vano
-**orre** verbs (**opporre**)	oppon**evo** oppon**evi** oppon**eva** oppon**evamo** oppon**evate** oppon**e**vano
-**urre** verbs (**produrre**)	produc**evo** produc**evi** produc**eva** produc**evamo** produc**evate** produc**e**vano

bere	bev**evo**	bev**evi**	bev**eva**	bev**evamo**	bev**evate**	bev<u>e</u>vano
dire	dic**evo**	dic**evi**	dic**eva**	dic**evamo**	dic**evate**	dic<u>e</u>vano
fare	fac**evo**	fac**evi**	fac**eva**	fac**evamo**	fac**evate**	fac<u>e</u>vano

- **Dare** and **stare** form the imperfect with regular **-are** endings: **davo, stavo,** etc.

USES OF THE IMPERFECT

The imperfect is used to convey past events which have no specific beginning or end.

A past state of affairs	**Era** tardi e **faceva** freddo *It was late and it was cold* **Eravamo** felici di vederli *We were happy to see them*	This can be physical, temporal, mental or emotional.
A habitual or repeated action in the past	**Pioveva** sempre in montagna *It always used to rain/It would always rain/* *It always rained in the mountains* **Andava** a messa tutte le domeniche *She used to go/would go/went to Mass every Sunday*	This is often expressed in English as 'used to' or 'would'.
Ongoing actions	**Pioveva** e la gente **correva** a casa *It was raining and people were running home* Lisa **piangeva** mentre sua sorella **urlava** *Lisa cried/was crying while her sister screamed/was screaming*	See also pp. 217–18 for the imperfect continuous.

A note on 'could'

Note the following differences from Italian.

| *Could:*
potere
sapere
riuscire | **Poteva** uscire solo la domenica
She could only go out on Sundays (permission)
Sapeva cucinare ma non sapeva usare un PC
She could cook but she didn't know how to/couldn't use a PC (ability)
Riuscivo a sentire/**Potevo** sentire la musica soltanto quando aprivo la porta
I could only hear the music when I opened the door (ability)
But: Lo **sentivo** benissimo
I could hear him clearly (<u>not</u> lo potevo sentire …) | When *could* expresses permission or ability it may correspond to the imperfect of **potere, sapere** or **riuscire**.
But: With verbs of perception (e.g. *to see, to hear*), there is no Italian equivalent of *could* unless permisssion or ability are involved. In the latter case, **riuscire** is often preferred to **potere**.
See also Conditional, p. 227. |

I   Things aren't what they used to be. Recall the good old days by completing the sentences.

     (a) Adesso la città è piena di macchine. Trent'anni fa … *there were very few cars.*

     (b) Al giorno d'oggi la gente ha paura di uscire di notte. Vent'anni fa … *no one was afraid.*

(c) Al giorno d'oggi tutti i giovani bevono tanto. Anni fa ... *they drank/used to drink very little.*

(d) Adesso nessuno va più a messa. Ai miei tempi ... *everyone went/used to go to Mass.*

2 There has been a break-in next door. Answer the questions, giving the Italian equivalent of the English.

(a) Non ha sentito niente quando hanno rotto il vetro della finestra? – *No, I was listening to the radio.*

(b) Sono passati per il giardino? – *I don't know, I was preparing supper in the kitchen.*

(c) Non ha visto nessuno fuori? – *It was dark, but yes, there was someone. He was wearing a ski jacket* (una giacca a vento) *and a woollen hat. I saw him as he was getting into a white van.* (un furgoncino)

3 Give the Italian equivalent of the following. There may be several possibilities.

(a) *I couldn't open the window.*

(b) *It was dark: I could hear them but I couldn't see them.*

(c) *I could only hear them if they shouted.*

(d) *I couldn't dance but I could sing.*

Use with da

How long since and for: **da** + imperfect	Nel 1988 **insegnava** già **da** cinque anni *In 1988 she had already been teaching for five years* **Abitavamo** a Genova **dal** 1990 *We had been living /had lived in Genoa since 1990* Lo **conoscevo** da quando avevo fatto il militare *I had known him (ever) since I had done military service* Era una settimana che non ci **vedevamo** *We had not seen each other for a week*	**Da** + the imperfect expresses the English pluperfect tense when referring to a past action which has not been completed or interrupted. **Essere che** + imperfect is a more colloquial equivalent.

Level 2

No imperfect: **da** + pluperfect	**Dalla** fine dell'anno precedente **aveva scritto** due libri *From the end of the previous year he had written two books.* **Da** quando **aveva perso** la moglie, non era più uscito *Since he had lost his wife he had not gone out*	When referring to completed past actions, as opposed to ongoing past actions, **da** is used with the pluperfect – as in English.

E 4 Give the English equivalent of the Italian.

(a) *I hadn't seen her since December.*   (c) *He had been waiting for her for an hour.*

(b) *I had known her since I was three.*   (d) *Since 1980 she had had three husbands.*

Level 2

5 Ancient history. You're quizzing your grandfather about his life. Complete the conversation in Italian, choosing between the imperfect and pluperfect tenses. (See p. 219 for the pluperfect.)

(a) **Question**: Quando è scoppiata la guerra ... *how long had you been teaching in Milan?* **Answer**: *I had been teaching for two years, since I had got married.*

(b) **Question**: Eravate fidanzati da molto tempo?
   Answer: *Yes, we had been engaged for six years.*
(c) **Question**: E poi la guerra ti ha separato dalla nonna. – Per quanto tempo?
   Answer: Per tanto tempo. Quando sono tornato dalla guerra ... *we hadn't seen each other for three years and I had never seen my daughter!*

Other uses of the imperfect

There are cases when the imperfect does not, strictly speaking, refer only to the indeterminate past.

To be about to: **stare per**	**Stavo per** uscire quando mi hai chiamato *I was about to go out when you called me*	When used in the imperfect, **stare per** expresses what was about to happen.
Referring to the future 'in the past'	Tu mi hai detto che non **veniva** più *You told me he wasn't coming/wouldn't come any more* Ci aveva spiegato che **pagava** più tardi *He had explained that he was paying/would pay later*	In Italian, as in English, the imperfect can refer to the future in a past tense narrative. This is common in informal Italian especially if the event referred to is definite. Otherwise a past conditional is often required See p. 229.
Hypothetical events	Hai già scritto? – Sì – Bene, altrimenti lo **facevo** io ... *Good, otherwise I was going to do it/would have done it myself* Non vengono più? Me lo **potevi** dire almeno! ... *You could at least have told me!*	In informal spoken Italian the imperfect is generally used to refer to events which might have, but didn't happen. See Past conditional, p. 229 for equivalent more formal written forms.
Impossible conditions with **se**	Se mi **chiamavi**, ti **venivo** a prendere *If you had called me, I would have come and picked you up*	The imperfect can be used very informally in both clauses. See pp. 229, 254 for more formal written constructions.
Immediacy of narrative	Quarant'anni fa **moriva** lo statunitense Herbert Kalmus, che nel primo decennio del XX secolo aveva inventato il 'tecnicolor' *The American H. K., who (had) invented 'technicolor' in the 1910s, died forty years ago*	The use of the imperfect instead of the **passato prossimo** or **passato remoto** (p. 220) is a particularly common feature in journalism. The effect is to make the events more immediate or dramatic. It is important to recognise rather than use the imperfect in this way.

6   You were not prepared for what was going to happen. Complete the sentences in Italian by substituting the English.

(a) Non sapevo che ... *they were coming so soon.*
(b) Mio figlio non mi aveva detto che ... *he was sleeping out.*
(c) Mio marito non mi aveva avvertito che ... *he was bringing twenty guests to dinner.*

Level 2

7 How might you have protested about the above situations?

(a) Loro me lo (potere) dire, almeno! *They could have ...*
(b) Me lo (dovere) dire, almeno! *He should have ...*
(c) Mi (potere) avvertire almeno! *You could have ...*

Level 2

8 You would have helped your friend out if you had known.

(a) Ho dovuto prendere un tassì. – Ma se lo (sapere) ti (venire) a prendere.
(b) Ho perso la mia carta di credito. – Ma se me lo (dire) ti (prestare) dei soldi.
(c) Giovanni non ha capito quello che bisogna fare. – Ma bastava chiamarmi e glielo (spiegare) subito!

• See also conditions with **se** and the subjunctive, Exercise 5, p. 255.

20.3 THE IMPERFECT AND *PASSATO PROSSIMO*

Deciding whether a verb should be in the imperfect or **passato prossimo** is not always straightforward. This is partly because in English the same word can be used for both imperfect and perfect tenses.

Ongoing v. completed action	Mentre Lina **guardava** la TV Gino **preparava** la cena *While Lina watched TV Gino prepared/was preparing supper* Mentre Lina **guardava** la TV Gino **ha preparato** la cena *While Lina was watching TV Gino prepared the supper*	**Preparava** expresses an ongoing past action taking place simultaneously with the watching of TV. **Ha preparato** is used to signify the fact that the action was completed while Lina watched TV.
Description v. completed action	Da bambino **non mi piaceva** il mio insegnante di storia *As a child I didn't like/used not to like my history teacher* Quando ho incontrato Michele per la prima volta **non mi è piaciuto** *When I first met Michele I didn't like him (didn't take a liking to him)*	**Non mi piaceva** is used to describe a state of affairs relating to an unspecified length of time, whereas **non mi è piaciuto** expresses an event that happened at a given time.
Was and were era/erano v. è stato/a, sono stati/e	**Era** una bella serata d'estate *It was a beautiful summer's evening* (D) Grazie, **è stata** una bella serata *Thank you, it was/has been a lovely evening* (E) **Erano** difficili gli esami? *Were the exams hard?* (D) **Sono stati** difficili gli esami? *Were the exams hard? i.e. Have the exams been hard (to do)?* (E)	Was and were are expressed by the Italian imperfect **ero**, **erano** and also by the **passato prossimo**, **è stato/a**, **sono stati/e**. The difference in use of the two tenses is usually one of description (D) versus event (E). Occasionally either tense is possible – with a only a slight shift in meaning.

Modal verbs and conoscere

There is usually a shift of meaning when these verbs are used in the imperfect as opposed to **the passato prossimo:** in the imperfect **dovere**, **potere** and **volere** often express actions which have not yet taken place, but when the **passato prossimo** is used the action has been completed. **Sapere** and **conoscere** have different shifts in meaning.

Verb	Imperfect	Passato prossimo
dovere	A che ora **dovevi** partire? *At what time were you supposed to/meant to leave?* **Dovevo** fare la spesa *I was supposed to do/ I used to have to do the shopping*	A che ora **hai dovuto** partire? *At what time did you have to leave?* (and did) **Ho dovuto** fare la spesa *I had to/have had to do the shopping*
potere	Ho chiamato per dire che non **potevo** venire presto venerdì *I called to say I couldn't come early on Friday*	Non **ho potuto** venire presto venerdì *I couldn't come early on Friday* (was not able to and didn't)
volere	**Voleva** offrirci da bere *He wanted to offer us a drink* (it was his intention) **Non voleva** studiare *She didn't want to/ wouldn't study* (but did she?)	**Ha voluto** offrirci da bere *He insisted on buying us a drink* (and did) **Non ha voluto** studiare *She (has) refused to/wouldn't study* (and didn't)
sapere	**Sapevo** che era in ospedale *I knew he was in hospital* **Non sapevano** rispondere alle domande *They didn't know how to/couldn't answer the questions*	**Ho saputo** che era in ospedale *I found out he was in hospital* **Non ho saputo** rispondere alle domande *I wasn't able to/couldn't answer the questions*
conoscere	A Londra **conoscevo** molti italiani *In London I knew/used to know/was acquainted with many Italians*	A Londra **ho conosciuto** molti italiani *In London I met/got to know many Italians*

I Express the following in Italian, choosing the correct tense.

(a) *On Tuesday while Anna listened to the radio Pietro made supper.*
(b) *On Wednesday Anna cleaned the house while Pietro prepared a lecture.* (una lezione)
(c) *Yesterday we went to a party. It was a wonderful evening.*
(d) *Yesterday we went for a walk because it was a lovely evening.*
(e) *Last year I went to Corsica. I liked it a lot.*
(f) *When I lived in London I liked visiting the museums.*

2 Complete the sentences, choosing the correct Italian form of the verb.

(a) (*I was supposed to*) partire alle tre ma il treno è in ritardo.
(b) (*I had to*) partire subito, mia figlia si è sentita male.
(c) Purtroppo (*I couldn't see*) il professore perché era malato.
(d) Mi hanno detto che (*I couldn't see*) il medico prima di lunedì.
(e) (*I found out*) dalla segretaria che il mio capo era in vacanza.
(f) (*I knew*) che il mio capo era in vacanza.

20.4 THE IMPERFECT CONTINUOUS

This English tense focuses on an activity which is in the process of taking place in the past. In Italian this is expressed by the normal imperfect tense or by the imperfect tense of the verb **stare**, followed by the gerund of the verb required.

Regular forms

Infinitive	stare + gerund	
	stavo	
parlare	stavi	parl**ando**
leggere	stava	leg**gendo**
finire	stavamo	fin**endo**
partire	stavate	part**endo**
	stavano	

Irregular forms

Verbs with contracted infinitives form the gerund by expanding their stem and adding -endo.

Infinitive	stare + gerund	
bere	stavo	**bev**endo
dire	stavi	**dic**endo
fare	stava	**fac**endo
trarre	stavamo	**tra**endo
proporre	stavate	**propon**endo
produrre	stavano	**produc**endo

USES

In Italian this verb form has a more restricted use than the past continuous in English.

An action in progress	**Stavo ascoltando** la radio quando ho sentito l'esplosione *I was listening to the radio when I heard the explosion* **or:** **Ascoltavo** la radio quando ho sentito l'esplosione	**Stavo** + gerund emphasises an action in the process of taking place in the past – often when something else intervenes. It can usually be replaced by the Italian simple imperfect with no significant change of meaning. **Stavo** + gerund is <u>not</u> used to express a state of affairs in the past, i.e. it must emphasise an action in progress.
<u>Not</u> a state of affairs	Che cosa **portava**? *What was she wearing?* Non so che cosa **faceva** a Roma *I don't know what she was doing in Rome*	

E 1 Look at Exercise 2 on p. 214 about the break-in. Which of the actions could be expressed using the imperfect continuous? Provide these alternative forms.

20.5 THE PLUPERFECT

The pluperfect (**il trapassato prossimo**) is a tense which expresses actions that have taken place before another in the past. It is often recognisable in English by the characteristic *had*: *I went to meet them, but they had already left.*

The pluperfect is composed of the imperfect tense of the auxiliary verb – **avere** or **essere** – plus the past participle of the verb required. The past participle of verbs with the auxiliary **essere** must agree with the subject.

Verbs with *avere*		Verbs with *essere*	
avevo avevi aveva	comp**rato** ricev**uto**	ero eri era	and**ato/a** cad**uto/a** part**ito/a**
avevamo avevate avevano	dorm**ito**	eravamo eravate erano	and**ati/e** cad**uti/e** part**iti/e**

- Irregular pluperfects simply have irregular past participles: see pp. 206–7.

USES

The pluperfect is used to express an action or situation occurring before another one in the past.

Expressing an action preceding another in the past	Quando siamo usciti **aveva smesso** di piovere *When we came out it had stopped raining* Una volta che **aveva finito** di studiare andava a trovare gli amici *Once he had finished studying he used to go and see his friends* **Era** sempre **stato** un marito modello finché un giorno sparì *He had always been a model husband until one day he disappeared*	The pluperfect is used with the other past tenses – the **passato prossimo**, the imperfect and the simple past. These express the past action nearest in time, while the pluperfect expresses what took place before then.
	Mi ha dato il numero che **avevo chiesto** *He gave me the number I (had) asked for* Mi ha chiesto dov'**ero nato/a** *He asked me where I was (had been) born*	Note that in English the pluperfect is not always rigorously used, but in Italian an action preceding another in the past must be pluperfect.

I   Complete the sentences using the pluperfect form of the verb given.

(a) Ieri Patrizio mi ha portato i libri che io gli (chiedere) l'altro giorno.

(b) Mio fratello (laurearsi) in medicina ma non aveva mai voluto fare il medico.

(c) Il funzionario voleva sapere dove (nascere) io e mio fratello.

(d) Quando Marcello (bere) era meglio non ascoltarlo.

Alternatives to the pluperfect

In Italian the pluperfect is often avoided by using more succinct constructions.

Level 2	Avoiding the pluperfect: infinitives and participles	**Dopo aver sentito** la notizia si è messa a piangere *After she had heard /After having heard the news she began to cry* **Una volta/Appena finito** di studiare uscivo con gli amici *Once I had/As soon as I (had) finished studying I used to go out with my friends*	If the subjects are the same in both clauses **dopo** can be used with a past infinitive and **appena** or **una volta** can be used with a past participle. The past participle can also be used alone. See also pp. 179, 240, 244.

E 2 Give the Italian equivalent of the English, avoiding the pluperfect where possible.

(a) As soon as I (had) left the house I was taken ill. *(sentirsi male)*
(b) After I had finished the exams I found myself a job.
(c) I had already left when they arrived.
(d) Once my wife had left hospital I was able to go back to work.

Level 2

20.6 THE SIMPLE PAST

In Italian the simple past is called the **passato remoto** and is used to express completed past actions. It corresponds to the English simple past or past historic: **ci andai** *I went.* It is used in formal written Italian but is also common in speech, for example in the south of Italy and in some parts of Tuscany. In northern Italy it is usually replaced by the **passato prossimo** in speech.

Regular forms

-are comprare *to buy*	**-ere** vendere *to sell*	**-ire** dormire *to sleep*
comprai	vendei	dormii
comprasti	vendesti/vendetti	dormisti
comprò	vendè/vendette	dormì
comprammo	vendemmo	dormimmo
compraste	vendeste	dormiste
comprarono	venderono/vendettero	dormirono

- The alternative -etti, -ette, -ettero endings of -ere verbs are widely used.

Irregular forms

A large number of verbs are irregular in the **passato remoto**, but most of them follow a consistent pattern. There are only three verbs whose **passato remoto** has no clear link to the stem, but they also follow the basic pattern, which is that the first person singular is similar in form to the third persons singular and plural.

essere	fui	fosti	fu	fummo	foste	furono
dare	diedi/detti	desti	diede/dette	demmo	deste	diedero/dettero
stare	stetti	stesti	stette	stemmo	steste	stettero

All other irregular verbs have regular **tu**, **noi** and **voi** -**ere** forms, based on the stem, i.e. on the infinitive. In the case of verbs with contracted infinitives the stem is an expanded version of the infinitive (see p. 192). It is essential to know the **io passato remoto** form of each verb to conjugate the whole tense, as this cannot be deduced from the infinitive. The following are some of the most common verbs. Most of the others are in the irregular verb appendix, pp. 281–8.

avere	ebbi	avesti	ebbe	avemmo	aveste	ebbero
conoscere	conobbi	conoscesti	conobbe	conoscemmo	conosceste	conobbero
chiudere	chiusi	chiudesti	chiuse	chiudemmo	chiudeste	chiusero
mettere	misi	mettesti	mise	mettemmo	metteste	misero
prendere	presi	prendesti	prese	prendemmo	prendeste	presero
rimanere	rimasi	rimanesti	rimase	rimanemmo	rimaneste	rimasero
rispondere	risposi	rispondesti	rispose	rispondemmo	rispondesti	risposero
scegliere	scelsi	scegliesti	scelse	scegliemmo	sceglieste	scelsero
togliere	tolsi	togliesti	tolse	togliemmo	toglieste	tolsero
vincere	vinsi	vincesti	vinse	vincemmo	vinceste	vinsero
nascere	nacqui	nascesti	nacque	nascemmo	nasceste	nacquero
vedere	vidi	vedesti	vide	vedemmo	vedeste	videro

Verbs with contracted infinitives have the same consistent pattern, based on the expanded stem.

bere	bevvi	bevesti	bevve	bevemmo	beveste	bevvero
dire	dissi	dicesti	disse	dicemmo	diceste	dissero
fare	feci	facesti	fece	facemmo	faceste	fecero
trarre	trassi	traesti	trasse	traemmo	traeste	trassero
porre	posi	ponesti	pose	ponemmo	poneste	posero
condurre	condussi	conducesti	condusse	conducemmo	conduceste	condussero

• Note also these verbs with double consonants in the first and third persons:

caddi (cadere), discussi (discutere), lessi (leggere), mossi (muovere), ruppi (rompere), scrissi (scrivere), seppi (sapere), tenni (tenere), venni (venire), vissi (vivere), volli (volere).

▌ USES

The **passato remoto** is essentially a written tense, although in some parts of Italy it is used in speech. Learners should avoid its use in speech in favour of the **passato prossimo** as the main past tense of everyday spoken or written Italian.

Used in literary and academic styles	I monaci **uscirono** in fila e la chiesa **rimase** deserta *The monks filed out and the church was left deserted*	The **passato remoto** expresses events which are over and done with and is the characteristic narrative tense of formal written Italian.
Not used if linked to the present	Lo hai visto di recente? <u>not</u> Lo vedesti di recente? *Have you seen him recently?*	Unlike the **passato prossimo** it does not express actions linked to the present.

Level 2 | *Combining the* passato remoto *and* passato prossimo

The **passato remoto** can be used in everyday spoken and written Italian – sometimes actually in conjunction with the **passato prossimo**. It expresses events that are distant – or 'history' in the mind of the speaker/writer, while the **passato prossimo** is used for more vivid, immediate events. Here is an example taken from a magazine:

Passato remoto with passato prossimo	Ci siamo innamorati ma poi **scoppiò** la guerra mondiale. La vita ci **portò** su strade diverse, **ci sposammo** con altre persone. Ora, rimasti vedovi tutt'e due, abbiamo scoperto che quell'antico sentimento non era mai finito.	*We fell in love, but the world war broke out. Life drew us along different paths, we married other people. Now that we are both widowed, we have discovered that our old feelings for each other had never died.*

E | 1 The following has been adapted from a story about a rabbit. Read the text, then answer (a) and (b).

Fu allora che vide un coniglio in una gabbia. Era un coniglio bianco, di pelo lungo e piumoso ... Fuori della gabbia, sul tavolo, c'erano dei resti d'erba e una carota. Marcovaldo pensò a come doveva essere infelice, chiuso là allo stretto, vedendo quella carota e non potendola mangiare. E gli aprì lo sportello della gabbia. Il coniglio non uscì ... Marcovaldo prese la carota, gliel'avvicinò, poi, lentamente la ritrasse per invitarlo a uscire. Il coniglio lo seguì ...

(Italo Calvino, 'Il coniglio velenoso', in *Marcovaldo*)

- chiuso là allo stretto – *cooped up in there*

  (a) Identify the nine **passato remoto** verbs. Give their infinitive, **io** and **tu** forms.
  (b) Substitute the **passato prossimo** for the **passato remoto** and rewrite the story in the first person as though you were telling it about yourself. Begin: È stato allora che ...

20.7 THE PAST ANTERIOR

To express past actions and events preceding the **passato remoto**, a tense called the past anterior or **trapassato remoto** is used in formal or literary Italian only. It has the same meaning as the English pluperfect. The **trapassato remoto** is formed with the **passato remoto** of **avere** or **essere** plus the past participle of the verb.

Verbs with *avere*	Verbs with *essere*
ebbi portato ebbi ricevuto ebbi finito	fui arrivato fui caduto fui uscito

USES

Andò a casa quando **ebbe mangiato** *He went home when he had eaten* Dopo che **furono partiti** Gemma si mise a piangere *After they had left Gemma began to cry*	Used when the main past tense is the simple past (**passato remoto**) and in a dependent clause, after **quando**, **appena**, **dopo che**.
Quando aveva mangiato andò a casa *When he had eaten he went home* Dopo che erano partiti Gemma si mise a piangere *After they had left Gemma began to cry* Appena entrò Angela, Giulio se ne andò *As soon as Angela (had) arrived, Giulio left*	The modern tendency is to use the **passato remoto** or the normal pluperfect tense rather than the **trapassato remoto**.

The conditional

The conditional form of the verb (**il condizionale**) generally expresses hypothetical or imaginary events and situations, as well as events dependent on a condition. This form often corresponds to *would* and *would have*: **Would you** go tomorrow? **Would you** have left so early?

21.1 THE CONDITIONAL

Regular forms

The conditional has some similarities with the future. Like the future there are two regular endings: one for -**are**/-**ere** endings and another for -**ire** endings.

-are and -ere		-ire	
portare	**prendere**	**finire**	**dormire**
port**erei**	prend**erei**	fin**irei**	dorm**irei**
pot**eresti**	prend**eresti**	fin**iresti**	dorm**iresti**
port**erebbe**	prend**erebbe**	fin**irebbe**	dorm**irebbe**
port**eremmo**	prend**eremmo**	fin**iremmo**	dorm**iremmo**
port**ereste**	prend**ereste**	fin**ireste**	dorm**ireste**
port**erebbero**	prend**erebbero**	fin**irebbero**	dorm**irebbero**

- As with the future tense, verbs with -**care** and -**gare** endings require the addition of an **h** to keep the hard sound of the infinitive: e.g. cercare – cercherei, pagare – pagherei.
- Verbs in -**ciare** and -**giare** drop the **i** of the stem, as it is not needed to maintain the soft sound of the infinitive: lasciare – lascerei, mangiare – mangerei.

Irregular forms

These also have similarities with the future. Apart from **essere**, there are two main patterns of irregularity. Many verbs omit the **e** or **i** of the regular conditional ending.

essere	sa**rei** sa**resti** sa**rebbe** sa**remmo** sa**reste** sa**rebbero**
andare	and**rei** and**resti** and**rebbe** and**remmo** and**reste** and**rebbero**
fare	fa**rei** fa**resti** fa**rebbe** fa**remmo** fa**reste** fa**rebbero**
potere	pot**rei** pot**resti** pot**rebbe** pot**remmo** pot**reste** pot**rebbero**

- Similar verbs include:

  avere, cadere, dare, dire, dovere, sapere, stare, udire, vedere, vivere.

  Other verbs omit the vowel of the regular conditional endings and double the **r**.

bere	be**rrei** be**rresti** be**rrebbe** be**rremmo** be**rreste** be**rrebbero**
tenere	te**rrei** te**rresti** te**rrebbe** te**rremmo** te**rreste** te**rrebbero**
venire	ve**rrei** ve**rresti** ve**rrebbe** ve**rremmo** ve**rreste** ve**rrebbero**
volere	vo**rrei** vo**rresti** vo**rrebbe** vo**rremmo** vo**rreste** vo**rrebbero**
trarre	tra**rrei** tra**rresti** tra**rrebbe** tra**rremmo** tra**rreste** tra**rrebbero**
porre	po**rrei** po**rresti** po**rrebbe** po**rremmo** po**rreste** po**rrebbero**
condurre	condu**rrei** condu**rresti** condu**rrebbe** condu**rremmo** condu**rreste** condu**rrebbero**

- Similar verbs include:

  ottenere (otterrei), parere (parrei), proporre (proporrei), ridurre (ridurrei), rimanere (rimarrei), tradurre (tradurrei), valere (varrei).

I Select the correct form of the conditional.

  (a) Mariella, tu lo lavaresti/laveresti veramente con acqua calda? (lavare)
  (b) Ma voi due cerchereste/cercereste davvero un altro lavoro? (cercare)
  (c) Lo prenderemo/prenderemmo, ma è troppo caro. (prendere)

2 Complete the sentences using the correct conditional forms.

  (a) (Venire – io) volentieri, ma ho un appuntamento.
  (b) (Volere – loro) partire, ma c'è sciopero.
  (c) (Rimanere – tu) fino a domani?
  (d) (Potere – voi) aiutare?
  (e) Mi (fare – tu) un favore?
  (f) Non (andare – io) mai con loro.

USES

Polite requests and diplomacy	Mi **faresti** un favore? *Would you do me a favour?* **Avrei** bisogno di almeno un chilo *I need/ I'll be needing at least a kilo* Ti sembra ubriaco? – Non **saprei** *Does he seem drunk to you? – I wouldn't know*	The use of the conditional, rather than the present, makes things less blunt and direct. The English equivalent is not always *would*.
Level 2 Hypothetical or uncertain events	**Uscirei** volentieri, ma non mi sento bene *I would love to go out, but I don't feel well* Al mio posto che cosa **faresti**? *What would you do in my place?*	The conditional is used to express actions which often depend on unspoken conditions.
Level 2 Conditions with **se**	Ti **accompagnerei** se avessi più tempo *I would go with you if I had more time* Se fossi in te, non ci **andrei** *If I were you, I wouldn't go*	The conditional is used with the imperfect subjunctive (see p. 254).

(a) A note on *would*

- *Would* can be used to express the Italian imperfect as well as the conditional.

   Mi daresti una mano? *Would you give me a hand?* (conditional)
   Mi dava spesso una mano *He would often give me a hand* (imperfect).

- *Would not* can also translate the **passato prossimo** or imperfect of the verb **volere**:

   Gli hanno chiesto di venire, ma non ha voluto farlo (**passato prossimo**)
   Gli hanno chiesto di venire, ma non voleva farlo (imperfect) (see p. 217).

E 3 Be polite and ask diplomatically. Rewrite the commands and statements below using the conditional.

(a) Umberto, dammi un bicchiere di vino.
(b) Anna e Cristina, fatemi un favore.
(c) Signora, ho bisogno di una crema più leggera.
(d) Signore, me lo prepari per stasera.

Level 2 4 What would you be willing to do if there were no obstacles? Use the correct form of the verbs given.

(a) Ti (dare un passaggio), ma devo andare a prendere mia figlia.
(b) (Tradurre) l'articolo, ma non ho tempo.
(c) Il vino lo (bere) volentieri, ma sto prendendo antibiotici.

Level 2 5 What would you do in someone else's shoes? Give the Italian equivalent of the English.

(a) Al tuo posto ... *I would not reply.* (rispondere)
(b) Al suo posto, signore ... *I would propose another solution.* (proporre)
(c) Al mio posto ... *he would get angry.* (arrabbiarsi)

- See also Exercise 5, p. 255 for the conditional used with the subjunctive.

Special meanings of the conditional

In the conditional the following verbs have a variety of meanings.

dovere	**Dovresti** chiedere uno sconto *You should/ought to ask for a discount* **Dovremmo** studiare domani *We should/ought to/are supposed to study tomorrow* **Dovrebbero** essere arrivati *They should/must have arrived*	There are three main uses: giving advice; expressing obligation – what you are meant or supposed to do; expressing probability.
potere	**Potreste** darci una mano? *Could you give us a hand?* **Potremmo** andare da Paolo oppure **potremmo** stare qui *We could go to Paolo's or we could stay here* La strada è buona, **potrebbe** essere a Roma ormai *It's a good road, he could be in Rome by now* Con questa nebbia **potrebbe** arrivare in ritardo *With this fog, he could/may/might arrive late*	There are three main uses: expressing polite requests – could; expressing a definite possibility; expressing a hypothesis or vague possibility – what could or is likely to be the case: could/might/may.
sapere	Mi **saprebbe** dire a che ora tornano? *Could you tell me what time they are coming back?* Non so se **saprebbe** rispondere *I don't know if he could/would be able to answer*	Polite requests (see also **potere**). Expressing ability.
volere	**Vorrei** delle informazioni *I would like some information* **Vorrebbe** venire martedì *He would like to come on Tuesday* Non **vorresti** venire con noi? *Wouldn't you like to come with us?*	Expressing wishes. Note that the conditional literally means *would want/be wanting*, but is expressed as *would like*.
piacere	Mi **piacerebbe** vederlo *I would like to see him* Ti **piacerebbe** venire con noi? *Would you like to come with us?*	Expresses what would give you pleasure. *Would like* is also the conditional of **volere** (see above).
essere	Ma questo, cosa **sarebbe**, scusa? *So what's this meant to be, may I ask?* E lui, chi **sarebbe**? *And who's he supposed to be?*	Can be used to express irritation or scepticism.

(b) A note on *could*

- Note that the English *could* can translate three tenses of the verb **potere**:

  Mi potresti aiutare? (conditional)

  Non potevano aiutare (imperfect)

  Non hanno potuto aiutare (**passato prossimo**)

  For full explanations see pp. 213, 217.

- Note also that *could* can be expressed by the verb **sapere** when it refers to ability:

    Mi sapresti dire l'ora? *Could you tell me the time?* (conditional)
    Sapeva leggere a tre anni *He could read at three* (imperfect) (see p. 213).

E **6** Give the English equivalent of the Italian.

    (a) Dovresti andare dal medico.
    (b) Dovrei partire alle tre, ma non ho fatto il biglietto.
    (c) Dovrebbero già essere a casa ormai.
    (d) Potresti venire alle due?
    (e) Hai detto che potevi venire alle due.
    (f) Potrebbero essere dalla zia oppure dalla nonna.
    (g) Mi sapresti dire se sono tornati?
    (h) Non sapeva dirmi niente.
    (i) Giulia vorrebbe rimanere a Pisa.
    (j) Le piacerebbe rimanere a Pisa.

21.2 THE PAST CONDITIONAL

The past conditional (**il condizionale passato**) generally corresponds to the English *would have*, and is made up of the conditional of the auxiliary **avere** or **essere** plus the past participle of the verb. (See p. 206 for which auxiliary to use.)

pagare	tornare
avrei pagato	**sarei** tornato/a
avresti pagato	**saresti** tornato/a
avrebbe pagato	**sarebbe** tornato/a
avremmo pagato	**saremmo** tornati/e
avreste pagato	**sareste** tornati/e
avrebbero pagato	**sarebbero** tornati/e

E **I** Supply the correct auxiliary verb to complete the past conditional.

    (a) (io) … venuto/a prima.   (d) Mi … arrabbiato/a.
    (b) (io) … telefonato ieri.   (e) Si … seccato/a.
    (c) (loro) … partiti/e più tardi.   (f) Ci … divertiti/e.

USES

(a) Hypothetical and impossible events

The past conditional very often refers to what did not happen.

Level 2	Hypothetical events	Hai scritto la lettera? – Sì. – Bene, altrimenti l'**avrei scritta** io *Did you write the letter? – Yes. – Good, otherwise I would have written it myself* Al tuo posto **sarei venuto** prima *In your place/shoes I would have come earlier* Me lo **avresti potuto** dire! *You could have told me!* *or*: Me lo potevi dire	The past conditional is used to refer to events which might have taken place but did not. It can also express wishes that could not have been realised. In colloquial Italian the imperfect may be used. See p. 215.
	I would have liked …	Mi **sarebbe piaciuto** venire, ma avevo un appuntamento *I would have liked (i.e. found it pleasurable) to have come but I had an engagement*	Note that the past conditional of **piacere** and **volere** are identically expressed in English.
	Impossible conditions with **se**	Ti **avrei accompagnato** se avessi avuto più tempo *I would have gone with you if I had had more time*	The past conditional is used with the pluperfect subjunctive to express events which could not have taken place. See also p. 254.

(b) Events which could take place

The past conditional can also express events and situations which could actually take place.

Level 2	The past conditional for the 'future in the past'	Ero sicuro che **sarebbe venuto** *I was sure he would come* Mi ha/Mi aveva detto che **avrebbe chiamato** presto *He told me/He had told me he would call soon* *or*: Ero sicuro che **veniva** *I was sure he was coming*	The past conditional expresses the future with respect to a past tense (imperfect, perfect and pluperfect) in a main clause. In English this is a simple conditional. The imperfect is a colloquial alternative. See p. 215.

(c) Unconfirmed facts: a special use

Level 2	A quanto dicono, la ragazzina **sarebbe** la figlia illegittima dell'attore *The girl is apparently the actor's illegitimate daughter* Secondo le rivelazioni del settimanale britannico, il ministro **avrebbe intrecciato** una torrida storia d'amore con la trentenne modella *According to the revelations of the British weekly, the minister had become involved in a steamy affair with the 31-year-old model*	The conditional and the past conditional are both used to report unconfirmed facts where in English present or past tenses are used. This is typical of news items.

E

2 Say how you would have reacted in the following circumstances.

(a) Non hanno fatto la fila, sono passati davanti a noi. Voi cosa avreste fatto? – *We would have protested.*

(b) Sono arrivati con tre ore di ritardo. Tu come avresti reagito? – *I would have been angry.*

(c) Mi hanno fatto pagare troppo. Tu cosa avresti fatto? – *I would have complained.* (lamentarsi)

3 *I would like ... I would have liked.* Answer in Italian using the appropriate conditional form of the verb used in the question: **piacere** or **volere**.

(a) Ti sarebbe piaciuto andarci? – *Yes, I would have liked to go (have gone). I would like to go tomorrow.*

(b) Avresti voluto parlargli? – *Yes, I would have liked to speak to him. I would like to speak to him soon.*

(c) Gli sarebbe piaciuto venire? – *Yes, he would have liked to come. He would like to come next week.*

(d) Avresti voluto finire il lavoro? – *Yes, I would have liked to finish the job. I would like to finish it soon.*

4 Give the Italian equivalents of the English. There are two alternatives each time.

(a) *I was convinced she would phone/she was going to phone.*

(b) *They knew she would leave/she was going to leave.*

(c) *He told me he would arrive at four/he was arriving at four.*

5 Give the English equivalent of the Italian.

(a) Il ministro non sarebbe disposto a dare le dimissioni.

(b) L'aereo sarebbe caduto dieci minuti dopo il decollo.

(c) Il rapinatore avrebbe sparato due volte.

● See also Exercise 5, p. 255 for conditions with the subjunctive.

22

The imperative

Imperatives (**gli imperativi**) are verb forms used for giving orders or making suggestions, e.g. *Wait! Don't come. Let's have a coffee.*

THE FORMATION OF THE IMPERATIVE

Regular forms

In Italian there are separate imperative forms depending on who is being addressed.

- The **tu** imperatives are used to address one person in a familiar way.
- The **voi** imperatives are used to address several people, and in some parts of Italy to address one person formally.
- The **Lei** imperatives are the most common way of addressing one person formally.
- The **noi** form of the verb is used to make suggestions (*let's ... let's not/don't let's ...*).

	-are aspettare *to wait*	-ere prendere *to take*	-ire finire *to finish*	-ire sentire *to hear*
tu	aspetta **non aspettare**	prendi **non prendere**	finisci **non finire**	senti **non sentire**
Lei	aspetti non aspetti	prenda non prenda	finisca non finisca	senta non senta
voi	aspettate non aspettate	prendete non prendete	finite non finite	sentite non sentite
noi	aspettiamo non aspettiamo	prendiamo non prendiamo	finiamo non finiamo	sentiamo non sentiamo

- The **tu** imperatives are identical to their present tense forms with the exception of -**are** verbs. These are the same as the third person singular forms (*he, she, it*).

- Noi and voi imperatives are identical to their present tense forms.
- The Lei imperatives are identical to their present subjunctive forms (pp. 245–6).
- Negative imperatives: **non** goes before the normal imperative except in the case of **tu** imperatives. These are formed by using **non** + the verb infinitive.

Irregular forms: verbs with an irregular present tense

If a verb has an irregular present tense its imperative forms are also irregular.
See also the list of irregular present tenses on p. 192. Below are a few examples.

Infinitive	**tu**: identical to present tense	**voi**: identical to present tense	**Lei**: identical to present subjunctive	**noi**: identical to present tense
venire	vieni (non venire)	(non) venite	(non) venga	(non) veniamo
salire	sali (non salire)	(non) salite	(non) salga	(non) saliamo
uscire	esci (non uscire)	(non) uscite	(non) esca	(non) usciamo
bere	bevi (non bere)	(non) bevete	(non) beva	(non) beviamo

Very irregular forms: eight verbs

These verbs are entirely or partly irregular. The list below is complete. Irregularities are marked in bold.

Infinitive	**tu**	**voi**	**Lei**
avere	**abbi**	**abbiate**	abbia
essere	**sii**	**siate**	sia
sapere	**sappi**	**sappiate**	sappia
stare	**sta'*/stai**	state	stia
andare	**va'*/vai**	andate	vada
dare	**da'*/dai**	date	dia
dire	**di'***	dite	dica
fare	**fa'*/fai**	fate	faccia

- Spelling changes: when the five forms asterisked above are followed by a pronoun the initial letter of that pronoun is doubled, except in the case of **gli**:

Fammi vedere *Let me see* Falle vedere *Let her see*
But: Fagli vedere *Let him see*

E

I Give the **tu** and **Lei** imperative forms of the verbs below.

(a) guardare il mare   (d) partire subito   (g) fare la doccia
(b) vendere la casa   (e) togliere la polvere   (h) avere pazienza
(c) finire il lavoro   (f) venire dentro   (i) stare fermo

2 Give the negative **tu** and **Lei** imperatives of (a), (b), (c) and (g) above.

Forms of reflexive imperatives

These are formed exactly like other imperatives. The important thing to note is the position of the reflexive pronoun and where the spoken stress is.

	accomodarsi *to come in, sit down*	**sedersi** *to sit down*	**divertirsi** *to enjoy o.self*
tu	accomodati non accomodarti/non ti accomodare*	siediti non sederti/non ti sedere*	divertiti non divertirti/non ti divertire*
voi	(non) accomodatevi	(non) sedetevi	(non) divertitevi
Lei	(non) si accomodi	(non) si sieda	(non) si diverta
noi	(non) accomodiamoci	(non) sediamoci	(non) divertiamoci

• Note that the negative **tu** imperatives (*) have two possible pronoun positions. For the rules of pronoun position see section below.

Imperatives with object and reflexive pronouns

tu, voi, noi: on the end of the imperative	Prendi**lo** *Take it* Lava**ti** *Wash yourself!* **(tu)** Prende**telo** *Take it* Lava**tevi** *Wash yourselves* **(voi)** Prendiamo**lo** *Let's take it* Laviamo**ci** *Let's wash ourselves* **(noi)**	Pronouns are usually attached to the end of the **tu**, **voi** and **noi** imperative forms.
Lei: before the imperative	**Lo** prenda *Take it* **Si** lavi *Wash yourself* **(Lei)**	Pronouns always come before the **Lei** form.
tu negative imperative; two positions	Non prender**lo**/non **lo** prendere *Don't take it* Non lavar**ti**/non **ti** lavare *Don't wash*	With negative **tu** imperatives the pronoun can be attached to the verb or precede it.

E

3 Give the Italian equivalent of the following using **tu** and **Lei** imperatives.

(a) *Do it at once.* (fare)   (d) *Go (there).* (andare)
(b) *Tell her to come.* (dire a)   (e) *Have fun.* (divertirsi)
(c) *Ask him to come.* (chiedere a)   (f) *Put on your coat.* (mettersi)

4 Give the negative **tu** and **Lei** imperatives of (a) and (d) above.

USES

To give orders	**Esci** di qui! Uscite di qui! *Get out (of here)!*
To give instructions	**Prenda** la prima strada a sinistra *Take the first road on the left* **Fate** soffriggere la cipolla *Fry the onion*
To make suggestions or invitations	**Facciamo** una pausa *Let's take a break* Non **prendiamo** un tassì *Don't let's take a taxi*
To make requests	**Abbi** pazienza! *Bear with me*
To advise and persuade (In advertisements the **tu** form is very common, although **voi** and **Lei** forms are also used.)	**Non fumare** tanto *Don't smoke so much* **Stammi** bene *Take care* **Siate** prudenti, ragazzi *Be careful, everyone* Per ricevere la tua calcolatrice, **spedisci** subito il buono! *To receive your calculator, send off the coupon immediately!*

E   **5**   Give the Italian equivalent of the following. Use the **Lei** imperative unless specified.

(a) *Do sit down.* (also **voi** form)
(b) *Pass me the salt.*
(c) *Give me a bit of bread, please.*
(d) *Make us a coffee, please.*
(e) *Bring us the bill, please.*

6   These are some of the instructions you gave when you took your nieces and nephews on an outing. What would you have said if you had only taken one of them?

(a) Guardate bene prima di attraversare la strada.
(b) State attenti!
(c) Non toccate niente.
(d) Non sedetevi lì!
(e) Uscite di qui.
(f) Sbrigatevi!

SPECIAL USES

The imperatives of **dare**, **sentire** and **dire** have common colloquial uses.

dai	Non te lo dico – Ma **dai**, non è mica un segreto! *I'm not telling you – Go on, it's not actually a secret!*	Literally *give*. Used for persuasion or encouragement.
senti senta	**Senti**, è inutile aspettare ... *Look, it's useless to wait ...* **Senta!** Mi porti un po' d'acqua? *Excuse me! Can you bring me some water?*	Literally *hear*, like the English *look* or *hey*. The **Lei** form is used to attract attention in a shop or restaurant.
dimmi mi dica non me lo dire	Carlo, ti voglio parlare – **Dimmi** *Carlo I need to speak to you – Go ahead* **Mi dica**, signora *Can I help you Madam?* **Non me lo dire!** *You don't say!* **But**: Non dirmelo *Don't tell me*	Literally *tell me*. The **tu** form is a common way of encouraging someone to speak, while the **Lei** form is used in shops to offer help.

The infinitive as imperative

Spingere *Push* **Lavare** in acqua fredda *Wash in cold water* **Non sporgersi** dal finestrino *Do not lean out of the window*	The infinitive is widely used in all kinds of written instructions aimed at an indeterminate audience.

7 What do you say? Pick the appropriate expression.

(a) You try to attract the shop assistant's attention: <u>Senti!/Senta!</u>

(b) You can't believe your ears: <u>Non dirmelo!/Non me lo dire!</u>

(c) You want your friend to pay attention: <u>Senti!/Ascolti!</u>

8 Here are some instructions on looking after a Christmas tree before bringing it into the house. Rewrite it as if you were telling an acquaintance (**Lei**) what to do.

Evitare le piante a radice nuda che perdono presto gli aghi. **Scegliere** piuttosto un albero in un vaso.

Mettere la pianta all'aperto e **annaffiare** abbondantemente quando la temperatura è sopra lo zero.

Nei giorni successivi **tenere** il terriccio (*compost*) umido. Prima di portarla in casa **spruzzare** i rami.

23

Non-finite verb forms

Non-finite verb forms have no specified subject or tense. The three main forms are the infinitive (*to eat*), the gerund (*singing*) and participles – present and past (*finishing, finished*). Unlike finite verbs, these forms cannot be conjugated because they do not have separate forms for each person or tense.

23.1 THE INFINITIVE

The simple infinitive

The simple infinitive (**l'infinito presente**) is the form used in the dictionary to identify a verb: *to see, to go*, etc. The past infinitive (**l'infinito passato**) corresponds to: *to have seen, to have gone*.

-are/-arsi	-ere/-ersi	-ire/-irsi	Italian infinitives generally end in **-are**, **-ere**
parlare	perdere	dormire	or **-ire** but also in **-arre**, **-orre** and **-urre**.
lavarsi	iscriversi	stupirsi	Reflexive infinitives end in **-si**.

-arre/-arsi	-orre/-orsi	-urre/-ursi
trarre	porre	condurre
sottrarsi	opporsi	ridursi

- Note that the reflexive infinitive **si** changes to match the subject of the verb on which the infinitive depends.

  Conviene iscriver**si** *It is advisable to enrol*   Vogliamo iscriver**ci** *We want to enrol*

  Devi iscriver**ti**, Maria *You must enrol, Maria*   Volete iscriver**vi** *You want to enrol*

USES OF THE SIMPLE INFINITIVE

The infinitive is used a great deal in Italian. It is used when there are two clauses and when the subject of the verbs in both clauses is the same. Note also that its English equivalents include gerunds (*shouting*) and finite verbs (*he shouts*) as well as the standard infinitive forms *to do, to speak*, etc.

After verbs taking prepositions	Ha cominciato a **gridare** *He began to shout/ shouting* Ricordati di **chiamarmi** *Remember to call me*	
After prepositions and prepositional phrases	Sono venuto per **aiutare** *I have come to help* È partito senza **salutarci** *He left without saying goodbye to us* Lavati le mani prima di **mangiare** *Wash your hands before eating/you eat*	Others include: **invece di, fuorché, oltre a, piuttosto che, tranne**.
After modal verbs	Devo **uscire** *I have to go out* Potrei **farlo** domani *I could do it tomorrow* So **nuotare** *I can swim*	**Dovere, potere, volere** always require an infinitive verb. For **sapere** see also p. 260.
After impersonal verbs and expressions	È importante **studiare** *It is important to study* Non vale la pena **farlo** *It is not worth doing* Bisogna **partire** *It is necessary to leave*	Compare the subjunctive use: **È importante che, non vale la pena che**, etc. p. 247.
After exclamations with **che**	Che bello **essere** qui! *How nice to be here!* Che peccato **dover** partire *What a pity to have to leave/that we have to leave*	Compare with subjunctive use: **che bello che, che peccato che**, etc. p. 247.
After verbs of emotion	Preferisco **stare** qui *I prefer to stay here* Le dispiace **ripetere**? *Do you mind repeating?* Non m'interessa **imparare** a guidare *I'm not interested in learning to drive*	Others include: **piacere, odiare, sperare, temere**. Compare with **che** + subjunctive when the subjects differ, p. 248.
After verbs of opinion, belief, knowing, and doubt + **di**	Crede di **essere** malato *He believes he is ill* Penso di **venire** *I am thinking of coming/I think I will come* Non credo di **poter** venire *I don't think I can come*	Others include: **dubitare, sembrare, parere, sapere**. Compare their use with **che** + (subjunctive) verb when the subjects differ, p. 248.
Suggesting a possibility	**Bombardarli?** A che serve? *Bomb them? What for?* **Perdonarlo?** Mai! *Forgive him? Never!*	This usually refers to an unwelcome possibility.
As a noun	**Piangere** non serve a niente *Crying is pointless/It's pointless to cry* Non sopportava **l'abbaiare** del cane *He couldn't stand the barking of the dog* Con il/col **passare** del tempo il dolore si attenua *As time passes the pain lessens*	Italian infinitives can correspond to the English -ing form used as noun. In formal Italian and in some set phrases the infinitive used as a noun can be preceded by the masculine articles **il/l'/lo**.
As an imperative	**Tirare** (on a door) *Pull* **Non correre!** *Don't run!*	See also p. 235.

I Complete the sentences by giving the Italian equivalent of the English.
(a) Non devi partire … *without paying.*
(b) Ti vedrò … *before I leave.*
(c) Bisogna … *change trains in Milan.*
(d) Che strano … *to see you here!*

2   Give the Italian equivalent of the English.

   (a) *I like travelling by train.*
   (b) *I'm thinking of leaving.*
   (c) *I hope to see you soon.*

   (d) *I doubt I can come.*
   (e) *Eat it? – You must be joking! (Ma scherzi!)*
   (f) *My favourite pastime is playing cards.*

Italian infinitive – English gerund

The following is very common in everyday speech. It is important <u>not</u> to use the Italian gerund.

Sta tutta la giornata **ad ascoltare** la musica *He spends (lit. stays) all day listening to music* **Ho passato** la giornata **a pensare** ai miei problemi *I spent the day thinking about my problems* I bambini **erano occupati a costruire** castelli di sabbia *The children were busy building sandcastles* **Era seduta a guardare** la TV *She was sitting watching TV*	Expressing simultaneous actions: **a** + the infinitive is used after **stare** to be, **rimanere** to stay, **trovarsi** to find oneself, **passare** to spend (time), **essere occupato** to be busy, or after verbs expressing position: **essere seduto/disteso**, etc. See also Verbs and prepositions, p. 273.

E   **3**   Complete the sentences by giving the Italian equivalent of the English.

   (a) Sta a letto tutta la giornata ... *reading novels.*
   (b) Erano seduti intorno al tavolo ... *playing bridge.*
   (c) Hanno passato la giornata ... *mending the car.*
   (d) Era distesa sul divano ... *eating chocolates.* (cioccolatini)

The past infinitive

This consists of the infinitive of **avere** or **essere**, plus the past participle. The final -e of **avere** (and sometimes **essere**) may be dropped. Reflexive forms have the pronoun **si** attached to **essere**, but the reflexive pronoun changes to match the subject on which the infinitive depends.

-are	-ere	-ire
aver mangiato	**aver** ricevuto	**aver** dormito/finito
essere andato/a/i/e	**essere** venuto/a/i/e	**essere** partito/a/i/e
essersi lavato/a/i/e	**essersi** seduto/a/i/e	**essersi** divertito/a/i/e

With the past infinitives of modal verbs the tendency is to use **avere**, whatever auxiliary the following verb normally takes.

	dovuto	
È assurdo ... **aver**	**potuto**	mangiare/vendere/andare/venire
	voluto	

4 *I am pleased to have …* Give the past infinitive form of the following simple infinitives.

Sono contento di:
(a) pagare i debiti   (b) ricevere il pacco   (c) uscire con te   (d) divertirsi

5 Complete the sentences, giving the Italian equivalent of the English.

(a) È un peccato … *to have had to leave.* (dover partire)
(b) Mi dispiace … *not to have been able to come.* (non poter venire)

Pronoun position and participle agreements

Position	Mio marito è contento di non aver**lo** comprato *My husband is glad he didn't buy it* (lit. *not to have bought*)	Object and reflexive pronouns are always attached to **essere** or **avere**.
Agreement	Credo di **essere partito/a** alle undici *I think I left at eleven* È un peccato **non essere arrivati** prima *It's a shame not to have arrived earlier/we didn't arrive earlier* È in carcere per **averla uccisa** *He is in jail for having killed her* **But**: È in carcere per aver ucciso Maria	The past participles of infinitives taking **essere** agree with the subject of the verb in the main clause. If this subject is indefinite the agreement is always **masculine plural**. The past participle of infinitives taking **avere** only agrees with a preceding direct object pronoun (see also pp. 101, 208).

6 Complete the following in Italian, making the necessary participle agreements.

(a) Sono contento di aver comprato i pantaloni. *I am pleased I bought them.*
(b) È un sollievo aver venduto la casa. *It's a relief to have sold it.*
(c) È un peccato *not to have left together.* (partire)
(d) È un peccato *not to have travelled together.* (viaggiare)

USES OF THE PAST INFINITIVE

The uses of the past infinitive often but not always coincide with those of the simple infinitive. Although its literal English equivalent is *to have eaten, to have seen,* etc., in practice it often corresponds to a past gerund (*having eaten*) or a finite verb: *I have eaten/I ate* or *I had eaten.* It is important to note that the past infinitive is used after a variety of tenses and that, like the simple infinitive, it is used when the subject of the verbs in both clauses is the same. Otherwise the subjunctive is used.

Used with a variety of tenses	Partirò/Parto/Sono partito/Ero partito senza **averlo visto** *I will leave/am leaving/left/had left without having seen him*	The past infinitive is used to refer to completed actions preceding the time of speaking, whether this is future, present or past.

After modal verbs	Devo **aver sbagliato** I must have made a mistake Potrei **averlo dimenticato** I might/could have forgotten it	
After verbs taking prepositions	Mi ricordo di **averlo letto** I remember having read it/I read it Ti ringrazio/Grazie per **avermi chiamato** Thanks for calling/having called me	Note that **grazie per** and **ringraziare** are only used with a past infinitive.
After prepositions	Andrò a Milano dopo **aver visto** Gianni I'll go to Milan after I have seen/after seeing (after having seen) Gianni Mi ha chiamato prima di **aver avuto** la risposta He called me before he (had) got (having got) the reply	**Dopo** is only used with a past infinitive.
After impersonal verbs and expressions with **che**	Bisognava **averlo capito** prima It was necessary to have understood that before Che peccato non **esserci andati** What a shame not to have gone/that we didn't go	If the subject of the second verb does not refer to the speaker, a subjunctive will be used. See p. 247.
With verbs of emotion, saying knowing, opinion and doubt	Sono contento/a di **esserci andato/a** I am pleased I went (lit. to have gone) there Dice di **essere stato** da Mario He says he has been at Mario's Eravamo sicuri di **averlo visto** We were sure we had seen him	Often used with the subjunctive when the subject of the verbs differ. (See **pensare che**, etc., p. 248.)

E **7** Complete these sentences in Italian.

(a) Che sollievo ... *to have found the keys.*
(b) È un peccato ... *not to have gone there.*
(c) Dubito di ... *(that) I have understood.*
(d) Mi dispiace ... *(that) I had to leave.* (dover partire)

8 Simple or past infinitive? Give the Italian equivalent of the English.

(a) *I went out without having breakfast.*   (c) *Thank you for helping us.*
(b) *They left without having paid.*   (d) *I'll come and see you after I've talked to him.*

9 Give the English equivalent of the following. Which two sentences mean the same?

(a) Penso di partire lunedì.
(b) Penso di essere partito lunedì scorso.
(c) Sono felice di vederlo domani.
(d) Sono felice di averlo visto ieri.
(e) Non posso sposarmi prima di finire gli studi.
(f) Non posso sposarmi prima di aver finito gli studi.

23.2 THE GERUND

A gerund (**il gerundio**) is used to provide additional information about the main verb:

Mi sono rotto la gamba **giocando** a calcio *I broke my leg playing football*

There are two forms: simple gerunds and past gerunds.

Simple gerunds

These are invariable except for the reflexive **si**, which changes to **mi**, **ti**, etc. depending on who the gerund refers to.

-are → ando	-ere → endo	-ire → endo
parlare **parlando**	ricevere **ricevendo**	dormire/finire **dormendo/finendo**
andare **andando**	venire **venendo**	partire **partendo**
lavarsi **lavandosi**	sedersi **sedendosi**	divertirsi **divertendosi**

Past gerunds

These consist of the gerund of **avere** or **essere** plus the past participle. They are invariable except for past participles, which follow the rules of agreement with the subject or object (see p. 208).

-are	-ere	-ire
avendo parlato	**avendo ricevuto**	**avendo dormito/finito**
essendo andato/a/i/e	**essendo venuto/a/i/e**	**essendo partito/a/i/e**
essendosi lavato/a/i/e	**essendosi seduto/a/i/e**	**essendosi divertito/a/i/e**

Pronoun position

Pronouns are normally attached to the end of simple gerunds and to the auxiliary of past gerunds unless they are part of a finite verb.

> Portando**lo** a casa *Bringing it home*   Avendo**lo** portato a casa *Having brought it home*
> *But*: **Lo** sto portando a casa *I am bringing it home*

▌ USES OF THE SIMPLE AND PAST GERUND		
Expressing simultaneous actions: *while/as*	**Svegliandomi** stamattina, mi è venuta in mente la soluzione *As I woke up this morning the solution came to mind* (lit. *waking up this morning ...*) L'appetito viene **mangiando** *One's/Your appetite comes while/as you eat (with eating)*	Simple gerunds only. The simple gerund expresses what is going on while another action takes place. The English equivalent is often a finite verb with *as/while*.
Modality: *how*	È entrata, **piangendo** *She came in crying* Risponde sempre sorridendo *He always replies smiling*	Simple gerunds only.

Under what conditions: *by* and *if*	**Leggendo** quel libro imparerai un sacco di cose *You will learn a load of things by reading/if you read that book* Ho imparato l'italiano **ascoltando** una cassetta *I learned Italian by listening to a cassette* **Sbagliando** s'impara *You learn by (making) your mistakes*	Simple gerunds only.
Cause: *since/because*	**Essendo** tardi ho dovuto partire *Since it was late I had to leave* **Avendo** fatto la spesa è tornata a casa *Since she had/When she had/Having done the shopping she went home*	Simple and past gerunds. Sometimes the gerund is used just for conciseness rather than to emphasise cause. This is typical of formal written Italian.
Concession: *despite/even though/ although*	**Pur essendo** ricco era tirchio *Even though he was rich he was mean* **Pur avendo** preso l'ombrello si è bagnato *Although he took/Despite having taken the umbrella he got wet*	**Pur** (*pure*) + simple or past gerund. See also p. 174.
In continuous tenses	Stiamo **uscendo** *We are going out* Stavano **pranzando** *They were having lunch*	**Stare** + the simple gerund expresses the English present and imperfect continuous. See pp. 195–6, 217–18.

(Level 2)

Same subject as main verb

It is important to note that the gerund usually has the same subject as the main verb. A gerund cannot be used if it refers to a subject which differs from the main verb subject: **che** or **mentre** + a finite verb must be used instead.

Passeggiando lungo il fiume **ho visto** tua figlia **Facendo** la spesa … **ho incontrato** Maria *But*: Ho incontrato Maria **che faceva** la spesa Ho incontrato Maria **mentre faceva** la spesa	*As I walked along the river I saw your daughter* *While (I was) doing the shopping I met Maria* *I met Maria (who was) doing the shopping* *I met Maria while she was shopping*

An exception to the above rule is with impersonal expressions.

Essendo buio, mi sono perso	*Since it was dark, I got lost*

E 1 How do you do it? Answer the questions in Italian using the correct form of the gerund.

(a) Che bella casa. Come hai fatto a comprarla? – (Lavorare) come un matto e (risparmiare) la metà dello stipendio.

(b) Studi tanto di notte, come fai a resistere? – (Bere) caffè e (fumare) come un turco!

(c) Gli affari vanno benissssimo, come ha fatto? – (Studiare) il mercato e (offrire) un servizio sempre migliore.

2   Why not? Explain why you didn't do the following things, using the correct form of the
past gerund.

(a) Perché non sei uscito con noi? – Beh, (essere) malato mi è sembrato più prudente.

(b) Come mai non hai voluto vedere il film? – Beh, (sentire) le critiche mi è passata la voglia.

(c) Come mai avete rifiutato l'invito? – Beh, (mangiare) così male l'altra volta, abbiamo
preferito andare da Laura!

3   While/as I was ... Express some of the events of your day in Italy, using a simple Italian
gerund where appropriate.

(a) *Going into town I met Giuseppe on the bus.*

(b) *As I crossed Piazza della Repubblica I saw the police arresting two men.*

(c) *On my way home/As I was going home, I saw Letizia talking to Adriano.*

4   Gerund or infinitive? Express the following in Italian.

(a) *I hate waiting.*   (c) *She ran off screaming.* (scappare via)

(b) *They were sitting there waiting for me.*   (d) *Screaming is pointless.*

23.3 THE PAST PARTICIPLE

The past participle (**il participio passato**) is the form of the verb which is used
with **avere** and **essere** in compound tenses. It is also used in passive constructions
(see p. 268). On its own, the past participle can be used to introduce a very concise
dependent clause.

Regular forms of the past participle end in **-ato**, **-uto** and **-ito**, but there are many
irregularities (see p. 207).

(bagnare) bagn**ato** *wet*	(temere) tem**uto** *feared*	(pulire) pul**ito** *clean/ed*

▌ USES

As a participle	**Data** la situazione, sarebbe meglio non partire *Given the situation ...*	This is like the English.
As an adjective	Mi devi mandare il contratto **firmato** (che è stato firmato) *You must send me the signed contract*	Used as adjectives, past participles agree with the noun they modify. They often replace a relative clause.
Expressing *having .../ when ...*	**Finita** la partita, torneremo a casa *When the match ends we'll go home* **Finita** la partita, siamo tornati a casa *When the match ended we went home* **Finita** la partita, eravamo tornati a casa *After the match had ended we had gone home*	The past participle can be used instead of a finite verb in a dependent clause. It is used with a variety of tenses, as the participle simply refers to actions preceding the main verb, irrespective of tense.

| Expressing *as soon as,* once | Una volta **arrivati** al semaforo, dovete girare a destra
Once you've got to the traffic lights you have to turn right | The past participle is often preceded by **(non) appena** or **una volta**, especially in speech. For the participle agreement see below. |

Pronoun position and participle agreements

| Agreement | Una volta **fatto**, non ci penso più
Once it's done I don't think about it any more/ I put it out of my mind
Una volta **arrivati** alla stazione, vi consiglio di prendere un tassì
Once you have arrived at the station I advise you to take a taxi
But: Una volta **imboccata** la strada,vedrete la casa a sinistra
Once you have turned into the road you'll see the house on the left | With verbs taking **avere**, the past participle is masculine singular. With verbs taking **essere**, past participles agree with the subject of the verb. With verbs taking **avere** followed by the object, the participle agrees with the object. |
| Pronoun position | Trovato**si** solo, si spaventò
On finding himself alone, he became frightened | Pronouns are attached to the participle. This is not used in speech. |

E   I   Rewrite the following, making each sentence more concise by using a past participle instead of the finite verb.

(a) Una volta che aveva fatto la spesa Luisa è tornata a casa.

(b) Appena le lezioni erano finite, siamo andati in centro.

(c) Una volta che siete arrivati in albergo, mi dovete chiamare.

(d) Appena hai passato il ponte e la farmacia, troverai la strada a destra.

(e) Avendo risolto il problema, mi sento più tranquilla.

The subjunctive

The subjunctive (**il congiuntivo**) is a form of the verb used to express a variety of attitudes such as uncertainty, hope, desire and fear. In Italian there are four subjunctive tenses, but in English subjunctive forms are rare and usually old-fashioned: *If your father **were** here, he would be happy. So **be** it.*

24.1 THE PRESENT SUBJUNCTIVE

Regular forms

The easiest way to form the present subjunctive is to start from the present tense and change the **io** form.

	parlare: o → i	vendere: o → a	dormire: o → a	finire: o → a
Indicative	io parl**o**	io vend**o**	io dorm**o**	io finisc**o**
Subjunctive	io parl**i**	io vend**a**	io dorm**a**	io finisc**a**

The full conjugations are as follows:

io	parl**i**	vend**a**	dorm**a**	finisc**a**
tu	parl**i**	vend**a**	dorm**a**	finisc**a**
lui/lei/Lei	parl**i**	vend**a**	dorm**a**	finisc**a**
noi	parl**iamo**	vend**iamo**	dorm**iamo**	fin**iamo**
voi	parl**iate**	vend**iate**	dorm**iate**	fin**iate**
loro	parl**ino**	vend**ano**	dorm**ano**	finisc**ano**

- Note that -**ere** and -**ire** verbs have identical endings.
- The singular forms of the present subjunctive are identical. If the context does not make the meaning clear, the subject pronouns are used.

- All the forms except **noi** and **voi** are based on the **io** first person form.
- The **noi** forms are identical to the indicative present, but the **voi** forms all end in -iate.
- Spelling. As with future and conditional tenses, verbs with -car*e* and -gare endings require the addition of an **h** to keep the hard sound of the infinitive: e.g. cercare – cerchi, pagare – paghi. Verbs in -**ciare** and -**giare** drop the **i** of the stem, as it is not needed to keep the soft sound of the infinitive: e.g. lasciare – lasci mangiare – mangi.

Irregular forms: verbs with an irregular indicative present

If a verb has an irregular indicative present tense then its present subjunctive is also irregular. It nevertheless follows the basic pattern of regular subjunctive endings shown above: i.e. all forms except the **noi** and **voi** forms are based on the first person **io** form. Here are some of the most common irregularities.

Infinitive	Present indicative	Present subjunctive
andare	vado	**vada** vada vada andiamo andiate vadano
bere	bevo	**beva** beva beva beviamo beviate bevano
dire	dico	**dica** dica dica diciamo diciate dicano
dovere	devo/debbo	**debba** debba debba dobbiamo dobbiate debbano
fare	faccio	**faccia** faccia faccia facciamo facciate facciano
potere	posso	**possa** possa possa possiamo possiate possano
rimanere	rimango	**rimanga** rimanga rimanga rimaniamo rimaniate rimangano
tenere	tengo	**tenga** tenga tenga teniamo teniate tengano
venire	vengo	**venga** venga venga veniamo veniate vengano
volere	voglio	**voglia** voglia voglia vogliamo vogliate vogliano
uscire	esco	**esca** esca esca usciamo usciate escano

- Although all the subjunctive **voi** forms end in -**iate**, there are some which are not based on the **voi** indicative forms:

  diciate, dobbiate, facciate, possiate, vogliate

- **Debba** is the most common form of the present subjunctive of **dovere**, but **deva** is also used.

Very irregular forms

The following five verbs are the only ones not derived from the present indicative **io** form.

Infinitive	Present indicative	Present subjunctive
avere	ho	**abbia** abbia abbia abbiamo abbiate abbiano
essere	sono	**sia** sia sia siamo siate siano
dare	do	**dia** dia dia diamo diate diano
sapere	so	**sappia** sappia sappia sappiamo sappiate sappiano
stare	sto	**stia** stia stia stiamo stiate stiano

- Note that the present continuous **stare** + gerund can be made subjunctive.
  sto leggendo → **stia** leggendo

1 Form the present subjunctive of the verbs given to say whay you want others to do.

  (a) Vuoi che io gli (mandare) il pacco?   (d) Vuoi che lo (finire) io?
  (b) Voglio che tu gli (scrivere) qualcosa. (e) Vuole che tu lo (pagare) adesso.
  (c) Voglio che loro (dormire) subito!   (f) Voglio che loro (cominciare) presto.

2 Ask what others prefer you to do by using the correct subjunctive form of the verb.

  (a) Preferisci che lo (fare) io?   (c) Preferisci che glielo (dare) io?
  (b) Preferisce che ci (andare) io? (d) Preferite che glielo (dire) io?

3 Have a guess. Can you form the present subjunctive singular form of the verbs below? – They have irregular indicative present tenses. If necessary consult the irregular present tense verb section on pp. 191–2.

  (a) contenere   (c) riuscire   (e) opporre
  (b) intervenire (d) produrre (f) attrarre

MAIN USES OF THE PRESENT SUBJUNCTIVE

The subjunctive is frequently used in Italian but its use is becoming increasingly flexible, especially in the spoken language. In many cases its use is a question of personal or stylistic choice. The following are guidelines to some of the most common uses.

In independent sentences: let ... may ...	**Che venga** quando gli pare *Let him come when he wants* **Viva** l'Italia! *Long live Italy!* (lit. *May Italy live*)	The subjunctive can express a wish – usually heartfelt.

In the following six cases a subjunctive is used in a subordinate clause when its subject differs from the subject in the main clause. If the subjects are the same, an infinitive is normally used (see pp. 236–7, 239). It is important to note that the present subjunctive refers to the future as well as to the present, as there is no future subjunctive.

After impersonal expressions and exclamations with **che**	**Bisogna che** tu venga presto domani *You need to come early tomorrow* **È facile/difficile che** arrivino lunedì *They are likely/unlikely to arrive on Monday* **Che peccato che** Barbara sia malata *What a shame that Barbara is ill*	Others include: **non importa che, basta che, conviene che, non vale la pena che, è incredibile/ bello/strano/meglio/ naturale/ essenziale/ importante ... che.**

With verbs expressing emotion and feeling	**Mi auguro che** tornino presto *I hope they will return soon* **Ho paura che** sia troppo tardi *I'm afraid it's too late*	Others include: **sperare, piacere, dispiacere, preferire, temere, non vedere l'ora** (*to look forward to*), **avere bisogno, essere contento.**
Verbs of thinking, believing, denial and opinion	**Mi pare che** vadano via domenica *I think they're going away on Sunday* **Ho l'impressione che** sia gelosa *I have the impression she is jealous*	Others include: **credere, pensare, ritenere, supporre, immaginare, sembrare, negare, non dire che.**
Verbs and expressions conveying hearsay, doubt, negation and uncertainty	**Si dice che** abbia una casa che vale 100 milioni *It is said she has a house worth 100 million* **Non so che cosa** lui stia leggendo *I don't know what he's reading* **Non è detto che** vengano *It's not definite that they are coming/They won't necessarily come* **Può darsi che** sia vero *It may be true/perhaps it's true* **But**: Forse è vero	Others include: **non so se, non capisco se, non è che, dubitare.** See also Negatives, p. 149. **Note**: forse means the same as **può darsi** but does not require the subjunctive.
Verbs for wishes, requests, orders and permission	**Vuoi che** lo faccia io? *Do you want me to do it?* **Permetti che** te lo spieghi? *Would you allow me to explain it to you?*	Others include: **chiedere, insistere, lasciare, pregare, pretendere, esigere, evitare, ordinare, proporre, suggerire.**
With some connectives of time	Chiamalo **prima che** vada via *Call him before he leaves* **È ora** che Ivo mi aiuti *It's time Ivo helped me* **But**: Chiamalo prima di andare via *Call him before you leave* È ora di aiutare Ivo *It's time to help Ivo*	Others include: **finché/ fino a quando (non).** Note also **aspettare che.** If the subjects are the same in both clauses, **prima, è ora** and **aspettare** are followed by **di** + infinitive. See also p. 179.

No subjunctive

It is important to note the following.

No subjunctive needed to denote certainty	È chiaro che sta male *It's clear he is unwell* Dicono che è brava *They say she is clever* **But**: **Si dice che** sia brava *It is said/they say …* **Direi che** sia brava *I would say …* **Non dico che** sia brava *I'm not saying …*	Expressions such as **essere evidente/ovvio/vero che** or **dire che** do <u>not</u> require subjunctives. **Si dice che, direi che** and **non dico che** <u>do</u> require them, since they express hearsay and negation.
The future indicative can replace the present subjunctive	Penso che sarà/sia difficile convincerlo *I think it will be hard to persuade him* Spero che verranno/vengano *I hope they come*	The future indicative can replace the present subjunctive after all verbs of thinking, of doubt, and some verbs of emotion.

4 You tell others what needs to happen. Express the English in Italian.

(a) Nicola, non hai ancora pagato l'affitto? *It's essential that you pay it soon.*
(b) Silvana e Giorgio non hanno spedito il pacco? *It's important that they send it tomorrow.*
(c) Voi non sapete se venite domani? *But it's necessary for me to know today.*

5 Discuss possibilities using the appropriate form of the verb. The English is given to help.

(a) È difficile che (venire) tutti quanti. (*It's unlikely that they will all come.*)
(b) È possibile che il treno (essere) in ritardo. (*It's possible that the train may be late.*)
(c) Non è detto che loro (tornare) stasera. (*They won't necessarily come back tonight.*)

6 Say how you feel, using the expressions in the order given to begin the sentences. Make the necessary changes to the verb.

> mi fa piacere che • mi dispiace che • temo che • che peccato che •
> ho paura che • non è giusto che

(a) Tu stai meglio.
(b) Lei non ha più tempo.
(c) Loro vogliono lamentarsi.
(d) Loro non possono venire.
(e) Lucio è malato.
(f) Lo fanno loro.

7 Express your thoughts and impressions using the correct form of the verb given.

(a) Ho l'impressione che Carlo (bere) troppo.
(b) Mi sembra che Luca (mangiare) tanto.
(c) Non credo che loro (rimanere) stasera.
(d) Non dico che (tradire) la moglie.

8 Make requests and demands using the correct form of the verb given.

(a) Giovanni, lascia che lo (fare) tuo fratello. (*Giovanni, let your brother do it.*)
(b) Lavinia permetti che io (finire) il mio discorso? (*Lavinia, will you allow me to finish what I'm saying?*)
(c) Voglio che Simone mi (dare) una mano. (*I want Simone to give me a hand.*)

9 Select the correct form of the verb. Beware, not all of the sentences require a subjunctive verb. In a few cases either form is possible.

(a) Sono sicuro che Anna è/sia infelice.
(b) Non dico che tu sei/sia antipatico.
(c) Dici che sono/siano tutti corrotti?
(d) Si dice che lui ha/abbia miliardi.
(e) Spero che tu torni/tornerai.
(f) Temo che sia/sarà troppo tardi.

10 Change the meaning by changing the subject. Rewrite the last part of the second sentence using the appropriate verb form.

(a) Mi dispiace non poter venire. – Mi dispiace che Lei ...
(b) Non credo di riuscire a farlo in tempo – Non credo che lui ...
(c) Prima di andar via voglio parlarti. – Prima che tu ...

11 Identify the sentences which require a subjunctive in Italian, and supply the correct form of the verb.

(a) *I prefer to do it.*
(b) *I prefer you to do it.*
(c) *I want to come.*
(d) *I want them to come.*
(e) *It's important to understand.*
(f) *It's important you understand.*

24.2 THE PERFECT SUBJUNCTIVE

This is formed with the present subjunctive of **essere** and **avere** plus the past participle
of the relevant verb.

	parlare	partire
io	abbia parlato	sia partito/a
tu	abbia parlato	sia partito/a
lui/lei/Lei	abbia parlato	sia partito/a
noi	abbiamo parlato	siamo partiti/e
voi	abbiate parlato	siate partiti/e
loro	abbiano parlato	siano partiti/e

• Irregularities concern the past participles only. To revise their use, see pp. 206–7.

Tense sequence of the perfect subjunctive

The perfect subjunctive is used in the same way as the present subjunctive but it refers
to an action preceding the time of speaking. It can follow a variety of tenses.

Present	Immagino che si **siano divertiti**	Note that the perfect
	I expect/imagine that they enjoyed themselves	subjunctive is used after
Future	Penseranno che tu non **abbia avuto** tempo	the present, future and
	di scrivere *They'll think that you haven't had/didn't*	(in some cases) the
	have time to write	**passato prossimo.**
Passato	Mi è dispiaciuto che tu **non abbia vinto** il premio	It may also sometimes
prossimo	*I was sorry you did not win the prize*	come after the
Conditional	Direi che **abbia sbagliato**	conditional.
	I would say he has made a mistake	

1 Complete the sentences by giving the Italian equivalent of the English.

    (a) Sono contento che tu... *you came/have come.*
    (b) Ho l'impressione che ... *he has not understood.*
    (c) Non credo che ... *they want to come.*
    (d) Direi che ... *they have forgotten.*

2 Give the Italian equivalent of the English.

    (a) *I imagine it has been difficult.*   (c) *It's odd that they haven't called.*
    (b) *Maybe he has already left.*   (d) *Do you think he has had an accident?*

24.3 THE IMPERFECT SUBJUNCTIVE

Regular forms

This is formed from the stem of the verb as follows.

	parlare	vendere	finire
io	parl**assi**	vend**essi**	fin**issi**
tu	parl**assi**	vend**essi**	fin**issi**
lui/lei/Lei	parl**asse**	vend**esse**	fin**isse**
noi	parl**assimo**	vend**essimo**	fin**issimo**
voi	parl**aste**	vend**este**	fin**iste**
loro	parl**assero**	vend**essero**	fin**issero**

- The **io** and **tu** forms of the imperfect subjunctive are identical. If the context does not make the meaning clear, the subject pronouns are used.

Irregular forms

The only irregularities are **essere**, **dare** and **stare** and verbs with contracted infinitives. The regular -**ere** endings are used in all cases except for **essere**.

essere	fossi	fossi	fosse	fossimo	foste	fossero
dare	dessi	dessi	desse	dessimo	deste	dessero
stare	stessi	stessi	stesse	stessimo	steste	stessero
bere	bevessi	bevessi	bevesse	bevessimo	beveste	bevessero
dire	dicessi	dicessi	dicesse	dicessimo	diceste	dicessero
fare	facessi	facessi	facesse	facessimo	faceste	facessero
trarre	traessi	traessi	traesse	traessimo	traeste	traessero
porre	ponessi	ponessi	ponesse	ponessimo	poneste	ponessero
condurre	conducessi	conducessi	conducesse	conducessimo	conduceste	conducessero

- Note that the imperfect continuous **stare** + gerund can be made subjunctive: stavo leggendo → **stessi** leggendo.

24.4 THE PLUPERFECT SUBJUNCTIVE

This is formed from the imperfect subjunctive of **avere** or **essere** plus the past participle of the verb.

	parlare	partire
io	avessi parlato	fossi partito/a
tu	avessi parlato	fossi partito/a
lui/lei/Lei	avesse parlato	fosse partito/a
noi	avessimo parlato	fossimo partiti/e
voi	aveste parlato	foste partiti/e
loro	avessero parlato	fossero partiti/e

- Irregularities concern the past participles only. To revise them, see pp. 206–7.

Tense sequence of imperfect and pluperfect subjunctives

Imperfect and pluperfect subjunctives are used after a past tense verb (imperfect, **passato prossimo**, pluperfect, etc.) or after a conditional.

Imperfect	Ero contento che **fosse** con me *I was pleased that he/she was with me* (now) Ero contento che **fosse venuto** *I was pleased he/she had come* (past) Sembrava che nessuno **avesse visto** niente *It seemed that nobody had seen anything* (past)	The use of the imperfect or pluperfect subjunctive also depends on what point in time is being referred to: the present, the future or the past.
Passato prossimo Pluperfect	Ho insistito che **scrivesse** subito *I insisted he write at once* (future) Avevo chiesto che **venissero** più tardi *I had asked them to come later* (future)	The imperfect subjunctive refers to actions happening at the time of speaking or to future actions; the pluperfect
Conditional Past conditional	Mi piacerebbe/mi sarebbe piaciuto che tu **imparassi** il francese *I would like you to learn French/I would have liked you to learn French* (future)	subjunctive refers only to actions which have taken place before the time of speaking.

E

I   Insert the correct imperfect subjunctive form of the verb given.

  (a) Voleva che (io – tornare) il giorno dopo.
  (b) Sperava che (tu – potere) aiutare.
  (c) Era contento che (noi – studiare).
  (d) Non sapevo se (voi – capire) anche l'arabo.

2   Provide the correct imperfect subjunctive form of the verb given.

  (a) Pensavo che Matilda (essere) in Australia!
  (b) Credevo che voi (avere) da fare.
  (c) Era contento che noi (stare) con lui.
  (d) Era ora che Marco ci (dare) una mano.
  (e) Mi dispiaceva che Giulio e Antonio (bere) tanto.
  (f) Volevo che tu lo (tradurre) in fretta.

3   Make the commands and requests below less abrupt by beginning with the expressions below in the order given and making the necessary changes to the verbs.

  > mi piacerebbe che tu • sarebbe meglio che Lei • mi farebbe piacere se tu •
  > vorrei che voi

  (a) Vieni con noi.   (c) Fallo subito.
  (b) Lo dica a loro, non a me.   (d) Me lo spiegate?

4   Insert the imperfect or pluperfect subjunctive, whichever is appropriate.

  (a) Era strano che … *no one was there.*
  (b) Era strano che … *no one had replied.*
  (c) Mi sarebbe piaciuto che … *them to come.*
  (d) Era un peccato che Angela … *had not come.*

24.5 FURTHER USES OF THE SUBJUNCTIVE

Subjunctive with indefinites and connectives

Most of the following indefinites and connectives can be used with all subjunctive tenses.

Indefinites	Non essere scoraggiato, **comunque** vadano le cose *Don't be discouraged, however things go* Io ti appoggio **qualunque cosa** tu abbia fatto *I support you whatever you've done*	Others include: **chiunque, qualunque/qualsiasi, dovunque.** See pp. 127, 130.
Concession and condition	**Benché** avesse voglia di venire, non è stato possibile *Although he felt like coming, it wasn't possible*	Others include: **nonostante, a condizione che, purché, sebbene.** See also pp. 176–7.
Contradiction, cause, purpose	Te lo dico **perché** tu sappia come regolarti *I'm telling you so that you know what to expect*	Others include: **non perché** (*not because*), **di/in modo che, affinché** (*so that*).
Exceptions	Lo troverai domani **a meno che (non)** sia fuori *You'll get hold of him tomorrow unless he's out*; Devo parlargli **senza che** gli altri lo sappiano *I have to talk to him without the others knowing*; **But**: Eravamo vicini senza saperlo *We were neighbours without knowing it*	Others include: **eccetto/ salvo che/tranne** (*except*). If the subjects are the same in both clauses these are all followed by an infinitive verb. See also p. 176.
Hypotheses	**Magari** fosse vero! *If only it were true!* **Caso mai** dovesse piovere, ti passo a prendere *If it should rain/If by any chance it should rain, I'll come by and pick you up*	The most common phrases are: **anche se, come se, caso mai, magari,** used with imperfect and pluperfect subjunctives. **Nel caso che** may be followed by any subjunctive tense.
	Nel caso che tu debba contattarmi ti lascio il mio numero *I'll leave you my number in case you have to contact me* Gli ho lasciato il mio numero **nel caso che** mi dovesse contattare *I left him my number in case he should need to contact me*	

Il fatto che and che

Il fatto che tu sia giovane non è una scusa *The fact that you are young is no excuse* **Che** avesse pianto era ovvio/probabile *It was obvious/likely she had been crying* **But**: Era ovvio che aveva pianto	**Il fatto che** is usually followed by the subjunctive whatever its position in the sentence. **Che** is always followed by the subjunctive when it precedes the main clause even when it would normally be followed by the indicative.

I Rewrite the sentences below, replacing **ma** and **se** with the words given and giving the correct form of the verb.

(a) È stanco, *ma* non ha fatto niente oggi. (benché/sebbene)
(b) Andremo in piscina *se* non fa freddo. (a condizione che)
(c) Possiamo stare a casa *se* tu non vuoi uscire. (a meno che)
(d) Uscirò *ma* nessuno lo saprà. (senza che)
(e) Ti lascio la chiave *se* ne hai bisogno. (nel caso che)

2   Complete the sentences by giving the Italian equivalent of the English.

    (a) *The fact that her son did not study* ... le pesava molto.

    (b) Le pesava molto ... *the fact that he did not study.*

    (c) Era evidente che ... *they were not willing to help.* (essere disposto a)

    (d) *That they were not willing to help* ... era evidente.

Subjunctive in relative and interrogative clauses

After a superlative antecedent to a relative clause	È la ragazza **più simpatica che** io **conosca** *She's the nicest girl I know* È la coppia **più generosa che** io **abbia** mai **conosciuto** *They are the most generous couple I have ever met* Era la città **più bella che** io **avessi** mai **visto** *It was the most beautiful town I had ever seen* È **l'unica** soluzione **che abbia** un senso *It's the only solution that makes sense*	The antecedent is the word or phrase to which **che** refers. A superlative antecedent is a phrase containing an adjective with **più, meno** or **solo, unico, primo, ultimo**.
After an indefinite antecedent to a relative clause	Non conosco **nessuno che** lo **abbia fatto** *I don't know anyone who has done it* Bisogna trovare **qualcuno che** lo **sappia fare** *You need to find someone who knows how to do it* **But:** Conosco qualcuno che lo sa fare *I know someone (specific) who knows how to do it*	Common antecedents are **qualcuno, qualcosa, uno, nessuno, niente**. These must refer to someone or something unspecified that may not exist.
After an interrogative antecedent (indirect questions)	**Non so chi** sia *I don't know who he is* **Non capisco come** l'abbiano fatto *I don't understand how they did it* **Voleva sapere dove** fossero andati *He wanted to know where they had gone*	These are words like **chi, che cosa, come, dove, quando, perché** or **se** after verbs and phrases such as **non sapere, non capire, chiedersi, domandarsi** and **voler sapere**. In spoken Italian the indicative is often used.

Imperfect and pluperfect subjunctive for conditions and hypotheses

Expressing a hypothesis or possible condition	Se **avessi** più tempo, ti aiuterei *If I had more time I would help you* Se **dovessi** vincere il Totocalcio, non so cosa farei *If I were to win/If I won the lottery I don't know what I would do*	If the action referred to could take place, an imperfect subjunctive is used after **se**, with a simple conditional in the main clause.
Expressing an unfulfilled or impossible condition	Se mi **avessi chiamato**, sarei andata a prenderti *If you had called me I would have gone to collect you*	In this case the pluperfect subjunctive is required after **se** and the main verb is in the past conditional. See also p. 229.

3 Express the following in Italian.

(a) *It's the most beautiful place there is.*
(b) *It's the most beautiful place I have ever seen.*
(c) *He was the only teacher who had ever helped me.*

4 Select the appropriate verb each time. In some cases either is possible.

(a) Non conosco nessuno che *sa/sappia* quattro lingue.
(b) Conosco qualcuno che *sa/sappia* quattro lingue.
(c) Hai comprato un abito che ti *sta/stia* molto bene.
(d) Devi trovare un abito che ti *sta/stia* bene.

5 What would happen if ... What would have happened if ...? Complete the sentences in Italian, substituting the English.

(a) *If you came to my place* ... potremmo partire insieme.
(b) *If they had arrived earlier* ... non avremmo perso il treno.
(c) *If I were to lose my job* ... sarebbe un disastro.
(d) *If he had not quarrelled with the boss* ... non avrebbe perso il posto.

25

Special verb constructions

25.1 REFLEXIVE CONSTRUCTIONS

Many Italian verbs can have a reflexive construction, i.e. they are always used with reflexive pronouns (see pp. 80–82) and use **essere** as the auxiliary verb in compound tenses. They can be divided into reflexive and reciprocal verbs.

Reflexive

Mi lavo *I wash myself* **Mi lavo** le mani *I wash my hands*	True reflexive verbs are those which express an action that a person does to himself/herself directly or indirectly.
Si chiama Adriana *Her name is Adriana* (lit. *She calls herself Adriana*) **Ci alziamo** alle sette *We get up at seven*	Note that the English equivalents may not include the words *myself, yourself, himself*, etc.
Mi sono preso una polmonite *I went and caught pneumonia* Ho preso una polmonite *I caught pneumonia*	Many common non-reflexive verbs followed by an object are made reflexive, especially in spoken Italian, simply for greater emphasis or dramatic effect. Others include **bere/bersi, comprare/comprarsi, mangiare/mangiarsi**.

Reciprocal

Ci siamo abbracciati *We embraced/hugged each other* **Si** sono scritti *They wrote to each other*	Some verbs with reflexive forms express reciprocal meanings – actions people do to each other. They are always used with **ci, vi** and **si** + plural verb forms.

- Similar verbs which can have reciprocal meanings include:

  aiutarsi, amarsi, baciarsi, conoscersi, insultarsi, odiarsi, parlarsi, picchiarsi
  (*to hit each other*), sentirsi (*to be in touch*), stimarsi (*to respect each other*),
  vedersi (*to see each other, to meet*), volersi bene (*to love each other*).

Non-reflexive forms

Mi **sono** fermato a Milano *I stopped in Milan* (lit. *stopped myself*) **Ha** fermato il treno *He stopped the train* Si **sono** salutati *They said hello to each other* Li **ho** salutati *I said hello to them*	Some Italian reflexive and reciprocal verbs have non-reflexive forms with the same or similar meaning. These, however, are used transitively, with a direct object (e.g. **treno**, **li**). Note that the auxiliary verb of the non-reflexive form is **avere**, not **essere**.

- Verbs used in this way include most reciprocal verbs and:

  alzarsi *to get up*/alzare *to raise, put up*, divertirsi *to enjoy o.self*/divertire *to amuse sb*, lavarsi/lavare *to wash*, muoversi *to get going*/muovere *to move sth*, pettinarsi/pettinare *to comb/do hair*, sentirsi/sentire *to feel*, spogliarsi/spogliare *to undress*, scusarsi *to apologise*/scusare *to excuse sb*.

Reflexive form, no reflexive meaning

Perché **ti** arrabbi? *Why are you angry?* Flavio **si** comporta male *Flavio behaves badly*	A number of Italian verbs with reflexive forms have lost their original reflexive meanings. The majority of these express a feeling, a state, or an attitude of mind.

- Other verbs used as above include:

  accorgersi *to notice/realise*, addormentarsi *to fall asleep*, annoiarsi *to be/get bored*, dimenticarsi *to forget*, lamentarsi *to complain*, meravigliarsi *to be amazed*, offendersi *to take offence*, pentirsi *to regret*, rendersi conto *to realise/be aware*, ricordarsi *to remember*, stufarsi *to get fed up*, stupirsi *to be amazed/surprised*, vantarsi *to boast*, vergognarsi *to be ashamed*.

I Give the Italian equivalent of the following: half of them are not reflexive constructions.

(a) *He washed himself.*
(b) *He washed the car.*
(c) *I dressed my daughter.*
(d) *I got dressed.*
(e) *We kissed each other.*
(f) *They kissed us.*
(g) *I felt unwell.*
(h) *I felt a pain* (un dolore).

- For further practice of reflexive constructions see Exercises 1–3, pp. 81–2; Exercise 4, p. 191; and Exercise 3, p. 207.
- For reflexive verbs used with parts of the body and clothing, see pp. 81, 109, and for agreements of the past participle of reflexive verbs, see pp. 102, 208.

25.2 CAUSATIVE VERBS

Causative verbs are verbs made up of two parts: **fare** or **lasciare** + an infinitive,
e.g. **far venire qlcu** *to get ('cause') sb to come*. They are used in two ways:

- to express making or letting someone do something: e.g. **far scrivere qlcu**
  to get/make sb (to) write, **lasciar ascoltare qlcu** *to let/allow sb (to) listen*.
- to express getting or having something done: e.g. **far pulire qlco** *to get/have
  something cleaned*.

Making or letting somebody do something

Object: position	Perché fai aspettare **i clienti**? *Why do you make the clients wait?* Perché **li** fai aspettare? *Why do you make them wait?* Ho lasciato passare **il camion** *I let the lorry past* **L'**ho lasciato passare *I let it past* Ha fatto arrabbiare **Pino** *He made Pino get angry* **Lo** ha fatto arrabbiare *He made him get angry*	In Italian the noun object comes <u>after</u> the verbs. The pronouns follow the regular rules of position of object pronouns (pp. 91–2). Note that if a reflexive verb such as **arrabbiarsi** follows **fare**, reflexive pronouns are omitted.
a before the noun subject	Perché non fai cantare quella canzone **ai bambini**? *Why don't you get the children to sing that song?* Perché non **gli** fai cantare quella canzone? *Why don't you get them to sing that song?* Lascia**mi/gli** finire il lavoro *Let me/him finish the work* Lascia finire (il lavoro) **a me/a lui** *Let me/him finish it*	If the infinitive verb has a noun subject (e.g. **bambini**) as well as an object, **a** goes in front of the subject. This is replaced by an indirect object pronoun (e.g. **gli**) or by a disjunctive, preceded by **a** (e.g. **a me, a lui**).

Getting or having something done

Object: position	Farò riparare la **macchina** *I'll get the car mended* **La** farò riparare *I'll get it mended* Mi faccio tagliare **i capelli** *I get my hair cut* Me **li** faccio tagliare *I get it cut*	Noun objects go after the verb and pronouns follow the rules of pronoun position. (See pp. 91–2.)
da before the noun subject	Farò riparare la macchina **da mio cognato** *I'll get my brother-in-law to mend the car/I'll get my car mended by my brother-in-law* **Gli** farò riparare la macchina *I'll get him to mend the car* Farà scrivere la lettera **dalla segretaria** *He'll get the secretary to write the letter* **Le** farà scrivere la lettera *He'll get her to write the letter*	**Da** is normally used before the person by whom a service is done if the infinitive has an object (e.g. **macchina**). An indirect object pronoun is normally used to replace that noun.

Using direct or indirect object pronouns

fare		If the construction has
+ one object	Fal**la** studiare di più *Get **her** to/Make her study more*	one object, a direct object
+ two objects	Fal**le** studiare **i verbi** *Get **her** to study **the verbs***	pronoun is required for
lasciare		the person. If there are
+ one object	**Lo** lasceremo scegliere *We will let **him** choose*	two objects, an indirect
+ two objects	**Gli** lascerei fare **quello che vuole**	object pronoun is required.
	or: **Lo** lascerei fare **quello che vuole**	Occasionally **lasciare** can
	*I would let **him** do **what he wants***	take a direct object
		pronoun for the person
		even when the infinitive
		has another object.

An alternative to lasciare + infinitive

Lasciare che + subjunctive	Lascia che lo facciano loro/i ragazzi (Lascialo fare a loro/ai ragazzi) *Let them/the children do it*	This is often used in place of **lasciare** + infinitive, but only when the dependent infinitive has a different subject from **lasciare**.

- **fare/lasciare** + infinitive also correspond to some common English verbs, for example:

  far sapere *to inform, let sb know*, far conoscere *to introduce sb, to acquaint sb with*, far notare *to point out*, far pagare *to charge sb*, fare vedere *to show*, farsi prestare *to borrow*, lasciar cadere *to drop*, lasciar perdere *to forget about, leave sth*, lasciar stare *to leave alone*.

1 Express in Italian what you get others to do and repeat it in shortened form.

   (a) *I get the house cleaned. I get it cleaned.*
   (b) *I make my son get up. I make him get up.*
   (c) *I always let my daughter go out. – I always let her go out.*

2 Now say who you got to do what and repeat it in shortened form.

   (a) *I got my sister to play the piano. I got her to play the piano.*
   (b) *I made Dino do the shopping. I made him do the shopping.*
   (c) *I let my brother drive the car. I let him drive the car.*
   (d) *I got the mechanic to adjust the brakes. I got him to adjust the brakes.*

3 This is the advice you get from your friends about your children. Complete the sentences in Italian.

   (a) *(Make him)* studiare di più.
   (b) *(Make him)* studiare medicina.
   (c) *(Let her)* uscire di più.
   (d) *(Let her)* scegliere le materie che preferisce.

25.3 VERBS OF PERCEPTION

Verbs of perception such as **sentire**, **vedere** and **guardare** may also be used before other infinitives, e.g. **sentir arrivare qlcu** *to hear sb arrive*, **veder partire qlcu**, *to see sb leave.* These follow slightly different rules from **fare** or **lasciare** + infinitive.

Using nouns: position	Sentirai cantare Pavarotti? *Will you hear Pavarotti sing?* Ho visto uscire di casa Elena *or*: Ho visto Elena uscire di casa *I saw Elena leave the house*	The noun direct object of the first verb often follows the infinitive, unlike English. But if the infinitive is modified by a phrase or if it has an object, the order can be similar to the English.
Using personal pronouns	**Lo** hai visto picchiare il cane? *Did you see him hit the dog?* **Li** ho sentiti dire che sei un bugiardo *I heard them say/I heard it said you are a liar*	When both the infinitive and the main verb have a direct object, the person is normally expressed as a direct object pronoun.
Alternatives to the infinitive after **sentire**, **vedere**, etc.	Sento piangere il bambino *I can hear the baby cry* **Sento** il bambino **che** piange *I can hear the baby (who is) crying* **But**: Sento che il bambino piange *I can hear that the baby is crying*	The relative **che** + a finite verb replaces the infinitive after **sentire**, **vedere**, etc. when the emphasis is on an action which is/was taking place. The subject precedes **che**. **But**: if **che** precedes the subject (**il bambino**), the meaning is different.

E 1 Rewrite the following, substituting the noun given for the pronoun.

(a) Dobbiamo sentirlo cantare. (Pavarotti)   (c) L'abbiamo visto passare. (il corteo)
(b) L'ho guardato giocare. (mio figlio)   (d) L'ho sentito uscire di casa. (il vicino)

2 There has been a robbery. Express in Italian the questions asked by the inspector.

(a) *Did you hear the dog bark?*   (c) *Did you hear them slam the door?*
(b) *Did you see the men leave?*   (d) *Did you hear the neighbours shouting for help?*

25.4 *SAPERE* AND *CONOSCERE*

Sapere can be used in two ways: as a modal verb and as a normal verb without a dependent infinitive.

Sanno scrivere *They can write/know how to write* Mi sa dire quando arrivano? *Can you tell me when they are arriving?*	As a modal verb **sapere** expresses knowing how to do something. It also expresses possibility. In the latter case **potere** can be used instead, without any significant change in meaning.
So che Tommaso è malato *I know Tommaso is ill* So tre lingue/il tuo indirizzo *I know three languages/your address* Lo sai a memoria? *Do you know it by heart?*	When **sapere** is used as a normal verb it implies complete knowledge of something and is used to express knowing a fact, a language or something by heart.

Sapere v. *conoscere*

Conosco Tommaso *I know Tommaso* Conosci 'la Primavera' di Botticelli? *Do you know Botticelli's 'Primavera'?* Non conosciamo la Sardegna *We don't know Sardinia*	**Conoscere** is used instead of **sapere** to express being or becoming acquainted with someone, something (e.g. a book or picture) or a place. For **conoscere** meaning *to meet*, see p. 217. It cannot be followed by **che** + clause.

I   Do you know? Complete the sentences choosing the relevant forms of **conoscere** and **sapere** from the list below.

> sai • conoscete • sappiamo • sa • conosci • so

(a) Io purtroppo ... solo l'italiano.
(b) Mark, tu non ... l'Italia?
(c) Signora, scusi, ... quando apre l'ufficio turismo?

(d) Ragazzi, ... quella poesia? – Certo, la ... a memoria!
(e) Fiorella, ... il mio indirizzo e il telefono?

25.5 *PIACERE*

FORMS

Piacere is used to express *to like* in English but it is not directly equivalent. The third persons **piace** and **piacciono** are the key. **Piace** (*it/he/she is pleasing*) is used if you like one thing and **piacciono** (*they are pleasing*) is used to say you like several things. Notice that the grammatical structure is different in English and Italian: the English subject + verb corresponds to the Italian indirect object (IDO) plus verb.

IDO + verb + subject	Subject + verb + direct object
Mi piace il gelato Mi piacciono i dolci	*I like ice cream (Ice cream is pleasing to me)* *I like desserts (Desserts are pleasing to me)*

Piacere *with indirect object pronouns*

The table above shows that in Italian the person who likes something is grammatically an indirect object. Therefore the indirect object pronouns **mi, ti, gli, le, ci, vi, loro** normally express the English subject pronouns *I, you, he, she, we, you, they*.

mi **ti** **gli, le** **Le** **ci** **vi** **(a) loro** **gli**	**piace** **piacciono**	*I like* *You like* *He, she likes* *You like (formal)* *We like* *You like* *They like* *They like (colloquial)*

- (a) **loro** is the formal way of expressing *they*, but in colloquial Italian it is usually replaced by **gli** (which is used to mean *he*). The context usually makes it clear whether **gli** means *he* or *they*. **Loro** is mostly used with **a**, though it can be used alone after the verb:

  Gli piace l'Inghilterra *He likes/They like England*

  A loro piace l'Inghilterrra *or*: L'Inghilterra piace **loro** *They like England*

Piacere *with nouns or with other types of pronoun*

Piacere can be also used with indefinite pronouns or with nouns. These always follow the preposition **a**. For emphasis, mainly in speech, disjunctive or stressed pronouns are used with **a** instead of **mi, ti, gli, le, vi, ci,** etc.

a me		*I* like	a Carlo		*Carlo likes*
a te		*You* like	a mia moglie		*My wife likes*
a Lei	**piace**	*You* like (formal)	a tutti	**piace**	*Everyone likes*
a lui/a lei	**piacciono**	*He/she/it* likes	a nessuno	**piacciono**	*No one likes*
a noi		*We* like	ad alcuni		*Some like*
a voi		*You* like	ad altri		*Others like*
a loro		*They* like	alla maggior parte		*Most (people) like*

E **1** **Piace** or **piacciono**? Insert the correct form of **piacere**, using an appropriate pronoun.

(a) (*I like*) il gelato.

(b) Non (*you like*) gli spaghetti?

(c) (*She likes*) cucinare.

(d) (*Do you like*) pranzare all'aperto?

(e) (*Does he like*) l'uva o preferisce le arance?

(f) (*Does she like*) le fragole o preferisce i lamponi?

2 Give two English equivalents for these sentences.

(a) Le piace viaggiare?

(b) Gli piacciono i film giapponesi?

3 Supply the missing words and ask who likes what.

(a) Tutti: la musica lirica? (*Does everyone like opera?*)

(b) I tuoi figli: andare a teatro?

(c) Chiara: le commedie di Pirandello?

USES

piace + singular noun or infinitive	Gli piace **il vino** *He likes wine* Ci piace **andare** al cinema *We like going to the cinema*	**Piace** is used with indirect object pronouns to say you like one thing or like doing something. It is followed by a noun or an infinitive verb.

piacciono + plural noun	Le piacciono le scarpe italiane *She likes Italian shoes* Le piacciono gli spaghetti? *Do you (formal) like spaghetti?*	**Piacciono** is used with indirect object pronouns to express liking several things. It is never followed by an infinitive verb.
Emphatic use	**A me** piace il pesce ma **a lui** no/**a lui** non piace *I like fish but he doesn't/he doesn't like it* **A lei** non piace la carne ma **a me** sì/**a me** piace *She doesn't like meat but I do/I do like it* Gli spaghetti piacciono **a lei** e anche **a loro** *She likes spaghetti and so do they* Il vino non piace neanche **a loro** *They don't like wine either*	**A** is used in front of disjunctive pronouns to express contrast or emphasis. It is also used with **anche** and **neanche**. In the first two examples note the use of **a me/te ... sì** and **a me/te ... no** to express *do/does* and *don't/doesn't*.
No direct object pronouns	È un bel film, ti piace? *It's a lovely film, do you like **it**?* Carlo è generoso, mi piace *Carlo is generous, I like **him*** I musei sono noiosi, non ci piacciono *Museums are boring, we don't like **them***	Note that there is no Italian equivalent of the English direct object pronouns *it, him, them,* etc. This is because in Italian what is liked is not the grammatical direct object of **piacere**. (See p. 261.)

Other uses of piacere

Compound tenses	Gli è **piaciuta** la pizza *He liked the pizza* Ti **sono piaciuti** i fagiolini? *Did you like the beans?*	**Piacere** always takes **essere**, so its past participle agrees with the subject (which in English is the object, i.e. the item liked).
Use with subjunctive	Gli piace che tu **sia** qui *He is pleased you are here* Mi piacerebbe che **venissero** *I would like them to come*	The subjunctive is used after **che** when the subject of **piacere** is different from the subject of the verb that follows. See Subjunctive, p. 248.

- Although **piacere** is mostly used in the third persons of the verb, it is also possible to use it in the first or second persons:

  Io piaccio a Aldo *Aldo likes me*
  Tu piaci a Mirella *Mirella likes you*

Other ways of expressing like/dislike

essere simpatico/ antipatico a	(Tu) mi sei simpatico/a *I like you* (Voi) gli siete simpatici *He likes you* (Io) le sono antipatico/a *She dislikes me* (Io) sono simpatico/a tutti *Everybody likes me*	The meaning is literally *to be likeable/not likeable to me, you, him, everybody*, etc. The subject pronouns **tu**, **voi**, **noi**, etc. are not essential.

E   **4**   Give the Italian equivalent of the English.

(a) *Franco, do you like the new course? – Yes, I like it very much.*
(b) *Signora Marini, do you like the flowers? – Yes, I like them a lot.*
(c) *Antonio and Roberto, do you like going to the gym? – Yes, we like it very much.*

5   Complete the sentences using the appropriate form of **piacere** with a pronoun subject.

(a) Ad Elena piace leggere, ma ... *he doesn't.*
(b) Ad Enrico non piace la frutta, ma ... *she does.*
(c) Ci piace il calcio. – *They like it too.*
(d) Non mi piace suonare il pianoforte. – *I don't like it either.*

6   You've been away as a family. Say who liked what.

(a) Mia moglie: l'albergo di lusso.
(b) Mia suocera: i negozi.
(c) I miei figli: la piscina.
(d) Io e mio suocero: le passeggiate in montagna.

7   Give the Italian equivalent of the English without using **piacere**.

(a) *He likes Mirella.*   (b) *She likes Bruno.*   (c) *They don't like me.*

25.6 OTHER VERBS USED IMPERSONALLY

Verbs used impersonally are nearly always used in the third persons. Apart from **piacere** there are many other common verbs used in this way.

Main verbs used impersonally

accadere *to happen*	importare *to matter, to mind*	spettare *to be up to sb*
avvenire *to happen*	interessare *to interest*	succedere *to happen*
bastare *to be enough*	occorrere *to be needed*	toccare *to have to, to be sb's turn*
bisognare *to be necessary*	parere *to seem*	volerci *to take, to be necessary*
capitare *to chance, happen to*	rincrescere *to regret*	mancare *to lack, to need, to be*
convenire *to be advisable/best*	sembrare *to seem*	*missing, insufficient, not to be there*
dispiacere *to be sorry*	servire *to be of use*	

█ USES

Depending on their meaning the verbs on p. 264 can be followed by nouns, adjectives or infinitives.

Singular verb + singular noun. Plural verb + plural noun	Mi **serve** una penna *I need a pen* Ci **servono** due bicchieri *We need two glasses* M'**interessa** il cinema *I'm interested in the cinema* Ti **interessano** i film francesi? *Are you interested in French films?*	The basic construction is the same as **piacere**: *A pen is of use to me. Two glasses are of use to us,* etc.
mi, ti, gli, le, etc. = *I, you, he, she,* etc.	**Le** dispiace *She is sorry* **Ti** conviene partire presto *You should leave early* (*It's best for you to leave early*)	Indirect object pronouns (**gli, le**, etc.) are often used to express English subject pronouns (*he, she,* etc.).
mi, ti, gli, le = *to/for me, you, him,* etc.	**Le** bastano due etti? *Are 200 gr. enough for you?* **Mi** pare ridicolo *It seems ridiculous to me* *But also*: **Basta** scrivere presto *It is enough to write soon* **Sembra** difficile *It seems difficult*	Indirect object pronouns are also used normally, to express *to* and *for*. Note that some constructions can be used without pronouns.
volerci	**Ci vuole** mezz'ora *It takes half an hour* **Ci vogliono** trenta minuti *It takes thirty minutes*	**Volerci** is always used with **ci**.
Use with nouns and pronouns	**A Giuseppe/A molti** manca un libro *Giuseppe has no book/Many people have no book*	An English noun or indefinite pronoun subject is preceded by **a** in Italian.
No DO pronouns	Mi serve *I need it* M'interessano *I am interested in them*	The English direct object pronouns *it, them,* etc. are not expressed in Italian.
With infinitive	Le dispiace farlo? *Do you mind doing it?* Capita spesso alle mie figlie di andarci *My daughters often go (happen to go) there*	Infinitives follow the third person singular of the verb. **Accadere, capitare** and **succedere** are followed by **di**.
Emphatic use	Tocca **a te** andare, non **a me** *You'll have to go, not me/It's <u>your</u> turn to go, not <u>mine</u>* Non spetta **a lui** decidere *It's not up to <u>him</u> to decide*	For emphasis **a** is used with a disjunctive pronoun instead of **mi, ti, gli, le, ci, vi** and **loro**.
Compound tenses	Che cosa gli è successo? *What's happened to him?* Ti sono successe delle cose strane! *Some odd things have happened to you!*	**Essere** is used as the auxiliary in compound tenses. The past participle agrees with the grammatical subject.

E

1 Complete the questions using the verbs given, with a pronoun where appropriate.

(a) Fabrizio, (bastare) due fette di prosciutto?

(b) Flavia, (servire) altro?

(c) Signor Mancini, (mancare) qualcosa?

(d) Nino e Sandro, (convenire) andare in aereo.

(e) Lidia, se non capisci (bastare) chiedere aiuto.

(f) Signori, (bisognare) stare molto attenti.

2 Rewrite the sentences putting the verb into the **passato prossimo**.

(a) Mi dispiace partire così presto.

(b) Ci succedono delle cose strane.

(c) Non gli capita mai di arrivare in ritardo.

(d) Gli tocca pagare una multa.

25.7 THE IMPERSONAL AND PASSIVE *SI*

In Italian the use of **si** with the third persons of a verb can give it an impersonal or passive meaning, e.g. **Si parla inglese** *One speaks English/English is spoken.*
Si has various other English equivalents which depend on the context: *we, they, people.*

Impersonal use	Come **si dice?** *How do you/How does one say it?* D'estate **si mangia** spesso all'aperto *In the summer people often eat outdoors* **Si partirà** verso le cinque *We'll leave around five*	Most verbs can be made impersonal by using **si** as the subject with the third person singular form of the verb. Its English equivalents vary.
Passive use	**Si parla** italiano *Italian is spoken* **Si parlano** molte lingue *Many languages are spoken* A casa **si parla** italiano *At home we speak Italian* **Si vende** *For sale* **Si vendono** cartoline alla stazione *Postcards are sold at the station/They sell postcards at the station*	Most transitive verbs (verbs with a direct object) can be used with **si** to express a passive meaning. The verb and object agree in number.
Use with adjectives	Quando **si è giovani**, non si pensa alla vecchiaia *When you're young you don't think about old age*	Adjectives referring to an impersonal **si** must always be masculine plural.
Use with pronouns	**Lo si** fa ogni tanto *It is done now and again* **Gli si** dice spesso di studiare *He is often told to study* Non **se ne** parla molto *It is not much talked about*	**Si** comes after direct and indirect object pronouns but before **ne**. See also Pronouns, p. 99.

Level **2**

Compound tenses and past participle agreements

Verbs normally taking **avere**	Si è **dormito** bene *Everyone/we slept well* Non si è **capita** la situazione ... *The situation was not understood* Si **sono sprecati** tanti soldi ... *A lot of money was wasted*	**Si** is always used with **essere**. If the verb normally takes **avere**, the past participle does not change unless there is a direct object, in which case it agrees with the direct object.
Verbs normally taking **essere**	Si è **partiti** presto per evitare il traffico *They/we left early so as to avoid the traffic*	If the verb normally takes **essere** the past participle is always masculine plural, but **essere** is singular.

I You need to know how things are done in your rented house. Select the appropriate form of the verb.

(a) Come si (accendere) il gas?

(b) Come si (spegnere) le luci?

(c) Come si (pulire) il fornello?

(d) Come si (chiudere) le persiane?

2 Insert the **passato prossimo** form of the verb, making past participle agreements if necessary.

(a) La fiera del libro è andata benissimo, mi hanno detto che si (vendere) tantissimi libri.

(b) I miei mi dicevano che lo zio era ricco sfondato. Non si (capire) mai come avesse fatto.

(c) Si doveva partire per Parigi, per cui si (andare) prestissimo a votare.

- For other exercises on **si**, see pp. 99–100.

25.8 THE PASSIVE

Verbs are said to be in the passive when the action is done <u>to</u> the subject, as opposed to the action being performed <u>by</u> the subject: e.g. *the Mafia **shot** the judge* (active); *the judge <u>was shot</u> by the Mafia* (passive). The passive form makes the performer of the action less important. This is why it is more common in academic or technical and scientific writing than in everyday speech. It is also common in journalism.

FORMS

Only transitive verbs, i.e. verbs which take a direct object, can be made passive. (You could not say, for example, *I was slept.*) The main way of forming the passive is by using **essere** in the appropriate tense followed by the past participle.

Simple tenses	Passive form	Compound tenses	Passive form
Present	**sono** rispettato	Passato prossimo	**sono stato** rispettato
Future	**sarò** rispettato	Future perfect	**sarò stato** rispettato
Imperfect	**ero** rispettato	Pluperfect	**ero stato** rispettato
Past definite	**fui** rispettato		
Present subjunctive	**sia** rispettato	Perfect subjunctive	**sia stato** rispettato
Imperfect subjunctive	**fossi** rispettato	Pluperfect subjunctive	**fossi stato** rispettato
Present conditional	**sarei** rispettato	Past conditional	**sarei stato** rispettato
Infinitive	**essere** rispettato	Past infinitive	**essere stato** rispettato

E I Make these sentences passive using **essere**.

(a) Le macchine inquinano la città.
(b) Troveranno il colpevole.
(c) A giugno gli insegnanti correggevano gli esami.
(d) Il pubblico accetterebbe queste nuove tasse?
(e) Non è giusto che il governo critichi gli insegnanti.
(f) Tutti hanno abbandonato il paesino incendiato.

USES

Past participle agreement	La casa sarà vendu**ta** The house will be sold Gli orari sono cambia**ti** *The timetables are changed*	The past participle always agrees with the subject in number and gender.
da	È stato ucciso **da** un pazzo/**dal** veleno *He was killed by a madman/by the poison*	To say who or what performs the action **da**, + definite article if necessary, is used.

The auxiliary **essere** is sometimes replaced by other verbs, most of which can be used in simple tenses only.

Using **venire**	Il portone **viene** (è) sempre chiuso a chiave *The door always gets/is always locked* Se non stai attento **verrai** (sarai) licenziato *If you're not careful you'll get/be sacked*	**Venire** is sometimes synonymous with **essere**, but tends to stress the action more and is often equivalent to 'get …'. It is only used in simple tenses.
Using **rimanere**	Il conducente **rimase** (fu) ucciso *The driver got/was killed* Il passante **è rimasto** (è stato) ferito *The passer-by got/was wounded*	Used mainly in the simple past, **passato prossimo** and pluperfect, it replaces **essere** to express a strong impact.
Using **andare**	Durante la guerra i quadri **andarono** (furono) perduti *During the war the pictures went missing/got lost/were lost* Tutta la casa **andò** (fu) distrutta *The whole house got/was destroyed*	**Andare** is normally used only in the third persons. In the simple past it expresses the idea of 'get …' with verbs like **perdere** or **smarrire** *to lose*, **distruggere** *to destroy*, **sprecare** *to waste*.

| andare for necessity or obligation | **Va** fatto subito (dev'essere fatto)
 It must be done at once
 Andrebbe fatto più tardi
 (dovrebbe essere fatto)
 It should/ought to be done later
 Andrà fatto domani (dovrà essere fatto)
 It will have to be done tomorrow
 Andava fatto ieri
 (avrebbe dovuto essere fatto)
 It should have been done yesterday | The present, the conditional, the future and the imperfect of **andare** are much used in this way and avoid the more complex use of **dover essere** + past participle. |

2 Substitute forms of **venire** or **rimanere** for **essere** as appropriate.

(a) Le finestre **sono** pulite ogni mese.

(b) I ragazzi **erano** spesso puniti.

(c) La città **è stata** distrutta.

(d) Noi tutti **siamo stati** stupiti dalle sue parole.

3 Say what must be done, using **andare** to complete the sentences.

(a) Il tetto (*must be*) riparato.

(b) La cucina (*ought to be*) rinnovata.

(c) I soffitti (*will have to be*) rifatti.

(d) Le finestre (*should have been*) pulite.

Alternative constructions to express the passive

In Italian, active verb constructions are often preferred to passive ones, especially in the spoken language, and some verbs actually cannot be used in the passive.

Third person construction essential	Mi **hanno detto** di venire *I have been told to come (They told me to …)* Ti **hanno dato** l'orario? *Were you given the timetable?* Gli **hanno consigliato** di aspettare *He was advised to wait*	In Italian verbs used with an indirect object person such as **dare a**, **dire a**, etc. cannot be used in the passive to express the English *I was given, I was told, I was advised*, etc. The third person plural of the active verb must be used.
Passive possible but uncommon	Il libro **gli è stato dato**/ **Gli hanno dato** il libro *The book was given to him/* *He was given the book* **Ci è stato promesso** un aumento/ **Ci hanno promesso** un aumento *A rise was promised to us/* *We were promised a rise*	Passive constructions can be used with all verbs with a direct object, but the third person active forms are usually preferred. This is especially the case with verbs like **scippare**, **rubare**, **rompere**, **distruggere** or **incendiare**, where the passive form is rare.
	Mi hanno scippato la borsa *I've had my handbag snatched*	

| Either passive or third person construction | **Sono stato invitato** alla festa
or: **Mi hanno invitato** alla festa
I was invited to the party
È stato convinto a partecipare/
Lo hanno convinto a partecipare
He was persuaded to participate | The third person construction is usually but not always preferred with verbs which have people as direct objects, e.g. **invitare qlcu, convincere qlcu.** (See Chapter 26, p. 276.) |
| Using **si** | **Si sentono** spesso strani rumori
Strange sounds are often heard | **Si** is often used with third person active verbs to express a passive meaning. See p. 266. |

E   **4**   Express the following in Italian.

(a) *I was told to arrive early.* (dire)
(b) *They were prevented from voting.* (impedire)
(c) *I was invited to a conference.* (invitare)
(d) *She was given the wrong timetable.* (dare)
(e) *I had my car stolen.* (rubare)
(f) *He had his shop burned.* (incendiato)

•   For exercises on **si**, see p. 267.

26

Verbs and prepositions

Prepositions such as **a** or **di** are often used with verbs to link them to nouns, pronouns or infinitive verbs and they can have a significant impact on the meaning. There are some major differences between their use in English and Italian:

1   Some English verbs require a preposition where Italian ones do not – and vice versa.
2   Many Italian verbs take **di** while others take **a** – and they may both be translated in English as *to*.
3   Other Italian verbs take prepositions such as **con**, **in**, **per** or **su** but these do not always correspond exactly to the English.
4   Italian prepositions precede the infinitive form of the verb, whereas English prepositions can also precede gerunds (the *-ing* form).

This chapter provides reference tables, plus an analysis of the main areas of difference between Italian and English use. The lists given are not exhaustive but include the most common verbs.

26.1 VERBS WITH NO PREPOSITION IN ITALIAN

(a) Before a noun or pronoun

Some of these verbs take **di** before an infinitive (p. 275), but never before a noun.

No preposition before a noun	ascoltare *to listen to* aspettare *to wait for* cercare *to look for* chiedere *to ask for*	guardare *to look at* pagare *to pay for sth* sognare *to dream about sb/sth*

Ascolta tuo padre *Listen **to** your father.* Ascoltalo *Listen **to** him*
Aspetto mia sorella *I am waiting **for** my sister.* La aspetto *I'm waiting **for** her*
Guarda la strada! *Look **at** the road!*
Ho sognato la guerra *I dreamed **about** the war*

(b) Before an infinitive

After verbs used impersonally and **essere** + adjective	bastare *to be enough to* bisognare *to be necessary to* convenire *to be a good idea/best to* dispiacere *to be sorry to, to mind ... ing* interessare *to be interested to/in ... ing* piacere *to like to/... ing* servire *to need to*	essere difficile *to be difficult to* essere facile *to be easy to* essere giusto *to be fair to* essere importante *to be important to* essere meglio *to be better/best to* essere necessario *to be necessary to* essere utile *to be useful to*

Bisogna uscire *You have **to** go out*

Non è facile capire *It's not easy **to** understand*

Non m'interessa vederlo *I'm not interested **in** seeing him*

Note that in some cases there is no preposition in English either:

Mi conviene partire *I had better leave*

Ti dispiace chiamare più tardi? *Do you mind calling later?*

All modal verbs	dovere *to have to* potere *to be able to*	sapere *to know (how to)* volere *to want to*
Verbs of liking/ disliking	amare *to like, to love to/... ing* desiderare *to wish, to want to* detestare *to detest, hate to/... ing*	preferire *to prefer to* odiare *to hate to ... ing* osare *to dare (to)*

Devo studiare *I have to study*   Detesto aspettare *I hate waiting/to wait*

26.2 VERBS TAKING *A*

(a) Only before a noun or pronoun

a before a noun or pronoun	assistere a *to attend sth* assomigliare a *to look like sb* aver diritto a *to be entitled to*	partecipare a *to take part in sth* sopravvivere a *to survive, outlive sb* voler bene a *to love sb*

Ho assistito alla cerimonia *I attended the ceremony*

Tu assomigli a tuo padre *You look like your father*

(b) Before a noun, pronoun or infinitive

a before nouns, pronouns and infinitives	abituarsi a *to get used to* dedicarsi a *to devote oneself to* fare bene a *to be good for, to be right to* fare male a *to be bad for, to be wrong to*	giocare a *to play (at)* rassegnarsi a *to resign oneself to* rinunciare a *to give up, refrain from* tenere/tenerci a *to be keen on/to value*

- For **pensare a** *to think about*, see p. 277.

Mi abituo al freddo/ad alzarmi presto *I get used to the cold/to getting up early*

Il fumo ti fa male/fa male alla salute *Smoking is bad for you/for your health*

Hai fatto male a non ascoltarlo *You were wrong not to listen to him*

(c) Only before an infinitive

a before an infinitive	affrettarsi a *to hurry/rush to*	impegnarsi a *to undertake to*
	aver torto a *to be wrong to*	mettersi a *to get down to/set about . . . ing*
	cominciare a *to begin/start to/. . . ing*	prepararsi a *to get ready to*
	continuare a *to continue to/go on . . . ing*	provare a *to try to*
	decidersi a *to make up one's mind to*	riuscire a *to manage to*
	iniziare a *to start/begin to/. . . ing*	scoppiare a *to burst into/out . . . ing*
	imparare a *to learn to*	tardare a *to delay . . . ing*

Hai torto a criticare il tuo amico *You're wrong to criticise your friend*

Hanno continuato a chiacchierare *They continued to chat/carried on chatting*

Sofia è scoppiata a piangere/è scoppiata a ridere *Sofia burst into tears/burst out laughing*

(d) Special uses before infinitives

The following verbs all take **a** before an infinitive as in (c) above, but **a** has several meanings.

a with verbs of position, movement and emotion	alzarsi a *to get up to/and*	rimanere a *to stay/stand and*
	andare a *to go to/and*	sedersi a *to sit and*
	annoiarsi a *to get bored . . . ing*	stare a *to stop, stay to/and*
	correre a *to run/race to/and*	stancarsi *to tire of . . . ing*
	divertirsi a *to enjoy . . . ing*	stufarsi *to get fed up . . . ing*
	fermarsi a *to stop to/and*	

With the verbs in (**d**) above, **a** is used in three ways:

1   As a synonym of **per** to express intention (*in order to*), as opposed to a definitely completed action.

Sono venuto **per/a** fare una telefonata *I have come to (in order to) make a phone call*

Mi sono alzato **per/a** salutare Gino *I got up to (in order to) greet Gino*

It is not clear whether the action actually took place.

2   To express an action which has taken place soon after the first one. This can be expressed in English as *and*.

Sono andato **a** fare la spesa *I went and did/to do the shopping*

Sono stato/rimasto **a** chiacchierare con loro *I stayed and chatted/to chat with them*

3   To express two simultaneous actions:

Si è divertito **a** guardare la partita *He enjoyed himself/had fun watching the match* (while he watched)

Si stanca **a** studiare tanto la sera *He gets tired studying so much in the evening* (while he studies)

See also Infinitives, p. 238.

E | **I** Refer to the notes on p. 273 and mark each sentence below 1, 2 or 3 according to which type you think it is. Then complete the sentences, giving the Italian equivalent of the English. In which sentence could **per** also be used?

(a) È venuto (*to make/and made*) una telefonata, dopodiché è andato via.
(b) Sono venuto qui (*to/in order to make*) una telefonata, ma il telefono è guasto.
(c) Siamo rimasti (*to see/and saw*) la partita.
(d) Si annoiavano (*hearing*) sempre le stesse canzoni.

26.3 VERBS TAKING *DI*

(a) Only before a noun or pronoun

di before nouns and pronouns	caricare di *to load, to burden* coprirsi di *to cover o.self, get covered in* innamorarsi di *to fall in love with sb/sth* macchiarsi di *to stain o.self with*	sporcarsi di *to dirty o.self, get dirtied with* riempirsi di *to fill o.self up with* sapere di *to taste/smell of* ubriacarsi di *to get drunk on*

Mi sono innamorato di Maria/di lei *I've fallen in love with Maria/her*
Si sono riempiti di caramelle *They stuffed themselves with sweets*
Sa di bruciato/di muffa *It tastes/smells burnt/musty*

(b) Before a noun, pronoun or infinitive

Before nouns, pronouns and infinitives	aver bisogno di *to need* aver paura di/a *to be frightened of sth* aver vergogna di/a *to be ashamed of* aver voglia di *to desire/feel like ... ing* accorgersi di *to notice, realise* chiedere di *to ask to, to ask after* dimenticar(si) di *to forget to* fidarsi di/a *to trust, rely on/dare (to)*	godere di/a *to enjoy, to enjoy ... ing* rendersi conto di *to realise, be aware of* ricordar(si) di *to remember to* scusarsi di *to apologise, be sorry for/that* stancarsi di/a *to get tired (of)/... ing* stufarsi di/a *to be fed up with/sick of* vergognarsi di/a *to be ashamed of*

Mi sono stancato del corso/di studiare *I've got tired of the course/of studying*
Mi sono accorto delle difficoltà *I have realised the difficulties*
Non ti sei accorto di aver perso la borsa? *Didn't you realise (that) you had lost your bag?*

Notes on **di** or **a**: Some of the verbs in (b) above may also be followed by **a** – usually with a slightly different meaning.

- In some cases the use of **a** or **di** is a matter of personal style or preference:

  Si vergogna **di/a** dirlo *He is ashamed to say it*
  Non mi fido **di/a** lasciarlo solo in casa *I don't dare leave him alone in the house*

- With some verbs **di** refers to a concrete possibility or specific instance, while **a** is used to refer to an unspecific or hypothetical action (*if/when*):

  Ho paura **di** vederlo *I'm frightened of seeing him/that I will see him*

La sera ha paura **a** uscire da sola *In the evening she's afraid of going out alone/when she goes out alone*

- Some verbs, e.g. **stancarsi**, **stufarsi** or **godere**, are mostly used with **di** but use **a** to express simultaneous actions (p. 273).

I   Give the Italian equivalent of the English, using the verbs given with either **di** or **a**.

(a) *I have got fed up with waiting.* (stufarsi)
(b) *I get tired studying in the evening.* (stancarsi)
(c) *Aren't you ashamed to cheat/of cheating people?*
(d) *I'm ashamed that I cheated Carla.* (imbrogliare)

(c) Only before an infinitive

Verbs taking **di** before an infinitive are very numerous. Here are a few.

di before infinitives: *to*	aspettare di *to wait to* aver il diritto di *to have the right to* aver intenzione di *to intend to* aver ragione di/a *to be right to* aver voglia di *to desire/feel like ... ing* cercare di *to try to* finire di *to stop* preoccuparsi di *to take care/the trouble to*	rifiutare/si di *to refuse to* rischiare di *to risk, be in danger of ... ing* scegliere di *to choose to* sforzarsi di *to strive, endeavour, try hard to* smettere di *to cease, stop, give up* sognare di *to dream of ... ing* tentare di *to attempt, try to*
di before infinitives: *that*	accettare di *to agree to/that* capire di *to understand that* credere di *to believe that* decidere di *to decide to/that* dire (di) *to say (that)* dubitare di *to doubt that* fingere/fare finta di *to pretend to/that*	negare di *to deny that* pensare di *to think that, to plan to* promettere di *to promise to, that* ritenere di *to consider (that)* sembrare/parere di *to seem/think that* sperare di *to hope to/that* temere di *to be afraid/fear that*

- For verbs of command and prohibition + **di**, see pp. 276–7. For more on **credere** and **pensare** see p. 277.

La sera Devi smettere di fumare *You must give up smoking*
Rischiamo di perdere tutto *We are in danger of losing everything*

(d) Expressing 'that'

In Italian **di** is used after a verb when the subjects are the same in both clauses (they take **che** + the subjunctive when they differ, pp. 247–8). The English equivalent for both constructions is nearly always *that*.

Dice di essere troppo stanco *He says (that) he is too tired*
Ha accettato di pagare *He has agreed to pay/that he will pay*
Ha capito di aver sbagliato *She understood that she had made a mistake*

2   Give an Italian equivalent of the following using a preposition with the verb given.

(a) *I think (that) I'll come early.* (pensare)
(b) *She hopes (that) she will get the job.* (sperare)
(c) *I doubt that I can help.*
(d) *I'm afraid (that) I am late.*

26.4 VERBS USED WITH *CON, DA, PER, SU*

With **con**	congratularsi con *to congratulate sb* cominciare/iniziare con *to begin with*	finire/terminare con *to end in* scambiare con *to exchange, swap for*
With **da**	dipendere da *to depend on*	
With **per**	finire per *to end up* preoccuparsi per *to be worried about*	scambiare per *to mistake for*
With **su**	contare su *to count on* dare su *to overlook/look out onto*	incidere su *to affect*

Mi sono congratulato **con** lui *I congratulated him*

La partita è terminata **con** un pareggio *The match ended in a draw*

Ho scambiato l'anello **con** un braccialetto *I swapped the ring for a bracelet*

Mi ha scambiato **per** mio fratello *He mistook me for my brother*

Dipende **dalla** moglie *He depends on his wife*

La finestra dà **sul** cortile *The window looks onto the courtyard*

26.5 VERBS WHICH ASK SOMEBODY TO DO SOMETHING

In Italian most common double object verbs expressing commands and prohibition are used in one of two ways: either with a direct object person plus **a** or with an indirect object person plus **di**. Knowing which pattern these verbs follow is important for the correct use of personal pronouns (Exercise 14, p. 88), and also to use the correct Italian equivalent of English passive constructions (p. 270).

Double object verbs

Direct object person + **a** + infinitive	aiutare qlcu **a** *to help sb to* convincere qlcu **a** *to persuade sb to* costringere qlcu **a** *to force sb to* forzare qlcu **a** *to force/push sb to* invitare qlcu **a** *to invite sb to* incoraggiare qlcu **a** *to encourage sb to*	obbligare qlcu **a** *to oblige sb to* persuadere qlcu **a** *to persuade sb to* spingere qlcu **a** *to push sb to* **But**: pregare qlcu **di** *to beg sb to*
Indirect object person + **di** + infinitive	chiedere a qlcu **di** *to ask sb to* comandare a qlcu **di** *to order sb to* consentire a qlcu **di** *to allow sb to* consigliare a qlcu **di** *to advise sb to* dire a qlcu **di** *to tell sb to* domandare a qlcu **di** *to ask sb to* impedire a qlcu **di** *to prevent sb from* offrire a qlcu **di** *to offer to do sth* ordinare a qlcu **di** *to order sb to* permettere a qlcu **di** *to allow sb to* proibire a qlcu **di** *to prohibit sb from* promettere a qlcu **di** *to promise sb that*	ricordare a qlcu **di** *to remind sb to* sconsigliare a qlcu **di** *to advise sb against ... ing* proporre a qlcu **di** *to propose sb does sth* suggerire a qlcu **di** *to suggest sb does sth* vietare a qlcu **di** *to forbid sb to* **But**: insegnare a qlcu **a** *to teach sb to* **Note also**: accadere a qlcu **di** *to happen to sb to* capitare a qlcu **di** *to happen to sb to* succedere a qlcu **di** *to happen to sb to*

Compare the use of personal pronouns in these examples.

Perché non **la** inviti **a** venire
Why don't you invite her to come?

Perché non **le** chiedi **di** venire?
Why don't you ask her to come?

Lo devi costringere **a** pagare
You must force him to pay

Gli devi proibire **di** fumare
You must forbid him to smoke

I   Give the Italian equivalent of the following.

(a) *I told Simona to come later.* (dire)
(b) *I invited Angelo to come.* (invitare)
(c) *I asked Martina to leave.* (chiedere)

(d) *I reminded Susi to phone.* (ricordare)
(e) *He made Susi phone.* (costringere)
(f) *She begged Fabrizio to write.* (pregare)

26.6 DIFFERENT PREPOSITION, DIFFERENT MEANING

Some verbs can take more than one preposition or no preposition at all, and this usually affects the meaning.

(a) *Credere a, credere in, credere*

Credi **a** Giorgio? *Do you believe Giorgio?* **Gli** credi? *Do you believe him?* Credi **alle** streghe/**agli** Ufo? *Do you believe in witches/in UFOs?* **Ci** credi? *Do you believe in them?*	**Credere a** indicates belief in a person or in the fact that something exists (but not God).
credere **in** Dio/**nello** Spirito Santo/**nella** giustizia/**nella** sua onestà *to believe in God/in the Holy Ghost/in justice/in his honesty* **Ci** credo (nella giustizia, in Dio) *I believe in it/him*	**Credere in** indicates belief in the existence of God or of human qualities. It means *to have faith in*.
Crede sempre quello che dice Ivo *He always believes what Ivo says (is true)* Lo crede *He believes it*	**Credere** without a preposition is used to mean *to think sth is true*.

(b) *Parlare di/a; pensare di/a*

Preferisco parlare **di** Lucia/**della** situazione politica *I prefer to talk about/discuss Lucia/the political situation*	**Parlare di** is used to refer to a topic of discussion: a person or a thing.
Vorrei parlare **a** Lucia *I would like to talk to Lucia* **Also**: Vorrei parlare **con** Lucia	**Parlare a**: this expresses talking <u>with</u> sb; **con** is also used.
Cosa hai pensato **degli** esami? *What did you think about/of the exams?* Pensi **di** venire? *Are you thinking of/planning to come?* Penso **di** partire presto *I think I'll leave early/I plan to leave early*	**Pensare di** means to have an opinion about sb or sth. Before an infinitive it can also mean *to plan to*.
Pensi **agli** esami? *Are you thinking about the exams?* Ha pensato **a** tutto *She has thought of/seen to everything* Hai pensato **a** prenotare i biglietti? *Have you seen to booking/Have you booked the tickets?* Penso sempre **a** te *I always think of you*	**Pensare a**: this expresses connection, not opinion. It also means *to see to, to arrange, to sort out*.

E

I Give the Italian equivalent of the following.

(a) *You can believe what you want.*
(b) *Do you believe Marina? Do you believe her?*
(c) *Do you believe in God?*

(d) *Can I talk to you about Gianni?*
(e) *Can I talk to Gianni?*
(f) *He talked to me about his job.*

2 Complete the sentences using **pensare** with **a** or **di** as appropriate.

(a) Che cosa pensi ... la proposta?
(b) Che cosa pensi ... Bruno?
(c) Pensi ... domani?

(d) Che cosa pensi ... fare?
(e) Hai pensato ... Bruno?
(f) Hai pensato ... prenotare?

Appendix 1: Spelling and pronunciation

The alphabet

In Italian there are 21 letters in the alphabet plus five letters, **j**, **k**, **w**, **x**, and **y**, which are only used in foreign words.

j, k, w, x, y	il **j**olly *joker* (in cards) il **k**imono *kimono* il **w**eekend *weekend* lo **x**ilofono *xylophone* lo **y**oga *yoga* **But w pronounced as v**: il **w**alzer *waltz* **W**alter *Walter*	These are mostly pronounced as in English, but in a few words of German origin **w** is pronounced like the English **v**.

Spelling

Italian spelling is fairly simple because the relationship between the letters and the sounds is consistent. On the whole there is no variation from one word to another. (Compare this with the English *comb*, *tomb*, *bomb*, etc.) However, some combinations of letters are pronounced and spelt differently from the English. The main ones are given here.

Spelling		Approximate English sound	Examples
ce	ci	English **ch**	cento (like *cherry*) Cina (like *cheese*)
che	chi	English hard **k**	anche (*monkey*) chilo (*keen*)
ge	gi	English **j**	geloso (*jealous/generous*) magico (*magic/Jill*)
ghe	ghi	English hard **g**	lunghe (*rogue*) larghi (*gear*)
sce	sci	English **sh**	scende (*shed*) scippo (*sheep*)
sche	schi	English hard **sk**	pesche (*sceptic/schedule*) boschi (*skip/skill*)

gli	No exact English equivalent	figlio, famiglia. The closest equivalent is _million_
gn	No exact English equivalent	lasagne, gnocchi, signore. The closest equivalents are _new_, _canyon_ or _onion_.
h	Not pronounced at the beginning of a word	ho, hobby (_honour_)

Accents

Grave accents	la citt**à** il caff**è** cos**ì** dormir**ò** pi**ù** da _from_ d**à** _gives_ e _and_ **è** _is_ si _one, you, him/herself_ s**ì** _yes_	Used to indicate that the stress falls on the final vowel. They also distinguish between words with the same spelling but different meanings.
Acute accents	perch**é** _because_ bench**é** _although_ ne _of it, of them_ n**é** _neither_	Much less common. Used to indicate a 'closed' e sound (like _Jill_) as opposed to an 'open' e (like _bed_). They also distinguish between words with the same spelling but different meanings.
With capitals	**È**/E' un mistero _It's a mystery_	The grave accent is required on capital letters but may also be written as an apostrophe.

Capital letters

In Italian capitals are less used than in English. Unless they begin a sentence, the following are <u>not</u> used with capitals:

• io (_I_)	Lo faccio io
• Titles (+ surname or organisation)	Il signor Perruta, l'avvocato Agnelli, il presidente della Repubblica
• Weekdays and months	sabato, domenica, marzo, aprile
• Languages and nationalities	l'italiano mi piace gli americani un paese europeo
• Streets	Abito in via Daniele Manin/in piazza del Duomo
• In book/play or film titles the first word only is capitalised, with the exception of newspapers	Il signore degli anelli (_The Lord of the Rings_), Sogno di una notte di mezza estate (_A Midsummer Night's Dream_) **But**: La Repubblica, Il Corriere della Sera

Capitals are otherwise used much as in English, but note that the formal personal pronouns (**Lei, La, Le**) and related possessives (**Suo, Sua, Suoi, Sue**) may be spelt with a capital letter.

Appendix 2: Verbs

Verbs taking *essere*

This list is not comprehensive.

andare *to go*	esistere *to exist*	ritornare *to return*
apparire *to appear*	essere *to be*	riuscire *to manage*
arrivare *to arrive*	fuggire *to flee, escape*	scadere *to run out*, *expire*
cadere *to fall*	giungere *to arrive at, to reach*	scappare *to dash, to run off*
costare *to cost*	intervenire *to intervene*	sparire *to disappear*
crollare *to collapse*	morire *to die*	stare *to stay, to be*
dipendere *to depend*	nascere *to be born*	svenire *to faint*
divenire *to become*	partire *to leave*	tornare *to return*
diventare *to become*	pervenire *to arrive, come to*	uscire *to go out*
emergere *to emerge*	restare *to stay*	valere *to be worth*
entrare *to enter, come in*	rimanere *to stay*	venire *to come*

Verbs used transitively and intransitively

Some verbs can take either **avere** or **essere**, depending on whether they are being used transitively or intransitively. These are some of the most common. See also pp. 209–10.

aumentare *to increase, to go up*	finire *to finish*	saltare *to jump**
cambiare *to change*	guarire *to get well, to cure*	scivolare *to slip*
cominciare *to begin*	iniziare *to begin*	servire *to be necessary, to serve*
correre *to run**	invecchiare *to grow old, to age*	scendere *to go down, get out of*
cessare *to cease*	migliorare *to improve*	terminare *to end, put an end to*
crescere *to grow, to bring up*	passare *to pass, to spend time*	toccare *to touch, to have to*
bruciare *to burn*	peggiorare *to get worse*	volare *to fly**
diminuire *to decrease, reduce*	salire *to go up, to get in*	vivere *to live**

- Verbs marked* may take the auxiliary **avere** even when used intransitively. See p. 210.

2 IRREGULAR VERB TABLES

Table 1 gives verbs whose simple past and/or past participle are all irregular and Table 2 lists verbs which are irregular in most tenses.

Table 1: Verbs with irregular simple past and/or past participle

Infinitive	Simple past	Past participle
accendere *to light, turn on*	accesi accendesti	acceso
accorgersi *to realise*	accorsi accorgesti	accorto
aprire *to open*	aprii/apersi apristi	aperto
assistere *to attend*		assistito
chiedere *to ask*	chiesi chiedesti	chiesto
chiudere *to close*	chiusi chiudesti	chiuso
conoscere *to know*	conobbi conoscesti	conosciuto
coprire *to cover*	coprii/copersi copristi	coperto
correre *to run*	corsi corresti	corso
crescere *to grow*	crebbi crescesti	cresciuto
decidere *to decide*	decisi decidesti	deciso
deludere *to disappoint*	delusi deludesti	deluso
deprimere *to depress*	depressi deprimesti	depresso
difendere *to defend*	difesi difendesti	difeso
dipingere *to paint*	dipinsi dipingesti	dipinto
dirigere *to direct*	diressi dirigesti	diretto
discutere *to discuss*	discussi discutesti	discusso
distinguere *to distinguish*	distinsi distinguesti	distinto
distruggere *to destroy*	distrussi distruggesti	distrutto
dividere *to divide*	divisi dividesti	diviso
emergere *to emerge*	emersi emergesti	emerso
escludere *to exclude*	esclusi escludesti	escluso
fingere *to pretend*	finsi fingesti	finto
fondere *to melt*	fusi fondesti	fuso
friggere *to fry*	frissi friggesti	fritto
giungere *to reach*	giunsi giungesti	giunto
includere *to include*	inclusi includesti	incluso
invadere *to invade*	invasi invadesti	invaso
leggere *to read*	lessi leggesti	letto
mettere *to put, place*	misi mettesti	messo
mordere *to bite*	morsi mordesti	morso
muovere *to move*	mossi muovesti	mosso
nascere *to be born*	nacqui nascesti	nato
nascondere *to hide*	nascosi nascondesti	nascosto

Infinitive	Simple past	Past participle
offendere *to offend*	offesi offendesti	offeso
offrire *to offer*	offrii/offersi offristi	offerto
perdere *to lose*	persi perdesti	perso/perduto
persuadere *to persuade*	persuasi persuadesti	persuaso
piangere *to cry*	piansi piangesti	pianto
prendere *to take, collect*	presi prendesti	preso
proteggere *to protect*	protessi proteggesti	protetto
ridere *to laugh*	risi ridesti	riso
risolvere *to solve*	risolsi risolvesti	risolto
rispondere *to answer*	risposi rispondesti	risposto
rodere *to gnaw*	rosi rodesti	roso
rompere *to break*	ruppi rompesti	rotto
scendere *to go down*	scesi scendesti	sceso
sconfiggere *to defeat*	sconfissi sconfiggesti	sconfitto
scoprire *to discover*	scoprii/scopersi scopristi	scoperto
scrivere *to write*	scrissi scrivesti	scritto
scuotere *to shake*	scossi scuotesti	scosso
soffrire *to suffer*	soffrii/soffersi soffristi	sofferto
sommergere *to submerge*	sommersi sommergesti	sommerso
sorgere *to arise*	sorsi sorgesti	sorto
sorridere *to smile*	sorrisi sorridesti	sorriso
spargere *to scatter, spread*	sparsi spargesti	sparso
spendere *to spend*	spesi spendesti	speso
spingere *to push*	spinsi spingesti	spinto
stringere *to squeeze, tighten*	strinsi stringesti	stretto
succedere *to happen*	successe	successo
tingere *to dye*	tinsi tingesti	tinto
uccidere *to kill*	uccisi uccidesti	ucciso
vincere *to win*	vinsi vincesti	vinto
volgere *to turn*	volsi volgesti	volto

Verbs with similar patterns. The following verbs have the same pattern as the ones given in the table above:

assistere: consistere, esistere, insistere, resistere; **deprimere:** esprimere, sopprimere; **giungere:** aggiungere; **leggere:** correggere, eleggere; **fondere:** confondere, diffondere; **mettere:** permettere, promettere, smettere; **muovere:** commuovere, promuovere; **piangere:** rimpiangere; **rodere:** corrodere, esplodere; **scrivere:** descrivere, iscriver(si); **scuotere:** riscuotere; **stringere:** costringere, restringere; **rompere:** corrompere, interrompere; **vincere:** convincere; **volgere:** rivolger(si), sconvolgere, svolgere.

Table 2: Very irregular verbs

- The following table lists the main Italian verbs with irregularities in most tenses. Only irregular forms are given. If a particular form of a verb does not appear in the table, this means it is regular: e.g. **andare** has a regularly formed imperfect, simple past and past participle, all based on the infinitive. These are therefore not given.

- Most irregular present tenses are given in full, but only the **io** forms of irregular future, conditional and subjunctive forms are given. Very irregular present and imperfect subjunctives are given in full. For the simple past, the first person (irregular) and second person (regular) are given, but the full forms are given for **dare, essere** and **stare**.

- Only one example each is given of **-arre, -orre** and **-urre** verbs. Their compounds have identical irregularities.

- The few imperative irregularities are not included. These can be found on p. 232 and are indicated in the following table with an asterisk (*) next to the infinitive form.

Infinitive	Present	Future and conditional	Imperfect	Subjunctive	Simple past	Past participle
andare* *to go*	vado vai va andiamo andate vanno	andrò, andrei		*Present:* vada		
apparire *to appear*	appaio appari appare appariamo apparite appaiono			*Present:* appaia	apparvi/apparsi apparisti	apparso
avere* *to have*	ho hai ha abbiamo avete hanno	avrò, avrei		*Present:* abbia abbia abbia abbiamo abbiate abbiano	ebbi avesti	
bere *to drink*	bevo bevi beve beviamo bevete bevono	berrò, berrei	bevevo	*Present:* beva *Imperfect:* bevessi	bevvi bevesti	bevuto
cadere *to fall*		cadrò, cadrei			caddi cadesti	
cogliere *to gather*	colgo cogli coglie cogliamo cogliete colgono			*Present:* colga	colsi cogliesti	colto

Infinitive	Present	Future, Conditional	Imperfect	Subjunctive	Passato remoto	Past participle
compiere to carry out, complete	compio compi compie compiamo compite compiono	compirò, compirei	compivo	Present: compia Imperfect: compissi	compii, compisti	compiuto
condurre to lead	conduco conduci conduce conduciamo conducete conducono	condurrò, condurrei	conducevo	Present: conduca Imperfect: conducessi	condussi conducesti	condotto
cuocere to cook	cuocio cuoci cuoce cuociamo cuocete cuociono			Present: cuocia	cossi cuocesti	cotto
dare* to give	do dai dà diamo date danno	darò, darei	davo	Present: dia dia dia diamo diate diano Imperfect: dessi dessi desse dessimo deste dessero	diedi/detti desti diede/dette demmo deste diedero/dettero	dato
dire* to say	dico dici dice diciamo dite dicono	dirò, direi	dicevo	Present: dica Imperfect: dicessi	dissi dicesti	detto
dovere to have to	devo devi deve dobbiamo dovete devono	dovrò, dovrei		Present: debba debba debba dobbiamo dobbiate debbano		
essere* to be	sono sei è siamo siete sono	sarò, sarei	ero	Present: sia sia sia siamo siate siano Imperfect: fossi fossi fosse fossimo foste fossero	fui fosti fu fummo foste furono	stato
fare* to do, make	faccio fai fa facciamo fate fanno	farò, farei	facevo	Present: faccia Imperfect: facessi	feci facesti	fatto
morire to die	muoio muori muore moriamo morite muoiono			Present: muoia		morto
parere to seem	paio pari pare paiamo/ pariamo parete paiono	parrò, parrei		Present: paia	parvi paresti	parso

Infinitive	Present	Future and conditional	Imperfect	Subjunctive	Simple past	Past participle
piacere to like, please	piaccio piaci piace piacciamo piacete piacciono			Present: piaccia	piacqui piacesti	piaciuto
porre to place	pongo poni pone poniamo ponete pongono	porrò, porrei	ponevo	Present: ponga Imperfect: ponessi	posi ponesti	posto
potere to be able to	posso puoi può possiamo potete possono	potrò, potrei		Present: possa		
rimanere to remain, stay	rimango rimani rimane rimaniamo rimanete rimangono	rimarrò, rimarrei		Present: rimanga	rimasi rimanesti	rimasto
riuscire to succeed	riesco riesci riesce riusciamo riuscite riescono			Present: riesca		
salire to go up	salgo sali sale saliamo salite salgono			Present: salga		
sapere* to know	so sai sa sappiamo sapete sanno	saprò, saprei		Present: sappia sappia sappia sappiamo sappiate sappiano	seppi sapesti	
scegliere to choose	scelgo scegli sceglie scegliamo scegliete scelgono			Present: scelga	scelsi scegliesti	scelto
sciogliere to dissolve	sciolgo sciogli scioglie sciogliamo sciogliete sciolgono			Present: sciolga	sciolsi sciogliesti	sciolto
sedersi to sit	mi siedo ti siedi si siede ci sediamo vi sedete si siedono	mi siederò, mi siederei		Present: mi sieda		

soddisfare to satisfy	soddisfo soddisfi soddisfa soddisfiamo soddisfate soddisfano	soddisferò, soddisferei	soddisfacevo	Present: soddisfi soddisfi soddisfi soddisfacciamo soddisfacciate soddisfacciano Imperfect: soddisfacessi	soddisfeci soddisfacesti	soddisfatto
spegnere to turn off	spengo spegni spegne spegniamo spegnete spengono			Present: spenga	spensi spegnesti	spento
stare* to be, to stay	sto stai sta stiamo state stanno	starò, starei	stavo	Present: stia stia stia stiamo stiate stiano Imperfect: stessi stessi stesse stessimo steste stessero	stetti stesti stette stemmo steste stettero	stato
tenere to hold	tengo tieni tiene teniamo tenete tengono	terrò, terrei		Present: tenga	tenni tenesti	
togliere to remove	tolgo togli toglie togliamo togliete tolgono			Present: tolga	tolsi togliesti	tolto
trarre to draw, pull	traggo trai trae traiamo traete traggono	trarrò, trarrei	traevo	Present: tragga Imperfect: traessi	trassi, traesti	tratto
udire to hear	odo odi ode udiamo udite odono	udirò/udrò, udirei/udrei		Present: oda		
uscire to go out	esco esci esce usciamo uscite escono			Present: esca		
valere to be worth	valgo vali vale valiamo valete valgono	varrò, varrei		Present: valga	valsi valesti	valso
vedere to see		vedrò, vedrei			vidi vedesti	visto/veduto
venire to come	vengo vieni viene veniamo venite vengono	verrò, verrei		Present: venga	venni venisti	venuto

Infinitive	Present	Future and conditional	Imperfect	Subjunctive	Simple past	Past participle
vivere to live		vivrò, vivrei			vissi vivesti	vissuto
volere to want	voglio vuoi vuole vogliamo volete vogliono	vorrò, vorrei		Present: voglia	volli volesti	

Similar verb patterns

Like **apparire**: scomparire to disappear; **cadere**: accadere to happen; **condurre**: dedurre to deduce, indurre to induce, produrre to produce, ridurre to reduce, tradurre to translate; **dire**: benedire to bless, contraddire to contradict, disdire to cancel; **fare**: disfare to undo, rifare to redo, stupefare to amaze; **piacere**: tacere to be silent; **porre**: comporre to compose, imporre to impose, opporre to oppose, proporre to propose, supporre to suppose; **seder(si)**: possedere to own; **tenere**: appartenere to belong, contenere to contain, ottenere to obtain, trattener(si) to stay, remain; **togliere**: cogliere to pick, accogliere to welcome, sciogliere to dissolve, to melt; **trarre**: attrarre to attract, contrarre to contract, estrarre to extract, distrarre to distract, amuse, sottrarre to subtract; **valere**: prevalere to prevail; **venire**: avvenire to happen, intervenire to intervene; **vivere**: sopravvivere to survive.

Glossary

You will find the main parts of speech defined at the beginning of each relevant chapter (e.g. Articles, p. 13). This section contains additional terms used in the book. If a term is in bold it is further defined in alphabetical order within this list or else at the beginning of the relevant chapter in the book itself.

Agreement	Refers to the matching of word endings in **number** and **gender** to other words they are linked to; e.g. in Italian the form of a noun affects the form of related adjectives or pronouns.
Auxiliary	Auxiliary or 'helper' verbs are used to form **compound tenses**. The main ones in Italian are **avere** *to have* and **essere** *to be*.
Clause	Part of a sentence which contains a **subject** and a **verb**. A **main clause** makes sense on its own. The meaning of a **subordinate** or **dependent clause** is usually unclear on its own, e.g. *I left the house* (main clause) *without speaking* (subordinate clause).
Complex sentence	A sentence which contains a **main clause** and one or more **subordinate** or **dependent clauses**, e.g. *When it stopped raining* (subordinate clause) *I left the house* (main clause).
Compound sentence	A sentence which contains more than one **main clause** linked by a **co-ordinating conjunction** such as *and*, e.g. *I left the house and I went to the station*. It can also contain **dependent clauses**, e.g. *After he had rung me* (subordinate clause) *I left the house and went to the station* (main/independent clauses).
Conjugation	Italian **verbs** are grouped into three conjugations defined by different **infinitive** endings. These are: **-are** (first conjugation), **-ere** (second conjugation) and **-ire** (third conjugation). Some second conjugation verbs have endings such as **-arre, -orre** or **-urre** and are known as **contracted infinitive verbs** (see p. 192). The conjugation of a verb (and also the **person**) determines the forms it takes in the different **tenses**.
Context	Refers to the surrounding text of written language or to the accompanying situation of speech. The context is often crucial in determining the meaning of a word, **phrase**, etc., e.g. *That's nice!* can be response to a genuine compliment or the ironic response to an unpleasant remark.

Co-ordinating conjunction	This is a word linking words or *clauses* of the same kind and of equal importance, e.g. *Do you want beer or wine? I drank beer but he drank wine.*
Countable noun	Also known as count nouns, these refer to people or things that have a singular and plural form and can be counted individually, e.g. *house/houses; boy/boys.*
Determiner	A word used with a noun to specify its meaning more closely. Typical determiners are **articles** (*a, the*), **demonstratives** (*this, that*), **possessives** (e.g. *my, your*) and **indefinites** (e.g. *all, many*).
Finite verb	A verb form with a definite **subject** and **tense**, e.g. *I sing, they played.*
Gender	In Italian all nouns are masculine or feminine, even if referring to things. The gender affects the form of the noun and sometimes its meaning.
Indicative	This refers to the most common **mood** used in verb tenses. It expresses fact and certainty.
Literal meaning	This refers to a word-by-word translation which may not be the natural equivalent to the word or phrase in the original language, e.g. **Mi piace il burro** literally means *Butter is pleasing to me*, but the normal equivalent is *I like butter.*
Mood	A category of verb tenses which indicates the attitude or perception of the writer/speaker. In Italian, verb tenses can be **indicative** (expressing fact), **subjunctive** (expressing uncertainty, hopes, desires), **conditional** (expressing awareness of conditions or limitations) or **imperative** (expressing commands).
Non-finite verb	This is a verb form with no specified subject or tense which is sometimes equivalent to a noun or adjective. There are four main types: **infinitive** (*to sing is fun*); **gerund** (*singing is fun*); **past participle** (*the song sung was sad*); and **present participle** (*the singing doll was very popular*). See Chapter 23.
Number	The **number** of a noun or verb refers to whether it is singular or plural.
Object	The **noun, pronoun** or noun phrase considered to be affected by the action of a verb, either directly or indirectly: e.g. *I see John/the tower – Who/what do you see?* (**direct objects**: John, the tower, who?, what?); *I speak to John. To whom do you speak?/Who do you speak to?* (**indirect objects**: John, who?/whom?).
Person of a verb	This refers to the particular form of the verb which depends on who or what performs the action. There are three singular and three plural persons. First persons: *I, we.* Second persons: *you, you (plural).* Third persons: *he, she, it, they.*
Phrase	A group of words lacking a **finite verb**, e.g. *the enormous house* (noun phrase), *having been working* (verb phrase).
Simple sentence	A simple sentence consists of one **clause** with only one **verb** and **subject**, e.g. *I left the house, I feel tired.*
Stem	Sometimes referred to as 'root', this is the basic part of the verb infinitive from which the different **tenses** are usually formed, e.g. **pens-** is the stem of **pensare**, **vend-** the stem of **vendere** and **fin-** the stem of **finire**.

Style	Style denotes variation in speech or writing. The style (or register) of someone's language may depend on who is being addressed or what the topic and purpose is. Style can be formal, colloquial, slangy, etc. It can also refer to a person's individual use of speech or writing, or to a way of using language at a particular historical period.
Subject	Generally the **noun**, **pronoun** or noun phrase which performs the action of a verb, e.g. <u>He</u> *is eating*, <u>Peter</u> *plays tennis*, <u>The black cat</u> *disappeared*.
Subordinating conjunction	A word which links a **main clause** to a **subordinate clause**, e.g. *He went to work <u>although</u> he was ill*
Tense	Forms of **finite verbs** which locate the action in time with relation to past, present and future. They may be simple tenses (formed of one word) or compound tenses (formed of an **auxiliary verb** plus a **past participle** or a **gerund**).
Uncountable noun	Also known as mass nouns, and used in the singular, these refer to indivisible masses such as foods, substances or abstract concepts, e.g. *gas, snow, bread, rice, housing, rudeness.*

Key to exercises

UNIT 1 NOUNS

1.1 REGULAR NOUNS

1 Ho bisogno di lampade, letti, armadi, tavoli, sedie, poltrone, tendine, specchi, tappeti.

2 Abbiamo bisogno di piatti, coltelli, forchette, cucchiai, bicchieri, tazze, scodelle, tovaglioli.

3 lattughe, asparagi, funghi, peperoni, fichi, albicocche, limoni, pesche, arance, ciliegie.

4 greci, polacchi, idraulici, medici, cuochi, tedeschi, parroci, turchi.

5 chirurghi and drammaturghi. *The others end in* **-gi**.

6 abitudine f, amore m, animale m, appendice f, azione f, elefante m, esame m, immagine f, incidente m, indagine f, indice m, infermiere m, ordine m, origine f, opinione f, unione f.

1.2 IRREGULAR NOUNS

1 gli atleti/le atlete, gli automobilisti/le automobiliste, i colleghi/le colleghe, i ginnasti/le ginnaste, i pilota, i poeti.

2 l'analisi, la crisi, il dilemma, il diploma, la moglie, il problema, il programma, il sistema.

3 *Masculine*: il clima/i climi, il/i delta, il pianeta/i pianeti.
Feminine: la cometa/le comete, l'/le eclissi, l'/le oasi.

4 *Masculine*: il/i frigo, lo/gli stereo, il/i video.
Feminine: l'/le auto, la/le foto, la/le moto.

5 computer m, database m, fax m, file m, software m, mouse m, modem m. Email *is feminine*.

1.3 COMPOUND NOUNS

1 gli accendisigari, gli apribottiglie, gli aspirapolvere, i cavatappi, i giradischi, i portacenere, i portasapone, gli stuzzicadenti, i tagliaerba, i tritacarne, i tritarifiuti.

2 *Regular plural*: i portafogli, i sottotitoli.
Invariable: i portachiavi, i portamonete, i/le portavoce, i doposcuola, i dopobarba, i senzatetto.

1.4 DEFECTIVE NOUNS

1 (a) I bagagli sono qui (Il bagaglio è qui). (b) Ho bisogno di informazioni. (c) Ha troppi soldi.
(d) Non ho spiccioli. (e) L'uva è senza semi? (f) C'è troppa gente qui.

1.5   COLLECTIVE NOUNS

1   (a) era   (b) non c'era   (c) sono arrivati   (d) sono stati

1.6   THE GENDER OF NOUNS

1   (a) le orecchie   (b) uova   (c) paia   (d) migliaia   (e) centinaia

2   l'arancia, il fico, la pesca, la mandorla, l'oliva.

3   le braccia, le ciglia, le dita, le ginocchia, le labbra, le mani (*odd one out because it is f. in the singular and its plural ends in -i*).

4   (a) la fine   (b) il capitale   (d) la capitale

5   contralto, mezzosoprano.

6   levatrice (*midwife*), regina (*queen*).

7   (a) Maria è diventata un architetto molto bravo.   (b) Mio figlio è diventato una guida molto conosciuta.   (c) James Bond, l'agente 007, è una spia famosa inventata da Ian Fleming.
(d) Le vittime più tragiche sono state *or* sono stati i bambini.

UNIT 2   ARTICLES

2.1   THE INDEFINITE ARTICLE

1   Ho fatto un frullato di frutta, un arrosto, un'insalata, uno zabaglione, una zuppa inglese, uno spezzatino, un sugo di pomodoro.

2   **uno**: studente, scienziato, spettatore, psichiatra, psicologo. **un**: signore, soldato, sacerdote, pediatra, profugo, produttore, poliziotto.

3   **un**: amico, appartamento, elicottero, etto, ingresso, ispettore, ombrello, operario, uccello, ufficio.
un': amica, automobile, enciclopedia, estate, inchiesta, isola, offerta, opinione, uscita, uniforme.

4   (a) una; un'   (b) uno; un   (c) un; uno   (d) un'; una

5   (a) Sono medico. *I'm a doctor.*   (b) È un bravo medico. *He's a good doctor.*   (c) È uno studente che studia tanto. *He's a student who studies a lot.*   (d) Sono studente. *I'm a student.*   (e) È cattolica tua zia? *Is your aunt a Catholic?*   (f) Mia zia è una cattolica molto tradizionale. *My aunt is a very traditional Catholic.*

2.2   THE DEFINITE ARTICLE

1   l'asciugamano, la carta igienica, il dentifricio, il sapone, lo shampoo, la spugna, il rasoio.

2   lo gnu, la scimmia, lo scoiattolo, il serpente, lo struzzo, lo yak, la zanzara.

3   lo zodiaco, il Capricorno, l'Acquario, i Pesci, l'Ariete, il Toro, i Gemelli, il Cancro, il Leone, la Vergine, la Bilancia, lo Scorpione, il Sagittario.

4   Mi fa vedere le espadrille, i mocassini, le pantofole, i sandali, le scarpe da tennis, gli scarponi, gli stivali, gli zoccoli.

5   (a) l'; il   (b) il; lo   (c) il; l'   (d) l'; lo

6 (a) Dottor Binni, le presento **il** signor Giusti.   (b) Mi piace **l'**italiano.   (c) Parli greco? Non, ma parlo bene **lo** spagnolo.   (d) Al liceo studio tedesco e inglese.

7 (a) **La** Gran Bretagna è un'isola.   (b) **Il** Messico confina con **gli** Stati Uniti.   (c) Cuba e Haiti non sono paesi ricchi.   (d) **La** Sardegna e **la** Sicilia sono isole e regioni italiane.

8 (a) Dammi **il** tuo libro.   (b) Mi presti la tua penna?   (c) Avete visto **il** mio cappotto?
(d) Questa è la tua giacca e questa è la mia.

9 (a) venerdì   (b) **il** martedì   (c) **il** 27 maggio   (d) **il** 5 febbraio 1993   (e) lunedì 10 giugno

10 (a) Faccio il medico.   (b) Maria sta facendo il bagno.   (c) Ho bisogno di fare la doccia.
(d) Non ho fatto il biglietto.

11 (a) Roma è una bella città.   (b) L'Aia si trova in Olanda.   (c) Lipari è un'isola affascinante.
(d) Mi ha fatto vedere la Parigi di Sartre e Camus.   (e) Oggi non è andato a scuola.
(f) Studia alla scuola di suo fratello.   (g) Siamo arrivati la primavera dell'anno scorso.
(h) Siamo arrivati in primavera.

12 (a) I cani sono animali fedeli. *Dogs are faithful animals.*
(b) I cani che abbiamo visto erano adorabili. *The dogs we saw were adorable.*
(c) In Italia i bambini vanno a scuola a sei anni. *In Italy children go to school at six.*
(d) Ieri i bambini erano stanchi. *The children were tired yesterday.*
(e) La guerra risolve poco. *War doesn't solve much.*
(f) La guerra nei Balcani è stata una tragedia. *The Balkans war has been a tragedy.*

13 (a) Non mi piace il tè, ma adoro il caffè.   (b) Mi piace tanto il tennis, ma non mi piace il calcio.
(c) Detesto l'inverno, ma adoro la primavera.

14 (a) L'Olivetti, la Pirelli e la Fiat sono famose società italiane.
(b) La Juventus è in testa alla serie A.
(c) Leonardo e Michelangelo erano grandi artisti.
(d) (Il) Petrarca e (il) Leopardi erano grandi poeti.
(e) La Morante e la Ginzburg sono note scrittrici italiane.
(f) Giuseppe Verdi è morto fra gli 86 e gli 87 anni, credo.

15 (a) Ha i capelli biondi, gli occhi azzurri, la pelle chiara e le orecchie a sventola. *He has got blond hair, blue eyes, fair skin and ears which stick out.*
(b) Ha il raffreddore e mal di gola ma non ha la tosse. *He has got a cold and a sore throat, but he hasn't got a cough.*
(c) Purtroppo si è rotto la gamba! *Unfortunately he has broken his leg!*

2.3   THE PREPOSITIONAL ARTICLE

1 (a) Vado al mercato, all'aeroporto, allo stadio, alla stazione.
(b) La carta è nel cassetto. I biscotti sono nell'armadio. La lampada è nello studio. Le matite sono nella scatola.
(c) Il pane è sul tavolo. La chiave è sull'armadietto. Il dizionario è sullo scaffale. La penna è sulla scrivania.
(d) Dai giardini si vede la casa. Dagli scalini si vede la fontana. Dalle montagne si vede la pianura.

2 (a) dei   (b) degli   (c) dell'

3 (a) **Centro visitatori <u>della</u> distilleria di Talisker**
L'unica distilleria <u>dell'</u>isola di Skye, situata in una zona di grande bellezza naturale <u>sulla</u> riva di Loch Harport. Aperta tutto l'anno <u>dal</u> lunedì <u>al</u> venerdì, <u>dalle</u> 9.30 <u>alle</u> 16.30.
(b) **Centro visitatori <u>della</u> distilleria di Oban**
Costruita <u>nel</u> 1794, la nostra favolosa ubicazione <u>nel</u> centro <u>della</u> città ci rende una <u>delle</u> distillerie più interessanti <u>della</u> Scozia. Aperta tutto l'anno <u>dal</u> lunedì <u>al</u> venerdì. <u>Da</u> dicembre <u>a</u> febbraio ore limitate <u>di</u> apertura. Ingresso <u>a</u> pagamento.

2.4 ARTICLES WITH GEOGRAPHICAL NAMES

1 (a) La capitale della Scozia è Edimburgo.   (b) La capitale d'Italia è Roma.   (c) La capitale d'Israele è Gerusalemme.   (d) La capitale del Canada è Ottawa.   (e) La capitale di Cuba è l'Avana.
(f) La capitale delle Filippine è Manila.

2 (a) Il futuro re di Inghilterra è Carlo, Principe del Galles.
(b) Carlo Alberto di Savoia abdicò nel 1849.
(c) Nel 1861 Vittorio Emanuele II, Re di Sardegna, fu proclamato Re d'Italia.

3 (a) Torino è in Piemonte. È il capoluogo del Piemonte.
(b) L'Aquila è negli/in Abruzzi. È il capoluogo degli Abruzzi.
(c) Cagliari è in Sardegna. È il capoluogo della Sardegna.

4 (a) Passo sempre le ferie in Francia, nella Francia del sud.   (b) Io lavoro in Gran Bretagna.
(c) Carlo è nato nel Regno Unito.

5 (a) Fiona abita nell'/sull'isola di Skye.   (b) Donald abita nelle Orcadi.   (c) Alberto abita a Capri.
(d) Barbara va all'Isola di Man.   (e) Alistair va alle Ebridi.   (f) Sandra va a Cuba.

2.5 THE PARTITIVE ARTICLE

1 (a) Mi dà del caffè macinato?   (b) Avete della pasta fresca?   (c) Devo comprare delle camicie nuove.   (d) Ho comprato dei pantaloni neri.   (e) Mi ha prestato degli scarponi da sci.
(f) Mi serve dello sciroppo per la tosse.   (g) Ho bisogno di aspirina.   (h) Non ho fratelli.
(i) Devo comprare olio, aceto, sale e pepe.   (j) Volevo mandarini, non arance.

2.6 PARTITIVE EXPRESSIONS AND THEIR ALTERNATIVES

1 (a) Mi dà un po' di zucchero?   (b) Mi porti un po' d'acqua frizzante?   (c) Mi dà un po' di fagiolini?   (d) Siamo senza burro.   (e) Sono senza soldi.   (f) Mancano le lenzuola.

2 (a) Ho alcune lettere/qualche lettera da scrivere.   (b) Ho alcuni dubbi/qualche dubbio da chiarire.
(c) Hai qualche articolo da leggere?   (d) Avete qualche impegno per domani?
(e) Non ho nessun dubbio.   (f) Non c'è nessun'altra possibilità?

UNIT 3 DESCRIPTIVE ADJECTIVES

3.1 REGULAR ADJECTIVES

1 (a) un uomo alto, vecchio, stanco, simpatico, ubriaco, importante, pessimista
una donna alta, vecchia, stanca, simpatica, ubriaca, importante, pessimista
uomini alti, vecchi, stanchi, simpatici, ubriachi, importanti, pessimisti
donne alte, vecchie, stanche, simpatiche, ubriache, importanti, pessimiste
(b) un discorso assurdo, necessario, lungo, breve
una vacanza assurda, necessaria, lunga, breve
discorsi assurdi, necessari, lunghi, brevi
vacanze assurde, necessarie, lunghe, brevi
(c) un cappotto nero, grigio, sudicio, magnifico, marrone
una giacca nera, grigia, sudicia, magnifica, marrone
cappotti neri, grigi, sudici, magnifici, marroni
giacche nere, grigie/grige, sudicie/sudice, magnifiche, marroni
(d) il pesce squisito, fresco, straordinario, marcio, inglese
la pera squisita, fresca, straordinaria, marcia, inglese
i pesci squisiti, freschi, straordinari, marci, inglesi
le pere squisite, fresche, straordinarie, marce, inglesi

2   (a) bel   (b) bell'   (c) bella   (d) bei   (e) begli

3   (a) buon   (b) buono   (c) buon'   (d) buoni   (e) buone

4   (a) San   (b) Sant'   (c) Sant'   (d) San, San   (e) Santo

3.2   MAKING AGREEMENTS

I   (a) È una collega depressa, lunatica e squilibrata.
   (b) Sua sorella è aggressiva, sensibile e dolce. (This is the person there is disagreement about.)
   (c) La professoressa è timida, pedante e conformista.
   (d) I miei cugini sono vanitosi, ignoranti ed egoisti.
   (e) Le mie zie sono colte, intelligenti e cosmopolite.
   (f) Gina e Franco sono bravi, simpatici e gentili.

2   (a) Che cosa fai di bello oggi?   (b) Vorrei bere qualcosa di caldo.   (c) Non ho fatto niente di male/sbagliato.   (d) Non danno nulla di bello al cinema stasera.   (e) Che cosa c'è di straordinario in tutto questo?   (f) Quello che c'è di strano è la sua indifferenza.

3   (a) tolleranti   (b) scortesi   (c) onesti   (d) giovani, ottimisti

3.3   SOME IRREGULAR ADJECTIVES

I   Ho visto   (a) una lampada liberty,   (b) tappeti multicolori,   (c) delle riviste gay,   (d) dei pappagalli verde smeraldo,   (e) dei pantaloni grigioverdi,   (f) un parasole viola,   (g) dei vestitini sexy,   (h) un boa con piume rosa.

2   (a) antidroga   (b) antinucleari   (c) antiaerei   (d) anticarro   (e) angloamericane   (f) russo-afgana

3.4   THE POSITION OF ADJECTIVES

I   (a) dei soldati americani   (b) un gruppo di suore sorridenti   (c) dei bambini annoiati   (d) dei giovani ubriachi   (e) un monaco buddista con la veste gialla   (f) una signora indiana con il sari di seta   (g) una donna strana con un cappello triangolare   (h) un gatto piccolino in una gabbia molto grande

2   (a) È una cara amica. Ho comprato una giacca cara.
   (b) Ci sono diverse soluzioni. Ci sono soluzioni diverse.
   (c) Ho parlato con lo stesso direttore. Ho parlato con il direttore stesso.
   (d) La ammiro, è una donna unica. È l'unica soluzione possibile.

3   (a) D, S   (b) S, D   (c) S, D   (d) D, S

4   (a) Due buste grandi e tre buste piccole, per piacere.
   (b) Un caffè lungo in una tazza grande/grande tazza, per piacere.
   (c) Prendo il solito caffè, per piacere, e un tè freddo.

3.5   USING TWO OR MORE ADJECTIVES

I   (a) guanti neri di pelle/guanti di pelle nera
   (b) un golf verde di cachemire/un golf di cachemire verde
   (c) una camicetta di cotone bianca e nera
   (d) una giacca a quadretti gialli e neri

2   (a) una compagnia aerea francese   (b) una nota società multinazionale   (c) un impianto nucleare russo   (d) un problema tecnico abbastanza/piuttosto complicato

3   (a) Sono uscito con dei compagni di scuola simpaticissimi.
   (b) Ho visto un documentario storico noioso.
   (c) Sono andato a un concerto rock veramente meraviglioso.
   (d) Ho incontrato una coppia canadese molto interessante.

4 (a) Tiziana era bellissima, con lunghi capelli neri e grandi occhi azzurri.

(b) Stanno cercando una giovane donna dai lunghi capelli neri *or, for specification*, una donna giovane, dai capelli lunghi e neri.

(c) È stata una decisione burocratica assurda.

(d) Non si può mica accettare quell'assurda decisione burocratica!

(e) Siamo stati in un meraviglioso albergo scozzese antico/un antico albergo scozzese meraviglioso.

5 Abita in: (a) un piccolo bungalow moderno (b) un vecchio quartiere di Roma (c) una bella casa grande (d) un'enorme stanza affittata/una stanza affittata enorme (e) uno stupendo attico antico/un attico antico stupendo.

3.6 NOTES ON MEANING

I (a) È un bel dipinto, è un dipinto magnifico. (b) È un buon vino, è un vino stagionato. (c) È un bravo/buon cuoco, è un cuoco geniale. (d) È un buon/bel libro di testo, è un libro di testo utile. (e) È un bel romanzo, è un romanzo originale. (f) Sono dei bravi bambini, sono bambini educati. (g) È una brava persona/È un uomo buono, aiuta sempre gli altri. (h) È un bravo studente, che studia tanto.

2 (a) È un brutto quadro. (b) È un vino cattivo. (c) È un cattivo cuoco. (d) È una persona cattiva. (e) Il tempo è brutto/cattivo. (f) È un brutto libro di testo. (g) È un brutto/cattivo romanzo. (h) Sono bambini cattivi. (i) È un cattivo studente. (j) È un brutto saggio.

3.7 ADJECTIVES AS OTHER PARTS OF SPEECH

I (a) We did everything possible/everything we could to help him. (b) The good thing is that in the end they gave me a discount. (c) The worst thing is the banks are closed. (d) Is that the best you can do?

UNIT 4 ADVERBS

4.1 THE FORMS OF ADVERBS

I (a) onestamente (b) brevemente (c) cordialmente (d) volgarmente (e) bene (f) male (g) meglio (h) peggio

2 *Used as adjectives, not adverbs*: (iv) (città) lontana, (vi) poco (vento), (ix) felici e contenti (*not modifying verbs*), (vii) tanto *modifies an adverb* (male), (viii) troppo *modifies an adjective* (caro)

4.2 ADVERBS OF MANNER, QUANTITY AND DEGREE

I (a) molto (b) molto (c) molte (d) molta (e) tanto (f) tanto (g) tanti (h) tanta

2 (a) Giocano bene a calcio. (b) Suona molto la chitarra. (c) Amava tanto i gatti. (d) Mi è piaciuto parecchio quel film. (e) Ha sbattuto forte la porta.

3 (a) Siamo appena arrivati. (b) Ti sento appena. (c) Gli piace mangiare molto. (d) Mi piacerebbe molto mangiare adesso.

4.3 ADVERBS OF TIME, FREQUENCY AND PLACE

I frequentemente, raramente, spesso, sempre, non ... mai, non ... mai più

2 (a) Marco è ancora a casa. Sta ancora studiando. *Marco is still at home. He is still studying.*

(b) Davide frequenta già l'università? Ha già dato gli esami? *Is Davide already at university? Is Davide at university yet? Has he taken any exams yet?*

(c) Studi sempre in biblioteca? Devi sempre studiare in bibioteca? *Do you always study in the library? Do you always have to study in the library?*

(d) Suo marito non aiuta mai in casa. Non ha mai aiutato in vita sua. *Her husband never helps at home. He has never helped in his whole life.*

(e) Usciamo spesso la sera. Siamo usciti spesso la sera. *We often go out in the evenings. We have often gone out/We often went out in the evening.*

3 (a) Faccio sempre io la spesa. (b) Mangiamo spesso fuori. (c) Guardo raramente la televisione. (d) Non mangiamo mai la carne. (e) Mi piace giocare spesso a tennis. (f) Ci piace spesso giocare a tennis.

4 (a) Bisogna sempre chiudere la porta a chiave. (b) Ha chiuso subito la finestra. Ha subito chiuso la finestra. (c) Hai portato dentro i piatti? (d) Ho mandato indietro il pacco. (*Less common –* Ho mandato il pacco indietro.) (e) Ho messo i documenti qui dentro.

5 (a) in ritardo (b) in anticipo (c) tardi (d) presto (e) con un'ora di ritardo/con un ritardo di un'ora (f) con dieci minuti di anticipo/in anticipo di dieci minuti

6 (a) No, non l'ho più visto. (b) No, non voglio più provare. (c) No, non ho ancora rifatto il letto. (d) No, non mi ha ancora scritto. (e) No, non sono ancora arrivati. (f) No, finora non ho avuto notizie.

7 (a) always (b) always (c) for ever (d) still (e) still (f) still (g) always (h) always/all the time

8 (a) Dorme ancora? (b) Paolo è ancora fuori? (c) Andrai ancora a Milano? (d) Doveva ancora andare in banca.

9 (a) still (b) again (c) still (d) again (e) still (f) again

10 (a) Ne vuoi ancora? (b) Mi/Me ne dà ancora quattro fette? (c) Mi fermo/rimango ancora dieci giorni. (d) Vorrei fermarmi/rimanere ancora un po'.

11 (a) Mi si è di nuovo bloccato il computer!/Mi si è bloccato il computer un'altra volta! (b) Ho perso le chiavi dell'ufficio un'altra volta./Ho perso di nuovo le chiavi dell'ufficio. (c) Mi si è rotta la stampante un'altra volta./Mi si è di nuovo rotta la stampante.

12 (a) Lo rimando? (b) Dovrà ridare l'esame. (c) Dovrai rifarlo.

13 (a) Lo mando un'altra volta? (b) Dovrà dare l'esame un'altra volta. (c) Dovrai farlo un'altra volta.

14 (a) Ne vuoi un altro po'? (b) Me ne dà altre quattro fette? (c) Mi fermo/rimango altri dieci giorni. (d) Vorrei fermarmi/rimanere un altro po'.

4.4 OTHER ADVERBS AND THEIR USES

1 (a) appunto (b) certo (c) magari (d) può darsi (e) esatto (f) senz'altro (g) d'accordo

2 (a) Purtroppo ha perso la chiave. (b) Per fortuna non si è fatto male. (c) Ovviamente non capiscono niente. (d) Francamente lo trovo antipatico. (e) Onestamente non mi sembra necessario.

3 (a) Non ho davvero/proprio capito niente. (b) Lo ha addirittura/perfino insultato! (c) Mi ha persino aiutato. (d) Lo troverai proprio davanti alla porta. (e) È solo un gioco.

4 (a) È addirittura/proprio incredibile! *It's really incredible!*
(b) Non è assolutamente possibile! *It's absolutely impossible!*
(c) Sono proprio matti! *They're really crazy!*
(d) Sono proprio seccati. *They are really annoyed.*

5 (a) eccezionalmente (b) terribilmente (c) eccessivamente (d) fortemente

6 (a) It's incredibly hot. (b) He's an exceptionally intelligent boy. (c) That film is depressingly stupid. (d) That man is horrendously ignorant. (e) The little girl was really sad: she had lost her kitten.

7 (a) Sono andato a Roma, Milano, Bergamo, Trento e Torino e poi sono anche andato a Bari.
(b) Davvero? Sei andato anche a Bari?
(c) Marta è intelligente. – Sì, ma anche Marina è intelligente.
(d) Marina è sensibile. – Sì, ma è anche allegra.

8 (a) Abbiamo solo una macchina. (b) Oggi studio solo geografia. (c) Siamo liberi solo lunedì …,
perché dopo partiamo. (d) Ieri ho letto solo due capitoli. (e) Hai comprato dei panini? –
No, ho comprato solo pane. (f) Possono solo venire la settimana prossima, non prima.

UNIT 5 COMPARATIVES AND SUPERLATIVES

5.1 ADJECTIVES, COMPARATIVES AND RELATIVE SUPERLATIVES

1 più bello, il più bello; più pesante, il più pesante; più ottimista, il più ottimista.

2 (a) più simpatico di (b) meno vecchia della tua (c) più simpatico della (d) meno frequentata
della (e) più cari del

3 (a) Gli Stati Uniti sono fra i paesi più ricchi del mondo. (b) Marilyn Monroe era fra le attrici più
belle di Hollywood. (c) Stromboli, Lipari e Capri sono alcune delle isole più affascinanti d'Italia.
(d) Il parmigiano è uno dei formaggi italiani più conosciuti.

4 migliore/più buono; il migliore/il più buono; peggiore/più cattivo, il peggiore/il più cattivo;
maggiore/più grande, il maggiore/il più grande; minore/più piccolo, il minore/il più piccolo; più, più
di tutti/il maggior numero di; meno, meno di tutti/il minor numero di.

5 (a) buone, più buone/migliori (b) buon, migliore (c) cattiva, più cattiva (d) maggiore/ più
grande, minore/più piccolo (e) più, meno

6 (a) migliore amico (b) peggiore stagione (c) fratello maggiore/più grande (d) più carte di
tutti/il maggiore numero di carte (e) meno carte di tutti

5.2 ADJECTIVES: ABSOLUTE SUPERLATIVES

1 (a) È una ragazza allegrissima/molto allegra. (b) È una persona molto egoista. (c) È un artista
eccellente/un ottimo/bravissimo artista. (d) È un pessimo linguista. (e) È una persona
buonissima. (f) È un cane terribile/molto cattivo.

5.3 ADVERBS: COMPARATIVES, RELATIVE AND ABSOLUTE SUPERLATIVES

1 più gentilmente, il più gentilmente possibile, molto gentilmente (*rare*: gentilissimamente)
più forte, il più forte possibile, fortissimo/molto forte
più tardi, il più tardi possibile, tardissimo/molto tardi
più vicino, il più vicino possibile, vicinissimo/molto vicino

2 (a) meno lontano di (b) più cordialmente (c) più presto/prima

3 (a) Sì, sono tornati tardissimo, più tardi di tutti.
(b) Sì, ha lavorato molto veloce/velocissimamente, più veloce di tutti.
(c) Sì, mi ha scritto molto regolarmente/ (*rare*: regolarissimamente), più regolarmente di tutti.

4 (a) bene, meglio (b) male, peggio (c) poco, meno (d) molto, di più

5 (a) Sì, hanno lavorato benissimo, meglio di tutti.
(b) Sì, ha aiutato pochissimo, ha aiutato meno di tutti.
(c) Sì, insegna malissimo, insegna peggio di tutti gli altri insegnanti.
(d) Sì, mi piace moltissimo, mi piace più di tutti.

6 (a) Devi venire il più presto possibile. (b) Devi mangiare il meno possibile. (c) Devi farlo il
meglio possibile.

7 (a) meglio, migliori (b) migliore, meglio (c) peggio, peggiori (d) peggiore, peggio

5.4 MAKING COMPARISONS OF INEQUALITY

1 (a) Ada è meno alta di sua sorella. (b) Gina studia più di me. (c) Mio nonno ha più di ottant'anni. (d) Fa più caldo di ieri. (e) Mi alzo prima/più presto dei miei genitori. (f) I trasporti pubblici sono più cari in Inghilterra che in Italia.

2 (a) che sorelle (b) che caffè (c) che mai (d) dell'ultima volta (e) che guidare a Roma (f) che intelligente

5.5 EMPHATIC COMPARATIVES

1 (a) È sempre più difficile/È ancora più difficile trovare un lavoro.
(b) L'idea mi piace sempre meno/ancora meno.
(c) È diventato sempre più triste/ancora più triste.
(d) Ottiene dei voti sempre peggiori/più brutti/ancora peggiori/più brutti.

5.6 MAKING COMPARISONS OF EQUALITY

1 (a) Elena è (tanto) generosa quanto Lisa. (b) Mirella è tanto ingenua quanto stupida.
(c) Io guadagno tanto quanto te. (d) Studiano tanto quanto dormono. (e) Carla ha tante amiche quante (ne ha) Rina. (f) Lucio lavora bene come te.

2 (a) È tornata dalla gara fresca come una rosa. (b) Mia nonna è sorda come una campana.
(c) Mio nonno è sano come un pesce. (d) Fumi come un turco.

3 (a) He isn't as stupid as you think. (b) I really find them as kind as you had said.
(c) I prefer you (just) as you are.

4 (a) altrettanto, che (b) altrettanto, che (c) altrettanto, che

5.7 OTHER COMPARATIVE CONSTRUCTIONS

1 (a) ma tu sei altrettanto alto. (b) ma il mio guadagna altrettanto. (c) ma io ne ho raccolto/i altrettanti. (d) io ho fatto altrettanto.

2 (a) Michele ha/porta la stessa camicia di ieri.
(b) Giovanna vota per lo stesso partito dei suoi genitori.
(c) Paolo ha lo stesso parrucchiere di suo fratello.

3 (a) Preferirei andare a comprare una pizza piuttosto che andare al ristorante.
(b) Ho intenzione di andare in campeggio piuttosto che dormire in albergo.
(c) Ho deciso di partire con il treno piuttosto che prendere la macchina.

4 (a) di quanto tu (non) pensi (b) di quello che sembra (c) di quanto dovresti

5 (a) iii (b) iv (c) ii (d) i

UNIT 6 SUFFIXES

6.1 NOUN AND ADJECTIVAL SUFFIXES

1 (a) paesino di montagna (b) deboluccio (c) dei paroloni (d) delle parolacce

2 (a) difettuccio (b) problemino (c) lavoraccio (d) stupidino/stupidello (e) Ha fatto un figurone. *He made a marvellous impression.* Che figuraccia ha fatto! *What a terrible impression he made!* Sembra un figurino. *He looks like a model/like a fashion plate.*

3 A 4 B 6 C 11 D 3 E 1 F 13 G 9 H 5 I 7 J 2 K 8 L 10 M 12

6.2 FALSE SUFFIXES

I (a) F mattone *brick* (b) F postino *postman* (c) T (d) F mulino *mill* (e) F bagnino *lifeguard*
(f) F rubinetto *tap*

6.3 ADVERBIAL SUFFIXES

I (a) un pochino (b) benino (c) prestino (d) maluccio

UNIT 7 PERSONAL PRONOUNS

7.1 SUBJECT PRONOUNS

I (a) Lei (b) tu (c) voi

2 (a) lui, lei (b) voi, noi (c) tu, io (d) Lei, noi due/tutti e due

3 (a) Mina e Elena, siete voi? – No, siamo noi, Marta e Lucia.
(b) Sei tu, Dario? – No, sono io, Giuseppe.
(c) Chi ha pagato? È stata lei? – No, è stato lui.
(d) Noi andiamo al cinema, e voi?

7.2 REFLEXIVE AND RECIPROCAL PRONOUNS

I (a) mi trucco (b) ti togli (c) ci lacchiamo (d) vi lamentate

2 (a) si addormenta (b) si lavano, si pettinano (c) ci svegliamo, ci alziamo

3 (a) si incontrano, si salutano, si danno (b) ci vediamo, ci sentiamo (c) si scrive, scambiarsi

7.3 DIRECT AND INDIRECT OBJECT PRONOUNS

I (a) He bought some roses (DO) and gave them (DO) to his wife (IDO).
(b) He bought her (IDO) some roses (DO).
(c) Did you ask Francesca (IDO) to leave?
(d) Did you ask her (IDO)?

2 *Direct object verbs*: ascoltare, aspettare, chiamare, guardare, pregare, scusare, sentire.
Indirect object verbs: comprare, dire, portare, spiegare, telefonare.

3 (a) li (b) la (c) lo (d) le

4 (a) ti (b) la, la (c) vi

5 (a) lo (b) l' (c) lo (d) ce l'ho (e) ce li

6 (a) Sì, l'ascolto spesso. (b) Sì, l'ho chiesto. (c) Le ho pagate 150 euro.

7 (a) gli (b) le (c) gli (d) le

8 a) Le (b) Le (c) vi (d) ti (e) vi

9 a) mi (b) le (c) ci

10 (a) si (b) gli (c) gli

11 (a) Gli ho chiesto di comprare il pane.
(b) Pino, gli hai detto di venire alle dieci?/Hai detto loro di venire alle dieci?
(c) Dario gli devi rispondere subito. Devi rispondere (a) loro subito.

12   (a) la   (b) le   (c) la   (d) le   (e) vi   (f) la

13   (a) La porterò al mare.   (b) Le porterò dei fiori.   (c) Lo manderò a Carlo.   (d) Gli manderò un fax.   (e) Lo leggerò a Dina e a Lucia.   (f) Gli leggerò il riassunto./Leggerò loro il riassunto.

14   (a) Le ho consigliato di partire presto.   (b) Dobbiamo convincerla ad aiutare.   (c) Non puoi costringerli a venire.   (d) Gli ho permesso di andare alla festa.

7.4   *NE*

1   (a) Quante ne prende? – Ne prendo mezzo chilo.
(b) Quanto ne vuole? – Ne prendo quattro scatole.
(c) Quanti ne vuole? – Ne prendo due

2   (a) Anch'io ne consumo pochissimi.   (b) Anch'io ne consumo tanta.   (c) Anch'io ne compro molto.

3   (a) La minestra è buona, ne vuoi un po'?   (b) La pasta è fresca, quanta ne vuole?
(c) Il vino è buono, ne vuole?   (d) Le salsicce sono eccezionali, ne volete?

4   (a) No, grazie, non ne ho bisogno.   (b) Ne sono sicuro.   (c) Anche noi ne abbiamo parlato.
(d) Ma non ne so niente.   (e) Non lo so, tu cosa ne pensi?

7.5   *CI*

1   (a) Sì, ci sono stato tante volte.   (b) Sì, ci andiamo fra poco.   (c) Sì, ci sono andato ieri.
(d) Ci vado adesso.

2   (a) Sì, ci sono abituato.   (b) Sì, ci siamo riusciti.   (c) Sì, (gli) ho risposto.   (d) No, non ci abbiamo pensato.   (e) Sì, li penso spesso/penso spesso a loro.

3   (a) Nel mio appartamento ci sono sei stanze, ma c'è un bagno solo.
(b) Cosa c'è da mangiare? – Ci sono gli spaghetti alle vongole e c'è l'insalata.
(c) C'è Piero? – No, non c'è.
(d) Ci sono Andrea e Massimo? – No, non ci sono.

4   (a) Ci metto un'ora   (b) Ci vuole un'ora   (c) ci mettono

7.6   OBJECT PRONOUN POSITION

1   (a) Preferisco vederti più tardi.   (b) Ho intenzione di divertirmi al mare.   (c) Abbiamo bisogno di comprarne altri.   (d) È meglio andarci domani.

2   (a) Angelica è uscita, lasciandola aperta.   (b) Luigi ha scritto pregandola di rispondere.
(c) È caduto, lasciandoli cadere.   (d) Gli sto leggendo un racconto.

3   (a) Gianna, mandala.   (b) Signora, lo spedisca.   (c) Parlatene oggi.   (d) Signore, gli parli domani.

4   (a) Sai dirmi se la cena è pronta?   (b) Voglio lavarmi le mani.   (c) Devo finirlo stasera.
(d) Non posso aiutarli.   (e) Non toccarlo!   (f) Non preoccuparti.

5   (a) ii   (b) iii   (c) iv   (d) i

7.7   DISJUNCTIVE PRONOUNS

1   (a) me, lei   (b) loro, lei   (c) me, lui   (d) noi, voi

2   (a) Porti me o lui al cinema?   (b) Vuoi telefonare a lei o a lui?   (c) Chiamerò loro e anche Gina.
(d) Manderò una cartolina a te e anche ai miei.

3   (a) sé   (b) lui   (c) lei   (d) sé

7.8 COMBINING DIRECT OBJECT PRONOUNS AND *NE* WITH INDIRECT OBJECT OR REFLEXIVE PRONOUNS

1 (a) me li (b) te le (c) glielo (d) ve la

2 (a) te le (b) gliela (c) ve lo

3 (a) gliene (b) gliene (c) ve ne

4 (a) Chi te l'ha detto? (b) Chi gliel'ha detto? (c) Chi ve l'ha detto?

5 (a) Sì, te lo farò sapere senz'altro, te lo prometto!
(b) Glielo dirò domani, signora, glielo prometto.
(c) Certo, ve lo racconterò di sicuro, ve lo prometto!

6 (a) Se non potete venire, ce lo dite? (b) Anna, quando parti, me lo fai sapere? (c) Ivo, se vuoi venire, glielo puoi dire? (d) Ti aiuterò, Mina, te lo prometto.

7 (a) Perché non te li lavi? (b) Perché non se lo toglie, signora? (c) Ce ne compriamo un po', allora? (d) Certo, me ne occupo io/lo faccio io. (e) Non possiamo permettercelo.

8 (a) È tardi, me ne vado. (b) Ma se ne frega! (c) Te la senti di venire al cinema? (d) Perché te la prendi? (e) Me la sono cavata all'esame.

7.9 OTHER PRONOUN COMBINATIONS

1 (a) lo si beve come aperitivo! (b) la si beve come digestivo! (c) lo si vende dappertutto!

2 (a) Ti si è bucata la calza. (b) Gli si è sporcata la cravatta. (c) Le si è strappata la giacca.
(d) Mi si è staccato il bottone.

3 (a) ci si dorme (b) ci si sta (c) Non ci si capisce (d) ci si riuscirà

4 (a) ci si alza (b) Ci si veste (c) ci si diverte (d) Ci si abitua

5 (a) Ce ne sono cinque. (b) No, non ce n'è. (c) No, ce n'è pochissimo. (d) È vero, ce ne sono pochissime. (e) Bene, quante ce ne sono?

6 (a) È troppo tardi, non ce la faccio stasera. (b) È troppo difficile, non ce la fa. (c) Dino, perché ce l'hai con me? (d) Ti ci vuole molto per arrivare a scuola?

7.10 DIRECT OBJECT PRONOUN AGREEMENTS

1 (a) No, non li hanno ancora scelti. (b) No, non le abbiamo ancora innaffiate. (c) No, non l'ha ancora mandata. (d) No, non li hanno ancora prenotati.

2 (a) Ne ho comprati tanti. Ne ho comprati/o due chili.
(b) Ne ho ordinate molte. Ne ho ordinate quattro.
(c) Ne ho ordinato parecchio. Ne ho ordinate/o tre bottiglie.
(d) Ne ho comprata poca. Ne ho comprato un barattolo.

3 (a) Li hai rotti tutti? (b) L'hai rovinata completamente? (c) L'hai sfasciata del tutto?
(d) L'hai distrutto totalmente?

4 (a) Ma te li ho prestati l'altro giorno! (b) Ma ve le abbiamo mandate la settimana scorsa!
(c) Ma te li ho comprati stamattina! (d) Ma ve la abbiamo portata ieri!

5 (a) se l'è slogata (b) se l'è storto (c) se le è bruciate (d) se l'è rotta

UNIT 8 POSSESSIVES

8.2 POSSESSIVE ADJECTIVES

1 (a) la tua   (b) il tuo   (c) il suo   (d) i vostri/i loro   (e) le vostre   (f) il vostro

2 (a) Non ho mai visto la sua casa.   (b) La sua casa è molto piccola.   (c) Ti piace la loro nuova casa?   (d) Il suo appartamento ha un balcone enorme.   (e) Il suo appartamento si trova al secondo piano.   (f) Il loro appartamento è in via Manin.   (g) Non mi piacciono le sue amiche. (h) Siamo usciti con le loro amiche.   (i) I suoi figli frequentano l'università.   (j) I loro figli vivono tutti all'estero.

3 (a) i miei figli   (b) i nostri nipotini   (c) le mie nipoti   (d) le nostre figlie

4 (a) mio, nostra   (b) mio, la sua   (c) la nostra, il suo   (d) mia, il mio   (e) mia, le nostre

8.3 POSSESSIVE PRONOUNS

1 (a) la mia   (b) le sue   (c) il tuo   (d) il mio   (e) ai tuoi

2 (a) tuo, mio, il mio   (b) sua, mia, la mia   (c) sue, sue, mie

8.4 EXPRESSING POSSESSION WITH 'S/S' ENDINGS

1 (a) La mamma di Leonardo è malata.   (b) La moglie del signor Palladino è in vacanza. (c) Il gatto dei vicini è nero.   (d) Ho trovato le scarpe di Elisabetta e anche quelle di Antonio. (e) Ho perso la lettera di Marta e anche quella di sua sorella.   (f) Ti vedrò/Ci vediamo da Giovanni.

8.5 POSSESSIVES WITH OTHER DETERMINERS + PROPRIO

1 (a) un mio amico/un amico mio   (b) una sua collega   (c) un loro conoscente   (d) (dei) nostri amici/(degli) amici nostri   (e) dei miei colleghi

2 (a) tre suoi amici/tre amici suoi   (b) alcuni nostri clienti   (c) quei tuoi amici/quegli amici tuoi

3 (a) proprio   (b) la propria   (c) propria/sua   (d) i miei propri

8.6 OMISSION OF THE POSSESSIVES IN ITALIAN

1 (a) l'ombrello   (b) la moglie   (c) il golf   (d) il piede   (e) il cappello

UNIT 9 DEMONSTRATIVES

9.1 DEMONSTRATIVE ADJECTIVES AND PRONOUNS

1 Ho preso in prestito questa lampada, queste sedie, questo divano, questi cuscini, quest'armadio, questo scaffale, questi specchi.

2 Mi fa vedere quella borsetta, quelle cravatte, quel maglione, quei pantaloni, quello specchio, quell'anello, quegli orecchini.

3 (a) quella, quell'   (b) quell', quell'   (c) quel, quello   (d) quel, quell'   (e) quei, quegli (f) quegli, quei

4 (a) quella (b) quello (c) quelli lì, quei tre (d) quelli lì, quelli verdi (e) quello?, quell'altro più piccolo

5 (a) Questa è la cucina e questo qui è il bagno. (b) Questa qui è la mia camera e quella là è la tua. (c) Quanto costa questa? E quella? (d) Quanto costano queste? E quelle?

9.2 OTHER WAYS OF EXPRESSING *THIS* AND *THAT*

I (a) Questo/Ciò non mi interessa. (b) Questo/Ciò non vuol dire che non venga/verrà. (c) Questo/Ciò non sembra giusto. (d) Non è vero.

2 (a) Che peccato/È un peccato, non può andare a sciare. (b) Che figura/È imbarazzante, cosa facciamo? (c) Che assurdità/È assurdo (questo)! (d) Che seccatura! Hai una chiave di riserva? (e) Grazie, sei molto gentile.

3 (a) È qui che vai a scuola? (b) È là/lì che compri la frutta e la verdura? (c) È qua/qui che hai avuto un incidente? (d) È lì che lavora tua figlia?

4 (a) Ecco perché/È per questo che sono in ritardo.
(b) Ecco perché/È per questo che la macchina non parte!
(c) Guarda, ecco come funziona …
(d) Mio fratello è un amico di suo marito, ecco come lo so/l'ho saputo.

5 (a) Per avere accesso all'Internet, ecco quello che si deve fare … (b) Ecco quello che mi ha detto … (c) Sì, è quello che ho intenzione di fare. (d) Non è quello che voglio/volevo dire.

UNIT 10 INTERROGATIVES

10.1 ASKING QUESTIONS

I (a) Quando viene l'avvocato? (b) Di dov'è la signorina? (c) Cosa vuole la dottoressa?

2 (a) La posta è arrivata, (non è) vero? (b) Ti chiami Carla, (non è) vero? (c) Partono lunedì, (non è) vero? (d) Non hai pagato, vero?

10.2 QUESTION WORDS

I (a) Come (b) Come (c) com'/dov' (d) quando e perché/quando e come (e) Dov'
(f) Perché (g) Come

2 (a) cosa vuole (b) a che cosa serve (c) di che cosa è fatto (d) di chi è (e) per chi è
(f) di chi è (g) di chi sono/siano (h) di chi è/sia.

3 (a) Che ora è? (b) Che lavoro fa? (c) Qual è il suo numero di telefono? (d) Qual è il suo sport preferito? (e) Com'è il suo insegnante? Che tipo è il suo insegnante?

4 *In sentence* (c).

5 (a) v (b) iv (c) ii (d) i (e) iii. *The mystery object is:* una palla *a ball*

6 (a) Quanti spaghetti vuoi? (b) Non so quanta gente c'è. (c) Quant'è lontano? (d) Quanto (tempo) impiegherai?

10.3 DISTINGUISHING INTERROGATIVES FROM RELATIVES

I (a) che cosa (b) quello che/ciò che (c) chi (d) che (e) chi (f) con cui (g) che
(h) quale

UNIT 11 EXCLAMATIONS

1 (a) Che bel giardino!   (b) Che panorama stupendo!   (c) Che magnifica scrivania antica!
   (d) Che bello quell'orologio!

2 (a) Che peccato!   (b) Che meraviglia!   (c) Che scarpe meravigliose! Che meraviglia quelle
   scarpe!   (d) Che bambini intelligenti!   (e) Come sono intelligenti! Che intelligenti che sono!

3 (a) Quanto rumore qui dentro!   (b) Che rumore tremendo!   (c) Che gente antipatica!
   (d) Quanta gente c'è in giro!

4 (a) Come/Quanto   (b) Quanti   (c) Come   (d) Come/Quanto

5 (a) ii   (b) iii   (c) ii, iii   (d) i, ii, iii

UNIT 12 INDEFINITES

12.1   INDEFINITE ADJECTIVES

1 (a) ogni   (b) Qualche   (c) ogni   (d) qualche   (e) Ogni   (f) qualche

2 (a) A qualunque/qualsiasi ora.   (b) Qualunque/qualsiasi colore va bene.   (c) Uno qualsiasi.
   (or, without qualsiasi: quello che vuoi tu.)   (d) Una qualsiasi.

3 (a) I'll accept your decision, whatever it may be/whatever it is.
   (b) Elisabetta would do anything for him.

12.2   INDEFINITE PRONOUNS

1 (a) Vuole qualcosa?   (b) C'è qualcuno alla porta.   (c) Qualcuno preferisce lavorare da casa.
   (d) Non voglio niente.   (e) Non c'è nessuno alla porta.   (f) Ognuno ha diritto/Tutti hanno
   diritto alla pensione.

2 (a) Sì, qualcuna.   (b) Sì, qualcuno.   (c) No, nessuno.

3 (a) qualcuno di noi   (b) qualcuno di voi   (c) nessuno di noi   (d) ognuno di voi

4 (a) Nessuno dei miei amici vuole fare il medico.
   (b) Non mi piace nessuna delle mie zie.
   (c) I miei genitori hanno un lavoro interessante, ma nessuno dei due ha fatto l'università.
   (d) Mio fratello ha fatto due foto, ma a me non piace nessuna delle due (or né l'una né l'altra).

5 (a) 65 euro l'uno/ciascuno   (b) tutte e due/l'una e l'altra   (c) o l'uno o l'altro   (d) né l'una né l'altra

6 (a) It's nothing: anyone would have done it.   (b) It's simple: anyone can do it.   (c) Whoever calls,
   tell them I'm out.

12.3   INDEFINITE ADJECTIVES AND PRONOUNS

1 (a) tutto   (b) tutti   (c) tutti   (d) tutti i   (e) tutta la   (f) tutte le   (g) tutti quanti
   (h) tutta quanta

2 (a) iii   (b) iii   (c) iii

3 (a) Ho un altro esame domani.   (b) Ci sono altri problemi?   (c) Hai altro da fare?

4 (b) Hai comprato troppa poca carne.

5 (a) Può chiederlo a qualcun altro?   (b) Prende altro?   (c) Nessun altro lo sa fare.   (d) Non ho
   (nient') altro da dire.   (e) Tutti gli altri sono andati a casa.   (f) Può prendere tutto il resto.

12.4 SINGULAR INDEFINITE ADJECTIVES AND PRONOUNS

1 (a) ciascun   (b) ciascuna   (c) ciascuno   (d) ciascun'/ciascuna

2 (a) nessun   (b) nessun'/nessuna   (c) nessuno   (d) nessuna

3 (a) Non c'è alcun problema.   (b) Non abbiamo alcuna/alcun'alternativa.

4 (a) ciascuna   (b) ciascuno   (c) ciascuna   (d) ciascuno

12.5 INDEFINITES AND QUANTITY

1 (a) Puoi mettere l'una o l'altra, ti stanno bene tutt'e due/entrambe.
(b) Puoi chiedere all'uno o all'altro, sono entrambi/tutt'e due degli esperti.
(c) Vanno bene tutt'e due, sono belli entrambi.

2 (a) Tutte e quattro le mie sorelle sono insegnanti.
(b) Tutte e quattro fumano.
(c) La maggior parte dei miei parenti abitano in Germania.
(d) La maggior parte di loro sono dottori.

12.6 INDEFINITES AND PLACE

1 (a) I left my diary somewhere.   (b) Let's go somewhere else.   (c) I'm not going anywhere.
(d) Don't they sell it anywhere else?   (e) You can find these shoes anywhere/everywhere.
(f) They have looked everywhere else.

UNIT 13 RELATIVE PRONOUNS

13.1 MAIN RELATIVE PRONOUNS

1 (a) Marta è un'amica che mi è molto simpatica.
(b) Edoardo è un lontano cugino che lavora a Parigi.
(c) I signori Colucci sono i vicini che litigano tanto.
(d) La Rinascente è un grande magazzino che si trova nelle maggiori città italiane.
(e) *Roma città aperta* è un film di Rossellini che non ho mai visto.

2 (a) L'appartamento che ho affittato è al primo piano.
(b) L'uomo che hai conosciuto/incontrato è il marito della padrona di casa, il quale
parte oggi.
(c) Hanno aumentato l'affitto, il che non è giusto.

3 (a) *Relative* – Quello/Ciò che fai è assurdo.   (b) *Relative* – Puoi fare quello/ciò che vuoi.
(c) *Relative* – Farò quello/ciò che posso.   (d) *Relative* – Quello/Ciò che non piace è il colore.
(e) *Exclamation* – Che colore orribile!   (f) *Interrogative* – Che cosa posso fare?
(g) *Interrogative* – Non so che cosa fare.

4 **Quanto** *can be used in* **3** (c); Farò quanto posso.

13.2 PREPOSITIONS WITH RELATIVE PRONOUNS

1 (a) Il professor Binni è un insegnante per cui/per il quale ho molto rispetto.
(b) Carlotta è la nipote a cui/alla quale ho regalato una bicicletta.
(c) Aldo e Stefano sono colleghi con cui/con i quali lavoro da due anni.
(d) Fiorella è la mia assistente senza cui/senza la quale non potrei lavorare.

2   (a) Ho due stampanti, di cui una non è mia.

      (b) Qui ci sono tre calcolatrici, due delle quali sono rotte.

      (c) Mi ha dato delle cartelle, alcune delle quali sono sparite.

      (d) Abbiamo cenato con degli amici di cui uno è deputato.

3   (a) Il 1905 è l'anno in cui è nato mio nonno.

      (b) Le ragioni per cui è emigrato non sono chiare.

      (c) La casa dove/in cui abitava è stata bombardata durante la guerra.

4   (a) a cui piace, che mi piace   (b) a cui, che   (c) che, a cui

13.3   *WHOSE*

1   (a) Ho appena incontrato una signora la cui nipotina conosce Anna.

      (b) Mia cugina le cui figlie abitano a Parigi si sente molto sola.

      (c) La signora i cui gioielli sono stati rubati è all'ospedale.

      (d) Il camion i cui freni non funzionavano ha provocato l'incidente.

      (e) Abita in un paesino di cui mi sono dimenticato il nome.

13.4   OTHER RELATIVE PRONOUNS

1   (a) tutto quello che   (b) tutto quello che   (c) Tutti quelli che   (d) tutti quelli che

2   (a) *Sentences* (a) *and* (b).   (b) Sentences (b) and (d).

3   (a) *Relative* – I'm afraid that those who haven't got a student's card can't eat in the canteen.

      (b) *Interrogative* chi *(indirect question)*

      (c) *Relative* – The deadline for those who want to enrol in the course is 3 September.

      (d) *Relative* – It's an ideal place for those who want to have a rest.

      (e) *Relative* – The Miramare Hotel takes care of those who want total relaxation.

      (f) *Relative* – There are those who prefer dogs and those who prefer cats instead.

4   Quelli che *can only replace the relative pronoun* chi; *therefore it cannot be used in sentence* (b).

UNIT 14   NEGATIVES

14.1   SINGLE NEGATIVES

1   (a) No, non mi chiamo Edda, mi chiamo Emma.   (b) Non credo. – Spero di no!

      (c) Perché vorrei sapere se ha pagato o no/o meno.

14.2   DOUBLE NEGATIVES

1   (a) Non ho visto nessuno.   (b) Non ha mai visto il Monte Bianco.   (c) Non è ancora partito.

      (d) Non voglio mangiare niente.   (e) Non vuole mai aiutare.   (f) Non voglio più venire.

2   (a) Non mi piace affatto.   (b) Non lo conosco per niente.   (c) Non è per niente antipatico.

      (d) Non devi assolutamente andare via.

3   (a) (i) Giacomo has not even called.   (ii) Not even Giacomo has called/Giacomo hasn't called either.

      (b) (i) I didn't go either.   (ii) I didn't even go.

      (c) (i) I don't even like it.   (ii) I don't like it either.

4   (a) Non ti sei mica dimenticato di imbucare la lettera?   (b) Non hai mica invitato i vicini?

      (c) Non hai mica lasciato acceso il forno?

5 (a) Non spiega mai niente. (b) Non offenderà più nessuno. (c) Non c'è (nient') altro. (d) Non ho ancora trovato niente. (e) Non ho mica trovato niente. (f) Non dirò niente a nessuno.

14.3 NEGATIVES USED WITHOUT *NON*

I (a) Mica male! (b) Nient'affatto (c) Niente (d) Mai! (e) Mai più (f) Assolutamente (no)/ Per niente!

UNIT 15 PREPOSITIONS

15.1 THE MAIN PREPOSITIONS

A

I (a) Abito all'ultimo piano. (b) Il ristorante è all'angolo, a destra. (c) La libreria è a 200 metri da casa mia. (d) Abito in una città/cittadina a sud ovest di Londra. (e) C'è un film interessante alla televisione. (f) C'è tua madre al telefono/Tua madre è al telefono. (g) Ci vediamo a/in dicembre, a Natale. (h) A che ora vieni, Ida?

IN

I (a) Devo andare in Francia. (b) Devo telefonare in Italia. (c) Vado in aereo. (d) Entriamo nel negozio. (e) Abiti/a in Inghilterra? (f) È nel cassetto. (g) Dormo in treno.

2 (a) Devo telefonare a mia cugina in Italia, a Roma. (b) No, s'impara in pochi mesi. (c) Siamo in sei. (d) Sono nato/a in aprile alle 5 di mattina, all'alba.

DA

I (a) I left London yesterday. (b) I left the office at seven. (c) The plane is leaving from gate 34. (d) We came in through the window. (e) Don't look out of the window. (f) When I was a student/As a student, I liked travelling. (g) I've been here since Saturday. (h) Wound you like something to drink?

2 (a) dalla (b) da (c) di (d) da

IN, A, DA

I Vado (a) in Italia (b) in Sicilia (c) in Toscana (d) a Capri (e) a Bari (f) al supermercato (g) alla Rinascente (h) in farmacia (i) in piscina (j) da Franco (k) dal parrucchiere (l) dal medico (m) allo zoo (n) al mare (o) a casa (p) in campagna

2 Ci vediamo (a) a casa mia (b) in biblioteca (c) da Franca (d) alla fermata dell'autobus (e) in trattoria (f) da mia sorella (g) al bar (h) in banca (i) dal fruttivendolo (j) al ristorante (k) da 'Gigino' (l) in centro

DI

I (a) a seat/safety belt (b) Mauro's house (c) a painting by Leonardo (d) a 2000 euro rise (e) a two-litre bottle (f) a winter's day

2 (a) un/un'insegnante di lingue (b) la moglie del primo ministro (c) un romanzo di Manzoni (d) una bambina di dieci anni (e) il volo delle otto (f) un viaggio di cinque ore (g) le otto di sera

3   (a) di   (b) da   (c) da   (d) di   (e) di   (f) da

4   (a) d'oro   (b) da sera   (c) a fiori   (d) di paglia   (e) da sole   (f) a quadretti

5   (a) dalla   (b) di *or* da   (c) dalla   (d) di *or* da   (e) da   (f) dal

PER

1   (a) Lavoro per una compagnia aerea.   (b) No, sono qui per affari.   (c) Sono qui per imparare l'italiano. È per il mio lavoro.   (d) Mi trattengo (per) un mese.   (e) Mi dispiace, ho molti appuntamenti (per) domani.

2   (a) ii   The car didn't start this morning because of the cold.
     (b) iii   He didn't come to the party out of shyness.
     (c) i   My daughter suffers a lot from her fiancé being away.

3   (a) per   (b) per terra   (c) per (la) strada

CON

1   (a) iii   (b) i   (c) ii

2   (a) ii   (b) i   (c) iii

3   (a) con la macchina   (b) con il treno   (c) con i baffi lunghi   (d) con i capelli biondi tinti

SU

1   (a) I left the documents on the desk.   (b) The cat climbed onto the roof.   (c) *The Bridge over the River Kwai* is a rather old film.   (d) It's a film about the war in Japan.   (e) We've been up Mont Blanc.   (f) The journey costs about two thousand euros.   (g) I read the news in the paper.   (h) I left my umbrella in the bus.

TRA, FRA

1   (a) I'm arriving between five and six.   (b) I'm arriving in a week's time.   (c) Mario is sitting between his cousin and his grandfather.   (d) Out of my cousins I prefer Luciano.   (e) We are amongst friends.   (f) The new house is between Genoa and Leghorn (Livorno).   (g) You can see the house through the trees.   (h) There is a special understanding between us. *or* We understand each other.

15.2   OTHER PREPOSITIONS

1   **di** *needed in*   (b) dopo di me   (d) verso di lui   (f) fuori dell'Italia   (h) senza di te

2   (b) dentro di me   (c) dietro alla/la porta   (d) dietro di/a te   (e) oltre a te   (f) oltre ai

3   (a) nel cortile   (b) accanto alla sua macchina   (c) di fronte al cinema   (d) dall'altra parte della strada   (e) in fondo alla strada   (f) davanti a casa sua

15.3   ADJECTIVES USED WITH PREPOSITIONS

1   (a) Pina è molto interessata ad imparare il greco.
     (b) Alberta è proprio decisa a cambiare casa.
     (c) Ida è ansiosa di partire, ma Delia non sembra disposta a muoversi.
     (d) Diego è molto soddisfatto del suo lavoro, è responsabile di tutto il reparto.

2   (a) Sono stufo/a del mio lavoro.   (b) Sono contento/a dei risultati.   (c) È gentile con me.
     (d) È sposata con un ingegnere.

3   (a) bravo a   (b) bravo a, in   (c) costituito di/da   (d) coperto con   (e) coperto di   (f) pronta a

15.4 NOUNS AND PREPOSITIONS

I (a) La causa dell'incidente non è chiara. (b) Mia sorella è un'esperta dell'Italia medievale.
(c) Il suo amore per gli animali è noto. (d) La sua avversione per i gatti era straordinaria.

UNIT 16 CONNECTIVES

16.1 ADDING INFORMATION

I e anche inoltre e oltre a in più

2 (a) Both Emilio and Elisabetta passed the exam. (b) Neither Emilio nor Elisabetta passed
the exam. (c) Emilio passed the exam, and so did Elisabetta. (d) Emilio invited some friends
and what's more he invited his mother.

16.2 CLARIFYING INFORMATION

I (a) cioè (b) meglio (c) in effetti (d) già (e) infatti

16.3 EXPRESSING ALTERNATIVES

I (a) altrimenti perderemo il contratto. (b) invece di mandare un'email. (c) invece di mangiare
caramelle, mangia piuttosto della frutta. (d) anziché/piuttosto che con loro.

2 (a) Prendi la birra o il vino? (b) Possiamo andare al cinema oppure rimanere qui. (c) Preferisco
andare da solo piuttosto che aspettare. (d) Non bere caffè, prendi piuttosto/invece un tè al limone.

16.4 COMPARING, CONTRASTING AND CONTRADICTING

I (a) ma (b) mentre (c) invece (d) d'altra parte

2 (a) ma invece ho cenato … (b) ma in realtà (c) ma in realtà

16.5 EXPRESSING REASONS, CAUSE AND EFFECT

I (a) dal momento che/dato che/visto che (b) siccome avevo perso (c) dato che/siccome

2 (a) Dato che/Siccome è il tuo compleanno, possiamo mangiare fuori.
(b) Non possiamo partire a causa dello sciopero/perché c'è sciopero.
(c) È merito tuo se/Grazie a te sono stato promosso.
(d) Sono in ritardo per causa tua./È colpa tua se sono in ritardo.

3 (a) ii The car has broken down, so I have to take it to the garage/mechanic.
(b) iii He broke his leg, so he couldn't go skiing.
(c) iv Profits have dropped, so as a result they have closed one factory.
(d) i I've organised things so as to save more.

16.6 MAKING EXCEPTIONS

I (a) meno/tranne/fuorché/eccetto (b) a parte (c) eccetto/tranne/salvo/a parte (d) fuorché

16.7 CONDITIONS AND CONCESSIONS

I (a) anche se (b) benché/sebbene/nonostante (c) pur (d) nonostante/malgrado

2 (a) Any time is fine for me as long as/provided I know beforehand. (b) We'll meet in the library
unless it's closed. (c) I know there is a strike, but I am going/leaving anyway. (d) We'll go on
holiday however business goes.

16.8   TIME SEQUENCE

1   (a) *The odd one is*: in questi giorni.   (b) *The odd one is*: nei giorni scorsi.   (c) *The odd one is*: nei prossimi giorni.   (d) *The odd one is*: in quel momento.

2   (a) ii   (b) iv   (c) i   (d) iii   (e) v

3   (a) fino a   (b) finché   (c) finché (non)/fino a quando (non)   (d) finché/fino a quando

UNIT 17 NUMERALS AND UNITS OF MEASUREMENT

17.1   CARDINAL NUMBERS

1   (a) un chilo   (b) una fetta   (c) diciassette libri   (d) diciannove pagine   (e) trentun studenti   (f) quarantotto ore   (g) tre capitoli   (h) ventitré ragazze   (i) cento sterline   (j) duecento sterline   (k) mille euro   (l) diecimila euro   (m) un milione di yen   (n) cinque milioni di dollari   (o) tre milioni cinquecentomila euro

2   (a) Il dieci per cento degli   (b) Il cinquantun per cento della   (c) venticinque euro   (d) il 2002   (e) il nove   (f) zero due trentanove ventiquattro ottantuno, interno settecentocinquanta   (*or* sette, cinque, zero)

3   (a) le dieci   (b) l'una/le tredici   (c) le otto/le venti   (d) le undici/le ventitré

17.2   ORDINAL NUMBERS

1   (a) il primo ottobre   (b) la seconda guerra mondiale   (c) il Terzo Mondo   (d) la decima volta   (e) il ventesimo anniversario   (f) Elisabetta seconda   (g) l'ottavo secolo d.C.

2   (a) il Novecento   (b) il Trecento   (c) il quindicesimo secolo   (d) il diciannovesimo secolo

17.3   OTHER NUMBERS

1   (a) un quarto   (b) un terzo   (c) tre quarti   (d) due terzi

2   (a) mezza bottiglia   (b) una bottiglia e mezza   (c) metà del vino   (d) mezza pagina   (e) metà (del) libro   (f) a metà prezzo

3   (a) C'era un centinaio di ospiti.   (b) C'era una ventina di studenti.   (c) C'è un migliaio di manifestanti.   (d) Ci sono migliaia di manifestanti.

UNIT 18 VERBS: THE PRESENT TENSE

18.1   PRESENT TENSE REGULAR VERBS

1   (a) abitano   (b) leggono   (c) scrivete   (d) studiate   (e) dorme   (f) mangia

2   (a) offrire -o   (b) preferire -isco   (c) partire -o   (d) soffrire -o   (e) seguire -o   (f) finire -isco   (g) capire -isco   (h) vestirsi -o

3   (a) mangi   (b) paghi   (c) cominciamo   (d) giochiamo

4   (a) si annoiano   (b) si perdono   (c) si divertono   (d) si stupisce

18.2   IRREGULAR VERBS

1   (a) hai, ho   (b) stai, sto   (c) fai, faccio   (d) dai, dò   (e) vai, vado

2   (a) usciamo, uscire   (b) andiamo, andare   (c) propongono, proporre   (d) dite, dire
(e) traduco, tradurre   (f) sono, essere   (g) sono, essere

3   (a) voglio, posso   (b) puoi, devi   (c) sappiamo, dobbiamo   (d) volete, potete

4   (a) rimani, rimango   (b) rimane, rimangono   (c) scegli, scelgo   (d) vengo, vieni
(e) mi trattengo, si trattengono   (f) mi siedo, vi sedete

5   (a) Mi alzo presto e faccio colazione alle sette.   (b) La Gran Bretagna è un'isola e l'Italia è una
penisola.   (c) Che cosa dice? Non lo sento.   (d) Bevete il caffè la mattina/al mattino?
(e) Non riesco ad aprire la finestra.   (f) Pranzano ancora?

6   (a) Quando parti per Parigi?   (b) Domani vado al cinema.   (c) Ti chiamo la prossima settimana.
(d) Ci sentiamo presto.   (e) Stiamo per partire.

7   (a) Imparo l'italiano da due anni. *or* Sono due anni che/È da due anni che imparo l'italiano.
(b) Ci conosciamo da tre mesi. *or* Sono tre mesi che/È da tre mesi che ci conosciamo.
(c) Sono in Italia da settembre./È da settembre che sono in Italia.
(d) Lo aspetto da sabato./È da sabato che lo aspetto.

8   (a) Porto   (b) Ho portato   (c) ho cambiato   (d) abito   (e) scrive   (f) ha scritto

18.3   THE PRESENT CONTINUOUS

1   (a) *and* (d) *are impossible as they refer to the future.*   (b) *is possible but unlikely.*

2   (a) stiamo studiando   (b) sto leggendo   (c) sto facendo/faccio   (d) fanno/stanno facendo, si
stanno divertendo/si divertono

UNIT 19 THE FUTURE

19.1   THE SIMPLE FUTURE

1   (a) scriverò   (b) dormirà   (c) torneranno

2   (a) giocherò   (b) spiegheremo   (c) cominceranno   (d) festeggerai

3   (a) andrò, farò   (b) dovrai, potrai   (c) rimarranno, vedranno   (d) avrò, sarò   (e) diremo,
verremo   (f) tradurrai, darai

4   (a) pioverà   (b) sarà   (c) arriveremo

5   (a) aumenteranno, resteranno   (b) affolleranno, inquineranno   (c) diventerà, lavoreranno,
otterranno

6   (a) Andrò a trovarla allora.   (b) Prenderemo la statale allora.   (c) Gli manderò una cartolina di
auguri allora.

7   (a) Domani vado a Torino.   (b) Prendiamo il treno alle cinque.   (c) Mando dei fiori a mia madre.

8   (a) Avrà almeno sessant'anni.   (b) Che lavoro farà?/Chissà che lavoro fa.   (c) Sarà sposato.
(d) Sarà ricca, ma è proprio stupida.

9   (a) Se mi dai una mano, ti compro/comprerò il gelato.
(b) Se mi impresti la macchina, pago/pagherò io la benzina.
(d) Se non ti sbrighi, facciamo/faremo tardi.

10 (a) gli insegnanti faranno sciopero. (b) la gente morirà di fame. (c) il clima della Terra cambierà.

11 (a) Resterò finché resta/resterà lui. (b) Resterò finché non arriva. (c) Ti telefonerò appena scriverà. (d) Quando mi pagheranno, ti comprerò un vestito.

19.2 THE FUTURE PERFECT

1 (a) l'avrai dimenticato (b) sarò già partito/a (c) Giovanni sarà tornato

2 (a) Avrà sbagliato strada? (b) Avrà avuto un incidente. (c) Avrà perso il nostro indirizzo.

3 (a) se avrò finito i compiti (b) quando l'avrò letto (c) una volta che avrò sistemato l'appartamento (d) dopo che avrò fatto la spesa

4 (a) se finisco i compiti (b) quando l'ho letto (c) una volta che ho sistemato l'appartamento (d) dopo che ho fatto la spesa (or: dopo aver fatto la spesa)

UNIT 20 THE PAST TENSES

20.1 THE *PASSATO PROSSIMO*

1 (a) ordinato (b) ricevuto (c) capito (d) andati/andate (e) caduto/a (f) partito/a

2 (a) ho fatto (b) ha risposto (c) hai aperto (d) sono stato/a (e) sono rimasto/a (f) sono venuti/e

3 (a) mi sono alzato/a (b) mi sono sentito/a (c) mi sono seduto/a (d) mi sono messo/a (e) mi sono tolto/a

4 (a) I know Sardinia well. I've been there many times. I've always liked it.
(b) Last year I went to Sardinia. I liked it a lot.
(c) Did you fly or did you travel by train? – I took the car, it's more convenient.
(d) Julia, I've taken the car. I'll bring it back tonight.

5 1 ci siamo alzati 2 siamo andati 3 sono arrivata 4 ho lavorato 5 mi sono annoiata
6 sono tornata 7 abbiamo fatto 8 abbiamo camminato 9 siamo tornati 10 abbiamo visto
11 è piaciuto 12 abbiamo dormito

6 (a) scritto, scritta (b) letto, letti (c) parlato, parlato (d) messo, messa

7 (a) mi è servita (b) non mi sono bastati (c) sono successe (d) mi è piaciuta

8 (a) Non ho potuto partire. (d) Hai dovuto tornare a casa?

9 (a) Abbiamo dovuto fermarci. (b) Elena ha dovuto riposarsi. (c) Mi sono potuto/potuta sposare presto. (d) Marta non si è voluta fidanzare.

10 (a) ho cambiato (b) è molto cambiata (c) non ha migliorato (d) non è migliorata (e) è volata (f) ho volato (g) sono corso (h) ho corso

11 (a) ha intenzione (b) ha dato (c) aveva intenzione (d) aveva dato

12 (a) Mi ha appena detto che ha prenotato ieri.
(b) Ieri mi ha detto che non aveva prenotato.
(c) Mi ha detto che aveva intenzione di prenotare la prossima settimana.

20.2 THE IMPERFECT

1 (a) c'erano poche macchine. (b) nessuno aveva paura. (c) bevevano pochissimo. (d) tutti andavano a messa.

2 (a) No, ascoltavo la radio.   (b) Non so, preparavo la cena in cucina.   (c) Era buio, ma sì, c'era qualcuno. Portava una giacca a vento e un berretto di lana. L'ho visto mentre saliva su un furgoncino bianco.

3 (a) Non riuscivo ad aprire la finestra.
(b) Era buio: li sentivo ma non li vedevo/non riuscivo a vederli.
(c) Li sentivo solo se gridavano forte./Li potevo sentire …/Riuscivo a sentirli ….
(d) Non sapevo ballare, ma sapevo cantare.

4 (a) Non la vedevo da dicembre.   (b) La conoscevo da quando avevo tre anni.   (c) La aspettava da un'ora.   (d) Dal 1980 ha avuto tre mariti.

5 (a) da quanto tempo insegnavi a Milano? – Insegnavo da due anni, da quando mi ero sposato.
(b) Sì, eravamo fidanzati da sei anni.
(c) non ci vedevamo da tre anni e io non avevo mai visto mia figlia!

6 (a) che venivano così presto.   (b) dormiva fuori.   (c) portava venti ospiti per cena.

7 (a) potevano   (b) doveva   (c) potevi

8 (a) sapevo, venivo   (b) dicevi, prestavo   (c) spiegavo

20.3   THE IMPERFECT AND *PASSATO PROSSIMO*

1 (a) Martedì, mentre Anna ascoltava la radio, Pietro ha fatto la cena.
(b) Mercoledì Anna ha pulito la casa mentre Pietro preparava una lezione.
(c) Ieri siamo andati a una festa. È stata una serata meravigliosa.
(d) Ieri abbiamo fatto una passeggiata perché era una bella serata.
(e) L'anno scorso sono andato/a in Corsica. Mi è piaciuta molto.
(f) Quando abitavo a Londra, mi piaceva visitare i musei.

2 (a) dovevo   (b) ho dovuto   (c) non ho potuto vedere   (d) non potevo vedere   (e) ho saputo
(f) sapevo

20.4   THE IMPERFECT CONTINUOUS

1 (a) stavo ascoltando   (b) stavo preparando   (d) stava salendo

20.5   THE PLUPERFECT

1 (a) avevo chiesto   (b) si era laureato   (c) eravamo nati   (d) aveva bevuto

2 (a) Appena uscito/a di casa, mi sono sentito/a male.
(b) Finiti gli esami, mi sono trovato un lavoro.
(c) Ero già partito/a quando sono arrivati.
(d) Quando mia moglie è uscita dall'ospedale, ho potuto tornare al lavoro *or* Dopo che mia moglie era uscita dall'ospedale, ho potuto tornare al lavoro.

20.6   THE SIMPLE PAST

1 (a) **fu:** essere – fui fosti, **vide:** vedere – vidi vedesti, **pensò:** pensare – pensai pensasti,
aprì: aprire – aprii apristi, **uscì:** uscire – uscii uscisti, **prese:** prendere – presi prendesti,
avvicinò: avvicinare – avvicinai avvicinasti, **ritrasse:** ritrarre – ritrassi ritraesti,
seguì: seguire – seguii seguisti
(b) **È stato** allora che **ho visto** un coniglio in una gabbia. Era un coniglio bianco, di pelo lungo e piumoso … Fuori della gabbia, sul tavolo, c'erano dei resti d'erba e una carota. **Ho pensato** a come doveva essere infelice, chiuso là allo stretto, vedendo quella carota e non potendola mangiare. E gli **ho aperto** lo sportello della gabbia. Il coniglio **non è uscito** … **Ho preso** la carota, gliel'**ho avvicinata**, poi, lentamente l'**ho ritratta** per invitarlo a uscire. Il coniglio mi **ha seguito** …

UNIT 21 THE CONDITIONAL

21.1 THE CONDITIONAL

1 (a) laveresti (b) cerchereste (c) prenderemmo

2 (a) verrei (b) vorremmo (c) rimarresti (d) potreste (e) faresti (f) andrei

3 (a) Umberto, mi daresti un bicchiere di vino? (b) Anna e Cristina, mi fareste un favore?
(c) Signora, avrei bisogno di una crema più leggera. (d) Signore, me lo preparerebbe per stasera?

4 (a) darei un passaggio (b) tradurrei (c) berrei

5 (a) non risponderei (b) proporrei un'altra soluzione (c) si arrabbierebbe

6 (a) You should go to the doctor's. (b) I am supposed/meant to be leaving at three, but I haven't
got my ticket. (c) They should already be at home by now. (d) Could you come at two?
(e) You said you could come at two. (f) They could be at auntie's or at granny's. (g) Could you
tell me if they've come back? (h) He/She couldn't/wasn't able to tell me anything. (i) Giulia
would like to stay in Pisa. (j) She would like to stay in Pisa.

21.2 THE PAST CONDITIONAL

1 (a) sarei (b) avrei (c) sarebbero (d) mi sarei (e) si sarebbe (f) ci saremmo

2 (a) Avremmo protestato. (b) Mi sarei arrabbiato/a. (c) Mi sarei lamentato/a.

3 (a) Sì, mi sarebbe piaciuto andarci. Mi piacerebbe andarci domani.
(b) Sì, avrei voluto parlargli. Vorrei parlargli presto.
(c) Sì, gli sarebbe piaciuto venire. Gli piacerebbe venire la prossima settimana.
(d) Sì, avrei voluto finire il lavoro. Vorrei finirlo presto.

4 (a) Ero convinto che avrebbe telefonato/che telefonava.
(b) Sapevano che sarebbe partita/che partiva.
(c) Mi ha detto che sarebbe arrivato/che arrivava alle quattro.

5 (a) The minister is apparently not prepared/unwilling to resign.
(b) The plane is reported to have crashed ten minutes after take-off.
(c) The robber is reported to have fired/apparently fired twice.

UNIT 22 THE IMPERATIVE

1 (a) Guarda il mare. Guardi il mare. (b) Vendi la casa. Venda la casa. (c) Finisci il lavoro. Finisca il
lavoro. (d) Parti subito. Parta subito. (e) Togli la polvere. Tolga la polvere.
(f) Vieni dentro. Venga dentro. (g) Fa'/Fai la doccia. Faccia la doccia. (h) Abbi pazienza.
Abbia pazienza. (i) Sta'/Stai fermo. Stia fermo.

2 (a) Non guardare il mare. Non guardi il mare. (b) Non vendere la casa. Non venda la casa.
(c) Non finire il lavoro. Non finisca il lavoro. (g) Non fare la doccia. Non faccia la doccia.

3 (a) Fallo subito. Lo faccia subito. (b) Dille di venire. Le dica di venire. (c) Chiedigli di venire.
Gli chieda di venire. (d) Vacci. Ci vada. (e) Divertiti. Si diverta. (f) Mettiti il cappotto.
Si metta il cappotto.

4 (a) Non farlo subito. Non lo faccia subito. (d) Non andarci. Non ci vada.

5 (a) Si accomodi. Accomodatevi. (b) Mi passi il sale. (c) Mi dia un po' di pane, per favore.
(d) Ci faccia un caffè, per favore. (e) Ci porti il conto, per favore.

6 (a) Guarda bene prima di attraversare la strada. (b) Sta'/Stai attento/a! (c) Non toccare niente. (d) Non sederti lì! (e) Esci di qui. (f) Sbrigati!

7 (a) Senta! (b) Non me lo dire! (c) Senti!

8 **Lei** *form*: eviti, scelga, metta, annaffi, tenga, spruzzi

UNIT 23 NON-FINITE VERB FORMS

23.1 THE INFINITIVE

1 (a) senza pagare (b) prima di partire (c) cambiare treno a Milano (d) vederti qui

2 (a) Mi piace viaggiare in treno. (b) Penso di partire/di andarmene. (c) Spero di vederti presto. (d) Dubito di poter venire. (e) Mangiarlo? Ma scherzi! (f) Il mio passatempo preferito è giocare a carte.

3 (a) a leggere romanzi (b) a giocare a bridge (c) a riparare la macchina (d) a mangiare cioccolatini

4 Sono contento/a di ... (a) aver pagato i debiti (b) aver ricevuto il pacco (c) essere uscito con te (d) essermi divertito

5 (a) aver dovuto partire (b) non aver potuto venire

6 (a) Sono contento di averli comprati. (b) È un sollievo averla venduta. (c) È un peccato non essere partiti insieme. (d) È un peccato non aver viaggiato insieme.

7 (a) aver trovato le chiavi (b) non esserci andato (c) di aver capito (d) aver dovuto partire

8 (a) Sono uscito senza fare colazione. (b) Sono partiti senza aver pagato. (c) Grazie di averci aiutato. (d) Verrò a trovarti dopo avergli parlato.

9 (a) I think I'm leaving on Monday. (b) I think I left last Monday. (c) I am happy to see him tomorrow. (d) I am happy I saw him yesterday. (e) I can't get married before finishing my studies. (f) I can't get married before I have finished my studies.
Sentences (e) and (f) have the same meaning.

23.2 THE GERUND

1 (a) Lavorando come un matto e risparmiando la metà dello stipendio.
(b) Bevendo caffè e fumando come un turco!
(c) Studiando il mercato e offrendo un servizio sempre migliore.

2 (a) essendo stato malato (b) avendo sentito le critiche (c) avendo mangiato così male

3 (a) Andando in città, ho incontrato Giuseppe sull'autobus.
(b) Attraversando Piazza della Repubblica, ho visto la polizia arrestare/che arrestava due uomini.
(c) Andando a casa ho visto Letizia che parlava con Adriano.

4 (a) Detesto aspettare. (b) Erano seduti lì ad aspettarmi. (c) È scappata via urlando.
(d) Urlare non serve a niente.

23.3 THE PAST PARTICIPLE

1 (a) Fatta la spesa, Luisa è tornata a casa.
(b) Finite le lezioni, siamo andati in centro.

(c) Una volta arrivati in albergo, mi dovete chiamare.

(d) Passati il ponte e la farmacia, troverai la strada a destra.

(e) Risolto il problema, mi sento più tranquilla.

UNIT 24 THE SUBJUNCTIVE

24.1 THE PRESENT SUBJUNCTIVE

I (a) che io gli mandi il pacco? (b) che tu gli scriva qualcosa. (c) che loro dormano subito! (d) che lo finisca io? (e) che tu lo paghi adesso. (f) che loro comincino presto.

2 (a) che lo faccia io? (b) che ci vada io? (c) che glielo dia io? (d) che glielo dica io?

3 (a) contenga (b) intervenga (c) riesca (d) produca (e) opponga (f) attragga

4 (a) È essenziale che tu lo paghi presto.
(b) È importante che lo spediscano/mandino domani.
(c) Ma è necessario che io lo sappia oggi.

5 (a) vengano (b) sia (c) tornino

6 (a) Mi fa piacere che tu stia meglio. (b) Mi dispiace che lei non abbia più tempo.
(c) Temo che loro vogliano lamentarsi. (d) Che peccato che loro non possano venire.
(e) Ho paura che Lucio sia malato. (f) Non è giusto che lo facciano loro.

7 (a) beva (b) mangi (c) rimangano (d) tradisca

8 (a) faccia (b) finisca (c) dia

9 (a) è (b) sia/sei (c) sono (d) abbia (e) tornerai/torni (f) sia/sarà

10 (a) non possa venire (b) riesca a farlo in tempo (c) vada via

11 (a) Preferisco farlo. (b) Preferisco che tu lo faccia. (c) Voglio venire. (d) Voglio che loro vengano. (e) È importante capire. (f) È importante che tu capisca.

24.2 THE PERFECT SUBJUNCTIVE

I (a) sia venuto (b) lui non abbia capito (c) vogliano venire (d) abbiano dimenticato/si siano dimenticati

2 (a) Immagino che sia stato difficile. (b) Può darsi che sia già andato via/partito. (c) È strano che non abbiano chiamato. (d) Pensi che lui abbia avuto un incidente?

24.4 THE PLUPERFECT SUBJUNCTIVE

I (a) io tornassi (b) tu potessi (c) studiassimo (d) capiste

2 (a) fosse (b) aveste (c) stessimo (d) desse (e) bevessero (f) traducessi

3 (a) Mi piacerebbe che tu venissi con noi. (b) Sarebbe meglio che Lei lo dicesse a loro, non a me.
(c) Mi farebbe piacere se tu lo facessi subito. (d) Vorrei che voi me lo spiegaste.

4 (a) non ci fosse nessuno (b) nessuno avesse risposto (c) venissero (d) non fosse venuta

24.5 FURTHER USES OF THE SUBJUNCTIVE

I (a) È stanco sebbene/benché non abbia fatto niente.
(b) Andremo in piscina, a condizione che non faccia freddo.

(c) Possiamo stare a casa a meno che tu non voglia uscire.
(d) Uscirò senza che nessuno lo sappia.
(e) Ti lascio la chiave nel caso che tu ne abbia bisogno.

2 (a) Il fatto che suo figlio non studiasse (b) il fatto che non studiasse (c) non erano disposti ad aiutare (d) Che non fossero disposti ad aiutare

3 (a) È il posto più bello che ci sia. (b) È il posto più bello che io abbia mai visto. (c) Era l'unico insegnante che mi avesse mai aiutato.

4 (a) sappia/sa (b) sa (c) sta (d) stia

5 (a) Se tu venissi a casa mia (b) Se fossero arrivati prima (c) Se io perdessi il lavoro/Se io dovessi perdere il lavoro (d) Se non avesse litigato con il capo

UNIT 25 SPECIAL VERB CONSTRUCTIONS

25.1 REFLEXIVE CONSTRUCTIONS

I (a) Si è lavato. (b) Ha lavato la macchina. (c) Ho vestito mia figlia. (d) Mi sono vestito/a.
(e) Ci siamo baciati. (f) Ci hanno baciato. (g) Mi sentivo/Mi sono sentito male.
(h) Ho sentito un dolore.

25.2 CAUSATIVE VERBS

I (a) Faccio pulire la casa. La faccio pulire.
(b) Faccio alzare mio figlio. Lo faccio alzare.
(c) Lascio sempre uscire mia figlia. La lascio sempre uscire.

2 (a) Ho fatto suonare il pianoforte a mia sorella. Le ho fatto suonare il pianoforte.
(b) Ho fatto fare la spesa a Dino. Gli ho fatto fare la spesa.
(c) Ho lasciato guidare la macchina a mio fratello. Gli ho lasciato guidare la macchina.
(d) Ho fatto aggiustare i freni dal meccanico. Gli ho fatto aggiustare i freni.

3 (a) Fallo studiare di più. (b) Fagli studiare medicina. (c) Lasciala uscire di pù. (d) Lasciala scegliere le materie che preferisce (*or*, Lascia che scelga ...)

25.3 VERBS OF PERCEPTION

I (a) Dobbiamo sentir cantare Pavarotti. (b) Ho guardato giocare mio figlio.
(c) Abbiamo visto passare il corteo. (d) Ho sentito il vicino uscire di casa.

2 (a) Ha sentito abbaiare il cane? (b) Ha visto andar via gli uomini? (c) Li ha sentiti sbattere la porta? (d) Ha sentito i vicini che gridavano aiuto?

25.4 *SAPERE* AND *CONOSCERE*

I (a) so (b) conosci (c) sa (d) conoscete, sappiamo (e) sai

25.5 *PIACERE*

I (a) Mi piace (b) ti/le/vi piacciono (c) Le piace (d) Ti/Le/Vi piace (e) Gli piace
(f) Le piacciono

2 (a) Do you like travelling? *or* Does she like travelling (b) Does he like Japanese films?
or Do they like Japanese films?

3 (a) A tutti piace/Piace a tutti la musica lirica? (b) Ai tuoi figli piace andare a teatro?
(c) A Chiara piacciono le commedie di Pirandello?

4 (a) Franco, ti piace il nuovo corso? – Sì, mi piace moltissimo.
(b) Signora Marini, le piacciono i fiori? – Sì, mi piacciono molto.
(c) Antonio e Roberto, vi piace andare in palestra? – Sì, ci piace moltissimo.

5 (a) ma a lui no/ma a lui non piace   (b) ma a lei sì/ma a lei piace   (c) Piace anche a loro.
(d) Non piace neanche a me.

6 (a) A mia moglie è piaciuto l'albergo di lusso.   (b) A mia suocera sono piaciuti i negozi.
(c) Ai miei figli è piaciuta la piscina.   (d) A me e a mio suocero sono piaciute le passeggiate
in montagna.

7 (a) Mirella gli è simpatica.   (b) Bruno le è simpatico.   (c) Io non gli sono simpatico/a.

25.6 OTHER VERBS USED IMPERSONALLY

I (a) ti bastano   (b) ti serve   (c) le manca   (d) vi conviene   (e) basta   (f) bisogna

2 (a) Mi è dispiaciuto partire così presto.   (b) Ci sono successe delle cose strane.   (c) Non gli è
mai capitato di arrivare in ritardo.   (d) Gli è toccato pagare una multa.

25.7 THE IMPERSONAL AND PASSIVE *SI*

I (a) Come si accende il gas?   (b) Come si spengono le luci?   (c) Come si pulisce il fornello?
(d) Come si chiudono le persiane?

2 (a) mi hanno detto che si sono venduti tantissimi libri.   (b) Non si è mai capito come avesse fatto.
(c) si è andati prestissimo a votare

25.8 THE PASSIVE

I (a) La città è inquinata dalle macchine.   (b) Il colpevole sarà trovato.   (c) A giugno gli esami
erano corretti dagli insegnanti.   (d) Queste nuove tasse sarebbero accettate dal pubblico?
(e) Non è giusto che gli insegnanti siano criticati dal governo.   (f) Il paesino incendiato è stato
abbandonato da tutti.

2 (a) Le finestre vengono pulite ogni mese.   (b) I ragazzi venivano spesso puniti.   (c) La città è
rimasta distrutta.   (d) Noi tutti siamo rimasti stupiti dalle sue parole.

3 (a) Il tetto va riparato.   (b) La cucina andrebbe rinnovata.   (c) I soffitti andranno rifatti.
(d) Le finestre andavano pulite.

4 (a) Mi hanno detto di arrivare presto. (*no passive*)
(b) Gli hanno impedito di votare. (*no passive*)
(c) Sono stato invitato/Mi hanno invitato a un congresso.
(d) Le hanno dato/Le è stato dato l'orario sbagliato. (*passive not common*)
(e) Mi hanno rubato/Mi è stata rubata la macchina. (*passive not common*)
(f) Gli hanno incendiato/Gli è stato incendiato il negozio. (*passive not common*)

UNIT 26 VERBS AND PREPOSITIONS

26.2 VERBS TAKING *A*

I (a) *Type 2*. È venuto a fare   (b) *Type 1*. È venuto per/a fare   (c) *Type 2*. Siamo rimasti a vedere
(d) *Type 3*. Si annoiavano a sentire

26.3 VERBS TAKING *DI*

1 (a) Mi sono stufato di aspettare.   (b) Mi stanco a studiare di sera.   (c) Non ti vergogni a imbrogliare la gente?   (d) Mi vergogno di aver imbrogliato Carla.

2 (a) Penso di venire presto.   (b) Spera di ottenere il posto/lavoro.   (c) Dubito di poter aiutare.
(d) Temo di essere in ritardo.

26.5 VERBS WHICH ASK SOMEBODY TO DO SOMETHING

1 (a) Ho detto a Simona di venire più tardi.   (b) Ho invitato Angelo a venire.   (c) Ho chiesto a Martina di andar via/andarsene.   (d) Ho ricordato a Susi di telefonare.   (e) Ha costretto Susi a telefonare   (f) Ha pregato Fabrizio di scrivere.

26.6 DIFFERENT PREPOSITION, DIFFERENT MEANING

1 (a) Puoi credere quello che vuoi.   (b) Credi a Marina? Le credi?   (c) Credi in Dio?
(d) Posso parlarti di Gianni?   (e) Posso parlare a Gianni?   (f) Mi ha parlato del suo lavoro.

2 (a) della proposta   (b) di Bruno   (c) a domani?   (d) di fare   (e) a Bruno   (f) a prenotare

Index

This index is designed for ease of reference so that you can locate what you need without necessarily knowing the relevant grammatical term. In many cases the same information appears in various places under different headings, for example: the grammatical category (e.g. indefinite adjective), the key English word (e.g. every) or an Italian word (e.g. *ogni*).